Opening the Gates to Asia

Opening the Gates to Asia

A Transpacific History of How America Repealed Asian Exclusion

Jane H. Hong

The University of North Carolina Press CHAPEL HILL

The University of North Carolina Press has been a member of the
Green Press Initiative since 2003.

Library of Congress Cataloging-in-Publication Data
Names: Hong, Jane H., author.
Title: Opening the gates to Asia : a transpacific history of how America
    repealed Asian exclusion / Jane H. Hong.
Description: Chapel Hill : University of North Carolina Press, [2019] |
    Includes bibliographical references and index.
Identifiers: LCCN 2019011077 | ISBN 9781469653358 (cloth : alk. paper) |
    ISBN 9781469653365 (pbk : alk. paper) | ISBN 9781469653372 (ebook)
Subjects: LCSH: United States—Emigration and immigration—Government
    policy—History—20th century. | Asians—United States—Social
    conditions—20th century. | Asian Americans—Social conditions—20th
    century. | Asia—Emigration and immigration—History—20th century.
Classification: LCC E184.A75 H66 2019 | DDC 305.895/073—dc23
    LC record available at https://lccn.loc.gov/2019011077

Cover illustration: Members of the Chinese American Citizens League,
Los Angeles. Y.C. Hong Papers, Huntington Library, San Marino, CA.

A version of chapter 3 was previously published in a different form as "Manila
Prepares for Independence: Filipina/o Campaigns for U.S. Citizenship and the
Reorienting of American Ethnic Histories," *Journal of American Ethnic History*
38, no. 1 (Fall 2018): 5–33. Parts of chapter 4 were previously published in
different form as "'A Cross-Fire between Minorities': Black-Japanese Relations
and the Empire Quota in the Postwar Campaign to Repeal Asian Exclusion,"
Pacific Historical Review 87, no. 4 (Fall 2018): 667–701 and is © 2018 Regents of
the University of California.

For my grandparents,
Hong Il Sun and Min Ae Ki,
with love and gratitude

Contents

Illustrations and Tables

ILLUSTRATIONS

TABLES

Abbreviations in the Text

ACLU	American Civil Liberties Union
ACPFB	American Committee for the Protection of the Foreign Born
AFL	American Federation of Labor
ARCI	Aid to Refugee Chinese Intellectuals
CACA	Chinese American Citizens Alliance
CCBA	Chinese Consolidated Benevolent Association
CEN	Committee for Equality on Naturalization
CIO	Congress of Industrial Organizations
CPFR	Committee for the Protection of Filipino Rights
FCC	Federal Council of Churches
ILA	India League of America
INC	Indian National Congress
INS	Immigration and Naturalization Service
IWL	India Welfare League
JACL	Japanese American Citizens League
JACL–ADC	Japanese American Citizens League–Anti-Discrimination Committee
JAWP	Japanese Agricultural Workers Program
NAACP	National Association for the Advancement of Colored People
NCIC	National Committee on Immigration and Citizenship
OFW	overseas Filipina/o workers

PRC	Philippine resident commissioner
RRA	Refugee Relief Act
SCAP	Supreme Commander for the Allied Powers
SEATO	Southeast Asian Treaty Organization
UCAC	United Caribbean American Council
UN	United Nations
UNESCO	United Nations Educational, Scientific, and Cultural Organization
USAID	U.S. Agency for International Development

Opening the Gates to Asia

Introduction

In 1907, Indian nationalist Taraknath Das fled the Indian subcontinent and the surveillance of British colonial authorities for the relative safety of the United States. There, he continued agitating for Indian independence from more than a century of British colonial rule. After brief sojourns in Seattle and northern California, he passed the U.S. Civil Service Examination and moved to Vancouver, Canada, where he worked as an interpreter at the British Columbia office of the U.S. Immigration Service for one short year. When Canadian authorities gave him a choice between keeping his job or continuing to publish the Indian nationalist newspaper he had founded, he chose the latter. Once back in the United States, he continued his revolutionary activities, rallying Indians and other anti-British forces toward the cause of India's independence. In 1917, Das was one of seventeen Indians convicted for their role in the Ghadar Conspiracy, a German-supported plot to overthrow the British Raj in India. He served a few years in prison for violating American neutrality laws during wartime, but, unlike most of his co-defendants, was not deported because he was a naturalized U.S. citizen. In 1923, the Supreme Court stripped him and dozens of other Indians of their naturalized status by ruling that Indians, as nonwhites, fell within the category of "aliens ineligible to U.S. citizenship."[1] Much as he had fought British colonial rule, he would spend the next two decades fighting in the U.S. Congress to get his citizenship back.

Histories of Asian exclusion in the United States often center around Chinese experiences, focusing on immigrant resistance to restrictive laws such as the 1882 Chinese Exclusion Act. But stories like Das's remind us that exclusion was a heterogeneous regime that affected Asian groups differently. Taraknath Das was born in West Bengal, India, in 1885, around the time that the U.S. Congress began restricting would-be Chinese migrants, and he died in New York City in 1958, seven years before the Hart-Celler Act eliminated the Asian exclusion regime altogether.[2] As a native of India, Das did not face the legal hurdles Chinese migrants faced when he entered the United States in 1906, as the U.S. Congress did not pass a law barring Indians until 1917.[3] He naturalized in 1914 and avoided deportation three years later because of uncertainty in the U.S. legal system surrounding Indians' racial heritage—a loophole that generally did not exist for East Asians.[4] The Supreme Court's 1923 ruling in *U.S. v. Thind* resolved that uncertainty, sanctioning the stripping of Das's U.S. citizenship.

The completion of the Asian exclusion regime followed one year after Das lost his citizenship. The 1924 Immigration Act created the national origins quota system that would remain in place until 1965, at first only permitting Europeans entry through country-based quotas. At the same time, the law solidified the exclusion of all Asians regardless of ethnicity or socioeconomic class by making the ability to immigrate contingent on eligibility for naturalization. Thus as "aliens ineligible to citizenship," no Asians now qualified for immigration. Moreover, the codification of Asians as permanent aliens in federal law made it harder for Indians stripped of their naturalized citizenship to get it back. Thwarted in his own personal efforts, Das lived several years in Europe before returning to teach political philosophy at Columbia University.

On May 25, 1943, the donnish professor was one of two non-Chinese Asians to testify in support of repealing Chinese exclusion at the U.S. House Committee on Immigration and Naturalization's widely publicized hearing on the subject. In a long and far-ranging statement, the now elderly Das recounted how, during the nineteenth century, the United States had initially pursued "oriental immigration" in its quest for "manifest destiny in the form of expansion in the Pacific," but later reversed this policy, leaving "poor, militarily weak China" to make "faint protest" against the 1882 Chinese Exclusion Act's "discriminatory" provisions. At the height of World War II, Das called not only for an end to Chinese exclusion but for the wholesale repeal of all Asian exclusion laws, which he denounced as a symbol of America's "Nazi-like race prejudice" against the "peoples of the Orient." His words enraged southern lawmakers, who told him he was pushing the demand too far; an "Oriental . . . born thousands of miles away" should not be able to come before Congress and "criticize [the United States'] country and courts," one protested. Another opponent of the bill dryly congratulated Das for having done the cause of repeal "more harm than anybody else."[5]

The twists and turns Das experienced broadly align with a historical puzzle: how did the United States go from excluding Asians for more than half a century to admitting more immigrants from Asia than from anywhere else in the world? Or, put simply, how and why did exclusion end, and who ended it? *Opening the Gates to Asia* recounts the largely untold history of Asian exclusion repeal by exposing it as a tool of U.S. empire building in postwar Asia.[6] The United States' unprecedented expansion in postwar Asia, this study shows, compelled a symbolic reopening of its borders to Asians as part of the price of empire.[7] Whatever damage Das caused with his testimony did not prove fatal: the Magnuson Act repealing Chinese exclusion passed U.S. Congress later that year. Within a few years, the 1946 Luce-Celler Act reversed Indians' exclusion from naturalization and immigration, enabling Das to reclaim his U.S. citizenship more than twenty years after losing it. Both laws also established small race-based quotas for Chinese and Indian immigration, while leaving all other aspects of the exclusion regime in place. The 1952 McCarran-Walter Act formally ended Asian exclusion by extending U.S. citizenship eligibility and small race-based immigration quotas to all Asians, assigned and structured in ways that nonetheless maintained greater rights for Europeans. It was not until the 1965 Hart-Celler Act that U.S. immigration policy toward Asians ceased to be based on race. The law's comprehensive reforms thus marked the true end of Asian exclusion some eighty years after its legal inception.

In the same way that the timing and shape of Asian exclusion's rise in the United States during the late nineteenth and early twentieth centuries tracked American expansionism in the Pacific, the movement for repeal charted the development of the United States' new informal empire in Asia after World War II. Framed most broadly, repeal was part of the larger transformation and expansion of U.S. empire during the era of Asian decolonization.[8] The United States had built a formal empire in the Pacific beginning in the late nineteenth century that ultimately encompassed the Philippines, Hawaii, Guam, and Samoa, among other Pacific islands. As Das testified in his statement, U.S. policymakers during this period often used immigration law as a tool to promote a fledgling America's global power; Washington flexed its national sovereignty through gatekeeping, even as it built loopholes into the Chinese exclusion laws to accommodate growing U.S. commerce and economic influence in the region.[9] The formal dismantling of the exclusion regime beginning in the 1940s saw the United States in a very different position: no longer struggling to match its older European counterparts, it was now a global superpower rivaled only by the Soviet Union. The political climate in Asia had also changed. A surge in anticolonial nationalism, coupled with the demands of U.S. wartime alliances with Asian powers, meant that Asians were less willing than ever to tolerate foreign powers who overtly ignored their claims to sovereignty and self-determination. As decolonization proceeded apace, Washington officials embraced more subtle and indirect tactics to insinuate U.S. influence. In short, if the old empire depended on formal colonial structures and coercion, the new U.S. empire was mostly informal and based on Asians' willing cooperation with and consent to U.S. power—or at least the appearance thereof.[10]

During the mid-twentieth century era of decolonization, repeal became part of the United States' efforts to create the appearance of equality and reciprocity in its dealings with Asian peoples. This project of racial liberalism was not merely a domestic one of incorporating racial minorities into a nation; during the World War II and postwar years, the U.S. state deployed some of its main tenets—in particular, its emphasis on nondiscrimination and inclusion—as a strategy to advance its empire-building projects in Asia.[11] Here I build on the work of Takashi Fujitani. Confronted by the demands of fighting a total war in Asia and Japanese propagandists excoriating the racial hypocrisy of the United States, he argues, Washington officials disavowed the exclusionary or "vulgar" racism associated with Nazism in favor of inclusionary or "polite" forms that could help mobilize racial minorities in the war effort at home and cultivate nonwhite allies on the global stage by persuading them of the United States' liberatory intentions toward them.[12] Applied to U.S. immigration and naturalization law, racial liberalism supported the belief, which steadily gained traction in Washington, that the United States simply could not seek to incorporate Asian peoples into its overseas sphere of influence if it continued to openly exclude them from entry and inclusion at home. Thus, the repeal laws did not so much represent an end to institutionalized U.S. racism against Asians. Rather, much like the United States' postwar empire itself, they repackaged racial hierarchy in ways that lawmakers felt they could present as polite, consensual, and in keeping with a decolonizing world order.

This book tracks the transpacific movement of Asians, Asian Americans, white American elites, and others who lobbied U.S. Congress for repeal between 1943 and 1965.[13] The movement was transpacific in a literal sense: advocates and the arguments they used drew from both sides of the Pacific.[14] My analysis of repeal rests on two main premises. First, repeal was not a one-time legislative event in Washington; rather, it came about as a result of a decades-long movement in which some people fought to dismantle only individual laws but others envisioned the dismantling of the entire Asian exclusion regime. Existing studies have tended to focus on single campaigns for repeal. One of the consequences has been an overarching emphasis on change rather than continuity as the story of repeal. In fact, I find great similarity between the symbolic measures of the 1940s and the more general repeal legislation of the Cold War years. All shared the same goal of continuing to restrict Asian immigration with laws that facilitated rather than hampered the expansion of U.S. power in Asia.

A second and related premise is that people, not geopolitics, were the primary drivers of policy change. International events and foreign policy pressures may have created political opportunities, but people's actions on those pressures made repeal possible. This study expands on current scholarship by considering the unique circumstances of colonial Asian groups, most notably Indians and Filipina/os. It also includes Asian actors on both sides of the Pacific, challenging binary distinctions of foreign versus domestic and Asian versus Asian American. This approach illuminates the strange duality and ambivalence which often accompany our view of U.S. immigration policy and practice. On the one hand, scholars generally acknowledge that immigration is a matter of foreign policy that involves U.S. relations with external powers. On the other hand, we tend to assume that immigration is primarily a domestic or internal conversation in which U.S. state actors alone decide who is allowed to enter or join the nation and on what terms. The corollary assumption is that people outside the United States—and especially members of foreign governments—do not have a role and that it would be inappropriate for them to have one.[15] This book challenges the conventional divides by incorporating different ways of addressing these historical developments, not only by analyzing U.S. archives regarding these issues, but also by utilizing records from the Philippines and India. When placed in conversation with the U.S. historical record, these documents from the global context reveal the extent of Asians' involvement in the U.S. repeal movement.

Among the forces spearheading the repeal campaigns, I am particularly interested in how the supposedly inclusive or antiracist imperatives of America's postwar empire empowered historically marginalized Asian and Asian American actors to wield unprecedented influence on Capitol Hill. In keeping with the patriarchal power structures of the time, these actors were overwhelmingly, though not all, men of some socioeconomic advantage. Nevertheless, their newfound influence illustrated an unexpected dynamic of U.S. ascendancy. By framing repeal as a tool of U.S. empire building in Asia, this volume makes visible a hitherto unnoticed paradox: the need for Asian consent to U.S. imperial expansion after 1945 gave historically marginalized Asian peoples unprecedented leverage to influence policy in Washington, DC. With the U.S. empire's new emphasis on a consensual relationship between U.S. power and the peoples that it sought to control, congressional lawmakers and executive branch officials alike had more reason to be receptive to Asian demands than ever before. With greater power, then, came greater vulnerability. During a time when few Americans knew much about Asia and when Asian faces remained a novelty on Capitol Hill, Asian Americans seized the moment to carve out a political niche as unofficial spokespersons for Asian audiences in ways that could offset their larger communities' lack of electoral power, even as Asians representing colonial governments in India and the Philippines championed U.S. repeal legislation as part of their own nation- and state-building projects.

By saying that repeal was a basic component of U.S. empire building, I do not mean to suggest that the promotion of American power was the ultimate goal of everyone involved in the repeal campaigns. Certainly, this was the case for many U.S. state actors, but advocates of repeal included both strong proponents *and* strong opponents of U.S. empire in Asia. In one way or another, however, all used or relied on U.S. power in their pursuit of repeal.

During a turbulent yet formative time in Americans' understanding of race and race relations, congressional debates over repeal served as a proxy for diverse contests over citizenship, national identity, and America's proper role in the world. That repeal could assume such expansive meanings was in part a function of many advocates' belief in the United States' prescriptive influence on the global stage. In this line of thinking, U.S. repeal measures granting greater recognition to Asian peoples could serve as an instrument or stepping stone to achieve loftier goals, such as increased status and legitimacy for long-subordinated peoples on the world stage. Some Asian colonial officials even expressed their hope that U.S. repeal measures might inspire other Western powers to follow the United States' lead in validating the equality of Asian peoples. Writing empire into the history of U.S. immigration reform can thus illuminate how national projects — whether U.S., Indian, or Philippine — became implicated in the U.S. imperial project in unexpected ways.[16] Specifically, the wide breadth of a transpacific approach allows us to see how the tensions and continuities between the transnational and national could help drive change in ways that were productive as well as destructive to the goal of repeal; national and transnational visions of repeal were not always in tension but could and sometimes did complement each other.

Das's experience, which opened this introduction, exemplifies the entanglement between exclusion and empire that this book interrogates. It was no coincidence that the desire to escape British colonialism in India drove both Das's migration to the United States and his initial pursuit of American citizenship, as he sought the protection of the U.S. state to safeguard his efforts to subvert the British empire. At the same time, when he fled to the United States, Das negotiated multiple imperial regimes in deciding his own political destinies, and many other Asian migrants followed a similar path.[17] His story further illustrates the importance of anticolonial struggle in shaping Asian migration, an element that narratives focused on the United States as a receiving site can sometimes ignore.[18] Indeed, as the coming chapters will show, repeal's bridging of diasporic communities with homeland governments at times led to discord among colonial Asian activists in the United States over their disparate visions of what independence and self-determination should look like in practice. In contrast to U.S.-focused diplomatic perspectives, which can devalue the role of Asian Americans as largely irrelevant to policy outcomes, this book's transpacific approach thus takes seriously the motives and actions of Asian *and* Asian American actors in their pursuit of repeal in a way that, in line with the call of cultural scholar Sau-ling Wong, avoids reinforcing the "American minority political enterprise."[19]

In addition to its transpacific lens, this book contributes to the scholarship by addressing how the movement for repeal reached across domestic racial lines. It was in constant conversation with other campaigns for race reform in the United States, including the movement for black civil rights. Putting Asian exclusion repeal into conversation with black civil rights gives greater insight into how Asian American activists negotiated their lack of electoral power.[20] One consequence of Asians' historical exclusion from both immigration and naturalization was that persons of Asian descent comprised less than half a percent of the total U.S. population and an even smaller share of the American electorate by the early 1940s; these numbers would not grow substantially until after 1965. This meant that while the success of the black civil rights movement relied in large part on the strength of northern black swing voters and the targeted legal strategies of well-established groups such as the National Association for the Advancement of Colored People (NAACP), Asian Americans in the repeal movement necessarily practiced different modes of political influence; the repeal movement had no equivalent of the black freedom struggle's Birmingham campaign. Here I draw on Lisa Levenstein's notion of a "movement without marches," which stretches our historical imaginations beyond traditional modes of protest to look for less easily recognized forms.[21] As the following chapters detail, in the absence of electoral power, Asians and Asian Americans cultivated distinct forms of political influence to overcome their political handicaps and wield influence for repeal. Their methods often played out behind the scenes in less public forums: Asian Americans wrote letters and petitions; testified before congressional committees; forged ties with a bipartisan network of U.S. officials and lawmakers; and partnered with white community organizations, church groups, and others. At times, they capitalized on white Americans' tendency to racialize Asian Americans as unofficial proxies for Asian audiences to secure meetings with U.S. policymakers, capture media attention, and otherwise amplify their voices. By taking this collective advocacy seriously despite its divergence from conventional models, this book expands our conception of how political influence works while enlarging our understanding of the uses of U.S. power—and who could deploy it toward what ends.

Those seeking to leverage U.S. internationalist imperatives eventually hit the strategy's inherent limit: most congressional supporters of repeal wanted the appearance of racial progress, not actual change.[22] From the repeal of the Chinese exclusion laws in 1943 to the comprehensive reforms of the 1965 Hart-Celler Act, U.S. lawmakers crafted repeal measures that removed overt anti-Asian discrimination from the law but sought—and largely succeeded—to maintain the status quo. Indeed, many Asian and Asian American advocates defined the removal of overt discrimination as their target. Many advocates considered more meaningful reform politically infeasible. Others hoped that piecemeal or nominal legislation would eventually lead to more substantive change in the future. But none of the laws that passed had the intent of allowing mass Asian immigration to the United States, and even the most optimistic of supporters did not necessarily expect the Hart-Celler Act to change the complexion of the nation. Yet it did precisely that, multiplying the number of Asians entering the country more than twentyfold between 1965 and 2015 and changing forever what constituted Asian America. This outcome was the movement's greatest and most lasting irony, and explaining how we got here—the twists and turns, the unexpected bedfellows—is the subject of this book.

The History of Exclusion and Empire

Scholars disagree on the precise point when Washington began to prioritize Asia as a significant focus of U.S. foreign policy interest, but it was Japan's attacks that focused Washington's attention on immigration and naturalization policy at a moment when U.S. policymakers saw their own security as increasingly dependent on the cooperation and goodwill of Asian peoples.[23]

The triggering event was Japan's World War II propaganda campaigns, which sought to woo Asians allied with the United States and Allied powers into the Axis camp by highlighting the racism of the U.S. Asian exclusion laws. A 1942 radio broadcast from Tokyo describing the Chinese Exclusion Act passed sixty years earlier as a "humiliation not only of the Chinese but of all Asiatics" was a case in point.[24] This and other Japanese critiques citing exclusion as evidence of U.S. racism and hypocrisy helped transform the U.S. immigration debates into a litmus test for American racial attitudes toward Asian peoples.

Asian governments had long condemned the racism of U.S. exclusion measures, with Qing officials protesting both restrictions on Chinese migration and Americans' mistreatment of Chinese migrants even before the 1880s. White American missionaries, businessmen, U.S. policymakers, and others had lobbied over decades for the repeal of discriminatory immigration laws on a variety of diplomatic, humanitarian, and economic grounds. But it was not until the Sino–American alliance of World War II made China central to Washington's own military interests that calls to end Chinese exclusion finally gained traction. So long as Washington continued to channel its resources toward Europe and the war against Germany, leaving the Chinese military to bear the brunt of the Allies' battle against Japan, Americans saw the goodwill of the Chinese government and people as critical to U.S. and Allied success in the Pacific War. By defining the insult of exclusion in pan-Asian terms, Japanese propagandists attacking the United States also set the stage for the expansion of repeal efforts to benefit not just Chinese but all Asians affected by exclusion.

This book shows how the complex relationship between repeal and Asian decolonization played out both independently of and in conversation with the Cold War.[25] As repeal unfolded over nearly a quarter century beginning in the early 1940s, Asia was remade as the first site of global decolonization, with more than ten Asian colonies gaining independence from the United States, Japan, and European imperial powers. The United States' informal empire building in this period reached across East, South, and Southeast Asia, often repurposing the formal colonial infrastructures left by departing European powers and imperial Japan as the basis for less overt and unofficial mechanisms of control. The goals of American intervention—to expand U.S. economic and military power—did not change, although their scale and the variety of tactics used both grew. The stakes were economic as well as political, as Washington vied to safeguard and promote U.S. dominance in contests with the Soviet Union and communist Asian powers on the one hand, and in negotiations with nationalists in Asia wary of the United States and other Western imperial powers on the other.

Scholars have explained the apparent contradiction in that U.S. empire building in Asia coincided with the dismantling of formal empire by demonstrating that decolonization was, as Simeon Man writes, "not antithetical to the spread of U.S. global power but intrinsic to it."[26] As they remind us, decolonization, or the formal process by which a colony transitioned to independent status, carried no guarantee that a former colony would ever achieve full sovereignty or self-determination. The strength of the U.S. postwar empire lay in its protean nature, its ability to adapt quickly to local circumstances and challenges. Postwar Asia was a case in point. Rather than replace formal colonies with fully sovereign and independent nation-states, in many cases decolonization featured the insinuation of U.S. dominance through indirect and often informal means. Between 1945 and 1953 alone, U.S. forces occupied and funded the rebuilding of a defeated Japan; occupied part of and then fought a war in Korea; and supported and then were cast out of mainland China with the communist victory in 1949. Further south, U.S. military involvement in present-day Vietnam and surrounding areas escalated to full-scale war by 1964. It also established a client state in Indonesia and attempted, with limited success, to engage an emerging neutralist power in a newly independent India. The Philippines exemplified the shift in U.S. empire most clearly, as Washington continued effectively to control the island nation's economy and military for decades after granting it formal independence in 1946.

Making Sense of Exclusion and Repeal

On the whole, existing studies have framed the rise and fall of Asian exclusion in the United States as two discrete chapters in U.S. history. In tracing the development of Asian exclusion in the United States, historians, legal scholars, and others have profiled the anxious white moralists, labor leaders, and calculating American politicians who championed the 1875 Page Law and the 1882 Chinese Exclusion Act restricting the entry of Chinese women and workers;[27] the anti-Asian groups in California whose appeals resulted in the 1907 Gentleman's Agreement which informally ended Japanese labor migration to the United States;[28] the nativists and exclusionists responsible for the 1917 Immigration Act's creation of an "Asiatic Barred Zone";[29] and the anti-Japanese forces supporting the 1924 Immigration Act, which completed and consolidated the Asian exclusion regime both by bringing Japan under exclusion and by making the ability to immigrate dependent on eligibility for U.S. citizenship.[30] Exclusion did not go uncontested. A parallel body of work has examined the diverse cast of actors who, together with Asians and Asian Americans, challenged the practice of exclusion from early on. Among others, they included internationalists in the U.S. State Department and the broader executive branch, American missionaries and religious groups, and commercially minded business interests.[31] As the story goes, the relative weakness of Asian powers vis-à-vis the United States and other Western countries made it politically possible for U.S. lawmakers to defend exclusion through decades of diplomatic protest and petition. Japan was the exception that proved the rule, illustrating the importance of empire and interimperial frameworks in shaping exclusion: Washington's reluctance to offend the imperial Asian power delayed the passage of formal legislation barring Japanese until 1924, when they became the last Asians not associated with a U.S. colony to be added to the list of racially banned groups.[32]

If scholarly narratives assign the origins of exclusion to racism and nativism, labor competition, and the demands of national party politics, they narrate repeal as a story of U.S. foreign policy and postwar internationalism.[33] With a few notable exceptions, analyses of repeal have been piecemeal, focused on specific laws, with studies scattered across a wide range of disciplines: history, legal and critical race studies, sociology, and political science.[34] They have concentrated on how Washington supported policy liberalization in the context of specific pressures or geopolitics related to World War II or the early Cold War. These accounts have tended to focus on China and Japan to the neglect of how diverse Asian peoples participated in the process. This study expands on current scholarship by considering the unique circumstances of colonial Asians—in this case, Indians and Filipina/os—as well as by thinking more broadly about repeal in three additional ways: first, in relation to U.S. empire building and expansion; second, in terms of how diverse coalitions of actors within the United States and across the Pacific worked together on repeal; and third, as the time span of the volume as a whole indicates, by periodizing repeal as a longer movement that extended past World War II into the era of decolonization and early Cold War years. Several scholars have drawn connections between the various repeal acts, but few have theorized them as a coherent movement that began with the repeal of Chinese exclusion in 1943 and culminated with the comprehensive reforms of 1965, as this book undertakes to do.[35]

Opening the Gates to Asia joins a growing body of work situating the rise and fall of the United States' Asian exclusion regime within global frameworks as well as within the longer history of U.S. empire in Asia.[36] Within this expanding literature, it makes several key interventions. First, it makes clear that repeal was about U.S. empire in Asia generally, not the Cold War alone. Contextualizing repeal within the history of U.S. empire writ large reminds us that the United States had a complicated relationship with anticolonial independence movements that far predated both the crystallization of the Cold War and the dismantling of formal empire after 1945. Washington officials struggled for years to articulate a clear position that reconciled the United States' own colonial identity with the interests of its European allies and the reality of anticolonial nationalism slowly shifting the international balance of power from the colonizers to those peoples on the cusp of decolonization. In what Erez Manela has called the "Wilsonian Moment" after World War I, U.S. President Woodrow Wilson appeared publicly to affirm the principle of self-determination but did little to enact this support for non-European peoples, alienating the loyalties of several Asian nationalists who would later become a thorn in Washington's side.[37] After World War II, the United States' dilemma became more urgent, as years of anticolonial struggle came to a head in nationalist wars for independence across the Asian continent. The weakening of long-entrenched European and Japanese colonial structures presented opportunities for the United States to gain a foothold in new parts of the region. U.S. military occupations in southern Korea and Japan, the creation of the People's Republic of China (PRC), and wars in Korea and Vietnam shaped U.S. immigration and naturalization policy in conversation with the Cold War and never merely as a symptom of it.[38] A longer timeline also reminds us that although the United States' empire building efforts to spread democracy were undoubtedly global in scope, its postwar projects in Asia—the first but not the last site of decolonization—were absolutely pivotal to U.S. global ascendance after World War II, even if most U.S. officials refused to acknowledge its importance. Asia's secondary status in the minds of many Washington policymakers helps account for the popularity of immigration and naturalization policy, as tools of diplomacy between the United States and Asian powers. U.S. policymakers reluctant to commit significant resources to Asia were often more amenable to using indirect or symbolic changes in such laws to further their goals in the region.[39]

Second, considering exclusion in the context of empire deepens our understanding of U.S. power vis-à-vis other white settler societies as well as in relation to other empires after World War II. In the former case, the discussion adds another dimension to recent work on Asians and settler colonialism.[40]

In its centering of U.S empire and its recognition of the United States' singular dominance in postwar Asia, this study elucidates why even though the United States was neither the first nor the only white settler state to initiate and construct an Asian exclusion regime, it was the first to dismantle the version it had created.[41] By the mid-twentieth century, Canada, New Zealand, and Australia had all enacted a medley of anti-Asian restrictions similar to those of the United States, with each regime reflecting the particular tensions of capitalism's clash with racial nationalism in that locale. Australian scholars have been at the forefront of the effort to globalize our current understanding of Asian exclusion by examining its history across several white settler societies. In the process, they have done the most to de-exceptionalize the United States by situating it within a global history of white supremacy in which white settler societies wanted Asian laborers but did not want to color their populations; their work reminds us that Australia, not the United States, was the first country to construct a broad exclusionary regime targeting Asians.[42] Nonetheless, U.S. power and its consequences during the postwar period set it apart.[43] The late Marilyn Young warned against downplaying these consequences; in trying to contextualize the United States within a wider world, she cautioned, scholars should be careful not to flatten U.S. hegemony after World War II.[44] When restored to an accurate and nuanced portrayal of global power inequities, the analysis demonstrates how the United States' greater power and need to protect imperial projects across the region made Washington that much more vulnerable to the pressures and petitions of Asian peoples. Among white settler societies, the United States alone had possessed a formal Asian colony.[45] By World War II, it had the most military troops on the ground and the most dollars invested in the region. Given that the stakes of continuing exclusion were the highest for the United States and its postwar empire in the region, it makes sense that Washington was the first to begin repackaging its regime in more inclusive terms.[46] It had the most to lose from potential backlash if it did not.

Recognizing the rise of U.S. hegemony during and after World War II is vital to this book's understanding of the inter-imperial nature of the repeal movement and how various campaigns sought to capitalize on shifting relations between the United States and other empires.[47] The United States' ascent to "preponderant power" saw it surpass the British and a defeated Japan as the preeminent imperial power in postwar Asia, challenged only by the Soviet Union and, to a lesser extent, after 1949, by the PRC.[48] As the United States' profile rose, some repeal advocates sought to use its newfound stature to advance their own causes. An inter-imperial lens, historian Augusto Espiritu writes, can be used to reveal instances of cooperation and conflict between empires as well as examples of "subaltern agency," or the many acts of resistance individuals and groups employed to manipulate larger powers or otherwise carve influence out for themselves.[49] I am particularly interested in examining this third category with relation to Asian and Asian American advocates for repeal. Some embraced U.S. supremacy as a pragmatic opportunity to realize their long-desired goals. Others viewed their support for repeal as part of an anti-imperial critique of the new U.S. empire, perceiving (correctly) that its innocuous appearance masked something more insidious.

Navigating their different relationships to U.S. supremacy was just one of the challenges Asians and Asian Americans faced. The third intervention of this book lies in examining how these advocates became actors in the drama of repeal in complicated and contradictory ways. Tensions inherent to the structure of the Asian exclusion laws created conditions ripe for conflict within Asian American constituencies. A case in point was Section 13(c) of the 1924 Immigration Act, which made eligibility to immigrate to the United States contingent on eligibility for U.S. citizenship.[50] By conjoining immigration and naturalization—two bodies of law with distinct histories—this provision made it necessary for any repeal measure to treat both arenas. It thus marked a sharp departure from precedent, in which immigration and naturalization policy had developed along largely independent paths. The entanglement necessarily complicated how advocates approached repeal. The mismatch between the foreign policy dimensions of immigration admission and the domestic focus of naturalization law would come to the fore in more than one campaign, at times creating schisms along class, religion, and other lines. This diversity in interests reminds us of the different stakes repeal carried even within a single community. Depending on one's class and citizenship status, eligibility for U.S. immigration and naturalization could be important on principle, or as a matter of daily survival.

By bridging U.S. Indian and Philippine communities in the United States with Asian colonial governments, the campaigns simultaneously set the stage for discord to emerge between homeland and diaspora over what national independence and self-determination should (and would) look like in practice. Many Indians and Filipina/os living in the United States had fought for their homelands' independence long before the repeal movement expanded the political opportunities and audience for their activism. The cause of repeal not only gave Indians and Filipina/os in the United States a new and timely platform from which to continue their calls for Asians' self-determination. Repeal measures also became their instrument to champion what was for many a long-standing and deeply personal cause. As the process of decolonization began in earnest, lofty nationalist ideals and goals gave way to concrete debates over policy and finances, and myriad proposals for how to enact the liberation for which so many had fought with deep passion and commitment. The repeal campaigns often felt the impact of the fissures and factionalism that resulted.

Even as the book broadens our understanding of repeal as a transpacific movement, it reminds us that repeal must always be understood in the context of U.S. domestic politics and their connections to imperial projects abroad. For example, the discussion of 1950s and 1960s repeal campaigns brings Asian American activism squarely into conversation with black civil rights and the burgeoning scholarship on comparative civil rights movements. Scholars of California and the U.S. West have documented rich histories of cooperation and conflict between Asian Americans and other nonwhite communities in sites such as Los Angeles and Sacramento. But as this book shows, Asian and black American advocates negotiated different political pressures and challenges in lobbying for federal legislation in Washington, DC.[51] Taking a long-term view of repeal allows for a broader and more nuanced understanding of the relationship between the repeal of Asian exclusion and black civil rights struggles, as they followed different timelines over the middle decades of the twentieth century. Following the paths of these two political efforts over an extended period allows us to see how the various campaigns that composed the longer movements converged, diverged, and proceeded independently of each other at different moments in time.

The black civil rights struggle and the movement for repeal were deeply entangled in the minds of the lawmakers whose votes determined the policy impact of these efforts. This was particularly true for southern Democrats, whose commitment to keeping America a white, preferably Anglo-Saxon, nation drove their broad opposition to ending the national origins quota system, desegregating public accommodations, and enacting federal protections for black Americans, among other policy proposals. Insofar as both movements challenged white supremacy, they faced the common ire of resistant lawmakers. But neatly conflating the two causes can obscure the very different politics and pressures that ultimately made legislative change possible in each. In just one example, during a time of unprecedented U.S. expansion in Asia, repeal acts that promised not to increase Asian immigration while making the United States look good abroad were arguably more palatable than civil rights measures that stood to destabilize long-entrenched racial practices at home.

This book shows that ultimately, the history of repeal was marked more by continuity than by change. The shift from Asian exclusion to repeal tracked concurrent transformations in U.S. empire, which changed forms but remained remarkably consistent in its goals. Just as exclusion went hand in hand with the historical rise of the United States' formal empire in Asia, repeal was a story about how a new, informal U.S. empire made Asians visible and important for a small window of time and how Asians, Asian Americans, and their allies seized this opening to realize what was for many a long-standing goal. This returns us to the reality that for most supporters of repeal, ending Asian exclusion was never supposed to increase immigration from Asia in any meaningful way. Repeal was exclusion's quick and timely antidote, promising the highest return in terms of advancing U.S. influence and empire for the least cost in resources expended and sacrifices made. And, for a time, it seemed to deliver on this expectation. The exclusion laws, once repealed, ceased to be a major talking point for U.S. rivals looking to undermine Washington's appeal to newly decolonized Asian peoples, and Asian immigration, though it increased steadily through nonquota categories, remained manageable as a small fraction of the overall migrant stream. We now know how serious of a miscalculation this was.[52] An immigrant stream that was more than 85 percent European before 1965 became overwhelmingly Asian and Latina/o by the following decade. The disruptions caused by U.S. imperialism in Asia could no longer be denied, and all the more so as the post-1965 immigrants were joined by refugees fleeing Southeast Asia in the wake of the U.S. wars in Vietnam.

OPENING THE GATES TO ASIA covers the repeal movement chronologically in five chapters. Each takes up a different campaign in recognition of the distinct origins, cast of actors, and politics behind the passage of the four major laws that together formally repealed Asian exclusion: the 1943 Magnuson Act; the 1946 Luce-Celler Act; the 1952 McCarran-Walter Act; and the 1965 Hart-Celler Act. Just as the history and timeline of exclusion looked different for individual Asian groups, so too did the process of repeal. The book's structure also reflects how cooperation between the different efforts was more episodic than sustained. Although advocates regularly adapted strategies used by other groups, each campaign mostly worked independently toward its own distinct goals. One of the consequences of these siloed efforts was that white American elites both in and out of Congress were often the most consistent throughline bridging the various efforts that together made up the movement for repeal.

The first phase of the movement comprised campaigns for piecemeal legislation that addressed barriers affecting individual Asian groups. During World War II and the immediate postwar years, Congress singled out Chinese, Indians, and Filipina/os for inclusion while leaving the general Asian exclusion regime intact. The book begins by tracing the passage of the 1943 Magnuson and 1946 Luce-Celler Acts, laws whose significance is often downplayed due to their largely symbolic nature. Framed within the longer history of U.S. immigration, however, the two pieces of legislation mark a turning point. They reversed the trend from restriction to liberalization for the first time since federal gatekeeping began in the late nineteenth century, and they laid the groundwork for the postwar trend toward relaxation, even if repeal came in fits and starts. Chapter 1 explains how the World War II campaigns to repeal Chinese exclusion created the foundational infrastructure for a longer repeal movement, with the Magnuson Act's success inspiring other Asian groups to revive or initiate similar demands. Departing from the overwhelmingly diplomatic focus of most accounts, I trace the roots of the 1943 campaign in community-based advocacy to reunite Chinese American citizens with their wives left behind in China. Long before white elites launched their media crusade for formal repeal, Chinese Americans had been fighting for the future of their families. White elites who formed the public face of the effort were critical to the success of Chinese exclusion repeal in the midst of war, but their victory came at a cost to Chinese Americans seeking to reunite families long separated by restrictive exclusion laws.

As World War II raged on, Indians, Filipino/as, and their transpacific network of allies seized on the political momentum of Chinese exclusion repeal to launch campaigns of their own. Chapters 2 and 3 chart how their efforts resulted in passage of the 1946 Luce-Celler Act at the start of the Asian decolonization era. The law granted immigration and naturalization rights to Indians and U.S. citizenship eligibility to Filipino/as upon their homelands' independence. While often dismissed as a nominal gesture by Washington to the decolonizing peoples of India and the Philippines, the 1946 law was critical in that it made repeal a longer, cumulative process rather than a one-time exception for Chinese. The Luce-Celler campaigns also illuminate how the projects of U.S. empire building and Asian exclusion were intimately linked. Although at least one scholar has described the act as a "sequel" to

Chinese exclusion repeal, from the start, the Luce-Celler campaigns were entangled with the anticolonial politics of the Indian and Philippine independence movements in ways that tested and often exposed the limits of the United States' oft-touted commitment to the self-determination of Asian peoples.[53] The focus on colonial groups not only expands the analysis beyond the scholarship's usual attention to Chinese and Japanese Americans. It also situates the Luce-Celler campaigns within the larger histories of Indian and Philippine struggles for national independence. I give special attention to the important, yet virtually unknown role of Indian and Philippine colonial government officials in lobbying for the law's passage by the U.S. Congress. Their work, as detailed in Asian and U.S. government documents, provides insight into the different ways that U.S. officials engaged with decolonizing Asians as well as with their imperial overseers—in this case, Great Britain and the United States itself—under pressure to relinquish their colonies. Centering the problem of colonialism through a transpacific lens allows us to take seriously the varied motives and actions of Asian *and* Asian American advocates.[54] In this case, Asian sources reveal how Indian and Philippine officials refashioned U.S. repeal legislation into tools that served their own state- and nation-building project in Asia.

The final two chapters chart a shift in the repeal movement from piecemeal to broad-based measures. The 1952 McCarran-Walter Act formally ended Asian exclusion by giving Asians nominal immigration quotas and naturalization rights, while the 1965 Hart-Celler Act eliminated the national origins quota system once and for all. In this last stage of the movement, observers commonly described repeal as an Asian American civil rights effort analogous to the black freedom struggles that were dominating news reports and political discussion in Washington, DC. Chapters 4 and 5 paint a more ambivalent picture of Asian Americans' negotiations with other nonwhite communities also fighting for rights and protections on Capitol Hill. These chapters situate Asian American advocacy for repeal alongside concurrent debates over black immigration and civil rights, the future of Mexican braceros, and calls by ethnic whites to end the national origins quota system's discrimination against southern and eastern Europeans. The resulting patchwork of legislation caused some groups to gain while others lost. This outcome reminds us that, as a driving theme of the repeal movement, racial liberalism was not intended to bring about racial justice, but to advance U.S. state goals.

In chapter 4, the Japanese American Citizens League (JACL) experienced the fallout of the United States' zero-sum racial logic when it supported the rights of Japanese immigrants at the expense of other nonwhite groups in lobbying for the McCarran-Walter Act. The 1952 law formally ended Asian exclusion as a feature of U.S. immigration and naturalization law, but it simultaneously cut off black immigration from the Caribbean, straining JACL's relationship with the NAACP and other black American groups in the process. Chapter 5 analyzes Chinese and Japanese Americans' efforts to make repeal meaningful amid the escalation of U.S. war in Vietnam and an apex in the black civil rights movement. An important but overlooked fact in the Hart-Celler campaigns was Hawaii's admission as the fiftieth U.S. state. Hawaiian statehood marked a new phase in the United States' postwar empire. Highlighting the work of Asian American lawmakers elected to Congress from Hawaii, I show how their pivotal role in the debates leading to passage of Hart-Celler in 1965 shaped the law, which brought migration from the Western Hemisphere under restriction for the first time even as it liberalized the overall policy.

The epilogue considers how the relationship between Asian migration and U.S. empire, exclusion and power, began changing in the 1960s through discussions of "brain drain" from Asia to the United States. Some of the same Asian powers that had once critiqued the United States for excluding Asians on racial grounds now accused the United States and other Western countries of strategically luring away the most educated and skilled members of developing societies, thereby ensuring their own economic hegemony for years to come.

Confronting the history of Asian exclusion repeal in the United States requires coming to terms with its deep and abiding entanglement with empire. In the late nineteenth and early twentieth centuries, the rise of the U.S. Asian exclusion regime went hand in hand with formal imperial projects in Asia, delimiting and defining the racial boundaries of the American nation against the scourge of nonwhite peoples from the Philippines and beyond then coming under U.S. control. Formal empire could change the United States in many ways, both imperialists and their critics argued, but not in its racial identity as a white nation. The expansion of the Asian exclusion regime, which reached its full articulation in 1924, tracked the popularity of Anglo-Saxon visions of the nation. By World War II, however, U.S. officials in Washington could no longer keep empire at arm's length. Excluding the very people it sought to control was no longer a tenable model. Repeal was part of the compromise, representing Washington's efforts to repackage itself as a racially inclusive state that would lead Asians by consent rather than coercion.

The U.S. exclusion regime may have ended in the 1960s, but the legacies of U.S. empire in Asia—most visible in the form of the millions of Asian peoples it drove to American shores—are not so easily erased. The number of Asian immigrants has grown from less than half a million in 1965 to more than 13 million half a century later. Over the same period, Asians have grown from 5 percent to more than 30 percent of the U.S. foreign-born population, and from less than half a percent to 6 percent of the U.S. population overall. Asians now exceed Latino/as as the top immigrant group coming to the United States, and if the trend continues, by 2055, Asians will make up the largest foreign-born population in America.[55] As Lisa Lowe writes, it is no coincidence that so many post-1965 immigrants have come from "countries deeply affected by U.S. colonialism, war, and neocolonialism." In her telling, they represent the "material legacy" of the "repressed history of U.S. imperialism," which may have changed tactics and form but remained inexorable as ever.[56] In the 1980s, Sri Lankan writer Ambalavaner Sivanandan coined the phrase, "We are here because you were there," to single out the role of British imperialism in driving black migration to the United Kingdom. His aphorism is equally relevant in this case. Asians came to the United States because Americans first went to Asia.[57] Framed in this light, the tremendous migration from Asia that followed repeal and the many diverse communities it created are perhaps the best reminders of how the transpacific ties first forged by U.S. empire continue to bind today.

CHAPTER ONE

Laying the Groundwork for a Movement
The World War II Campaign to Repeal Chinese Exclusion

Storekeeper Jew Lou, known as "Charley" to his customers, was born in San Francisco in 1877, five years before Congress passed the first Chinese exclusion act restricting the immigration of Chinese workers to the United States.[1] As a young man Lou traveled the Deep South, in search of opportunities outside California. He eventually opened a grocery store in Pace, Mississippi, as one of the small town's earliest settlers. By the time he was of marrying age, exclusion and antimiscegenation laws were in full effect, and in any case, he preferred to marry a Chinese woman. So, like many Chinese Americans at the time, he traveled to China, where he married and had a son. At the time, loopholes in the exclusion laws permitted U.S.-born citizens such as Lou to bring their Chinese wives and foreign-born children to the United States. Nevertheless, the process was lengthy and onerous, and Lou had a financial responsibility to his business partner in Pace. In 1905 he returned to Mississippi on his own and continued to support his family from abroad. It would be another fifteen years before Lou returned to China with paperwork in hand to bring his son K. C. to the United States. When K. C. Lou, in turn, wanted to start a family, he made the same journey across the Pacific for a wife. Like his father, K. C. married in China, had a child, and began the legal process to bring his family to the United States. It was now 1925, however, and the Johnson-Reed Act of the year prior had closed the loophole in the law allowing citizens to sponsor immediate family members for entry outside of the general restrictions on Chinese immigration. K. C. Lou also returned to Pace alone. Over the next two decades, he traveled to China regularly, and he and his wife had a second child, a son named Charles. Concerned for their safety amid Japanese expansionism, Lou initiated paperwork to bring his family to the United States after the outbreak of the Pacific War, but his case made no progress due to the 1924 Immigration Act. A private relief bill passed in 1952 eventually enabled Lou's mother to bring Charles, now a young man, to the United States, where they settled in California.[2] But there would be no reunion. By then, K. C. was dead, of complications associated with appendicitis. His separation from his wife and two children, always meant to be temporary, thus became permanent, like that of tens of thousands of "trans-Pacific" families created by the U.S. Chinese exclusion regime.[3]

The Lou family's experience epitomizes how Chinese "exclusion" operated more like a sieve than a solid wall for much of the period the 1882 Chinese Exclusion Act and the laws extending it were in effect.[4] Before 1924, Chinese continued to enter the United States through class- and family-based exemptions that permitted merchants and elites—along with their wives and the wives and children of Chinese American citizens—to immigrate despite race-based restrictions. Chinese Americans such as K. C. Lou relied on these loopholes to create families as restrictive immigration policies, antimiscegenation laws, and other structural and social barriers made it difficult for Chinese men living in the United States to partner with non-Chinese women. Given their importance, when the 1924 act unexpectedly ended these practices, it was not surprising that Chinese Americans from across the country launched a campaign to restore them. As detailed below, this effort was in progress by the time the World War II campaign to repeal the Chinese exclusion laws began gaining momentum and quickly supplanted it. Taking these family and community histories as a starting point, this chapter analyzes the Chinese exclusion repeal campaigns as a dialogue and negotiation between a community-based effort driven by the needs of Chinese Americans and an elite white American campaign rooted in Washington's wartime imperatives.

The role of U.S.–China diplomacy and elite white lobbyists in the World War II campaigns to repeal Chinese exclusion has been well documented.[5] Existing studies often begin with a speech Soong Mei-ling, wife of Chinese Nationalist leader Chiang Kai-shek and "First Lady" of China, delivered to a joint session of the U.S. Congress on February 18, 1943. Her message was simple but strong: Chinese troops had for "four and a half years of total aggression . . . borne Japan's sadistic fury unaided and alone," and needed greater aid and assistance from the United States. The Allies had it wrong, she asserted, if they believed Germany to be a greater threat than Japan, which had far "greater resources at her command."[6] Soong's speech created a sensation in the American press: journalists lauded her "bravery" and "courage" in making China's case before the American people.[7] Although Soong never mentioned U.S. exclusion laws in her speech, several House lawmakers seized the moment to introduce Chinese exclusion repeal bills to Congress. They hoped that the demands of the Sino–American alliance and of winning the Pacific War would persuade U.S. lawmakers finally to undo the longtime restrictions.

Over the first half of 1943, lawmakers introduced nine measures to repeal the Chinese exclusion laws enacted between 1882 and 1902. Some versions proposed a straightforward repeal, whereas others provided naturalization rights for Chinese and an annual immigration quota for China. Such petitions were not new but, as the story typically goes, the wartime demands of a faltering Sino–American alliance against Japan gave calls for repeal unprecedented urgency. The Citizens Committee to Repeal Chinese Exclusion and Place Immigration on a Quota Basis (hereafter, Citizens Committee), a group of white elites with ties to U.S. diplomatic and missionary circles, skillfully catalyzed pressure groups and played on Washington's fears of losing a Chinese ally to create momentum for repeal legislation during the spring and fall of 1943. Over just seven months, this committee successfully popularized the case for Chinese exclusion repeal as a wartime measure to defeat Japan in the Pacific and as an exceptional act of wartime diplomacy needed to meet the demands of an exceptional time. Their efforts even prompted President Franklin Roosevelt to appeal personally to Congress. The result was the passage of the Magnuson Act, or the Chinese Exclusion Repeal, in December of that year.

Much in this account is true, but its portrayal of the Magnuson campaign as a stand-alone effort by white elites that began in early 1943 and ended in victory that fall is incomplete. Situating Chinese exclusion repeal within a longer history of Chinese American community activism, this chapter describes the Citizens Committee campaign as the culmination of historical efforts to liberalize U.S. immigration policy toward Chinese on the one hand, and as the beginning of a longer movement for repeal on the other. On the first point, I will recover the origins of the repeal campaign in its ongoing conversation—and at times, contest—with a grassroots effort led by Chinese American citizens seeking to reunite with their wives and families stranded in war-torn China. In what became a pattern over several subsequent campaigns, the Citizens Committee interrupted and ultimately superseded a community-based effort, in this case, one intended to restore nonquota admission for the alien wives of Chinese American citizens.[8] Charting this context makes clear how the Magnuson Act, far from a product of wartime geopolitics alone, more accurately represented the convergence of transnational and national, diplomatic and community-based pressures. Tracing the interaction of the two campaigns highlights a fundamental tension between those individuals who wanted immigration policy to address concrete concerns rooted in the community and those who privileged its symbolic value as a foreign policy tool. The interplay between these two imperatives was generative at times and limiting at others; in this case, it had the paradoxical effect of helping to drive the success of Chinese exclusion repeal as a diplomatic gesture, while delaying gains desired by Chinese American communities.[9]

This chapter charts how the Citizens Committee campaign for repeal planted the seeds of a longer movement. Profiling some of the white Americans who became mainstays in subsequent campaigns to repeal exclusion for other Asian groups, it explains how the Citizens Committee campaign served as a launching pad for later repeal efforts. The threat of setting a precedent that other groups could use to demand similar gains proved one of the hardest objections for supporters of repeal to overcome in the face of U.S. lawmakers determined to keep the nation white. Exclusionists' fears only grew as Indians, Koreans, and others seized on the momentum surrounding Chinese exclusion repeal to make claims of their own.

A Brief History of Chinese Exclusion

The 1882 Chinese Exclusion Act was one of a constellation of laws passed between 1875 and 1924 that together constructed a Chinese restriction regime sensitive to differences of class and gender. Women were some of its earliest targets; seven years before the first Chinese Exclusion Act, the 1875 Page Law barred all Chinese seeking entry to the United States for "lewd and immoral purposes." Although the law did not single out Chinese women specifically, their exclusion was widely understood to be one of its goals based on the highly racialized assumption that most Chinese women seeking entry to the United States were prostitutes.[10] Indeed, the Page Law proved so effective at excluding Chinese women that their share of the total U.S. Chinese population fell from 7.2 percent in 1870 to just 3.6 percent in 1890.[11] Before 1924, most Chinese women gained entry to the United States through the sponsorship of their husbands, who were either U.S. citizens of Chinese descent or part of the exempted class of Chinese merchants.[12] While these loopholes explain how women composed 30 percent of Chinese American citizens by 1940, the consequences of the community's historical gender imbalance and ongoing restrictions were still evident by the war years. The division of Chinese families such as the Lous, for example, took a generational toll.[13]

Challenges to U.S. immigration restriction began even before the 1882 Chinese Exclusion Act passed Congress and continued in different forms through World War II.[14] A low rumble of protest initiated in the late nineteenth century never completely disappeared. In May 1905, Chinese merchants in China boycotted American goods to express their opposition to recent U.S. legislation extending the exclusion laws indefinitely. Chinese throughout Asia and the United States protested in what one scholar has called an expression of "trans-Pacific Chinese nationalism."[15] Chinese Americans of varied backgrounds—elite and nonelite, citizen and noncitizen—employed a range of creative strategies to challenge and circumvent legal restrictions.[16] For example, organizations such as the Chinese Six Companies of San Francisco and other chapters of the Chinese Consolidated Benevolent Association retained lawyers to defend persons threatened with deportation in U.S. courts and before state immigration boards. Of the various repeal campaigns, the battle to overturn Chinese exclusion attracted the most significant and sustained interest from white Americans.[17] American Protestants, particularly missionaries with ties to Asia, and businessmen interested in the China trade, were the two most prominent white constituencies.[18] Until the organization went defunct in the late 1930s, leaders of the American Asiatic Association, a group of American merchants and business interests active in the Far East, lobbied Congress for a loosening of restrictions on Chinese immigration as the key to preventing further disruptions to U.S. commerce in the region.[19] At different times, liberal and humanitarian organizations including the YMCA and YWCA, the National Institute of Immigrant Welfare, the National Council of Jewish Women, the American Civil Liberties Union, and individual Americans with an interest in China joined them, forming a diverse coalition of support for Chinese exclusion repeal.

Nevertheless, several factors conspired to undermine the strength of the repeal movement before World War II. Most immediately, a conservative coalition of southern Democrats and western Republicans supporting exclusion used their influence on the House and Senate Committees on Immigration and Naturalization to keep bills relaxing existing restrictions off the congressional agenda. Attentive to foreign policy, the White House and executive branch had tended historically to support liberalization, but Congress controlled immigration and naturalization policy, and China's weakness on the international stage—it was at best a semicolonial power—gave lawmakers little incentive to act on Chinese objections. In this regard, it becomes clear that Washington's interest in repeal during World War II was as much, if not more, about undercutting the power of an expansionist Japan as it was about bolstering a wartime Chinese ally. Through the interwar years, U.S. officials were content to let Chinese officials stew over the insult of exclusion while Washington focused on the main threat to American interests in the region: imperial Japan. In the years after World War I, U.S. diplomats devised the Washington order to neutralize it; the United States, Great Britain, and other European naval powers curbed the size of their navies in exchange for Japan's pledge to do the same. But this new order would not last. Tokyo chafed at the efforts of Western powers to curb Japan's military power, and Japanese leaders and citizens alike roiled at the racial insult of the United States' 1924 Japanese exclusion clause. Japan's invasions of Manchuria and the Chinese mainland in the 1930s dashed any hope of a quick or meaningful rapprochement. By the start of the Second Sino-Japanese War in 1937, Washington was firmly on the side of the Chinese and sending aid to Chiang Kai-shek's government based on the belief that only a strong China could offset the rising Japanese threat and safeguard the United States' own fortunes in the Pacific. Within a few years, repeal advocates began using Japan's actions to elevate the issue of exclusion from a minor irritant in Chinese-American relations to a major problem of wartime diplomacy that demanded the attention of even the staunchest exclusionists in Congress.[20]

The Fight for Chinese Wives

In September 1941, Albert Lee, a Chinese American merchant in Boston, sent a petition to the local office of the American Board of Commissioners for Foreign Missions. Citing reports of Japanese brutality in occupied China, he asked for help on behalf of Chinese Americans seeking to reunite with their Chinese wives and children and get them out of harm's way.[21] Lee understood the urgency of the situation firsthand. Japanese soldiers had killed his own wife a few years earlier, and now he devoted his energies to ensuring that other Chinese men could "avoid this same fate."[22]

The reinvigorated anti-exclusion movement during World War II may have traced its origins to Lee's petition, but in partnering with the northeastern chapter of the Chinese American Citizens Alliance (CACA), Lee and his white American allies joined an effort first launched nearly twenty years earlier. In October 1924, the CACA and other Chinese American organizations across the country created the fourteen-member Committee to Challenge the 1924 Immigration Act (*Boli ju*). Its goal was to reopen the loophole allowing the Chinese alien wives of U.S. citizens and of merchants to enter the United States outside of existing restrictions. Working with prominent white lawyers, the *Boli ju* had successfully won readmission for the latter; beginning in 1925, Chinese merchants could once again bring their alien wives into the country outside of the 1924 ban on all Asian immigration. But the 1925 court ruling not only excluded the wives of U.S. citizens. It also foreclosed the courts as a site for future appeal on the issue.[23] Chinese Americans responded by shifting their attention to Congress, where they appealed to individual lawmakers for relief.

The *Boli ju* disbanded following the court ruling, and West Coast leaders in the CACA, a fraternal organization of U.S.-born citizens of Chinese descent founded in 1895, became the public face of the cause. CACA membership was selective: before 1976, it was limited to prominent male community leaders, and prospective members had to be sponsored by two current members and approved by a screening committee before gaining admission. Compared with the Chinese Consolidated Benevolent Association (CCBA) and other community organizations open to noncitizens, the CACA had several advantages as a legislative vehicle. Since all members were U.S. citizens, they could vote, allowing them to claim at least a modicum of electoral power; indeed, for decades, certain chapters of the CACA actually required its members to vote in U.S. elections or pay a penalty. CACA members, drawing largely from the middle and elite classes, were often well educated and fluent in English. Many were professionals, and some even had American legal training.[24]

Y. C. Hong, who served as president of the CACA's Los Angeles chapter from 1926 to 1949 and Grand President of the whole Alliance from 1949 to 1953, was the first person of Chinese ancestry to pass the California Bar and be admitted into practice in the state. Hong served a mostly Chinese American clientele at his law office in Los Angeles's Chinatown. Just twenty-six years old when he began leading the community-based campaign for a Chinese wives bill, Hong embodied the CACA's ideal of Chinese American assimilation and middle-class respectability. Born in San Francisco, he received his JD and LLM degrees from the University of Southern California Law School, where he wrote his graduate thesis on the 1882 Chinese Exclusion Act. In 1925, Hong authored a pamphlet titled *A Plea for Relief*, which the CACA circulated to members of the House and Senate Immigration Committees in Congress. In this document, he argued that the state's practice of excluding the alien wives of Chinese American citizens violated their rights as U.S. citizens. He further suggested that permanently separating Chinese American men from their Chinese wives encouraged miscegenation and thereby endangered "the safeguard of public morals."[25] Interracial marriage between "persons of the Mongolian race" and whites, he pointed out, was

Portrait of Y. C. Hong, 1930s. Y. C. Hong Papers, The Huntington Library, San Marino, California.

illegal in at least eleven states, including Arizona and California. By affirming rather than critiquing lawmakers' fears of racial mixing between Chinese and others, Hong's piece reflected the conservative tendencies and accommodationist bent of the CACA as a whole.

The CACA's approach achieved limited success. Sympathetic lawmakers sponsored two rounds of Chinese wives bills in 1926 and 1928.[26] Speaking before the Senate Committee on Immigration in 1928, CACA member Wu Lai Sun of the Portland Lodge reassured lawmakers that the wives admitted would not compete with white American workers. But none of the measures made it past a committee hearing.[27] In 1930, the CACA won a partial victory in the form of a law admitting those Chinese wives of U.S. citizens who had married *before* the Immigration Act of 1924 went into effect, up to a quota of sixty women per year through 1940.[28] Amid the economic hardship and resurgent nativism of the Great Depression years, however, a general wives measure remained elusive as congressional lawmakers searched for ways to reduce, not increase, immigration overall.[29]

Change did not come until the outbreak of World War II and the United States' formal entry into it. By the time Madame Chiang Kai-shek visited Capitol Hill in early 1943, Albert Lee of Boston and other CACA leaders had successfully secured two congressional sponsors for a Chinese wives bill. Rep. Sheridan Downey of California had personal ties with the local CACA and with Chinese Americans throughout his southern California district. Rep. John Lesinski Sr. of Michigan, the son of Polish immigrants and a devout Catholic with seven children, regularly used his seat on the House Immigration Committee to champion the liberalization of U.S. immigration policies, particularly those related to family reunification. On the first day of the new congressional session in January 1943, Lesinski introduced to the House a bill providing for the "admission to the U.S. of alien Chinese wives of American citizens" regardless of marriage date or citizens' country of origin. The legislation caught the attention of House Immigration Committee chairman Samuel Dickstein (D-NY), who scheduled a hearing over the objections of several southern members. Months before Chinese exclusion repeal had its first formal hearing, discussion of the Lesinski bill highlighted some of the main questions animating the debate. Perhaps most pressingly, lawmakers asked, for whom was immigration liberalization primarily intended: Asian allies in Asia, Asian Americans, or another constituency altogether? And what would be the consequences of passing a Chinese immigration bill? Would it address a specific problem or begin a cascade that imperiled the United States' Anglo-Saxon heritage and its identity as a majority white nation?

Between the time the hearing was scheduled and when it actually took place in early March 1943, Madame Chiang Kai-shek's Washington visit and famous speech to Congress, followed by the introduction of the first Chinese exclusion repeal measures by Rep. Kennedy (D-NY), transformed the Lesinski hearing into a proxy for the larger debate over Chinese exclusion repeal. To the chagrin of Chinese American supporters, House lawmakers and witnesses alike spent more time comparing the two pieces of legislation than discussing the wives bill on its own terms. Still, the hearing was instructive, offering valuable lessons for advocates of both Chinese immigration measures on ways to maximize support.

A major factor hurting the Lesinski bill's cause, advocates widely agreed, was its main base of support among religious organizations and church groups with only modest influence in Washington, DC.[30] As David Hollinger notes, Protestant leaders had more political sway than scholars often assume, but the influence of white American missionary figures in particular was on the decline by the 1940s. During World War II, skeptical U.S. officials were as likely to question the loyalties of religious leaders as they were to dismiss them for being out of touch with the reality of power politics.[31] Discussion at the hearing revealed the weakness of religious proponents' reliance on principled and humanitarian arguments, such as the sanctity and integrity of the family. Albert Lee was the only Chinese American witness to appear and even he devoted the first part of his short statement to reading the endorsements of Catholic clergy and other prominent religious leaders. Like Y. C. Hong twenty years earlier, Lee sought to use lawmakers' fears of miscegenation between Chinese men and white women to scare them into supporting the wives bill. Given their long history of calls to protect white womanhood from the sexual threat of black men, he rightly predicted that southern Democrats would fear a similar intermingling of white women with Chinese immigrants.[32] Indeed, it is notable how many northern Democrats, including liberals who touted their commitment to racial equality, claimed to share the sentiment. As House Immigration Committee chairman Samuel Dickstein stated bluntly: "The situation is this: Here is an American-born Chinese. We do not want him to mingle except with his own kind. We all agree to that."[33] It is difficult to say how sincere Dickstein was—the sentiment was certainly strategic—but his statement was just one instance when advocates of repeal publicly affirmed some of the same racist beliefs as their proexclusion peers.

Lawmakers opposed the wives bill on several grounds. Southern Democrats at the Lesinski hearing made clear their strong opposition to not just the wives bill but any measure that proposed a liberalization of immigration policy. As a voting bloc, they were formidable due to their strength in numbers, their control of many congressional committees due to seniority, and their power to filibuster in the Senate. As a group, they were restrictionist, segregationist, and federalist, and they based their objections to repeal on all three grounds. Rep. A. Leonard Allen of Louisiana led the opposition group within the House Immigration and Naturalization Committee. A cantankerous man of humble origins who had passed the bar without attending law school, Allen was known for his colorful fishing and farming metaphors. He repeatedly voiced critics' fears that easing Chinese immigration to the United States in any way would set a precedent for more sweeping change to come. Like the committee's other southern members, Allen was especially wary of Chairman Dickstein, a naturalized immigrant from New York, who by the early 1930s, was well known for championing the controversial admission of Jewish refugees from Europe[34] and the elimination of the 1924 act's national origins quota system more generally.[35] Walter Judd, a former missionary in China turned newly elected Republican congressman from Minnesota, was a less likely adversary of the wives bill, but a highly influential one. He argued that a bill repealing Chinese exclusion was a better use of Congress's wartime goodwill toward China and opposed the wives bill to the extent that it would jeopardize repeal.

Repeated disagreement between Judd and Dickstein reflected their individual commitments and priorities, but it also exposed a larger dichotomy between lawmakers who believed that the first priority of congressional legislation should be to promote domestic civil rights justice for Chinese Americans, and those who saw immigration policy primarily as a tool to advance U.S. interests overseas. For Dickstein, the wives bill was imperative for upholding the equal rights of Chinese American citizens; as a result, he saw the Lesinski bill as a purely domestic matter.[36] This view was consistent with his general approach to immigration policy. The child of Lithuanian Jewish immigrants and a naturalized immigrant himself, Dickstein began his career by voting against the 1924 Immigration Act and spent the rest of his twenty-year term in the House fighting to overturn its national origins quota system.[37] While he was active on foreign policy matters throughout his time in Congress, the New York lawmaker remained most interested in how overseas developments affected people living in the United States.[38] As chairman of the House Committee on Immigration and Naturalization from 1931 to 1945, he had broad discretion to bring liberal measures up for hearings, but as the committee's most polarizing member he was rarely successful. Anti-Semitism was at least partly to blame for his unpopularity, which was not limited to southern lawmakers: during a time when 40 percent of Americans believed that Jews had too much power, Judd was one of several lawmakers who accused Dickstein of adding "a loophole" to admit Jews to the United States into every bill he proposed.[39] Anti-immigrant sentiment also played a role.[40] Dickstein's vocal support for refugee legislation therefore made him a double target.

In contrast, Judd used the Lesinski bill hearing as an opportunity to articulate the case for Chinese exclusion repeal as a tool of U.S. wartime diplomacy aimed primarily at a Chinese rather than an American audience.

Whereas Dickstein dismissed anyone outside the United States as a secondary factor, Judd argued that the millions of Chinese in China "courageously" fighting Japan should be the main audience U.S. lawmakers considered when deciding which Chinese immigration bill should pass. Judd spoke at length about the people he had met in China while stationed there as a medical missionary. Citing the wisdom he had personally gleaned about the Chinese people and how they think, he devoted most of his statement to explaining why repealing the Chinese exclusion laws was the superior option. For one, repeal would admit fewer Chinese to the United States while making a larger symbolic statement about U.S. commitment to the Chinese and to the principle of racial equality by "removing the color bar." By contrast, the wives bill would potentially allow in thousands of Chinese women without removing the racial stigma of the exclusion laws, and Chinese families, Judd warned, would begin "propagating." Finally, from the "standpoint of international goodwill," the wives legislation would do little for the "450 million Chinese" whom the United States should "have as friends in the next hundred or two hundred years."

In the short term, Judd's objections were highly influential in the Lesinski hearings. At a closed-door meeting of the House Immigration Committee's main leadership in April, several lawmakers echoed Judd's contention that repeal would simultaneously have greater symbolic value and smaller practical impact than the wives bill. Rep. Carl Curtis of Nebraska (R-NE), for example, cautioned against letting "hordes and hordes of Chinese" come into the country.[41] In reality, his argument was a ruse; all eight southern Democrats on the committee would have likely opposed the bill anyway. But Judd's eloquent objections provided them with a convenient excuse, and indeed, southern critics would continue to paraphrase Judd's foreign policy critique throughout the early days of the campaign. On April 7, 1943, the House Immigration Committee rejected the Lesinski bill by a vote of nine to six.

When confronted with the choice of whether to try again, CACA leaders agreed to put the wives bill on hold in favor of a repeal measure whose passage would presumably pave the way for more legislation in the future.[42] It was a pragmatic decision. Chinese American community leaders recognized that absent the support of powerful white elites, their cause could never hope to attain the same level of political momentum the Citizens Committee had achieved. Over subsequent months, they supported its repeal measure in various ways. They published pieces advertising the Citizens Committee's efforts in Chinese-language newspapers.[43] They offered financial support:

funds collected by Chinese community groups in Hawaii, for example, made up one-fourth of the Citizens Committee's total operating budget.[44] The CACA thus hoped to serve the Chinese American community's long-term interest, even if it meant working through an all-white campaign not of their own creation. In the words of Xiaojian Zhao, Chinese Americans "well knew that the repeal was only a wartime strategy of the government," but they were open to using it as a stepping stone to achieve their own goals.[45]

The Citizens Committee to Repeal Chinese Exclusion

Relative to the Chinese wives campaign, the origins of the Citizens Committee effort among white American elites with connections to China are better known and documented.[46] In 1941, a U.S. consul in Hong Kong named Donald Dunham contacted New York publisher Richard Walsh to discuss the possibility of repealing the U.S. Chinese exclusion laws as a way to improve the United States' sullied image among Chinese.[47] Alarmed at what he saw as the exclusion laws' embarrassing effects on U.S.–China diplomacy, Dunham asked Walsh, the husband of China missionary turned Nobel Prize–winning author Pearl Buck, to initiate a popular campaign for repeal. Walsh would ultimately become the chairman of the Citizens Committee, which comprised a small executive committee and a mailing list of thousands of Americans by the spring of 1943. While Lee and other Chinese American advocates had to rely on the goodwill and patronage of white American influencers, the Citizens Committee had many more resources from which to build. To start, Walsh mobilized his extensive professional network and influence in media and culture to advertise the case for repeal to people in power as well as among religious Americans broadly. At Walsh's suggestion, East Asia expert Charles Spinks called for repeal in the monthly journal *Asia and the Americas*.[48] Hundreds of private citizens and American organizations sympathetic to the cause contacted the Citizens Committee after reading the piece. Walsh also marshaled his connections and resources to hold town halls, where he publicized the case for repeal as a wartime imperative. Reports published in newspapers and religious publications garnered the nascent organization even more followers.

Early supporters of the Citizens Committee were a diverse group whose different interests and motives presented a challenge as well as a strength. In addition to chairman Richard Walsh, more liberal members included Pearl Buck; labor leader Monroe Sweetland of the Congress of Industrial Organization; Read Lewis of the Common Council for American Unity;

sociologist Bruno Lasker of the National Council on Naturalization and Citizenship; and Roger Baldwin of the American Civil Liberties Union (ACLU). Among the group's more politically conservative members were Rep. Walter Judd, *Time-Life* editor-founder Henry Luce, and his wife, Rep. Clare Boothe Luce (R-CT). From the start, an internal debate broke out over questions of scope, or how broad the group's goals should be. Namely, should the Citizens Committee lobby for simple repeal or more substantial change? Should it advocate only for Chinese or fight for the rights of several or even all Asian peoples?

Internal discussions surrounding the group's formal launch in May 1943 suggest how, in recruiting supporters to lobby the cause of China, the Citizens Committee effectively created a network of advocates committed to more comprehensive reform. The Citizens Committee may have officially begun as a group focused on repealing Chinese exclusion, but as late as April up to half of its mailing list reported a strong preference for a broad-based measure that repealed exclusion for all Asian peoples.[49] Much of the final negotiations featured efforts by the core leadership to persuade would-be supporters that a Chinese-only agenda was the best path forward. To be clear, many of the Citizens Committee's main leaders, including Walsh and Buck, personally desired comprehensive repeal. But they believed it was politically infeasible. So long as the United States was at war with Japan and more than 120,000 Japanese Americans—two-thirds of them U.S. citizens—remained incarcerated in state-run camps along the West Coast, they felt a general Asian immigration bill would never pass Congress.[50] As evidence, Walsh cited the failure of a general naturalization bill Rep. Vito Marcantonio (D-NY) introduced earlier that year; the mere suggestion that the bill could one day benefit the Japanese had doomed its chances from the start.[51] Judd and other supporters proposed limiting legislation to apply to friendly allies only (thereby excluding enemy nations such as Japan), but several committee leaders remained skeptical.

Christian organizations were among the most insistent on the need for a more expansive bill that repealed exclusion for many Asian peoples, not just Chinese. Because they opposed racial restriction in U.S. immigration policy on principle, some even wanted to include Japanese. The Federal Council of Churches (FCC) did not go that far, but it remained one of the most outspoken and stalwart of the bunch. As an umbrella group representing thirty-two mainline Protestant denominations, the FCC was one of the most influential ecumenical organizations of the time with strong political connections and support in Washington, DC.[52] For nearly two decades, it had also been one of the most active and consistent champions of ending Asian exclusion. Through the spring of 1943, when hearings on the repeal bill began, the FCC's executive committee continued to resist Walsh's requests to narrow their demands to repeal for Chinese only. Indeed, just days before the House Immigration Committee hearings on repeal were set to begin, FCC leaders adopted a resolution asking Congress to modify existing laws to allow all persons from "friendly" nations, including Asian ones, to enter the United States under the current quota system. According to the resolution, racial exclusions in the current law did "violence to the Christian view of one humanity under God" and, as such, were "contrary to the democratic principles upon which the country was founded."[53] Since even devout southern lawmakers were often content to ignore arguments rooted in religious beliefs or morality, the FCC's advocacy arguably did little to win new converts to the cause. But as an important Protestant organization, it typified the preference of many religious groups for broader legislation on the grounds that exclusion was morally problematic, not just in relation to Chinese but for all Asian peoples.

The debate could have stretched on much longer, but news that the House Immigration Committee had scheduled a May hearing on Chinese exclusion repeal forced Citizens Committee leaders to make an executive decision. With just weeks to spare, Walsh and a core group moved to make membership in the newly formed Citizens Committee contingent on the acceptance of three goals: (1) the repeal of the Chinese Exclusion Acts; (2) an annual immigration quota for Chinese; (3) Chinese eligibility for U.S. citizenship as an exception to the racial ban on Asiatic naturalization. While some continued to press for a broader bill, most supporters were mollified by Walsh's encouragement to see the Chinese campaign as the first step in a gradual process of repealing exclusion laws for all Asian peoples. Judd was among them: since earlier in the year, he had been working with officials in the Justice Department to draft a comprehensive bill for Asian exclusion repeal. But after gauging the political climate, they decided to put the broader-based legislation on hold until the Chinese measure passed. This general repeal measure would resurface after the war; its reintroduction and eventual incorporation into the 1952 McCarran-Walter Act was just one example of how the wartime campaign for Chinese exclusion repeal laid the organizational and legislative infrastructure that ultimately made the wholesale repeal of Asian exclusion possible.

A Missionary Crusade for Repeal

White American missionaries to Asia had long been active in the effort to undo exclusion laws targeting Asians, and they would continue to play a key role in campaigns during and after World War II.[54] As the three most prominent "missionary-connected Americans" within the Citizens Committee leadership, Walter Judd, Pearl Buck, and Henry R. Luce exemplified three important functions missionaries played in the longer repeal movement. First, they translated foreign cultures and peoples to a white American audience. According to David Hollinger, missionaries often served as "point persons" opening the "public ear to nonwhite voices" and guiding Americans' "engagement with peoples beyond the United States and Europe." One observer of the time credited Buck's 1931 book, *The Good Earth*, with having "'created' the Chinese . . . for a whole generation of Americans."[55] Second and related, they used their platforms and their racial capital as white Americans to promote the cause; as "whites," Hollinger writes, the missionaries could "get a hearing for things Asian."[56] Before World War II, all three figures were affiliated with the American Committee for Non-Participation in Japanese Aggression. The group called on the United States to take a harder line on Japanese expansionism in Asia and successfully lobbied for a U.S. embargo on Japanese oil and metal in 1937. Third, although personal experience always informed their actions, missionaries often took care to cast their petitions in pragmatic terms to stave off criticisms of being overly sentimental or, as in the case of Walter Judd, of lacking patriotism as a globalist more interested in helping Asians than Americans.

No lawmaker or missionary figure would become more closely identified with the repeal movement than Walter Judd, whose faith-based service in China anchored a two-decade-long congressional career. Born into a devout midwestern family, Judd earned his medical degree and then worked as a traveling secretary for the Student Volunteer Movement of Foreign Missions during the 1920s. During that time, he came under the influence of legendary missionary and occasional U.S. diplomat John R. Mott and his idea of "Christian missions" as the "great and true internationalism." Mott's vision of "missionary statesmanship" casting individual student volunteers as "ambassadors, interpreters, and mediators in the most vital aspects of international and inter-racial relationships" inspired Judd and instilled in him a deep belief in his Christian responsibility to serve other peoples of the world.[57] Judd's ten years as a medical missionary serving rural Chinese populations shaped his lifelong interest in Asia and China, in particular. During the 1920s and 1930s, he witnessed firsthand the human impact of Chinese civil unrest and Japanese expansion into the Chinese countryside; these experiences cemented his opposition to the U.S. policy of appeasement and drove his calls for Washington to defend Chiang Kai-shek's besieged Nationalist government, a position Judd later championed as one of the founders of the Cold War "China Lobby." Escalating violence and repeated bouts with malaria forced his return to the United States. Once stateside, he ran for Congress based on a growing belief that he could "do China more good" from within the U.S. government than anywhere else.[58] He specifically cited a desire to "remove the stupid and insulting immigration measures which stigmatize all non-Caucasians as hopelessly inferior peoples" as one of the main reasons he left medicine to seek public office.[59]

As a lawmaker elected on an internationalist platform, Judd felt the tensions between his cosmopolitan past and his national office perhaps most keenly. From the beginning of his House term, he successfully parlayed his decade of missionary service into proof of his expertise on Asian affairs, especially those involving China. In this, he both played on and benefited from Washington's heightened receptivity to missionary voices at a time when they were among the few white Americans with deep knowledge of Asian cultures and languages.[60] In his first major address on the House floor in February 1943, Judd claimed that his experiences helped him understand what Asian peoples "really want, what they feel, what they are after." Likening the United States' situation in the Pacific to "the body of a patient at the autopsy table" and himself to a "doctor" studying the patient, he prescribed "true understanding" and "knowledge" as the remedies to improve U.S. relations with Asian powers.[61] House members, including many southern lawmakers, cheered his speech with a standing ovation, and American media outlets, including liberal ones, joined the applause: a piece in the *Nation* magazine profiled the Minnesotan as one of eight new congressmen to watch.[62] Nevertheless, Judd initially avoided the spotlight in the repeal campaign for fear that his missionary past would undermine the effort. Through early 1943, he privately lobbied for repeal bills but refused to sponsor any, and he intentionally kept his name off Citizens Committee letterhead and other campaign materials.[63] As he wrote to a missionary colleague, he was concerned that his participation in the Citizens Committee's public effort would paint it as a quixotic religious or moral crusade driven by the "starry-eyed idealism" of a "sentimental and impractical missionary." Critics already accused him of being "more interested in China than in America" based on the length of time he had spent there and the many Sinophile causes he had championed after his return.[64] The last thing he wanted was to do more harm to the cause.

At first glance, Pearl Buck and Henry Luce shared the most in common. Both were missionary kids who had grown up in China and become fixtures in the elite New York publishing world, where their work interpreted and publicized Asia for the consumption of white American readers. Buck was probably the more famous of the two, even if Luce was just as influential. While both were primarily interested in China, they were also members of the New York–based India League of America, which, as discussed in the next chapter, figured prominently in the Indian repeal campaign. The daughter of two Presbyterian missionaries, Buck grew up in rural China, attended college in the United States, and returned to northern China for nineteen years as a missionary alongside her first husband. It was during this time that she wrote *The Good Earth* (1931), the book that earned her a Pulitzer Prize in literature. Shortly thereafter, she divorced and returned to New York where she married Citizens Committee chairman Richard Walsh, who was also her publisher at John Day. Her work set in China earned a Nobel Prize in 1938. Like Buck, Henry Luce spent his childhood in China, though he never lived there as an adult. According to Luce's biographer, Robert Herzstein, two main forces shaped his "character and worldview": "Protestant Christianity" and "a fervent faith in America's God-ordained global mission in Asia."[65] As the cofounder and president of Time-Life Inc., Luce used his influential publications to champion U.S. intervention in Asia generally and the containment of communism specifically. Throughout the longer movement for repeal, Luce used his editorial power over *Life* and *Time* magazines to publicize the cause and the activists who lobbied for it with favorable profiles and editorial pieces. This was no small matter, as *Time* and *Life* magazines reached upward of 10.5 million Americans and a quarter to half of the middle-class American reading public by the late 1940s and *Time* was the most popular magazine among every income bracket, including Luce's monied and influential colleagues in publishing and government.[66] Rep. Clare Boothe Luce, Henry's second wife, served two terms in the House between 1943 and 1947 and would go on to cosponsor repeal legislation for Indians after the war.

Politically, however, Luce and Judd were more like-minded. Beginning in the 1930s, Buck's outspoken criticism of Chinese Nationalist leader Chiang Kai-shek increasingly put her at odds with her missionary colleagues, who remained devoted allies of Chiang for decades to follow. Judd famously helped cofound the China Lobby in the early 1950s; for two decades, China Lobbyists played a pivotal part in the decision of the

United States and the United Nations to recognize Chiang Kai-shek's anti-communist Republic of China (ROC) government in lieu of the People's Republic of China's (PRC) communist regime.[67] In the words of Buck's biographer, beginning in World War II Luce came to regard Buck as "his adversary . . . wrong on Chiang, soft on Communism, sentimental about equality, and unreliable on the use of American power."[68] In fact, around the time that the Citizens Committee campaign officially began, he explicitly forbade his magazines from publishing anything positive about Buck or her writings. Even so, the disagreement did not stop him from joining the Citizens Committee under the leadership of Buck's husband.[69] Buck and Luce would not be the only advocates of repeal to have profound disagreements—though theirs may have been the most public—as the movement attracted supporters with diverse backgrounds and political affiliations.

The Citizens Committee Strategy

In preparation for the House Immigration Committee's hearing on repeal scheduled to begin in May of 1943, leaders of the Citizens Committee made several important decisions that would continue to inform the longer repeal movement. The first was to limit membership in the organization to white Americans. They argued that lawmakers would see them as objective and dispassionate, unlike people of Chinese descent. T. C. Hsu, the only person of Chinese descent in attendance at the Citizens Committee's April meeting, agreed.[70] The second was to emphasize the military and diplomatic importance of repeal over principled or humanitarian arguments for passage—that is, to frame the cause as a wartime or diplomatic effort, rather than as a racial or ethnic one. In so doing, the Citizens Committee established geopolitics and wartime expediency, rather than civil rights and humanitarianism, as the main language of a successful repeal campaign. Strategies originally adopted to maximize the campaign's short-term success had longer-term implications for subsequent efforts, including over who could best champion the cause and what kind of arguments they should use.

Most immediately, the Citizens Committee's all-white membership policy prompted careful negotiation by Asian and Asian American advocates seeking to retain some influence. In effect, the policy marginalized Chinese American voices, except in highly staged ways. Committee secretary Geneva Cranston recruited two Chinese American citizens to speak at the House repeal hearings as models of assimilated, hardworking, and therefore deserving community members.[71] Both used the same strategy, downplaying their Chinese heritage as secondary or otherwise irrelevant to their identity as Americans. Fred Yee, an electronics engineer for the U.S. War Department, spoke the language of an unhyphenated Americanism. As a third-generation Chinese American citizen, Yee opened his testimony by disavowing any personal association with Chinese organizations and emphasizing that he was not there to speak for any particular group. He then went on to reaffirm his U.S. citizenship status *in spite of* what he called his "Chinese" features. Dr. Li Min Hin, a medical doctor and former commander of the American Legion in Hawaii, likewise downplayed his Chineseness. As a lifelong resident of Hawaii, he told the congressmen that he no longer felt "conscious" of his Chinese roots and that other Chinese Americans shared his single-minded commitment to the United States: "The only home we have is America," he asserted. "What else is there to fight for?" With House Immigration Committee member and Hawaii Territorial Delegate Joseph Farrington (R-HI) chiming in to agree, Li described the assimilation of persons of Chinese descent in Hawaii and their unique contributions to the war effort as skilled, educated workers. In doing so, he suggested a color-blind understanding of American patriotism that did not differentiate based on race. But race did matter, and not simply as an obstacle to explain away. The statements of both men suggested their awareness of racial novelty's power at a time when Asian Americans made up less than 1 percent of the mainland U.S. population and many white Americans had never seen an Asian face in person.[72] Yee, for example, offered himself as proof that Chinese could be assimilated; "I like to be here just to show you," he stated.[73]

The Citizens Committee's all-white policy further constrained Chinese government officials from playing a prominent role at the hearings. Members of Chiang Kai-shek's administration generally believed that the Japanese government's attempts to stop congressional exclusion in 1924 had backfired. To avoid causing similar backlash, they eschewed a visible role in the public campaign, while promoting the legislation's success in other ways. Over the spring of 1943, Chinese consular officials helped recruit witnesses for the congressional hearing and wrote letters to local newspapers expressing the Chinese government's support for the cause. The Chinese ambassador to the United States visited the State Department twice to convey China's support for passage. During the hearings, representatives of the Chinese Embassy even made unofficial visits to members of the House Immigration Committee and the Immigration and Naturalization Service (INS), prompting southern lawmakers to complain about foreign officials

Soong Mei-ling (Madame Chiang Kai-shek) addresses U.S. Congress, 1943. Bettmann / Getty Images.

overstepping the lines. While Madame Chiang Kai-shek did not explicitly refer to the Chinese exclusion laws in any public speeches during her 1943 U.S. visit, she discussed the issue several times in private conversations with U.S. lawmakers, including Rep. Martin Kennedy, who sponsored the first repeal bill in the House.

The Citizens Committee's pragmatic focus established wartime expediency and geopolitics as the primary languages of the longer repeal movement. The leadership determined early on that war-related appeals citing repeal's value to winning the Pacific War tended to evoke the least opposition, while those based on abstract principles such as racial equality and human rights antagonized certain segments of Congress.[74] Framing repeal as a wartime measure had several additional advantages. First, even the most reluctant congressional lawmakers felt hard-pressed to deny a critical wartime ally during a time when Allied victory on the Pacific front was by no means assured.[75] Second, the tactic appealed broadly to voters. Finally, and perhaps most important, framing repeal in terms of wartime interests allowed supporters to dodge thorny questions about domestic race relations and racial tensions amplified by the war.[76] Scholars often describe World War II as a watershed in U.S. race relations, but in 1943 it was a shift still in the making. A. Philip Randolph's threatened March on Washington had forced Roosevelt to act on fair employment practices in 1941, and the African American media launched its "double V" campaign for victory against racism at home and fascism abroad in the same year. Jim Crow was under attack and southern Democrats were on the defensive. By locating the locus for reform in Asia, advocates sought to recast domestic questions of race as secondary concerns less relevant to a discussion primarily about U.S. military and security interests overseas.

For their part, the House Immigration Committee's large contingent of southern Democrats rejected this argument on its face. Repeal, they countered, was a domestic matter whose passage would almost certainly exacerbate the nation's already tense racial climate and the "Negro problem" in particular. Pearl Buck's participation undermined the Citizens Committee's ability to rebut this argument; at one point during her testimony, Louisiana Congressman A. Leonard Allen prodded her about a recent radio appearance in which she had called for "full and complete social equality among Negroes and whites, and all other groups."[77] Buck tried to dodge by claiming that the war context made her views on domestic race relations irrelevant, but Allen had won the point. Along with measures to address Jim Crow, such as anti–poll tax bills, Allen and other restrictionists easily derided repeal as federal government outreach infringing on southern states' rights.[78] Rep. W. Arthur Winstead (D-MS), a farmer turned first-term congressman, warned that allowing more Chinese into the United States would set the United States back "5 to 10 years" by worsening an already "serious" "Negro problem" and otherwise increasing "hatred between the races" by introducing a third "surly minority on the white side that [would] go out and insult any Negro."[79] In other words, he argued that as a third-party quasi-white group, Chinese immigrants would exacerbate African American militancy by feeding their sense of racial oppression, and this was another reason to continue excluding Chinese. This statement may have had its roots in a Reconstruction-era practice in which southern planters recruited Chinese workers as an idealized labor source to replace emancipated black slaves; the assumption, in both historical moments, was that the two groups were naturally inclined to be opposed.[80]

However far-reaching some of their arguments, southern Democrats clung hard to their objection that passing repeal for Chinese would set a precedent for other Asian peoples to demand admission to the United States, threatening its status as a white nation. "Hundreds of millions of other Asiatics," Rep. Allen declared, would "ask for that same thing," beginning with the "400,000,000 Hindus or Indians" living in Asia. Over the course of the nine-day hearing, Rep. Allen's tirade against setting a precedent grew into a crusade: the lawmaker revisited the threat of the Chinese measure inviting an Asian flood into the United States no fewer than twenty-five times. He was particularly keen on rooting out witnesses' personal sympathies, seizing on any hint of support for broader immigration reform toward Asia. As part of this effort, he quizzed witness after witness on whether they believed repeal should be extended to Indians, Koreans, and the other Asian groups whom he insisted were "watching" the hearings in the hope of making similar demands.[81]

While Fred Yee and Li Min Hin, the Citizens Committee's two handpicked witnesses of Chinese descent, generally stayed on script, other Asian American witnesses at the hearing were less predictable. When asked, Kilsoo Haan, the lone Korean American to speak at the hearing, quickly sidestepped the question of similar gains for Koreans by reiterating that China's role in winning the war was the "first consideration."[82] The words belied his private actions, however. One month earlier, Haan had petitioned Rep. Magnuson, one of the Chinese exclusion repeal bill sponsors, for an amendment that named Koreans the cobeneficiaries of an immigration quota and U.S. citizenship eligibility. As Japan's "number one enemy" and China's longtime military partner in the fight against Tokyo, he wrote, Koreans deserved whatever form of relief the United States could provide.[83] As recounted in the book's introduction, Indian witness Taraknath Das played no such games. When questioned, he stated bluntly his belief that Congress should extend repeal to all Asian groups and then proceeded to expand the scope of the statement to address social equality. To the horror of many he cited his belief that a "Jew from America or a Negro from this country" had the "right" to become president of the United States and even lamented the United States' past enslavement of African Americans.[84] Southern Democrats, who comprised eight of the House committee's twenty-one members, were none too pleased, and as discussed earlier, Das's testimony elicited a roar of outcry.

Ultimately, the decision to base the Chinese immigration quota on race rather than nationality was the compromise that made it possible for repeal legislation to advance. By the time the spring 1943 hearings ended, a majority of the House Immigration Committee's twenty voting members favored straight repeal but disagreed over the wisdom of a quota. The race-based quota, which was incorporated into the Magnuson bill that fall, counted persons of Chinese descent from anywhere in the world against an annual quota of 105; it thus closed a key loophole of concern to restrictionists. As its main architect, Rep. Gossett (D-TX) explained that it prevented persons of Chinese descent from outside of China from flooding the United States. It also set the Chinese quota apart from the nationality-based ones granted to Europeans, thus perpetuating the stigma of inferiority. With this compromise, the Magnuson Act ended wholesale Chinese exclusion in the narrowest terms and with the least impact possible.

On October 7, the House Immigration Committee passed the amended measure by a vote of eight to four. Political scientist Fred Riggs has described the various factors that tipped the vote, which could easily have gone the other way; key among these was the absence of eight committee members inclined to oppose it.[85] Five days later, President Roosevelt sent Congress an endorsement letter calling on members to pass the amended Magnuson bill as "important in the cause of winning the war and of establishing a secure peace."[86] The White House statement, combined with the support of key southern senators such as Georgia's Richard Russell, was enough to persuade the Senate Immigration Committee—and eventually the full Senate—to pass the legislation without major issue; meetings with Chiang Kai-shek and other Chinese leaders had convinced Russell, a staunch exclusionist and segregationist, of the need to support the bill as a wartime measure.[87] On December 17, President Roosevelt signed the bill into law. Citing the removal of an "unfortunate barrier between allies," he declared that the Pacific war effort could now continue, for both Chinese and Americans, with a "greater vigor and a larger understanding of our common purpose."[88]

The Principle of Nondiscrimination

Not everyone was satisfied with the final shape of Chinese exclusion repeal. The Magnuson bill may have passed, but the process left many of its staunchest supporters dissatisfied in ways that created momentum for future change. One could even argue that the disappointment and frustration the Chinese campaign caused sowed the seeds of more sweeping and impactful reform. Even before the campaign was over, the truce calling for Citizens Committee supporters to commit to a narrow focus on Chinese repeal as a wartime measure started to fray. A day after the Magnuson bill passed the House, leaders of the lobbying vehicle began debating the addition of an amendment that incorporated the main provisions of the Lesinski wives bill abandoned earlier that year. The discussion was prompted in part by a letter from a white American soldier who "fell in love and married a Chinese girl" while deployed only to discover that he could not bring her home to the United States "because of her ancestry."[89] The Committee's "Washington group" led by Judd and labor leader Monroe Sweetland decided against the amendment on the grounds that adding it would certainly doom the entire legislation. Mollified but not fully persuaded, Reed Lewis of the Common Council for American Unity warned that the failure to include a wives provision would become a "fester which will spread poison for years to come."[90] Around the same time, a supporter named "Miss Smith" wrote the committee's leadership to complain that giving the Chinese equal treatment and "fighting for a principle" had been, to her mind at least, the "whole point of the campaign." Yet the effort had yielded only a symbolic victory: "107 is what we will have gotten . . . and NOT the principle of no discrimination," she lamented.[91]

Perhaps the clearest proof of how committee members' dissatisfaction laid the groundwork for subsequent campaigns were the actions of Citizens Committee leaders themselves. Once it became evident that the measure had enough votes to be enacted, the Citizens Committee's executive team tasked secretary Cranston with compiling the names and addresses of supporters who had written letters to Congress for use in future efforts. In their final report to members issued after President Roosevelt signed the bill in December 1943, committee leaders expressed their hope that the passage of the Magnuson bill would mark "the beginning" of the "elimination of all racial discriminations from our immigration and naturalization laws."[92] In other words, they indicated their desire that the repeal of Chinese exclusion serve as the starting point of a longer movement—a first step toward the larger goal of comprehensive repeal—rather than as an end in itself.

The tension between the rhetoric and reality of repeal can be seen in the Magnuson Act's consequences for Chinese wives. Even as the law formally ended Chinese exclusion and gave China an annual immigration quota, it made it more difficult for many Chinese wives of U.S. citizens to join their husbands in America. The Magnuson Act not only blocked relief for those Chinese alien wives who married after 1924. It closed a loophole in the law that had previously allowed women who married before the 1924 Immigration Act took effect to enter the United States outside of any quotas or restrictions; after 1943, they, too, became subject to China's immigration quota of 105 per year. In sum, as historian Meredith Oyen has written, "instead of ending racial exclusion," the repeal law "revised it and codified the unequal citizenship of Chinese Americans."[93]

The Citizens Committee soon disbanded, its goal of repealing Chinese exclusion successfully achieved, but Chinese Americans continued to agitate for a wives bill. It would take three years for a modified version of Lesinski's proposal, buoyed by a postwar rush of legislation providing for the admission of military brides and fiancées, to pass Congress under different sponsorship. Between 1945 and 1950, more than five thousand Chinese women married or engaged to U.S. soldiers gained admission to the United States as nonquota immigrants under the War Brides Act (1945) and the War Fiancées Act (1946), but the Chinese wives of U.S. citizens who had not served in the military remained barred.[94] Prompted by Chinese American constituents and the war's rapid warming of public attitudes toward Chinese, several lawmakers from California sponsored a slate of bills addressing the plight of Chinese wives still struggling to reunite with their families. Reps. George P. Miller, Franck Havenner, and Helen Gahagan Douglas were all liberal Democrats representing urban areas, and both Havenner and Douglas served districts with significant Chinese American populations.[95] Along with their CCBA colleagues, CACA leaders were at the forefront of the campaign for passage; taking a page from the Citizens Committee's playbook, they hired a white lawyer based in Washington, DC, to present their case at the legislation's fall 1945 hearings before the House Committee on Immigration and Naturalization. The committee's discussion was short and relatively uneventful, with restrictionist members most interested in ascertaining how many Chinese women the legislation would likely admit and how many Chinese men had tried to wed white women due to the dearth of available Chinese women. Mollified by the bill's limited scope and perhaps prompted by their fears of miscegenation, they and their counterparts on the Senate Immigration Committee gave their approval. The Chinese Alien Wives of American Citizens Act went into effect on August 9, 1946. Local Chinese American leaders in San Francisco, who had done nothing to mark the Magnuson Act's passage during the war, commissioned gold plaques for Rep. Miller and other California congress persons as a show of gratitude for their support of the wives act.[96] Their tribute commemorated twenty years of community-based lobbying by the CACA and other Chinese Americans seeking to reunite Chinese families long separated by U.S. exclusionary laws: a feat that the formal repeal of Chinese exclusion three years earlier had not been able to achieve.

Other Asian groups that had been watching the progress of the Magnuson Act soon seized on the Citizens Committee's victory to revive and, in some cases, initiate new repeal campaigns of their own. They thus sought to do precisely what southern Democrats and other critics of the law had warned: make Chinese exclusion repeal a precedent for broader change. Encouraged by the Chinese victory to rethink what was possible, Indians and Filipina/os on both sides of the Pacific looked to the tactics and strategies modeled by the Citizens Committee to Repeal Chinese Exclusion to guide their efforts. Fundamental differences between China and their homelands soon became apparent, however, complicating their attempts to build directly on the Chinese success. As the next two chapters will explore, chief among these was the problem of colonialism.

CHAPTER TWO

Entangling Immigration and Independence

Indians and Indian Americans in the Campaign for Exclusion Repeal

Just as southern lawmakers had predicted, news of the congressional hearing on Chinese exclusion repeal in May 1943 sparked a flurry of discussion on both sides of the Pacific about the possibility of a similar bill for India. In the words of one *New York Times* writer, "If China, why not India?"[1] Like China, India was critical to the Allies' Pacific war against Japan. It offered a geographically strategic base for military operations and supplies, and its large population promised much-needed manpower for combat. A New York–based Indian relief group called the India Welfare League (IWL) seized the moment to send an open letter to members of the U.S. House and Senate Immigration and Naturalization Committees urging support for an Indian citizenship bill the league had first championed four years earlier. IWL president Mubarek Ali Khan called for its passage as a logical "next step" to a Chinese measure.[2] Behind the scenes, Indian officials serving in the British colonial government at Delhi discreetly tested the Roosevelt administration's receptivity to an Indian immigration and naturalization bill similar to the one under consideration for Chinese. Encouraged by the warm response, Sir Girja Shankar Bajpai, the Indian colonial government's representative to Washington, suggested to his colleagues in Delhi that if the campaign for Chinese exclusion repeal "bore fruit," they should plan to "skillfully rid[e] the high tide of American Sinophilism to bring Indians within the scope of the proposed relief."[3]

Conspicuously missing, however, was discussion of India's status as a longtime colony of the United States' British ally and the complications this potentially introduced. When the Citizens Committee formally launched its Chinese exclusion repeal campaign in the spring of 1943, it had been less than a year since British authorities imprisoned Mahatma Gandhi, Jawaharlal Nehru, and other leaders of the Indian National Congress (INC) as punishment for their ultimatum demanding immediate independence as the price of Indians' full cooperation with Britain in the Allied war effort. The Quit India Movement marked a turning point in Indians' decades-long battle for independence. After the public showdown gave way to a stalemate, the struggle between Indian nationalists and British imperialists moved to the court of international opinion, with each side seeking to rally powerful allies such as the United States. But Washington was not so easily wooed. During the war, U.S. officials were torn between their immediate need to maintain a wartime alliance with Great Britain on the one hand, and the United States' long-term interests in courting Indians, for whom independence appeared just a matter of time, on the other. Confronted with this conundrum, first Roosevelt and then Truman largely refrained from pushing the reluctant Winston Churchill to grant India independence while taking steps to avoid alienating Indian nationalists altogether.[4] Advocates for the repeal of Indian exclusion likewise proceeded carefully.

Centering the work of actors on both sides of the Pacific, this chapter charts how Indians and Indian Americans sought to use U.S. repeal legislation as an instrument or tool to achieve their own national and anticolonial goals. During and immediately after World War II, they cultivated transpacific networks of support for repeal spanning Delhi, Whitehall, and Washington, DC. By pairing Indian and British sources with U.S. archives, the analysis upends conventional accounts of the Luce-Celler Act as a cause originated and spearheaded by elite white racial liberals and conservative internationalists.[5] Instead, it reveals how white Americans and later, British officials, did not take concrete action until Indians prompted them. Ultimately the effort only succeeded because Britain decided to support the change in U.S. immigration law, and as the chapter shows, Indian colonial officials were the intermediaries who made it happen.

The first half of the chapter foregrounds the conflicts that emerged among Indian Americans, as exemplified by the split between the IWL and the India League of America (ILA). Both were New York–based Indian American organizations; the IWL provided relief to Indian workers, while the ILA was an elite Indian and non-Indian vehicle dedicated to promoting Indian independence. From the start, the contest brought to the fore differences in class, religion, and political affiliation. The IWL's campaign to relieve the economic struggles of its members clashed from the start with the ILA's lofty, symbolism-oriented approach. In part, their divergent priorities registered how Indian exclusion in 1917, by stopping large-scale migration from the subcontinent, had stratified Indian American communities between elites and nonelites, East Coast and West Coast populations. As part of the pre-exclusion generation, Taraknath Das, an educated Hindu, spent summers between classes at the University of California at Berkeley picking celery alongside Sikh farmers and sharing in their experiences of marginalization and oppression. By contrast, the post-exclusion waves of students and intellectuals who flocked to East Coast college towns and groups such as the ILA had little interaction with the West Coast farmers and workers who made up the majority of the nation's Indians on the eve of World War II. That said, both the IWL and ILA believed that the repeal campaign could be used to promote Indian independence and were eager to do their part. This chapter shows how repeal came to serve as a platform from which Indian nationalists and their white allies in the United States could simultaneously return attention to the plight of colonized Indians and increase pressure on Washington to support the Indian struggle for independence. Both leagues drew strength from the diasporic alliances they forged with leading politicians and parties in India. But these transpacific bonds also brought the influence of Hindu–Muslim conflict and the debate over different visions of Indian independence then wreaking havoc on Indian politics into the U.S.-based repeal campaign.[6]

The second half of the chapter focuses on the critical role Sir Girja Bajpai, the Indian agent-general to Washington, DC, and other members of the Government of India at Delhi played in the passage of the 1946 Luce-Celler Act.[7] Indian colonial officials had long monitored the treatment of overseas Indians as part of their regular oversight, but beginning in the 1930s, they made the welfare of Indians abroad a critical component of their efforts to secure greater concessions from Great Britain and, increasingly, to gain the goodwill of Washington. In the case of repeal, the back-channel lobbying of Indian agent-general Bajpai and his Delhi colleagues was the key to securing British approval of an Indian immigration and naturalization bill, which in turn was critical to winning the votes of southern holdouts in Congress.

Viewed through a transpacific lens, the Indian campaign for exclusion repeal models a way of thinking about American empire building in Asia that decenters the U.S. state, even as it foregrounds the instrumental uses of U.S. power.[8] Indian and Indian American nationalists, it shows, sought to marshal the U.S. state's imperial projects toward their ultimate goal of Indian independence. This strategy not only reflected Indians' widespread recognition of America's preponderant power after World War II.[9] It demonstrated a belief that they could use that power to advance their own anticolonial agendas. In this view, the United States' imperial ambitions were not simply foreign impositions to be resisted; insofar as they subverted British dominance, they also presented new opportunities for Indians seeking self-determination.

Indian Immigration and Independence before World War II

Indians began arriving in the United States in significant numbers in 1908, when legal restrictions targeting Chinese and Japanese workers left West Coast farmers and other employers looking for a replacement source of inexpensive labor.[10] Despite the tendency of many white Americans to lump them all together as "Hindu," Indians in the United States included people of diverse ethnicities, caste identities, linguistic traditions, class and educational backgrounds, as well as religious faiths. The majority were Sikhs from the Indian state of Punjab living and working as farmers in California. Another third were Muslims concentrated in the West and the Southwest. Many fewer Indians were high-caste Hindus such as Taraknath Das, who came to the United States as students and intellectuals to earn degrees and teach at colleges; they were mostly scattered throughout the Northeast and Midwest, with a few in the South. As their numbers grew on the West Coast—peaking at 6,000 during World War I—Indians increasingly became a target of California exclusionists, who complained that Indian workers displaced white labor and resisted assimilation into American society. With the restriction of Chinese, Japanese, and Korean workers largely complete by 1908, the San Francisco–based Asiatic Exclusion League (formerly the Japanese and Korean Exclusion League) joined with local California officials and media outlets such as the McClatchy Company's *Sacramento Bee* to stop the "tide of turbans" entering the United States, as Das himself had done several times, from across the Canadian border and via British merchant ships.[11] Congressional lawmakers were especially blunt: in 1911, a special House-Senate joint immigration committee declared Indians the "least desirable race of immigrants thus far admitted to the United States."[12] At the time, however, most lawmakers were more interested in limiting the entry of the less desirable peoples of southern and eastern Europe than in the so-called Oriental problem. Thwarted in their early attempts to pass federal legislation, West Coast exclusionists turned to local and state measures. Over the next decade, the legislatures of at least thirteen western states, including California, Arizona, and Washington, passed alien land laws designed to prevent Asian immigrant farmers from competing with whites; Indians were among those most directly affected, although Japanese farmers were often the main target.

The historical entanglement of Indian exclusion with Indians' anticolonial struggles against the British empire began with the complete ban on Indian immigration put into place by Congress's passage of the 1917

Immigration Act.[13] The timing was no coincidence: momentum for the law benefited from public outcry and media attention to Indian nationalist activities in the aftermath of the Ghadar, or Hindu-German Conspiracy, in which the global Ghadar Party sought to "overthrow the British rule by using force and free India from foreign domination." Hundreds of Indians along the West Coast were accused of participating in the plot to overthrow the British Raj in India. According to one count, more than 400 Indians left the United States for India during World War I to take part; Das, already in Asia, was named as one of the plan's masterminds.[14] American media accounts portraying Indians as revolutionary and violent, coupled with British intelligence describing Indians' long history of revolutionary activities on U.S. soil, bolstered exclusionists' cause and crystallized congressional support for Indian exclusion. The Immigration Act of 1917 accomplished this by creating the "Asiatic Barred Zone." While the geographical designation technically banned the immigration of peoples from a large swathe of the Asian continent, India was widely understood to be its primary target since earlier policies had already curbed the entry of Chinese and Japanese workers into the United States.[15] The "Hindu Conspiracy Trial" concluded in 1918 with an American jury finding seventeen of the Indian defendants guilty in a dramatic San Francisco trial that ended in the murder of one Indian witness by another in front of a full courtroom. According to Seema Sohi, the widely publicized scene only cemented in many white Americans' minds the link between Indians' radicalism and their racial threat to the nation.[16]

Because the Asiatic Barred Zone dealt only with future immigration, however, it left unclear the status of Indians already living in the United States, including whether they were eligible for U.S. citizenship. Indians' racial identity had long been contested; through World War I, scores of Indians became U.S. citizens by citing their "Caucasian" or "Aryan" heritage to establish their eligibility under the "free white persons" provision of the 1790 Naturalization Act.[17] The Supreme Court decision in *Thind v. U.S.* (1923) ended this practice,[18] ruling that even if Indians were "Caucasian," they were not "white" according to the commonsense understanding of the term and were therefore ineligible for naturalization.[19] The fallout was swift and far reaching. As "aliens ineligible to citizenship," Indians came under the restrictions of the 1924 Immigration Act, which consolidated their exclusion as a function of their racial ineligibility for naturalization. By 1925, U.S. federal authorities had cancelled the naturalization certification of at least fifty Indians—including Das—and continued to pursue other cases well into the 1930s. Sikh and Muslim farmers on the West Coast and elsewhere scrambled to shift their land deeds to the names of sympathetic white friends or of their U.S.-born children lest they lose their property under alien land laws. These restrictions prohibited "aliens ineligible to citizenship" from owning agricultural land in West Coast states including California, home to more than 60 percent of the Indian American population. Members of the Indian Central Legislature in Delhi passed the Indian Naturalization Act of 1926 in protest. The reciprocity measure barred Americans from Indian citizenship as long as Indians remained "aliens ineligible to citizenship" under U.S. law.[20]

Forming another link between Indians' anticolonial advocacy and their campaigns for rights in the United States, veterans of the Ghadar movement took the lead in seeking redress for Indians' loss of citizenship through legislation. This was consistent with the Ghadar Party members' under-standing of their fight for India's freedom as tied to their struggles for ra-cial equality in the United States. Specifically, they believed that Indian Americans' poor treatment was a direct consequence of their homeland's colonial oppression on the international stage. As Ghadar Party leader Gobind Lehari Lal explained the connection, it was "no use to talk about the Asiatic Exclusion Act, immigration, and citizenship" without talking about a "strike at the British because they [are] responsible for the way Indians [are] being treated in America."[21] By this logic, party members argued, se-curing India's independence from British oppression would advance Indians' status and treatment not only in the United States but in white settler soci-eties across the globe. Like CACA leaders were doing in their concurrent campaigns for a Chinese wives bill, Ghadar movement veterans Sailendra Ghose and Taraknath Das enlisted influential white congressmen to advo-cate on their behalf. Pennsylvania senator David Reed had commanded Indian American soldiers during World War I; his measure would have restored the citizenship of denaturalized Indians. New York Congressman Emmanuel Celler, a longtime critic of U.S. immigration restriction, pro-posed to reclassify Indians as white and therefore eligible for naturalization. To no one's surprise, neither gained traction amid the heightened nativism and growing economic hardship of the time. And things would get worse before they got better, as state governments moved to strengthen and en-force laws circumscribing alien rights during the Great Depression.

A Tale of Two Leagues

Mubarak Ali Khan had had enough. Since entering the United States through New York City Harbor in 1920, the scrappy Indian had worked as an auto mechanic, a store clerk, and even, for a short time, as a farmer.[22] Khan was one of the thousands of Indian Muslim sailors who deserted their British ships at U.S. ports after the passage of the 1917 Immigration Act made obtaining legal entry virtually impossible. Many were fleeing religious persecution and seeking economic opportunities generally not afforded to Muslims in many parts of the subcontinent. When Khan jumped ship, he became part of what Vivek Bald has called the "undocumented labor migration networks" through which hundreds of deserter seamen from China, India, and elsewhere ended up working in East Coast port cities and factory towns; Indians made up the largest group of nonwhite seamen deserting by the 1920s.[23] Although most eventually left the United States, Khan stayed and moved to Arizona, where he had Punjabi Sikh neighbors. By the time the Great Depression reached its peak, Khan was back in the New York area, but he was struggling. Not only were factory jobs scarce. Due to citizenship restrictions on federal jobs and many assistance programs, Indians—now classified as "aliens ineligible to citizenship" under U.S. law—rarely received any form of state relief. Roosevelt's New Deal was not for Indians like him, it seemed, but he was determined to change this by obtaining U.S. citizenship.

Having learned that the House Committee on Immigration and Naturalization was in the process of redrafting a comprehensive nationality law, Khan and a small group of like-minded Indians representing the India Welfare League (IWL), a community-based mutual aid organization founded in 1937, took a bus to Washington, DC.[24] Their plan was simple: visit each committee member in person and ask for Indians to be added to the list of groups eligible for U.S. citizenship. The change would benefit all of the country's roughly three thousand Indians: those living in urban areas such as New York City would have greater access to New Deal employment and relief programs that gave preference to U.S. citizens, while others along the West Coast would have legal protection from alien land laws threatening their livelihoods as farmers.

Upon their fourth visit to his office, Rep. Samuel Dickstein (D-NY), chair of the House committee, offered them ten minutes of his time, and as one IWL leader later recounted, a "ten-minute interview stretched out, at the Congressman's initiative, into an hour-long conference."[25] Over the next two years, a sympathetic Dickstein used his position to get the group's citizenship proposal put on the docket.[26] At hearings before the House Immigration Committee in 1939 and 1940, Khan and other IWL members testified to the material harm and legal deprivation that longtime Indian residents of the

United States suffered due to their inability to naturalize. Indians were always among the "last to be hired and the first to be fired," he lamented, because they could claim few legal rights or recourse.[27] In short, the problem of Indian workers was one of incorporation. "These people are here. They intend to remain here the rest of their lives," one leader testified. "[S]hall we let them remain as permanent aliens or almost in the status of refugees who are not permitted to avail themselves of the various advantages that the American Government agencies extend to citizens, or shall we incorporate them?"[28] But lawmakers were unmoved, and the IWL members went home and waited for the right time to revive their campaign.

The introduction of Chinese exclusion repeal, coinciding with Madame Chiang Kai-shek's February 1943 visit and address to Congress, became that moment. Within days of her widely publicized speech, Khan sent petitions to House and Senate lawmakers appealing for an Indian bill as a natural next step to the Chinese repeal bill recently introduced to the House. The open letter caught the attention of North Dakota senator William Langer (R-ND), who was well positioned to shepherd legislation through Congress as a member of the Senate Committee on Immigration and Naturalization. In the fall of 1943, while the Chinese repeal bill was still pending, Langer introduced an Indian measure granting U.S. citizenship eligibility to the approximately 3,000 Indians living in the United States who had entered the country before the 1924 Immigration Act took effect. Over the following months, Khan devoted himself to gathering support; as he later recounted, he slept "many a night . . . on the Union Station bench" to stay near Capitol Hill and knock on lawmakers' doors.[29] Early the next year, Khan and Langer traveled to California, where they visited Indian communities to solicit funds to support the campaigning efforts ahead. Alarmed by rumors of Khan's shady dealings, a local Indian leader in the state's Central Valley wrote J. J. Singh, president of the ILA in New York, to ascertain whether the North Dakota senator and his Indian colleague could be trusted. Singh quickly alerted his fellow ILA board members, who convened an emergency meeting about what to do next.

As a group of elite Indians and their influential white allies, the ILA and its leader were a world apart from Khan and IWL members riding buses and sleeping on park benches in Washington, DC. Born in 1897 in Rawalpindi, India, Singh served briefly in the Punjab Provincial Congress Committee and, later, in the All-India Congress Committee before leaving the subcontinent in 1922, demoralized by the abuses of British colonial rule. After a few years in England, Singh traveled to Philadelphia as part of an Indian

Sirdar Jagjit (J. J.) Singh, president of the India League of America. William Auerbach-Levy (1889–1964) / Museum of the City of New York. X2013.165.64.

merchants group, stayed when the others left, and eventually established a stable import-export business in Manhattan. In 1940, he became president of the ILA, and under Singh's leadership, the ILA became one of the most prominent U.S.-based vehicles for Indian independence. In the wake of the August 1942 Quit India Movement, it ran a full-page advertisement in the *New York Times* calling on President Roosevelt and Chinese leader Chiang Kai-shek to "use their good offices" to bring the British government and INC back into negotiations.[30] The action solidified the ILA's reputation as an unofficial mouthpiece for the INC and its spokesmen, Mahatma Gandhi and Jawaharlal Nehru, and registered its connections with a long list of white elites across media, industry, and government. For the rest of World War II, American policymakers, journalists, and academics regularly cited the ILA's monthly newsletter *India Today*, and the *New York Times* and other prominent media outlets often consulted Singh as an expert on Indian affairs. The ILA's executive board and advisory committee included some of the most powerful figures in the American publishing world. Several veterans of the Citizens Committee to Repeal Chinese Exclusion were also involved, connecting the two campaigns in concrete ways. For example, as they had done for Chinese repeal, former Citizens Committee chairman and publisher Richard Walsh, novelist Pearl Buck, and *Time-Life* editor Henry Luce all used their extensive connections to place articles in strategic forums and rally public support through the printed word.

The ILA was deeply invested in crafting a positive image of India and Indians to white American audiences, and its leaders quickly concluded that Senator Langer and Mubarek Ali Khan made poor spokesmen for their cause. As the governor of North Dakota, Langer had been forced to resign on charges of corruption. His reputation for graft followed him to Congress, where after his election, the Senate Committee on Privileges and Elections tried to prevent him from taking office on the grounds of "moral turpitude"; it took a full Senate vote to seat him. Khan's integrity was similarly questionable. The IWL leader regularly introduced himself as a doctor from a well-connected Indian family, even though none of it was true. Even at the IWL's 1939 and 1940 hearings before the House Immigration Committee, Khan had claimed blood ties to powerful politicians in India to bolster his position. The ILA's reluctance to let Khan serve as the public face of an Indian legislative campaign had classist overtones as well.[31] With the exception of Singh, the ILA's cadre of Indian members were mostly academics with PhDs and diplomats who had come to the United States on temporary visas and planned one day to return to India. Many believed that they had little in common with Sikh farmers and Muslim working-class immigrants like Khan, and this contributed to their general distaste for the IWL campaign as an undesirable reflection on Indians in the United States.

It did not take ILA leaders long to decide they should launch their own legislative effort. In taking on the issue, they hoped to address several deficiencies of the Langer bill, which, in their eyes, fell far short of the legislation they believed was most needed. They specifically objected to how the Langer bill's clause limited citizenship eligibility to longtime U.S. Indian residents, rather than granting it to all Indians. By failing to address the principle of racial discrimination that the 1923 *Thind* decision had codified in law, some argued the measure positioned India below China in terms of the rights accorded the two peoples.[32] Within weeks, ILA leaders enlisted New York Democrat Celler and Connecticut Republican Clare Boothe Luce to serve as bipartisan sponsors of an Indian immigration and naturalization bill in the House. The unconventional pairing of a well-known liberal Democrat with a conservative Republican exemplified repeal's wide appeal. Celler supported it as a matter of principle and racial equality, while Luce, an early anticommunist, saw it as a preemptive measure to offset Soviet Communism's growing footprint in Asia. Modeled after the 1943 Magnuson Act that repealed Chinese exclusion, the Luce and Celler bills (hereafter, Luce-Celler) included two main provisions: an annual immigration quota for India of 100 persons and U.S. citizenship eligibility for persons of Indian descent. Unlike the Langer bill, the Luce-Celler bill's naturalization provisions imposed no temporal restrictions for citizenship eligibility based on date of entry, bringing it more into line with the Chinese measure that preceded it.

As an organization committed to advancing India's independence from British rule, the ILA was an unlikely vehicle to interfere with a community-based effort to help struggling Indian workers in the United States. But, as with the Citizens Committee's efforts, Asian communities living in the United States were conspicuously absent from the ILA's petitions in support of the Luce-Celler bills. Instead, the group of white and Indian elites followed the geopolitical or internationalist strategy the Citizens Committee campaign had modeled under Walsh. At rallies in New York City and Washington, DC, ILA speakers echoed the war-related arguments that had featured in the previous effort and explicitly connected the two causes. In one representative statement, Luce asserted that the logic framing Chinese exclusion repeal as a step toward Allied victory "applied with equal measure to India."[33] Using this logic, J. J. Singh claimed to have "canvass[ed] all the forty-eight states" and received "1300 replies" in favor of its passage.[34] Within a few months, the Luce-Celler legislation received the editorial endorsements of the *New York Times*, the *New Republic*, and the *Los Angeles Times*, all prominent but politically diverse publications. In line with the arguments the ILA had made, the various outlets stressed India's similarity to China as an important Pacific ally as well as the military contributions that made Indians especially deserving of recognition.[35] The *New York Times* encapsulated this sentiment especially well with its concluding plea: "We have lifted the bars for the Chinese. We can afford to do the same for the Indians. We can't afford to do otherwise."[36]

The impact of the ILA's publicity efforts crossed the Pacific. Several members of the INC in Delhi responded with a resolution expressing their support for the Luce-Celler bill and reaffirming that Indian' contributions to the Pacific War had earned them a place in the United States' national quota system.[37] In yet another transpacific exchange, the Indian Congress's action caught the attention of the *New York Times*, which described the resolution as further evidence that U.S. passage of the Luce-Celler bills was an urgent matter of American wartime diplomacy.[38] The INC thus upheld the ILA's decision to adopt an India-focused wartime strategy as the most universally compelling way to persuade U.S. lawmakers. The belief that what was good for India was good for Indian independence was likely also part of their motivation to respond.

The ILA's anticolonial orientation also helps explain why the Indian campaign enjoyed the greatest support from African American leaders of any effort in the longer repeal movement. Most immediately, the endorsements were a by-product of J. J. Singh's close working relationship with Walter White, president of the NAACP, and A. Philip Randolph of the Brotherhood of Sleeping Car Porters; the two men were among the first public figures and the first black leaders to endorse the Luce-Celler bills in 1944.[39] Indians and African Americans shared a long history of fighting colonialism, with special enmity for the British, who had dominated both the African continent and Asian subcontinent. The fight for Indian independence became an especially meaningful and rich site of overlap and cooperation, as black Americans and Indians forged solidarities in recognition of their common oppression.[40] These sentiments and history account for why, in the aftermath of the 1942 Quit India Movement, more than eighty black intellectuals issued an open letter calling on President Roosevelt to intervene in the impasse between the INC and the British. Black community leaders, including White and Randolph, had prompted the move. They embraced the logic that the J. J. Singh and the ILA would later advance: that repeal served the larger goal of Indian freedom and thereby advanced the rights of nonwhite peoples everywhere.[41]

Black intellectuals in the United States had long rallied around Indian nationalists, and specifically, around INC figures such as Mahatma Gandhi and Jawaharlal Nehru, whom they saw as powerful and eloquent spokespersons for the world's colonized and nonwhite peoples. As Gerald Horne and Nico Slate have shown, during World War II, African American leaders made India central to their global double victory campaign, arguing that U.S. racism threatened Allied victory in the Pacific by turning Indians against the United States in favor of Japan.[42] In turn, Indian leaders publicly likened the oppression of blacks in the United States to that suffered by Indians chafing under the yoke of British colonialism. The Indian campaign was an exception in an increasingly ambivalent interplay between Asian exclusion repeal and black activism after the war. Unfortunately, it probably did little to boost the ILA's chances of success, given the precarious standing of many African American groups with the Roosevelt administration after the threatened March on Washington and southern lawmakers' skepticism toward the same. Indeed, those whose votes mattered the most may have stiffened their resolve against an Indian repeal bill given its apparent connection to black civil rights. Some Indians, at least, were undeterred by the potential pitfalls of identifying too closely with black Americans. When an advisor questioned her about it, for example, Indian politician and sister of Nehru, Madame Pandit, famously replied, "What do you mean—I am colored myself and so are my people."[43]

In theory, the IWL could also have sought black support, but cooperation between the elite ILA and the middle- and upper-middle-class NAACP reflects how a shared class identity and networks could facilitate solidarities across racial lines. During the war, Khan and other IWL members were equally, if not more, vocal than ILA members in expressing their solidarity with the plight of black Americans; a February 1945 piece in which Khan observed that "98% of the Indian community in the U.S." shared the "social and economic segregation" of black Americans was typical.[44] Yet there is no evidence of meaningful communication between the working-class Indian American group and black leaders. Differences of geography certainly played a role. As black elites who interacted disproportionately with other elites in northeastern cities like New York and Washington, DC, figures such as Walter White were mostly disconnected from the plight of Indian farmers living in central California and workers such as Khan based in less expensive northern New Jersey cities. The distance had longer-term consequences. Inasmuch as black leaders followed the ILA's lead in ignoring the plight of Indian American farmers and workers in favor of the struggles facing Indians in Asia, it arguably contributed to a tendency by black organizations to disassociate the civil rights struggles of Asian Americans seeking to overcome racial barriers in the United States from the struggles of Asians suffering the impact of U.S. imperial projects and militarism in postwar Asia.[45]

As Washington officials struggled to maintain their neutrality in the Indian-British impasse over independence, both supporters and opponents of the Luce-Celler bills seized on the ILA's work for Indian independence to articulate the relevance of a U.S. repeal bill to Indian affairs. All perceived a connection, even if they did not agree on what it was. Southern Democrats and American academics such as Charles Colby of the University of Chicago alike warned that the legislation could alienate the United States' British allies by implying a U.S. endorsement of Indian independence.[46] Indeed, many Indian nationalists on both sides of the Pacific welcomed the bill as an indirect signal of Washington's support for Indian independence and its growing desire to help Indians more generally. It was good news to P. N. Sapru, a member of the Indian legislature's upper house, who suggested that the bills could be leveraged to promote more equitable treatment for Indians living in Australia and Canada and across the globe. "If we can establish the principle of racial equality," he declared, "we shall have achieved a very great deal."[47] Indian ILA members described the potential in much the same terms. In a 1944 letter to J. J. Singh, Mumtaz Kitchlew and Dr. Tarani Sinha welcomed the "great international prestige" the Luce-Celler bills promised to give Indians by removing their "present stigma" of exclusion on racial grounds. By making Indians' rights under U.S. law a proxy for India's standing and status within the international community, they thus reframed U.S. repeal legislation as an instrument to advance the ultimate goal of Indian independence.

As unlikely as the logic might seem in retrospect, several factors facilitated the link Indians drew between their fight to pass U.S. repeal bills and their independence struggles. The first was long-standing uncertainty regarding Washington's position on India, which led to all kinds of speculation among nationalists and imperialists alike. In the absence of formal U.S. policy, people on both sides of the Indian-British impasse read Washington's actions as a barometer on the sympathies of individual U.S. officials. For Indian nationalists, the hope was that Americans would soon come around and begin providing material support as well as use its considerable diplomatic sway to persuade Whitehall that relinquishing India was the best action. The viability of the British war effort depended on continued U.S. support, they reasoned, and even if Prime Minister Winston Churchill was not willing to discuss India, other British officials were more sensitive to Washington's views. Also germane was the longer history of Indian American activism that entangled Indians' status and treatment in the United States with India's standing in the world.[48] The Ghadar Party had long connected the struggle for U.S. citizenship to India's freedom and "national self-respect" on the world stage.[49] As discussed earlier, for Taraknath Das, whose blunt testimony angered southern lawmakers at the House committee hearings on Chinese exclusion repeal in spring 1943, U.S. citizenship had afforded practical protection from British reprisal for his nationalist activities, even preventing his deportation after World War I.[50] On an ideological level, Das also described the act of claiming American citizenship as a deeply symbolic one, an official renunciation of his status as a British colonial subject. During World War II, media outlets echoed this tendency to interpret help for India as an implicit critique of British imperial policy and of the British more generally. In 1943, for example, a writer in *Time* magazine memorably described the U.S. Congress's decision to support sending famine relief to India as one of America "buck[ing] the British Empire."[51]

Sinha and Kitchlew's 1944 letter to Singh laid out the related logic underwriting the ILA's symbolic understanding of repeal. The two Indian elites emphasized that they had no practical or personal motives for supporting the Luce-Celler bills.[52] They had "no intention whatsoever of ever becoming American citizens," they assured Singh and the ILA leadership, and planned to "remain [and] die Indians." The statement reflected an active choice to maintain a transient orientation toward the United States. Many of the ILA's Indian members had remained in America to escape the upheavals of World War II on the subcontinent, but they planned to return to India after the war ended.[53] It was one more distinction between them and the working-class members of the IWL who sought American citizenship as a means of survival. Many IWL members shared their ILA counterparts' strong desire for Indian independence from Great Britain, but since they planned to stay in the United States indefinitely, the campaign for a U.S. bill also carried immediate, material implications to shape their lives.[54] The difference between legislative success and failure could mean their family's survival versus starvation, and they brought this urgency with them to Capitol Hill.

Confrontation on Capitol Hill

The tension between the ILA's idealism and the IWL's pragmatism was on full display at a hearing on the Langer bill before the Senate Immigration and Naturalization Committee in the fall of 1944. The Luce-Celler bill's greater support and visibility notwithstanding, Senator Langer had skillfully used his position on the committee to get his measure on the docket first. Although it was the same body of lawmakers who had voted in favor of the Chinese repeal measure one year earlier, it was not an easy crowd. Presiding as the acting committee chair was Tom Stewart, a Tennessee Democrat who, in the wake of Pearl Harbor, had introduced a bill to strip all U.S.-born Japanese Americans of their birthright citizenship. Six Indian American witnesses from both the IWL and ILA spoke during the proceedings. Khan and other IWL leaders attempted to clarify the merits of the Langer bill over current policy, but the hearing quickly became a losing battle to articulate its strengths over the Luce-Celler bill. Khan and Ramlal Bajpai of the IWL, along with two representatives of a group called the India Association for American Citizenship, faced off against Singh and two other ILA members arguing for the Luce-Celler measure as a more sweeping and symbolically significant alternative that incorporated all of the provisions of the Langer bill.[55] Disagreement erupted in vitriolic confrontation during the testimony of ILA supporter Dr. Krishnanal Shridlani, as he listed the advantages of the broader Luce-Celler immigration bill to "inspire Indians toward greater collaboration with the United States" and to uphold Washington's moral claims to "world leadership." Khan interjected, challenging the ILA's right to speak for a majority working-class Indian American community. As a group of "lecturers, emotional blackmailers, businessmen, and other claimed 'authorities' on India" who came to the United States for "transient and propaganda purposes," he questioned how ILA members could possibly understand the "experience of their country brothers."[56]

The conflict was not over goals so much as priority and practicality. Indian witnesses generally shared a desire for Indian independence, but because of their different class backgrounds they disagreed about whether immediate survival for Indians in the United States or the future freedom of Indians everywhere should take precedence. When asked by a puzzled lawmaker why the IWL would not simply support the Luce-Celler bill, which incorporated the Langer bill's citizenship provisions, Khan cited concerns about practicality. In the event that the Luce-Celler bills could not get enough votes to pass Congress, he did not want naturalization to become a casualty of the independence issue. The Langer bill, he argued, was the more politically feasible of the two measures since it would not increase immigration; it was a reasonable assessment, given the restrictionist climate of Congress. Another IWL witness was more blunt. Do not "destroy" the Langer bill's promise to bring urgent "justice for law-abiding, tax-paying Indians in the U.S." by linking it to "India's freedom," he beseeched. Indian elites in the ILA might have the luxury of time, but for the IWL and other Indian workers living in the United States, relief was needed now.[57]

In addition to class differences, growing religious acrimony between Hindus and Muslims in India came to influence the U.S.-based campaign through the efforts of both the ILA and the IWL to foster closer ties with politicians and parties in India. By the time the Langer bill hearing began, the communal battle over the future of Indian independence had reached new heights as the All India Muslim League's call for the subcontinent's partition into a separate Muslim state gained traction. The demand to partition India along religious lines had long threatened the policy of secular nationalism Indian Congress leaders such as Nehru and Gandhi adopted in their pursuit of a unified, pluralistic Indian nation.[58] A series of highly anticipated talks between Muslim League leader Mohammed Ali Jinnah and INC leader Mahatma Gandhi, less than two months earlier had shifted the power dynamic, which historically favored the INC. The Muslim League gained greater legitimacy from these talks, as did the plan for a separate Pakistani state.[59] As Jinnah's profile rose, Khan sought to bolster the IWL's profile and legitimacy through closer association with him and the All India Muslim League based in Bombay, to the benefit of the campaign for the Langer bill. In anticipation of the 1944 House hearing on the Langer bill, Khan submitted letters of support from Jinnah and Sir Firoz Noon, a prominent Muslim politician in India and Sir Girja Bajpai's former colleague in the Viceroy's Cabinet. In his note, Jinnah specifically expressed his approval of the legislation for the "betterment of the Indians and particularly of the Musalmans" in attaining the status of "full-fledged American citizens."[60] While most congressional lawmakers had no idea of the implications or even knew who Jinnah and Noon were, the Indian Americans in the room would have recognized the invocation of religious tensions.[61] The Hindu-Muslim and religious-secular divisions that were plaguing the Indian independence debate on the subcontinent thus seeped into the Washington repeal campaign.[62]

For the IWL, the outreach to Jinnah and the Muslim League was also part of its wartime reinvention as a Muslim organization. Founded in 1937, the IWL did not start as a Muslim organization, but it assumed an overtly religious identity under Khan's leadership; so sharp was the change, in fact, that most non-Muslim members left the group. The shift put the IWL even more at odds with Singh, a nonobservant Sikh, and the ILA, which actively described itself as a mouthpiece for the INC in America.[63] Relations between the two New York–based Leagues steadily worsened over the course of the campaign. In an effort to make peace, Richard Walsh insisted on an ILA resolution calling on members to make "special efforts for relations with Muslims in New York and elsewhere" in the summer of 1944.[64] By contrast, Khan's writings in the IWL newsletter *New India Bulletin* exemplify his use of religious differences to intensify the organizational rivalry. The self-described "devoted Muslim" began framing the legislative contest as the result of a more fundamental religious conflict. In letters to ILA members and others, Khan denounced the Luce-Celler lobby's actions as a diasporic extension of class and communal dynamics in India and lambasted the ILA's "two Sikhs and one Hindu"—here he referred to J. J. Singh, Anup Singh, and Shridlani—as following in the Indian Congress's elitist tradition of "fail[ing] to place the needs of the Indian people first." Extending his communalist critique into Koranic exegesis, Khan described the IWL's Indian citizenship bill as an expression of the Islamic imperative to "translate" the "'Golden Rule' into deeds, to 'clothe the naked and feed the hungry' throughout the 'Muslim world.'"[65] Such language was popular in Indian politics at the time. What had begun as a class conflict between two New York–based Indian groups over the scope of reform to U.S. law thus assumed greater diasporic significance as IWL leaders infused class-based differences with religious significance.

The theme of Hindu-Muslim conflict made a brief but striking appearance at the Langer bill hearing, as Georgia Democrat Robert Ramspeck seized onto Indians' history of religious strife as another reason for pause. Citing a 1943 congressional report on India, Ramspeck argued that India's religious conflicts made an Indian bill a "different proposition" from the Magnuson Act. China was far easier to Christianize than India, which had "fifty-odd different religious sects" full of "fanatics in their religion." Indeed, this was a view commonly expressed in American missions publications by World War II. The implication was that Indians would be harder for an American society founded on biblical tenets to assimilate relative to the more pliable Chinese. Allowing Indians to enter the United States thus promised "more complications" and should be opposed on religious grounds, Ramspeck concluded.[66] Ultimately, the senators present at the 1944 hearing voted unanimously to table the IWL's Langer bill, having concluded that the ILA's repeal legislation had greater support. The decision cleared the path for the Luce-Celler measure to have its first hearing early the following year. Much as in the case of Chinese repeal, a higher-profile campaign featuring strong white elite support had supplanted a community-based effort. Unlike Chinese American groups, however, the IWL would not step aside so quietly.

Entwining Immigration and Independence: The India League of America

Advocates of the Luce-Celler bill received a strong boost during the early months of 1945 as the measure attracted greater official and popular support.

Using language nearly identical to his endorsement for the Magnuson bill more than a year earlier, President Roosevelt called for passage of the Luce-Celler bill as vital to helping "win the war and to establish a secure peace."[67] In letters to the House Immigration Committee, the U.S. State Department described the measure as necessary to prevent future antagonism in U.S. relations with an independent India. Growing executive support coincided with a drift in Anglo-American relations that made U.S. officials more willing to express support for India, even if they never explicitly called for independence. Other groups also mobilized.[68] One of the bill's most significant commendations came from the Congress on Industrial Organizations (CIO), which broke with the American Federation of Labor (AFL) to endorse the measure.[69] The Hindustan Welfare Society of America and the India National Congress Association of America, two California-based Indian American groups claiming to represent the "overwhelming majority of East Indian residents" in the United States, similarly expressed their "whole-hearted" approval of the Luce-Celler bill.[70]

Emboldened by the outpouring of support, ILA affiliates transformed the House Immigration Committee's March 1945 hearing into an official forum where they voiced their nationalist grievances and desires while dispelling any lingering doubts about Indians' commitment to the Allied cause. J. J. Singh's statement replicated the tendency of internationalist arguments to erase Asian communities in the United States. As Walter Judd had done with Chinese in the Magnuson bill campaign, the ILA president sought to win the support of U.S. lawmakers by describing the impact of the Luce-Celler bill on Indians, rather than on Indian Americans. He rightly surmised that a transnational strategy playing on India's anticipated importance to Washington would be more effective than a domestic one in light of the fact that the Indian American community was small and lacked political influence.

If observers had been uncertain about the relationship between the ILA's Luce-Celler campaign and the Indian independence struggle before, the link was now unmistakable. While ostensibly a forum on Indian immigration, the hearing effectively became a platform for Indians in the United States and their allies to advertise the plight of colonized Indians and to increase pressure on U.S. officials to intervene on Indians' behalf. J. J. Singh quickly emerged as the most charismatic spokesman of these views. Noah Mason of Illinois (R-IL) declared the Sikh leader's speech the "most spectacular" presentation at the hearing, doing more to sway him in favor of the bill than "all the other witnesses put together."[71] Singh's scathing critique of British wartime policies in India echoed the grievances of nationalist leaders like

Nehru and thereby reinforced the ILA's unofficial role as a mouthpiece for the INC in the United States. Addressing popular criticisms of Indians' contributions to the war as "half-hearted," Singh maintained that if any Americans "found fault" with India's "lack of war effort," the responsibility lay "at the door of the British imperialists and not on the Indians." If the British had really wanted to mobilize Indians effectively, they would not have put a "great disciple of democracy" like INC leader Nehru in prison; even today, a "great man who should be sitting in the conferences at Yalta and San Francisco, is rotting in jail in India," Singh lamented.[72] In one of his boldest statements, he contended that had it not been for British intransigence on the Indian independence issue, more than five times the number of current enlistees in the Indian volunteer army would have joined the Allies in the fight against Japan. Moreover, if an Indian nationalist movement allied with Japan had been able to gain followers, it was precisely because of British inflexibility on Indian independence, not due to any inherent Indian sympathy with imperial Japan. Either way, he asserted, the exceedingly small number of Indians who had joined Subhas Bose's Indian National Army compared with the number fighting alongside the British was proof positive of Indians' overwhelming loyalty to the Allied cause.

In statement after statement, ILA witnesses testified to the geopolitical significance of the Luce-Celler bill and its promise to promote the United States' anticolonial image and distance Washington from Whitehall's imperial sins. According to Singh, the Luce-Celler bill was already "front-page news" in India, where Indian officials were touting it as a "test case" of the United States' "professions of democracy and equality." He called on House lawmakers to pass the legislation not only as a way to increase Indians' already "tremendous amount of friendly feeling toward the people of the United States" but also as a way to draw a "line of demarcation" between the United States and British colonialists in Indian minds. The legislation's co-sponsor, Clare Boothe Luce, echoed the pressing need to distinguish between the United States and Great Britain, particularly before the United Nations Conference began later that spring in San Francisco. In Luce's telling, the United States needed a strong platform from which to pressure its European allies—here she meant Great Britain, though she never singled out the U.S. ally by name—to relinquish their colonial possessions. A refusal by the U.S. Congress to pass this bill, she argued, would handicap the United States' position at the conference by ensuring that American criticisms of European imperialism "suffer" from a "certain degree of hypocrisy" since the United States could not "successfully deplore a policy which we practice."[73]

In fact, American and British leaders would successfully dodge any substantive discussion of colonialism at the San Francisco conference, much to the chagrin of Indian nationalists, including J. J. Singh, who reported from the meeting as a guest correspondent for the Bombay-based Indian newspaper the *Hindustan Times*.[74]

Southern Democrats at the hearing ascribed to the legislation a different kind of diplomatic significance and messaging in their attempts to quash it: simply put, they argued that it would imperil Anglo-American relations. According to Rep. Gossett, the audience U.S. lawmakers should worry about was the British government, which might view passage of the act by Congress as an American attempt to coopt or otherwise "alienate the affections" of Indians.[75] Gossett's warning tapped into a mounting sense of competition and threat among the British, who were still coming to terms with the United States' growing dominance over the continent.[76] Short of a formal statement from Whitehall, southern critics insisted that they could not vote for the Luce-Celler measure in good conscience. As restrictionists, southern Democrats would almost certainly have opposed any proposal to liberalize immigration anyway; nonetheless, the colonial objection provided a compelling, and not easily resolved, screen for their restrictionist views. Perhaps feeling that his argument about the difficulty of Christianizing India and therefore of assimilating immigrants would have no weight in the face of anything that might imperil victory in World War II, Georgia Democrat Robert Ramspeck did not raise the issue of religion. Sensing the bill was poised for passage, however, he discreetly recruited several of the committee's southern Democrats and conservative Republicans to attend the last day of the hearing and vote against the measure; the absence of three lawmakers who supported the bill clinched its defeat in committee by a margin of ten to six. Suggesting how powerful the narrative of a British audience eventually became, House Immigration Committee chairman Samuel Dickstein later reported that the vote failed in executive committee "solely upon" the fear that passing it "might embarrass the British Government."[77]

News of the bill's defeat by the House committee spurred supporters in both the United States and India into action.[78] Decrying the vote as motivated by "racial antagonism," a writer in the Bombay-based *Free Press Journal* asked if the disappointment was a "foretaste of things to come at San Francisco?"[79] In an interview with the U.S. Office of Wartime Information, House Immigration Committee chairman Dickstein insisted that Indians "should not be alarmed" since U.S. lawmakers would soon revive the legislation. The *Hindustan Times* quoted Dickstein in a front-page story titled

"Immigration Bill to Be Revived?," which recorded both the disillusionment of U.S. officials and other advocates as well as their determination to carry on the fight.[80] Citing negative press in the Indian media and grumbling in official Delhi circles, Rep. Celler promptly wrote President Roosevelt and the State Department requesting their intervention to keep the legislation alive. Given that Indians were watching to see what American lawmakers would do, he argued, the United States could little afford to offend them by refusing to repeal the racial exclusions they found so insulting. That so many people in both the United States and India saw the legislation as a proxy for Washington's position on Indian independence raised the stakes even higher.

The View from Delhi

By the time Sir Girja Bajpai formally approached U.S. State Department officials about the possibility of an Indian exclusion repeal bill in spring 1943, Government of India officials at Delhi had been monitoring the treatment of Indians living outside the subcontinent for years, if not decades.[81] As one more cynical observer described it, the colonial government had strategically leveraged "Indian sentiment over the woes of Indians overseas" to "acquire a certain amount of popularity" with the Indian people.[82] As early as the World War I era, the Indian government had asked their British overseers to help end discriminations imposed on Indians living in other parts of the empire, particularly South Africa and Kenya, where figures including Gandhi had made headlines battling local restrictions on Indians' economic and political activities.

Protests over Indians' mistreatment resurged with force during World War II. Shortages and pressures stemming from the war effort prompted colonial legislatures in southern and eastern Africa to place new restrictions on Indian populations living there, and Indian officials in Delhi were ready to renew their efforts. They lodged formal protests and petitions, appealing to the British government to intervene on local Indians' behalf. The Indian colonial government did not act alone. At least twice during World War II, the Indian Legislative Assembly debated a bill proposing reciprocal restrictions on the natives of countries that discriminated against Indians overseas. Most assembly members had members of the British empire and Commonwealth in mind, but others extended the principle to Indians living in the United States. This became even more common as the United States surpassed Britain in military and financial strength.

Within the U.S. campaign, no Indian figure did more than Bajpai to en-sure the Luce-Celler bill's success. An Oxford-educated don with a distin-guished career in the Indian Civil Service, Bajpai became India's first agent-general, or direct representative, to the United States after the posi-tion was created in the summer of 1941. India, the United States, and Brit-ain had each embraced his appointment as a diplomatic liaison between Washington and Delhi for different reasons. Indians serving in the British colonial government in Delhi liked the idea of a direct report to speak for their interests in Washington, DC, while U.S. officials were eager to in-crease American influence on the subcontinent and to strengthen the U.S.-India relationship without straining the Anglo-American alliance. For their part, British officials at Whitehall hoped that the agent-general, as a symbol of Indians' political autonomy under British rule, could help counteract the growing influence of Indian nationalists like Singh in the United States.[83] After being knighted in 1932, Bajpai had just been named to the prestigious Viceroy's Executive Council, the cabinet of the British Governor-General's office of India, when he was tapped for the newly created job. Bajpai was widely respected throughout the ranks of the colonial government; even the ILA's New York–based leaders initially welcomed his appointment, de-claring it "a step in the right direction" on the grounds that "Indians them-selves should speak for their country." Bajpai was specifically praised as an "expert on the status of emigrated Indians."[84] His many qualifications not-withstanding, however, the ILA's J. J. Singh voiced the belief of Indian na-tionalists throughout the world when he called Bajpai a "British stooge" who would ultimately speak only for the "present British government and not for the people of India."[85]

For years Bajpai supported the ILA's lobbying efforts from behind the scenes, embracing the cause of the Luce-Celler bill in a way that promoted the ILA's cause rather than upstaging it. It did not take long for Bajpai and other Delhi officials to decide their preference for the ILA's Luce-Celler mea-sure over the IWL's Langer bill in early 1944. In contrast to Khan's assertion that the Langer bill was an easier sell, Bajpai argued that the Luce-Celler bill's similarity with the Chinese measure would facilitate its passage: "Con-gress will not wish, for the sake of political harmony, to deviate from the lan-guage of the Chinese Act even by a comma," he asserted. "The more the changes, the greater the risk of controversy."[86] He further echoed the ILA's misgivings about IWL's patron, Senator William Langer, whose "unsavory reputation" and status as "persona non grata with the [Roosevelt] Adminis-tration" made him an "undesirable ally" and "unwelcome champion of Indian rights" who might have to "be tolerated but ought not to be wooed."[87] Shortly after the bill was first introduced to Congress, Bajpai promoted Luce-Celler during a tour of Indian American communities of California, which in his report to Delhi he notably called the "Indian colonies," the term conveying a sense of responsibility and oversight. Indeed, Bajpai and other Government of India officials regularly referred to the Luce-Celler legislation as "our bills" in internal documents, suggesting a feeling of ownership.[88] As the IWL's Khan had done during his visit months earlier, the Indian official spoke at several Sikh temples and Indian community centers, rallying support among local Indian residents for congressional action. He also met with local newspaper editors and California state officials to solicit their aid; in a note to Delhi, he personally claimed credit for the *Los Angeles Times'* endorsement.

It is worth asking why Bajpai remained so committed to the cause given that the ILA and Singh, his occasional rival and frequent critic, stood to receive the credit for its passage. There was no love lost between the two men: Singh continued publicly to dismiss Bajpai as a British mouthpiece, while Bajpai once likened Singh's ego-driven leadership style to that of a "Turk who can bear no rival near the throne."[89] Powerful sponsors of Singh's such as Henry Luce fueled the sense of competition. For example, a *Time* magazine piece in late 1943 unfavorably described Bajpai as "India's timid official delegate," while crediting Singh's more aggressive lobbying style with galvanizing congressional support for an Indian famine relief bill. This unflattering depiction may have contributed to a melee at the Sikh temple in Stockton, California, two months later. A group of local Indians attacked the visiting agent-general for his ineffectiveness in representing them; they reportedly harassed Bajpai so severely that he cut his speech short and escaped through the back door to avoid physical harm.[91]

There are several ways to understand Bajpai's support of Luce-Celler. For one, it was consistent with Delhi's general efforts to rehabilitate Indian American communities as part of its public relations outreach to Washington and the American public, whose good opinion was seen as especially important at a time when the words of U.S. leaders and American media outlets could greatly influence international opinion. Accordingly, as Major General Shah of the Indian government's Office of External Affairs warned his colleagues, Indian Americans' "very dirty habits" and addictions to "social vices, drink, and violence against each other" threatened to "disgrace" all Indian people.[92] It was therefore in Delhi's best interest to improve the living situations of Indians in places like California as soon as possible. Given that he left most of the public advocacy to the ILA, Bajpai's views on the Luce-Celler bill's relevance to the cause of Indian independence remain unclear, as do his personal desires for India's future. That said, J. J. Singh's dismissals of him as a British mouthpiece oversimplify the case. Although appointed by the British, Bajpai quietly shaped his office into something quite different from Whitehall's vision. On several occasions, he promoted greater U.S. involvement in Anglo-Indian affairs and reportedly even lobbied discreetly for India's independence. In correspondence with U.S. State Department officials outside the purview of British officials, he criticized his British superiors, including Prime Minister Winston Churchill, and expressed support for an independent Indian republic rather than the Indian Commonwealth that Whitehall officially endorsed.[93] It is hard to say for sure without explicit evidence, but it is certainly possible that Bajpai was willing to tolerate Singh because he recognized the other man's skill and believed that his advocacy could advance India's bid for independence.

Bajpai was one of many Indian officials serving in the Delhi-based Government of India who lobbied the British government to support U.S. legislation for Indians. Even as the Chinese exclusion repeal campaign was still in full swing, Major General Shah of the External Affairs office argued that British support for Indian American rights via a U.S. bill was imperative as an act of public diplomacy.[94] In a report to Whitehall, Shah credited Singh with convincing Indians in America that the British government's "intransigence on the India question" had produced their unequal treatment and status under U.S. law.[95] In this way, the ILA was successfully "spreading anti-British propaganda amongst Indians." To stop it, he argued, Whitehall must appear a champion of Indian American rights or risk imperiling the Anglo-American alliance and with it Britain's position on the international stage. Although there is little evidence that Roosevelt was willing to weaken the U.S. alliance with Britain and Indian Americans had virtually no electoral power, Whitehall may not have been so confident. At least one member of the Far Eastern Bureau of the British Information Ministry was receptive. In a letter to Shah, G. C. Ryan agreed that inaction in the face of rising American support for Indian nationalists and a corresponding rise in anti-British sentiment was no longer an option; Whitehall had to respond. He also emphasized that Indians in the United States were a direct "reflection upon the good name of India and the Empire." Exclusion made many Indian Americans poor, and poverty made for bad publicity. Consequently, Whitehall must either work to "raise [Indian Americans'] standards of behavior and civilization" or "arrange large-scale repatriation to India."[96]

Southern House Democrats' claim to have stopped the Luce-Celler bill for fear of endangering the Anglo-American alliance was an overstatement, but Whitehall continued to provide them this excuse by ignoring Delhi's advice. In the end, Bajpai was the one who convinced Great Britain to act. Though lacking Singh's style, his official position and regular contacts in the White House allowed him to navigate back channels and to mobilize a response. On the same day the House tabled the Luce-Celler bill, the agent-general met with U.S. attorney general Francis Biddle to ask whether the administration might intervene on the measure's behalf.[97] On Biddle's recommendation, Acting Secretary of State Joseph Grew pledged the State Department's "continued and active sympathy" and "confidentially" informed Bajpai of his private recommendation to the president that a "fresh initiative" was needed in the matter. Having learned of the bill's tabling from Emanuel Celler, Roosevelt apparently wrote to Rep. Ramspeck to ask that the measure move forward, but he died before the lawmaker could respond. As Truman took office amid a climate of confusion, Bajpai turned his attention to London. He met with Lord Halifax, the British ambassador to Washington, and asked him to use his influence. When Halifax delayed, Bajpai again pressed the issue. Among other tactics, he played on Whitehall's uncertainty about the impact of Roosevelt's death on the future of the Anglo-American relationship. In contrast to Roosevelt, with whom British officials had enjoyed a close rapport, he reminded Halifax that Truman's views on India and the future of the British empire were largely unknown.

Whitehall's approval came within weeks. In a letter to the U.S. State Department dated May 3, 1945, the British ambassador "welcome[d]" enactment of the Luce-Celler bill as a "gesture of friendship to India which had played, and is playing, so important a part in the war."[98] The war he was referencing was half over; Germany was in the midst of surrendering. That a U.S. immigration and naturalization bill could garner this much attention and support from the British, Indian, and American governments suggests the degree to which all three powers came to see it as an important instrument serving their other goals. For Britain, the endorsement served its immediate goal of bolstering Indians' military participation in the Allied war against Japan. Germany's surrender in the spring of 1945 only amplified the importance of the British Indian Army, which at 2.5 million men was the largest volunteer force ever assembled, nearly equal to the size of the army in Great Britain itself. For India and the United States, the imperatives remained largely unchanged: Indians continued to welcome any U.S. measure that recognized them, implicitly or explicitly, as an entity independent of and distinct from the British, while U.S. officials sought to cultivate a positive future relationship with an independent India.

Britain's formal endorsement was the catalyst the White House needed to bring renewed pressure on the House Immigration Committee to reconsider the legislation. Despite the procedural questions it raised, committee chairman Samuel Dickstein again used his authority to schedule another hearing on the Luce-Celler measure over the objections of several southern members. Bajpai's intervention had near single-handedly saved the bill.

With British opposition no longer a viable objection, advocates of repeal turned their efforts to alleviating the racial anxieties of southern critics. At Rep. Celler's request, Truman met personally with Rep. Ramspeck in an effort to preempt further deadlock in the House. In his letter to Truman, Celler advised the new president to emphasize that "East Indians" were "not Negroes" but "of the Caucasian race."[99] The two official witnesses to speak in support of the measure at a hastily scheduled House Immigration Committee hearing that June took a different tack: playing on southerners' racial fears, Ambassador William Phillips and Rep. Clare Booth Luce cited the threat of a global race war in an effort to sway them in *favor* of passage. Phillips, speaking for the White House, warned his congressional audience that if they allowed U.S. exclusion laws to stand, India would be "thrown more and more into alignment with other Asiatic people" and result in the formation of a "resentful color block against the white races."[100] Luce, the bill's Republican cosponsor, echoed Phillips's emphasis on Asia as critical to the United States' own future security, but she framed the conflict in terms of a nascent Soviet–U.S. rivalry. "When the imperial designs of Soviet Russia clash with those of Great Britain, in the near or middle east, and another world war conflagration starts," she cautioned, America will "surely need 400,000,000 Indians and 350,000,0000 Chinese who will still call America the land of freedom, generosity, and principle."[101] Anticipating the role that the Cold War would play in immigration debates that followed, she maintained that repealing exclusion was a small price to pay for Asians' loyalties. For their part, southern critics continued to protest the bill on procedural grounds. House Committee chairman Dickstein overruled them, however, and the House Immigration and Naturalization Committee reported the measure out favorably in June to face a full House vote that fall.[102]

The Final Legislative Battles

Two developments in the summer of 1945 changed the course of the Indian independence movement and with it the Luce-Celler debates over their final year. First, Labor Party leader Clement Attlee succeeded Churchill as British prime minister in late July 1945, removing one of the greatest impediments to Indian independence. Unlike his predecessor, Attlee had supported the cause for years as a means of unburdening Britain economically and militarily. Under his leadership Whitehall immediately began drafting plans for the transfer of power on the subcontinent. Around the same time, the Simla Conference, a meeting of India's political leaders convened by the British government to decide the terms of Indian self-government, pushed political disagreements over the Muslim League's demand for a separate Muslim state to the forefront of the independence debate. Both INC leader Nehru for a unified India and Muslim League leader Jinnah for partition were intractable, but virtually all the major American media outlets attributed the conference's failure directly to Jinnah's insistence that his party choose all Muslim representatives in the Indian government. In addition to introducing many Americans to the Muslim League leader as a major player in Indian politics for the first time, the U.S. news coverage foregrounded religious disunity as a major source of conflict threatening India's independent future.[103]

With the question of India's future at least preliminarily resolved, advocates of the Luce-Celler bill seized on pragmatic arguments to make the final push for passage. Celler harped on the promise of the Indian market for American goods, while Luce focused on the legislation's "political expediency" during a time when "Asiatic colonial peoples" were "shopping for political ideologies" and "inclined" to look to "Moscow."[104] Rep. Walter Judd's lengthy statement to the House expanded on Luce's warnings of a mounting Soviet Communist threat that would one day challenge the United States. He also traced a direct line from the 1943 Magnuson Act to the measure at hand. Just as repealing Chinese exclusion had had an "extraordinary" effect on Chinese morale at the height of the Pacific War, he argued that the Luce-Celler bill offered Washington a tool to counter the growing influence of Soviet Communism among the "billion people in Asia" now "deciding whether to go with the communists or with all the nonwhite people, or with the democracies."[105] In reality, Judd's statement revealed as much about his own preoccupation with communism as about the actual state of affairs on the subcontinent.[106] By 1946, as U.S. conflict with the Soviet Union was still crystallizing, the terms and timetable of Indian independence remained a pressing concern.

After a long and contentious floor debate, House lawmakers passed the Luce-Celler bill by an overwhelming margin of three to one; nevertheless, the many vitriolic statements made over the four-hour discussion registered lasting opposition among southern Democrats, who remained a vocal and powerful minority. As he had done during the Chinese campaign, Rep. A. Leonard Allen of Louisiana led the charge. He made the hearing's only reference to religion: citing recent reports of Hindus and Muslims "killing each other on the streets," he questioned the wisdom of allowing any amount of Indian immigration to the United States given the state of religious disunity that was plaguing the subcontinent. Why "transport to America" an "internal quarrel" that has been "going on for ages over there?" he asked. In another statement, Allen turned Halifax's endorsement into a critique of Whitehall's general inaction on India, which now compelled U.S. lawmakers to compensate in the form of this bill. "The British will not give the Indians or Hindus what they want," he complained, "but they tell us to do this."[107] Clearly, even though independence was a settled question, it had become inseparable from the proposed repeal legislation in some lawmakers' minds.

Having passed in the House, the bill now moved to the Senate, where Georgia Democrat and chairman of the Senate Immigration and Naturalization Committee Richard Russell led the opposition. Russell was a well-known segregationist and restrictionist who had spent years working to preserve Jim Crow segregation in the South and prevent changes to the national origins quota system, which he believed was needed to protect the United States' Anglo-Saxon culture.[108] To this end, he opposed all nonwhite immigration from Asia and Africa, and in fact, had already made clear his objections to Indians when he rejected a refugee bill citing his fear that it would open a door for "tens of thousands of Indians and Moslems from India" to demand admission on similar humanitarian grounds.[109] From the fall of 1945 through the spring of 1946, Russell successfully used his power as committee chair to keep the Luce-Celler bill from progressing further.

The final months of the Luce-Celler campaign revolved around an inter-branch standoff that pitted the Truman administration's commitment to an interventionist, peace-keeping foreign policy against the more overtly U.S.-centric and conservative vision of the southern bloc that Russell represented. The United States' formal entry into the war after Pearl Harbor had brought a temporary truce, as southern Democrats joined with the White House and the northern contingent of the party in rallying around the common goal of an Allied victory.[110] A self-described "isolationist . . . by instinct," Russell had nonetheless accepted the need for foreign intervention during World War II, based on his belief that the "flag" was in "danger."[111] With the end of World War II, however, southern Democrats largely withdrew their support for overseas intervention. Like Russell, many opposed Roosevelt's postwar vision of the country as a permanent world policeman, a role Truman inherited and embraced. While they did support a strong U.S. military, often their main goal in building one was precisely to avoid having to maintain a large international presence and commit to long-term foreign aid: that is, they wanted to strengthen the United States in order to keep the world at a distance.

Evidence of growing anti-American sentiment in India coupled with postwar activism by Indian nationalists on the subcontinent eventually cemented Truman's determination to shepherd the legislation through the Senate as quickly as possible. In October 1945, Nehru's outspoken criticisms of Washington's wartime policies as indirectly reinforcing British colonial policies put U.S. officials on edge. Reports of U.S. support for European colonial entrenchment in Indonesia and Indochina, where Dutch soldiers were using U.S.-issue weapons to kill local nationalists, fueled condemnations of Washington's continued support for European colonialism in the region. In February 1946, anger erupted in violence; Indians attacked U.S. military units, diplomatic staff, and businesses in Calcutta. With their independence assured if not yet actualized, Indian nationalists began systematically challenging anti-Indian policies and practices in white settler societies other than the United States. That same year, Madame Pandit, addressing the General Assembly as India's unofficial spokesperson to the United Nations, protested the poor treatment of Indians living in apartheid-era South Africa. Her petitions, among many others, compelled a UN vote to censure South Africa's racial policies; the United States voted with India in favor of censure. It was a symbolic victory; real change would not come for decades. Similarly, one of India's proposals upon joining the Commonwealth of Nations several years later was that citizenship eligibility in all independent member countries be interchangeable. Canada, Australia, and South Africa quickly dismissed the idea. With these and other demands for the equal treatment of its citizens living abroad, India thus positioned itself to replace a now-defeated Japan as Asia's most vocal champion of international antiracist diplomacy.

These developments incentivized the White House to expedite passage of the Luce-Celler bill as a tool to offset falling U.S. prestige in the region, and

U.S. president Harry S. Truman signs the Luce-Celler Act, 1946. J. J. Singh is third from the right and Filipino American leader Diosdado Yap is second from the left. Harris and Ewing, courtesy of the Harry S. Truman Library.

Russell's acquiescence was key. Three years earlier, it had taken no less than a personal meeting with Chinese Nationalist leader Chiang Kai-shek and President Roosevelt's personal reassurance that the Magnuson bill would not create a precedent to persuade the Georgia senator to allow a favorable report by the Senate Immigration Committee under his control. Several other factors had mitigated Russell's opposition in the Chinese case. First, due to its timing and framing, the Magnuson bill could more easily be justified as a wartime measure, and while he disagreed with Roosevelt on many issues of domestic policy and social reform, Russell had great trust in the president when it came to international affairs. Second, Russell shared a long friendship with Madame Chiang Kai-shek from her time attending Wesleyan College in Macon, Georgia, where she and the senator first met. Indeed, the two dined together in China just a few months before the Magnuson bill reached the Senate and shortly after the Chinese leader returned from her visit to the United States.

This time, with Truman an unknown quantity and no personal connections to India, Russell was more cautious.[112] In his mind, passing the Luce-Celler bill would do worse than violate the White House's earlier pledge not to set a precedent: it would allow immigration from India, a society he personally despised for being "primitive" and "full of religious fanaticism."[113] It took three more meetings with Truman before the Georgia senator finally relented to schedule a hearing on the legislation. Finally, in April 1946, the Senate Immigration Committee gave the bill a favorable report. Following another round of petitions from Delhi and the White House, Russell permitted the committee to report the bill out to the Senate floor for a vote, with the stipulation that he personally opposed it. Marking an anticlimactic finish to a long and dramatic journey, the Luce-Celler bill passed easily by voice vote on a day that Russell was absent from the chamber.

The Legacies of Luce-Celler

On July 2, 1946, President Truman signed the Luce-Celler bill into law, with J. J. Singh and another ILA colleague on hand to witness the event in the Oval Office.[114] News of its enactment unleashed a wave of congratulatory and jubilant reports in the American and Indian media. Singh received wide praise for his part in the victory. A group of Indians from California pledged to "remember forever [his] untiring efforts on their behalf." Indian officials applauded his "critical role" in the bill's passage. Having watched the progress of the campaign from Delhi, Indian Congress leader Nehru noted the "striking tenacity" behind Singh's "single-handed piloting" of the Indian immigration bill. Even Gandhi praised the ILA president's lobbying work as "solely responsible" for its successful enactment.[115] The *Time* reporter covering the bill's journey through Congress described Singh's efforts in detail, citing the many letters sent and visits the "handsome, swarthy . . . 6-ft. Sikh from Kashmir" had made while "tirelessly stalk[ing] Capitol Hill hallways" to secure its passage.[116] Unlike Singh, Khan was not present at the signing of Luce-Celler, but that did not stop him from taking credit for the citizenship gains it brought.[117] Sir Girja Bajpai appeared in none of these accounts; his involvement in the campaigns was the most forgotten of all. After independence, he went on to have an illustrious political career, serving as the Indian Republic's first foreign minister under its first prime minister, Jawaharlal Nehru.

None of the ILA lobbyists ever became U.S. citizens and, true to their word, most of them returned to the subcontinent soon after the bill's passage—even J. J. Singh. Dr. Shridlani, Khan's antagonist at the 1944 hearing on the Langer bill, settled in Delhi as a journalist. Dr. Anup Singh, the former editor of the ILA's newsletter, served several terms in the Upper House of the Parliament in Delhi and later as India's representative to the UN Commission on Korea. Several others took up academic posts at Indian universities. Singh stayed in the United States for another twelve years and continued to lead the ILA, which floundered for a new focus without the unifying goal of Indian independence. Despite his central involvement in the Luce-Celler campaign, he also never naturalized. In his fifties, Singh married a white American woman and they had a son. He moved the whole family to India in 1959, writing about his decision in a *Times of India* article titled "Why I Came Back to India." Above all, he explained, he wanted to spare his child the challenge of "dual loyalties."[118]

Khan's public life after Luce-Celler was far more active than Singh's. The former IWL president moved to Phoenix, where he continued to lead the newly renamed Pakistan Welfare League (PWL); the group would eventually claim congressional lawmakers, former governors, and the associate curator of the American Museum of Natural History in New York as members of its advisory board.[119] The organization's partnership with the All India Muslim League in Bombay eventually came full circle. Just as Khan had drawn on his homeland ties to Jinnah and the Muslim League to shore up the IWL's legitimacy in the Langer campaign, Jinnah later came to rely on Khan and the PWL community to promote the Muslim League's case for Pakistan in the United States. In November 1946, four months after the Luce-Celler bill's passage, Khan accompanied two Muslim League spokespersons on a cross-country speaking tour intended to raise American support for the cause.[120] They, along with millions worldwide, celebrated the founding of the new Muslim state of Pakistan and Jinnah's inauguration as its first president on August 15, 1947.[121] Few among them could have anticipated the unspeakable violence and bloodshed that the subcontinent's formal division, once achieved, would bring.

Conclusion

The Luce-Celler bill assumed multiple meanings in the final years of the Indian independence movement, in the context of war and an impasse between the British and the Indian National Congress over the latter's demands for India's immediate independence. For Indian nationalists, its passage marked a welcome, if indirect, signal of American support for Indians' self-determination. For Indians permanently settled in the United States, the legislation promised to improve their economic and political prospects. And for the British, endorsing the bill was an expedient act of migration diplomacy intended to mobilize Indians in the Allies' final battles against Japan without necessarily leading to Indian independence. A transpacific perspective shows how these different visions intersected. Centering Indians in both the United States and Asia broadens the story from a Washington-based tale of repeal as a U.S. imperial project to a multifaceted campaign in which Indians and Indian Americans sought to instrumentalize repeal toward their own goals, perhaps most notably as an anticolonial tool to further Indian independence.

There are many ways to assess the significance of the Indian bill's success. On the one hand, although the 1,772 Indians who became U.S. citizens under the Luce-Celler Act's naturalization provisions by 1965 included Dalip Singh Saund, the first Indian American and the first Asian American to be elected to U.S. Congress, the immediate impact of the law's Indian immigration quota and naturalization provisions remained largely symbolic.[122] Yet as part of the longer movement for repeal, the Indian legislation established repeal as more than a one-time act of wartime emergency or exceptional measure for Chinese only. Indeed, as its critics had most feared, the victory of the Luce-Celler Act transformed the Magnuson Act into precisely what its staunchest opponents said it should never become: a precedent for other Asian groups to follow.

No group of activists was more attuned to the rhythms of the Indian campaign than Filipinos, who, like Indians, had been seeking new rights and greater recognition from the U.S. government for years, albeit under different circumstances. Due to a technicality, the Indian immigration and naturalization provisions of the Luce-Celler bill were combined with a Philippine naturalization measure that made all Filipina/os eligible for U.S. citizenship upon the islands' independence. Many Washington observers described the joining of the two bills as fitting insofar as they both stemmed from a common impetus to affirm Washington's commitment to the self-determination of all Asian peoples. Thus it was that Filipino intellectual Diosdado Yap and other Filipino American community leaders stood alongside J. J. Singh in the Oval Office as President Truman signed the act into law on July 2, 1946; two days later, the Philippines celebrated its independence from nearly half a century of U.S. colonial rule. Chapter 3 tells the story of how they got there. As in the Indian effort, the Philippine bill's entanglement with independence struggles already in progress complicated its passage. And because the imperial power in question was the United States, the complexities took on even greater weight.

CHAPTER THREE

Manila Prepares for Independence

Filipina/o Campaigns for U.S. Citizenship on the
Eve of Philippine Decolonization

In 1940, Joaquin Elizalde appeared before the U.S. House Committee on Immigration and Naturalization to speak in support of legislation making Filipina/o residents of the United States eligible for U.S. citizenship. He began his statement by acknowledging an apparent impropriety: Elizalde was a member of the Philippine colonial government appearing on behalf of Filipina/os seeking to renounce all of their legal ties to the Philippines and make the United States their place of nationality. As the Philippine resident commissioner, Elizalde served as the islands' direct representative and nonvoting territorial delegate to the U.S. Congress in Washington, DC. The Commonwealth government at Manila, he reassured U.S. lawmakers, would continue to "do everything in its power to induce Filipinos in the U.S. to return to their [own] country." But committee members should recognize the many Filipina/os who nonetheless planned to stay. "Innocent victims of circumstance," they had "spent the best part of their adult lives" in the United States, with many now "permanently rooted" by American wives and U.S. citizen children. Now, as the economy worsened, many found it increasingly difficult to find jobs and relief under New Deal policies that privileged citizens over aliens. Given their plight, Elizalde argued, it "behoove[d] the governments of both the U.S. and the Commonwealth to find [an] equitable way of solving [these immigrants'] difficulty," including the possibility of U.S. citizenship.[1]

Philippine officials featured prominently in every aspect of the campaign for Philippine naturalization from Joaquin Elizalde's first appearance in front of the House Immigration and Naturalization Committee in the late 1930s, through the incorporation and enactment of a Philippine citizenship bill as part of the Luce-Celler Act of 1946. The few accounts of the World War II Philippine citizenship campaign have focused on the advocacy of Filipina/o Americans, narrating their activism as part of the history of Philippine labor leaders, workers, and leftists fighting for rights in their workplaces and communities.[2] Without discounting their contributions, this chapter tells a broader, transpacific story detailing the critical role Manila officials played as some of the most consistent and visible lobbyists in the Washington, DC–based naturalization campaigns. Drawing from both U.S. and Philippine archives, I place Filipina/o advocates in conversation with Filipina/o Americans and their allies. I show how the effort was an attempt by Philippine officials to prepare for what they feared would be the catastrophic financial costs of national independence from U.S. colonial rule. With the future of trade and stable income to sustain the new nation's infrastructure uncertain, members of the Manila government looked to cultivate Filipina/o Americans as a reliable source of revenue and investment in the form of remittances and other support sent from the United States to the islands. Centering Manila's role in the Washington-based naturalization campaign thus reveals Philippine officials' instrumental understanding of the U.S. citizenship bill as a means to achieve their own national goals. It also suggests their loose view of national citizenship. Through their support of naturalization rights, Manila officials sought to inculcate in Filipina/o Americans a sense of responsibility to the islands that transcended a formal legal status alone. Viewed from Asia, then, Manila's campaigning for the Luce-Celler bill can be seen as an act of Philippine state-building intended to safeguard and promote the islands' economic welfare and stability after independence.

Focusing on Manila's role makes clear how important the Philippine independence struggle was in shaping the timing, argumentation, and ultimate success of the U.S.-based naturalization campaign. The islands' imminent transition to independence not only provided the motive for Manila's involvement. It fundamentally framed the legislative debate and the politics of passage in Washington, DC. In total, Philippine independence was a process more than a decade in the making. This chapter charts how Filipina/os' battle for U.S. citizenship eligibility became entangled in the protracted struggle between Manila and Washington to negotiate its timetable and terms. Not simply an interstate struggle among Philippine and U.S. officials, the naturalization campaigns brought to the fore long-standing tensions between the Philippine colonial government in Manila and Filipina/o American communities over questions of representation and interests. In a parallel with the Indian campaign, Philippine colonial officials supported the legislation for their own nation-building purposes, while for many Filipina/o Americans, it was an immediate matter of daily survival.

Nevertheless, categorical differences between the Indian and Philippine campaigns exemplify how varying histories and timelines of exclusion could give rise to distinct stories of repeal. First, unlike the Indian case, because Philippine migration was never completely closed off, advocates generally eschewed discussion of quotas and focused on addressing the material and social harms caused by Filipina/os' exclusion from U.S. citizenship. Second, Filipina/os in the United States and Asia renewed the fight for U.S. citizenship with the promise of Philippine independence already in hand. The 1934 Tydings-McDuffie Act, or Philippine Independence Act, established a Philippine commonwealth and laid out a ten-year transition period to independence. Thus they differed from Indians who instrumentalized repeal to serve their fight for homeland independence. Third, Indian challenges to empire may have contributed to their formal exclusion during World War I, but only in the Philippine case was exclusion effectively a condition of independence.[3] Even as it set forth the terms of Philippine independence, the 1934 act notably reversed a long-standing U.S. policy of open migration from the islands. It stipulated that for the purposes of immigration, the "Philippine Islands shall be considered to be a foreign country" and Filipina/os "considered as if they are aliens."[4] Filipina/os had previously struggled against racial ineligibility to U.S. citizenship, but never before had it been used to restrict their migration. The Philippines was given an annual migration quota of fifty persons. Before World War II, this represented a symbolic advantage over other Asian countries, which were allowed none, but it was still a fraction of the quotas given to European countries, including ones with much smaller populations; according to Paul Kramer, the Philippine quota was supposed to reflect the islands' transitional status "halfway between a sovereign, quota country and an Asiatic, excluded one."[5]

The Philippine campaign offers a unique example of how empire and exclusion were connected during the era of Asian decolonization.[6] As a U.S. colony, the Philippines was directly implicated in the United States' recalibration of empire in Asia after World War II, and in fact, was its exemplar.[7] U.S. policymakers widely touted Washington's decision to grant the Philippines independence as the clearest proof of its support for the self-determination of all peoples. During World War II, U.S. policymakers, such as Secretary of State Cordell Hull in 1942, expressed their hope that Great Britain and other European powers might follow the United States' lead and begin dismantling their own empires in Asia.[8] But the practical realities of Philippine independence belied the rhetoric. As Takashi Fujitani writes, the United States "trumpeted" Filipina/os' self-determination "as a gift" even as it "compromised" the new state's sovereignty in myriad ways.[9] It was therefore fitting that Philippine naturalization should take effect upon the formal separation of the islands from U.S. colonial rule. The move upheld the fiction of Philippine sovereignty during a time when U.S. officials were eager to tout Washington's relinquishing of its Philippine colony as a prescriptive other Western powers should emulate.

The Strange Case of the Filipino in the United States

Due to their special relationship with the United States, Filipina/os have long been an aberration in the history of Asian immigration and naturalization. Washington annexed the Philippines in 1898, in the aftermath of the Spanish-American War.[10] As U.S. colonial subjects, Filipina/os were insulated from early exclusion laws, but their status was often unclear. An act of Congress in 1902 declared most residents of the islands to be Philippine citizens, but it did not clarify their status under the law or indicate whether they could become American citizens. U.S. lawmakers attempted to resolve the ambiguity by creating "U.S. national" as a catch-all category that included those individuals born in unincorporated territories who were otherwise deemed ineligible for naturalization. As U.S. nationals, Filipina/os were generally treated the same as U.S. citizens for the purposes of travel and migration, but they could not vote in federal elections or exercise citizens' other political rights. Congressional decrees granting certain territorial residents American citizenship on a piecemeal basis (e.g., Puerto Ricans in 1917), while continuing to deny it to others (e.g., residents of Guam before 1950), further complicated Filipina/os' status by creating an uneven patchwork with no consistent logic or reason.[11] According to legal scholar Charles McClain, by World War I, federal courts were "divided evenly" on whether Filipina/os were eligible to become U.S. citizens, but no higher court had yet resolved the issue.[12] In the meantime, Rick Baldoz writes, Filipina/os "took advantage of the uncertainty surrounding their administrative status to challenge their subordination, exploiting loopholes in statutory language to claim rights and creating headaches for authorities."[13] A 1925 federal court ruling ended this legal limbo, establishing that the racially restrictive language of previous naturalization laws barred Filipina/os, along with other Asian groups, from American citizenship. Their racial ineligibility thus confirmed, U.S. military service became Filipinos' only viable pathway to naturalization before World War II.[14]

The rules governing Philippine migration were more clear-cut, at least before 1934. As colonial subjects of the United States, Filipina/os remained exempt from the legal exclusions that barred all other Asian groups by 1924. In fact, Congress's passage of the Johnson-Reed Act prompted an unprecedented number of Filipina/os to enter the continental United States over the next decade, as agricultural interests and other industries in search of inexpensive workers looked to the United States' largest Pacific colony as a ready source of inexpensive replacement labor. Filipina/o migration jumped to record levels: over the next decade, more than 45,000 Filipinos and a smaller number of Filipinas entered the U.S. mainland and settled in states along the West Coast, bringing the total population of Filipina/os in the United States (including Hawaii) to over 100,000 by the 1930s.[15] Public outcry over a "third Asiatic invasion" harped on the sexual and racial threat posed by the new arrivals, the majority of whom were males under the age of thirty.[16] Filipinos' tendency to fraternize with white women made headlines and led to anti-Filipino riots in places such as Watsonville, California, where in 1930, hundreds of white men attacked a dance hall frequented by local Filipinos and even killed one man during five days of violence. Popular fears provided fodder for exclusionists' support and eventual passage of the 1934 Tydings-McDuffie Act, which as one writer described it, made Filipina/os "at once part of the American empire [and] outsiders within it."[17] Efforts to address this included a state-sponsored incentive whereby the U.S. government would pay return transportation for all Filipina/os in the United States who departed voluntarily. Between 1935 and 1940, the Philippine Repatriation program subsidized return travel to the islands for roughly 2,500 Filipina/os in exchange for their promise never to return to the United States; the U.S. Supreme Court eventually ruled it unconstitutional. In a testament to the roots many Filipina/os had already begun laying in the United States, fewer than 2,500 of the nearly 150,000 eligible took advantage of Washington's offer, prompting one *Time* magazine writer to dub the program the "Philippine Flop."[18]

A 1938 pamphlet titled *The Strange Case of the Filipino in the United States* described the consequences of Filipina/os' unique status under the Tydings-McDuffie Act of 1934 and as targets of the Philippine Repatriation program. Its author, California-based Filipino writer Maximo C. Manzon, recounted how subjecting Filipina/os to exclusion had exacerbated their economic hardships during the Depression. It made them vulnerable to unscrupulous employers who sought to "strangle" them "legally and economically" on the one hand, and of U.S. state officials seeking further restrictions on the other. Since their change in legal status from American nationals to aliens had contributed so centrally to their economic plight, Manzon argued that Congress should enact a naturalization bill making all Filipina/os eligible for U.S. citizenship. Such a bill not only would align with

American values. It would also "signify an important contribution to democracy" and "help to maintain the friendliest relations between" the United States and the Philippines, the "two democratic countries on the Pacific."[19]

Manzon's pamphlet, published and distributed by a New York City–based left-wing group called the American Committee for the Protection of the Foreign Born (ACPFB), caught the attention of Rep. Vito Marcantonio (D-NY) and inspired him to sponsor the first of several naturalization bills on the community's behalf.[20] With slight variations, all proposed to extend U.S. citizenship to Filipina/os who had entered the United States before the Tydings-McDuffie Act went into effect on May 1, 1934. "Marc," as he was often called, was a Labor Party member known as much for his radical support of racial equality and workers' rights as for his striped suits, beige fedoras, and high-pitched voice. Although he had few Filipina/o constituents in his East Harlem district, Marcantonio cited his great sympathy for all "underdogs" as the main reason for his support.[21] While his third-party affiliation meant that he was ineligible to lead any House committees, his close working relationship with the chair of the House Immigration Committee, New York Democrat Samuel Dickstein, created opportunities. Over the next three years, versions of the Marcantonio bill would have three hearings before the committee over the objections of its southern members; as eight of the committee's seventeen members, they could not block a hearing, but as a voting bloc, needed only two allies to table any bill.

While ACPFB leaders and publications spread awareness of Filipina/os' plight among a wider national and northeastern audience, Filipina/os living along the West Coast mobilized what would be the campaign's largest show of community advocacy in the form of the Committee for the Protection of Filipino Rights (CPFR). In *America Is in the Heart* (1946), Filipino writer and labor activist Carlos Bulosan recounted how leftists, communists, and labor leaders representing Filipina/o American communities from Seattle to San Diego formed the CPFR in 1939 as a "broad organization" committed to advancing the interests of Philippine workers in the West. Hopes ran high that the CPFR could succeed where other groups had failed, and sure enough, Bulosan described how the committee, boasting "vitality and direction at a time when intelligent leadership was . . . sorely needed," quickly became the "most effective weapon of the Filipinos on the West Coast." Between 1939 and 1940, CPFR members in southern California collected more than 20,000 signatures in support of Marcantonio's naturalization bill, but unemployment, labor repression, and nativism ran high during the Great Depression and their efforts went no further. Bulosan ultimately credited the opposition of "race-haters," protectionists, "big farmers," and other right-wing groups such as the "Liberty League of California, Daughters of the Golden West, Daughters of the American Revolution, and the Parent–Teacher Association" with killing the bill in congressional committee. According to Bulosan, their opposition defeated "every bill favorable to Filipinos in Congress and in the state."[22] As an organization, CPFR did not fare much better: the group ceased to exist by the early 1940s and its dissolution left other entities to continue the fight for naturalization legislation on Capitol Hill.[23] In the absence of a community-based vehicle for lobbying with the expertise and connections of the ILA or even the CACA, the Philippine resident commissioner's (PRC) office quickly emerged as the most active and organized force for passage.

Manila Begins Looking Ahead

By the late 1930s, Philippine Commonwealth officials were already thinking ahead to the economic challenges of independence and devising ways to mitigate them. In short, the islands would have no guaranteed income or tax base once it separated from U.S. rule.[24] Under the current system, the profits Philippine elites made through the U.S. colonial trade relationship supported the Manila government's operations through a complex web of patronage called *utang na loob*. By the 1930s, sugar revenues accounted for as much as two-thirds of the entire profit made from the export of goods from the islands, and most of that sugar was sold in the U.S. market, where it could be priced cheaply because goods from the colonial Philippines were exempt from American tariffs. Nick Cullather has explained how the patronage system operated: the sugar revenues made by Philippine elites selling in the U.S. market "flowed through the government to local caciques [leaders] in the form of patronage and largesse, while political allegiances and votes flowed back to the top." The system worked because it was mutually beneficial. Commonwealth president Manuel Quezon's mastery of patron relationships enabled him to centralize control in his office, producing what many U.S. officials derided as a "one-man government" by World War II.[25] Many Philippine elites were unsure what independence would mean for their business, and some fully expected to lose their livelihoods if, as anticipated, independence ended the islands' favored trade status and tariff exemptions. In the scramble to identify new revenue streams, Manila seized on Filipina/os in the United States, whose remittances at the time totaled more than five million U.S. dollars annually.[26]

The Commonwealth government in Manila had other reasons for taking an interest in Filipina/o Americans. Like their state counterparts in Delhi, Philippine officials believed that this community was negatively shaping Americans' attitudes toward their homeland. As Francisco Varona explained in an internal report to Manila, the "past conduct" of Filipina/o American communities had served as the "worst possible propaganda" for the Philippines "among the masses of the American people who have come into contact with them." A Philippine naturalization bill offered an opportunity for uplift that would demonstrate Filipina/os' capacity for full inclusion in American society.[27] In the longer term, Philippine officials welcomed anything that promoted a positive image of Filipina/os in U.S. policymakers' minds as a way to help them secure more favorable terms in the final negotiations regarding independence. More immediately, Manila representatives hoped to leverage American goodwill for Filipina/os into greater military aid for the islands. As Japanese expansion continued across the continent, Quezon and other Commonwealth officials grew increasingly desperate for U.S. assistance as fears grew of an imminent Japanese invasion of the islands. Many officials in Washington agreed that the islands would likely become Tokyo's target at some point, but as one historian put it, they "could not bring themselves to abandon the Philippines entirely, but neither could they summon the will to protect them adequately."[28]

With these imperatives in mind, the Philippine Commonwealth government began taking proactive steps to secure the support of Filipina/os living in the United States. In 1938, the office of the Philippine resident commissioner, a diplomatic arm of Manila based in Washington, DC, opened a Pacific Coast branch in San Francisco to promote greater interaction with the mainland's largest Filipina/o communities in California's Central Valley. Quezon posted longtime Philippine civil servant Francisco Varona to the new office as a labor commissioner charged with advocating for Filipina/o workers in the area, which was already known for a history of tense worker-employer relations and labor unrest. As the editor-owner of a Philippine newspaper famous for its exposés of poor working conditions, he was a strategic choice. Varona had spent only six months in office as a temporary labor commissioner in Hawaii between 1920 and 1921, but even in his short tenure, he had earned a reputation as a tireless and effective advocate, proactively filing complaints about workers, mistreatment, obtaining a pay raise for them, and even securing them the guarantee of return passage to the Philippines after three years of plantation labor paid for by their employers.[29] Internal notes suggest how the PRC's office under Elizalde envisioned the appointment as an ideal way to bring Filipina/os living in the United States "closer to the Philippine Government and vice-versa."[30] Early reports indicate that the plan was working: according to one Seattle community leader, Varona distinguished himself from other colonial officials with the amount of time he spent with Filipina/o American community members listening to their grievances and expressing genuine concern over their plight. In the words of one observer, "many people who were critical of [Varona] at a distance, learned to like him at close range."[31] Varona's popularity peaked in 1939, when he worked with Filipino leaders in Stockton, California, to create the Filipino Agricultural Laborers Association as an independent, all-Filipino union. Even writer and labor leader Carlos Bulosan, highly critical of many Manila officials, praised him as a "spectacular figure in Filipino life."[32]

Also contributing to Varona's popularity were the annual Inter-Community Conferences sponsored by the San Francisco PRC's office. The meetings gathered delegates representing Filipina/o communities from Seattle down to San Diego, fostering a strengthened sense of unity and shared purpose among them. For Commonwealth officials, the main objective of the conference was to have local leaders discuss issues of common concern under Manila's watchful eye, but these meetings also served their financial goals. In addition to encouraging remittances, the PRC's office used these forums to promote stronger financial ties between the Manila government and U.S. Filipina/o communities. At the 1942 Inter-Community Conference, for example, Manuel Adeva of the PRC's office presented the idea of a savings plan in which Filipina/o Americans would deposit their U.S. war bonds directly with the Philippine government. In his telling, the program had dual appeal: in the short term, it gave U.S. residents the opportunity to assist the United States "in the successful prosecution of the war"; in the long term, it promised to "lay the foundation of economic security in the Philippines after the war."[33]

But the effort to court Filipina/o communities in the United States required confronting years of accumulated resentment built up through the colonial government's history of neglect, condescension, and at times, outright antagonism toward the very people it was charged with protecting. In addition to representing Philippine interests as territorial delegates to the U.S. Congress, PRCs were supposed to oversee the welfare of Filipina/os living and working in the United States. By the 1930s, however, the PRC office had instead developed a reputation for neglecting and even undercutting Filipina/o Americans' interests. In one infamous episode from the Higher

Wages Movement in 1920s Hawaii, Cayetano Ligot, Varona's successor as the islands' Philippine resident labor commissioner, and other Philippine officials tasked with ensuring worker safety and rights had sided with employers and undermined unionization efforts in order to guarantee continued revenue for the Philippine government and line their own pockets.[34] According to JoAnna Poblete, this was consistent with the training of many U.S. colonial officials to "prioritize U.S. interests over those of the Philippines."[35] Distrust among Filipina/o Americans toward the Manila government only grew when it failed to offer protection from the resurgence of nativism and anti-alien policies targeting Filipina/os during the Depression.

The Manila government's poor relationship with Filipina/o American workers was unsurprising. As Poblete explains, stark differences in their "class status, imperial training, and colonial background" meant that the Philippine elites who invariably staffed the colonial bureaucracy were more likely to blame working-class Filipina/os for causing their own problems than they were to sympathize with them.[36] Ethnic and linguistic differences only compounded the sense of distance; Philippine elites such as Elizalde took great pride in their Spanish mestizo identity and Spanish-language skills, a legacy of Spain's centuries of colonial rule over the islands, and saw themselves as sharing little in common with the ethnically Ilocano and Visayan workers who made up the majority of West Coast Filipina/o communities. Even Varona, beloved as he was, shared many of his elite colleagues' views. In a 1938 interview, for example, he blasted the "irresponsibility" of Filipinos for "discredit[ing]" the Philippines as a whole. Rather than single out "discreditable Filipinos," however, he ultimately blamed the Manila government for "foolishly" allowing them to migrate in the first place.[37] It was in this context that President Quezon expressed hope that Varona's appointment as labor commissioner would ameliorate the severity of these class prejudices alienating Manila from Filipina/o workers, but Varona's abrupt death in 1941 scuttled that possibility.

The Philippine Resident Commissioner on Capitol Hill

When Joaquin Elizalde first became the PRC in 1938, many Filipina/o American observers lamented his selection as the next in a line of sinecures for the regime's wealthy supporters.[38] Labor leader Carlos Bulosan's published assessment of Elizalde as someone "primarily concerned with affairs in the islands" seemed to support the idea that Filipina/os in the United States should expect more of the status quo.[39] Certainly, few Filipina/os in the

United States would have chosen Elizalde, a sugar businessman and million-aire widely believed to have bought his position, to serve as their official advocate.[40] Although born in the islands, he spent his youth at boarding schools in Switzerland and Spain before graduating from the London School of Economics. The scion of an elite Spanish-mestizo family, he was actually a Spanish citizen until his late thirties, when he adopted Philippine citizen-ship for financial reasons. New York City businessman Porfirio U. Sevilla voiced the doubts of many Filipina/o Americans when he asked how "such a man" could possibly represent the Philippine people, much less the working-class farmers and manual laborers who made up the majority of the U.S. community. Indeed, Elizalde would spend the first two years of his term battling a lawsuit filed in U.S. courts to challenge his Philippine citizenship, and with it, his qualifications to serve as commissioner.[41] The case was dis-missed in 1940—two weeks after he addressed the House Immigration Committee—but ongoing reports surrounding the litigation only reinforced allegations that he was not fit for the government position.

Legal troubles did not stop Elizalde from embracing his new job. Between 1939 and 1942, he became the face of the colonial government's concern for Filipina/o Americans, appearing before the House Committee on Immigra-tion and Naturalization no fewer than three times to advocate on their be-half. His participation in the naturalization campaign had at least two impacts. On the one hand, Manila's demonstration of interest made it more difficult for congressional critics simply to dismiss the Marcantonio bill as a radical congressman's quixotic crusade. Even if they did not support its pas-sage, southern Democrats felt some pressure to accord the bill at least a modicum of consideration, particularly in light of the Philippines' growing importance to the Pacific War against Japan. By the same token, however, Elizalde's conspicuous involvement complicated any attempt to paint Phil-ippine naturalization as a purely domestic or internal factor completely di-vorced from transpacific debates over Philippine independence or Filipina/o migration. Even Elizalde tried to make this argument. The "issue here is not one of admission to this country," he asserted more than once, but the future fate of the "people who are . . . legally and lawfully" already in the United States.[42] To the chagrin of many, the Marcantonio bill would ulti-mately prove inextricable from both.

No sooner was a Philippine naturalization bill introduced than it got caught up in an interbranch debate over the timeline of Philippine indepen-dence that ultimately doomed it. By the time Rep. Marcantonio introduced his version to Congress in 1939, the Roosevelt administration was in a standoff with Senator Millard Tydings, a cosponsor of the original independence law, over his one-man crusade to expedite the date of Philippine independence by five years from 1946 to 1941. Tydings argued that the earlier separation was better for the United States because it absolved Washington of any responsibility to intervene or support the islands militarily in the event of a Japanese attack.[43] Roosevelt and other executive officials shared Tydings's desire to remove American troops from the islands, but they did not believe it was in the U.S. interest to withdraw so quickly. With the timeline to independence still in flux, U.S. Secretary of State Cordell Hull—breaking from the State Department's long record of support for Asian immigration and naturalization measures—withheld the agency's support from any version of a Philippine citizenship bill until "shortly before complete independence" took place.[44] In turn, southern lawmakers seized on this statement as a pretext to put the measure on hold. California exclusionist Rep. Welch, congressional architect of the 1930s repatriation program, joined them to form a coalition that collectively ensured the bill's defeat.[45]

Resentments built through decades of distrust between Filipina/o American communities and the colonial government in Manila surfaced with force the following year at a House Immigration Committee hearing on a newly revived Philippine naturalization bill. Leon Foronda and F. Aguire Palmares of the Brooklyn-based Filipino American Citizenship Council of New York agreed with Elizalde that the naturalization bill should pass, but they flatly rejected his right to speak on their behalf. Philippine colonial officials from Manila had determined the islands should be independent, they protested, and Filipina/o Americans were suffering for that choice. When Philippine officials spoke of widespread support for independence, they were "speaking for the Philippine Islands and the Filipinos there," Foronda insisted. Filipinos in the United States—many of them "family men" married to U.S. citizens—had different considerations to weigh; the "majority" planned to "live here permanently unless . . . ejected forcibly." Palmares was blunter: he accused Philippine officials of having "dump[ed]" Filipina/o Americans like himself "overboard" to get what they wanted. Unlike their counterparts in Asia, he explained, Filipina/o Americans saw their futures in the United States and were "willing and ready" to forsake their Philippine nationality for the chance to become American citizens. The 1934 Tydings-McDuffie Act, a law negotiated and passed without Filipino American involvement, had sent the opposite message: by changing Filipina/os' legal status from national to alien, he argued, it had encouraged white Americans to treat them—including native-born U.S. citizens like himself—like "foreigners."[46] As such, it illustrated why Philippine officials were ill qualified to speak for Filipina/o Americans; they simply did not have the same interests.

Arguably as important as what Palmares said was what his mixed-race heritage represented to lawmakers. The nonwhite racial identity of the Philippine people had long figured centrally in debates over the islands' relationship with the United States. Many southern lawmakers had opposed the 1898 annexation of the Philippines because they did not want the United States to incorporate a majority nonwhite territory, and even supporters regularly referred to Filipinos as America's "little brown brothers."[47] Palmares's self-identification as the "product of the intermingling of two races"—the child of a Filipino father and a white mother—recalled a recent history of racial hatred centered around Filipinos' perceived sexual threat.[48] Scholars have traced the origins of anti-Filipino violence to fears of miscegenation and illicit sexual relations between Philippine men and white American women.[49] So strong were anxieties over Filipino migrants' hypersexualized masculinity that David Barrows, then the president of the University of California, had described Filipinos' vices as "almost entirely based on sexual passion" during an appearance before a congressional committee in 1930.[50] That so few witnesses explicitly invoked race in their statements suggests how much the norms regarding acceptable language had changed by the World War II years. Even if they were now unspoken, however, the influence of racial fears persisted and continued to fuel lawmakers' opposition—no doubt contributing to the bill's failure in committee.

By the time the House body held its second hearing on Philippine naturalization in early 1942, the islands had become a Pacific battle site. Japan invaded the Philippines ten hours after its attack on Pearl Harbor and proceeded to capture control of Manila and other key sites over the months that followed. The United States' formal entry into World War II renewed a debate over how Americans should understand Filipinos' military service.[51] After World War I, Filipino Americans and their allies had successfully capitalized on their service, using arguments of martial patriotism to win a few hundred Filipino veterans the right to U.S. citizenship.[52] At the Marcantonio bill's February 1942 hearing, supporters of the naturalization measure redeployed the strategy, citing Filipinos' high rates of enlistment and relating stories of their loyalty and courage to make the case for passage. Their appeals elicited sharp pushback from southern Democrats and other congressional critics more inclined to see Philippine military participation as a matter of self-interest than of loyalty to the United States.

As Virginia Democrat Robert Ramsay protested, if Filipinos were "so loyal" to America, why did they want independence so much? By asking "to be released from the United States government," they had made clear that they "don't want to be in the United States" or "have anything to do with us," he contended. In fact, it was "repulsive" to say their military service was about America at all; Filipina/os should never claim "special credit" from the United States for simply defending their own "native land."[53] In reality, Japan had targeted the Philippines precisely because of its status as a U.S. colony, and after four decades of U.S. colonial rule, many Filipino soldiers made no distinction between loyalty to the United States and to the Philippines. Ramsay and other critics made no mention of these complexities.

The Commonwealth Goes to Washington

Commonwealth President Manuel Quezon was a man on a mission. In the early months of 1942, he astonished White House officials with a letter outlining a seven-point plan to "save" the Philippines that called for the "immediate and complete independence" of the islands as well as the withdrawal of all U.S. and Japanese troops, the removal of U.S. military bases, and the evacuation of all Philippine nationals who wished to leave the islands. The underlying implication—debatable at best and absurd at worst—was that Japan would lose interest in the Philippines and leave if it were no longer part of the United States. In the spring, Quezon continued to press the point. Shortly after Japanese forces captured Manila, U.S. forces under General Douglas MacArthur evacuated Quezon and several of his cabinet members to Washington DC, where they set up a Philippine Commonwealth government in exile. Proximity gave Quezon a better vantage point from which to pursue what he framed as in the best interest of Filipina/o self-determination. Most observers saw the campaign as Quezon's personal ploy to remain in power, however. The 1934 Philippine Constitution had originally limited the president to a single six-year term. A 1940 plebiscite allowed Quezon to run for reelection in 1941, but if the new rules remained in place, he would have to step down in 1945 with no possibility of a third term. If the United States liberated the islands before then, however, as president of an independent Philippine Republic he would face no such restriction and could theoretically stay in office.[54]

Quezon found in Washington, DC, a stronger opposition than he had expected. The career politician had long had his detractors, among them

Americans who publicly decried the "one-party dictatorship" he had created in the Philippines.[55] Many U.S. policymakers had expressed hope that the islands' transition to a Commonwealth would promote a more democratic government in Manila, but the new structure actually allowed Quezon to consolidate executive power, creating what one historian called a "unipersonal" government in which he exercised "nearly absolute power."[56] Other critics questioned his loyalty to the United States. In the years before the Japanese invaded the Philippine islands, reports of his regular correspondence with and trips to Tokyo brought him under suspicion of sympathizing with the enemy, and his self-serving campaign to stay in power did little to reassure U.S. officials of his trustworthiness. Exacerbating matters was Quezon's advanced tuberculosis, the effects of which left him bedridden for weeks at a time. The illness took both a physical and political toll: upon seeing Quezon for the first time, one White House observer memorably described him as a "hacking shell."[57] His frequent absences from Washington for extended stays at convalescent homes in Florida and upstate New York only further weakened his position.

Facing a dearth of white American support, Quezon began courting Filipina/o Americans to compensate. He hoped to retain the presidency by positioning himself as the most effective champion of overseas communities' rights. As a former PRC (1912–13) himself, the Philippine politician had long recognized the importance of Filipina/o Americans in places like California to shape not only white Americans' impression of the Philippines but Washington's policy toward the islands more broadly. His record reflected a clear understanding of how migration policy could serve as an influential tool of diplomacy, and his great adeptness in using diplomatic arguments to oppose greater restrictions on Filipina/os' movement and legal status under U.S. law.[58] While his health did not allow him to travel there in person, Quezon focused on cultivating closer ties with the large Filipina/o communities on the West Coast. At his direction, the PRC office in San Francisco became involved in state-level campaigns to exempt Filipina/os from alien land laws barring them from holding or leasing agricultural land. In 1943, the state legislatures of California and Arizona successfully overturned this ban for Filipina/os, who were declared a special category of noncitizen. While the changes were a shared victory achieved after years of legal challenge and appeals by Filipina/o community leaders and their white allies, the PRC's office in Washington claimed much of the credit.[59] For Quezon and the Commonwealth government, image or appearance could be just as, if not more, important than reality.

California-based journalist J. C. (Johnny) Dionisio was a major impetus for Quezon's use of the naturalization bill as a bid for Filipina/o American support.[60] Filipina/o communities along the West Coast were "ready and eager to follow whatever plan the government has for them," he asserted, but they were also "tired of promises" and wanted their leaders to offer "GUIDANCE" and "action" on their behalf. Like the PRC's office, which would formally hire him in 1944, Dionisio recognized Filipina/o Americans' incredible financial strength: "100,000 Filipinos in the United States, Hawai'i, and Alaska" together generated an "annual income of more than 100 million dollars," he estimated, a sum that "top[ped] the yearly income of any province in the Philippines before the war." If Quezon could claim a hand in winning the naturalization bill, he contended, it would not only bolster his political profile but it could also benefit Manila—and presumably his future regime—materially. It was critical that Filipina/o Americans continue to send money to relatives in the Philippines, where it could be "invested in agricultural or industrial projects" on the islands.[61] To facilitate this, Dionisio argued that the Manila government had a moral "responsibility" to "guide" Filipina/os in "conserving their earnings instead of dissipating them . . . in gambling houses."[62] To this end, he called for speedy implementation of the cooperative savings plan proposed by the PRC's office during the war; since Filipino workers could not manage their own earnings, he concluded, the Philippine government should do it for them. With such careful management, whether or not Filipina/os chose to stay in the United States, they could play an important role in the rebuilding of an independent Philippine Republic through their remittance dollars. But it was important to plan ahead. Forging strong ties between Manila and U.S. communities now would ensure that any benefit Filipina/os in the United States received from the war and its aftermath would also accrue to the new Philippine state after independence.

In the meantime, a new piece of legislation, sponsored by a new kind of lawmaker, was giving the naturalization cause renewed political momentum on Capitol Hill: the McGehee bill proposed to institute an exam process that would give U.S. citizenship to all Filipina/os who could pass it and who had lived in the United States since 1934, when the Commonwealth of the Philippines was created.[63] As a southern Democrat, Rep. Dan McGehee of Mississippi was an unlikely champion of any measure liberalizing naturalization restrictions. His interest in Philippine affairs had begun with his attendance at the 1935 inauguration of the Commonwealth as a member of the U.S. congressional delegation and deepened with his service on the Philippine

Philippine Commonwealth Officials in conference with U.S. president Truman at the White House, 1945; *left to right*: Truman; Philippine president Sergio Osmena; Paul V. McNutt, high commissioner of the Philippines; General Carlos Romulo, Philippine resident commissioner. Bettmann / Getty Images.

Rehabilitation Commission from 1944 to 1946. His involvement was circumstantial but nonetheless opportune; insofar as McGehee's southern Democrat colleagues remained the bill's greatest critics, his sponsorship promised to soften their opposition. In short order, the McGehee bill became the version the House Committee on Immigration and Naturalization preferred, superseding Marcantonio's nearly identical measure. Quezon died before he could take advantage of the newfound momentum, but his successor, Sergio Osmena, continued the practice of using the naturalization issue to court Filipina/o American support, which he would ultimately need just as much as Quezon to retain the presidency.

Carlos P. Romulo, who succeeded Elizalde as PRC, also used the Philippine naturalization bill to nurture personal political aspirations. Addressing House lawmakers shortly before he and Osmena accompanied General

MacArthur to take back the Philippines in the fall of 1944, Romulo called for passage of the citizenship measure as a matter of simple wartime justice, a reward for Filipina/os' loyalty to the United States in the face of a Japanese threat. "Japan had promised [the Filipino] independence, brown supremacy, Asia for the Asiatics, and the white man in the dust!" he declared. Yet even when offered such pledges of pan-Asian solidarity, Filipina/os had "chose[n] the white man's side in the dust of Bataan." The latter was a reference to the Japanese army's forced march of 70,000 U.S. and Philippine prisoners of war that resulted in the death of thousands.[64] Again drawing from the logic of martial patriotism, Romulo questioned how any American could "hold unworthy of naturalization, the countryman, brother, cousin, father, of the Filipino who fought under the American flag to save the Philippines for an America that had not yet given him the independence he so desired."[65]

Under Romulo, the PRC's office became an important lobbying vehicle for Filipina/o American community members and their allies, in many respects assuming the role that California-based community organizations like the CPFR had sought to cultivate before the war.[66] Romulo was in the Philippines during the McGehee bill's first hearing before the House Committee on Immigration and Naturalization in November 1944, but his staff coordinated a centralized campaign to build public support from their office in Washington, DC. A week before the hearing, PRC officer Manuel Adeva issued an eleventh-hour call soliciting telegrams of support on behalf of the "Committee on Naturalization of Filipinos," a lobby group ostensibly based at the PRC's Washington office; he delivered these to committee chairman Dickstein the day before the hearing.[67] Most of the endorsements came from Philippine organizations and individuals in California and the Pacific Northwest, but East Coast groups were represented, too: notes came from the Filipino Executive Committee for New England, the Filipino Association of Philadelphia, and the Filipino National Council in New York, among others. While he did not speak in any formal capacity, Adeva was present at the hearing; from the congressional gallery, he took notes on the committee's discussion and drafted a memorandum outlining next steps in the PRC's strategy.[68]

The PRC office's proactive approach was consistent with earlier efforts by Elizalde and his staff to promote closer ties with Filipina/o Americans, but Romulo's heavy-handedness reflected his personal belief that they were incapable of advocating for themselves. Like Quezon, Romulo spent several years in the United States as a younger man; while Quezon came as a civil servant, however, Romulo experienced America as a *pensionado*, or a

U.S.-sponsored Philippine student, studying at Columbia University between 1918 and 1922.[69] Whereas Quezon encountered a wide range of Philippine workers in Hawaii and the West Coast, Romulo's social circles were largely limited to elite Filipina/os living in New York and Washington, DC. Consequently, the World War II years marked the first time he interacted with working-class Filipina/o American communities in any sustained way. In his writings, he described them as a "shy and unorganized group" that had "never looked beyond achieving the independence of [its] native land" for political goals.[70] As Augusto Espiritu writes, Romulo frequently represented Filipina/o Americans as nameless victims in a narrative that erased years of community-based struggle not only for U.S. citizenship but also for better wages and working conditions, and even the right to marry across racial lines.[71] Under Romulo's leadership, therefore, the PRC's office may have come to fill a need within the community but in positioning itself as a patron for marginalized Filipina/o communities, it generally failed to acknowledge their long history of self-advocacy and organizing in the United States.

Romulo's meticulous management of his image in the naturalization campaigns spoke to how completely he personalized the success of the McGehee bill both as a measure of his leadership ability and as an important factor in shaping his reputation as a colonial government official. He had only recently returned from several months in the Philippines when the McGehee bill passed the House on April 7, 1945; although much of the congressional wrangling had happened in his absence, he took great pains to ensure he received credit. Press releases sent by the PRC's office to every member of Congress described Romulo's speech to a joint session the day before the vote as the "catalyst" that made victory possible; Romulo reiterated this dubious idea in a series of private letters to U.S. officials. Later that year, when the *Nation* magazine accused his office of delaying the bill's progress in the Senate Immigration Committee by "ignor[ing]" Filipino Americans' multiple requests to send a "memorial," he very publicly demanded an apology.[72] An ambitious man, Romulo was sensitive to his image not just in the United States but in Asia. He was already looking ahead to his political future in the Philippines and did not want criticisms alleging inaction or incompetence tarnishing his reputation as an effective statesman on either side of the Pacific.[73] While it is unclear how direct a role he envisioned Filipina/o Americans playing in future Philippine elections, at a minimum he believed his reputation in the United States could inform his image in the Philippines. He may also have seen Filipina/o Americans as a potential source of campaign funds.[74]

Romulo's efforts to claim credit notwithstanding, over the next year, Filipina/o American communities took their own steps to further the naturalization bill after it stalled in the Senate committee, blocked by powerful southern Democrats James Eastland of Mississippi and Richard Russell of Georgia. In July 1945, Filipino leaders from Hawaii mounted a last-minute attempt to push the measure through Congress before the Pacific War ended and any momentum generated by U.S. military imperatives in Asia was lost. A delegation representing the Territorial Filipino Council of Hawaii paid visits to Senators Eastland and Kenneth McKellar (D-TN), the chairman and a member of the Senate subcommittee charged with reporting on the measure, respectively. When asked in person for their views, the two southerners reportedly expressed their full support, with Eastland assuring them that the legislation would receive consideration soon. But the meetings yielded no immediate legislative action.[75] It probably did not help that the Hawaii delegation paired its support for the naturalization measure with petitions to allow the special entry of 6,000 Philippine laborers to the Hawaiian Islands.[76] With the end of both the European and Pacific wars in sight, many lawmakers were looking to limit migration, not expand it, in anticipation that tens of thousands of returning U.S. servicemen would soon flood the American workforce.[77] Frustrated by the delay, Andrew Escalona of Delano, California, wrote the PRC's office to blame Romulo's "complacent" and "inconsistent" behavior for the McGehee bill's lack of movement. PRC officer Leonides Virata quickly defended his boss; more than inaction by Romulo, he insisted, the problem was Senator Eastland's "natural prejudice . . . against colored peoples."[78] Eastland, then in his first congressional term, would spend the next three decades in the Senate as a leading foe of racial integration and other measures strengthening federal protections for racial minorities.

In line with advocates' worst fears, the bill made no further progress before the Japanese surrender that August. Late that month, a "discouraged and depressed" Romulo described a growing sense of indifference on Capitol Hill regarding all matters related to the Philippines. Many U.S. officials had not been "ready for the surrender of the Japanese," he wrote in a report to President Osmena, and now that the government had its "hands full with America's domestic problems," lawmakers saw the Philippine question as a "drop in the bucket" that could "either wait or let well enough alone." Further complicating matters were the elaborate and often overlapping structures of U.S. state oversight governing the islands' affairs. Every proposal related to the Philippines involved "five or six executive departments," Romulo complained. There were no clear precedents for how to proceed, given that the

United States had never relinquished a formal colony before; everything was "absolutely new ground." But perhaps most pernicious was a "disturbing" attitude "in the highest circles of the administration" supporting the belief that, with the liberation of Philippines, "America has done its duty by us" and Filipina/os were "not entitled to any more damages." With the attention of Congress thus "diverted" and Americans' eyes turning inward, he advised Commonwealth President Osmena to visit Washington, DC, personally and meet with Truman in the hope that "prodding from above [could] shake off this officialdom from its inertia."[79]

Osmena was willing, but by the end of the Pacific War he also found himself in a compromised position facing an imminent presidential election against Manuel Roxas, a longtime Philippine politician most Filipino elites and prominent U.S. figures like General Douglas MacArthur favored.[80] As Manuel Quezon's vice-president during the Philippine Commonwealth government's U.S. exile, Osmena had inherited the presidency without contest when Quezon died, but few Filipino politicians welcomed his return to Manila with open arms. Not only was Osmena ethnically different as a Chinese-mestizo whom the Spanish-mestizo Roxas and his supporters liked to call "El Chino."[81] There was also the matter of the war. The Japanese occupation irrevocably disrupted the political structures of the colonial period. Before the war, Quezon had used his mastery of the patronage game—of money in exchange for political support—to cultivate a solid base of supporters. Amid the destruction of war and a Japanese occupation government, however, the money stopped, leaving Osmena with no leverage or tools to rebuild Quezon's network. It also mattered that Osmena had been in exile for some of the hardest periods of the war, which invited the resentment and suspicion of those politicians, such as Roxas, left behind. Roxas had not only weathered the Japanese occupation of the Philippines. Like many of Quezon's and Osmena's former supporters, he now faced Washington's charges of collaboration with Tokyo during it. The actions of one U.S. leader saved him. General MacArthur's intervention cleared his name and near single-handedly enabled Roxas's swift return to political office after U.S. troops recaptured the islands. In July 1945, Roxas was elected interim president of the Philippine Senate. By that fall, he was widely seen as Osmena's main competition for president of the new Philippine Republic.[82]

Increasingly marginalized within Philippine politics, Osmena turned to Filipina/o American communities for support, but there, too, he encountered a mixed reception. Whereas California community leaders had once praised him as proactive and effective, they now accused him of being "afraid and hesitant to lead" with a "tendency to vacillate and temporize" based on his recent actions in Manila. Their initial approval had come in response to one of Osmena's first actions after becoming Commonwealth president in August 1944: to create a committee to "investigate the needs of Filipinos in America and to decide how best to fill these needs."[83] But the goodwill quickly dissipated after he returned to the Philippines, where powerful political rivals thwarted his agenda at every turn. With an eye toward the spring 1946 presidential elections, Osmena sought to "endear himself" to Filipina/o Americans once again by demonstrating that he would be "fighting for their rights" in the form of the McGehee naturalization bill.[84] To this end, he personally met with Senate holdouts Russell and Eastland during his Washington trip and in follow-up correspondence from Manila, urged speedy action on the measure. In a last-ditch attempt to work around the strong congressional opposition that yet remained, Osmena also appealed to President Truman to act directly.

Truman, still less than a year into the presidency, did his best to bypass the congressional deadlock. His executive strategy, as outlined in a White House memorandum in early February, was to include a reciprocity clause in the Bell Trade bill giving Filipina/os in the United States the same rights that U.S. citizens would enjoy under Philippine law. Assuming that the Senate had not passed a stand-alone immigration or naturalization bill by the time of Philippine independence, the clause was a fail-safe ensuring that Philippine citizens would receive "privileges of immigration and naturalization not less favorable than the same privileges accorded by the Philippines to citizens of any other nation."[85] The assumption was that southern Democrats were unlikely to block the entire trade package based on the naturalization issue alone. The language of reciprocity also played on Filipina/os' growing resentment over the trade bill's so-called equal rights clause, which required the Philippine government to treat Americans and American corporations as if they were Philippine citizens in economic matters. That said, the clause further required an amendment to the Philippine Constitution, and it was unclear whether legislators in Manila would approve a measure that many colonial officials—including Osmena himself—regarded as a "blatant infringement on Philippine sovereignty."[86]

Whatever its envisioned purpose, Congress ultimately did not implement the White House plan. In what one scholar has called a "study of manipulatory democracy," the trade bill's sponsor, Missouri Democrat Rep.

Jasper Bell, used his position as chair of the House Committee on Insular Affairs to hold U.S. rehabilitation aid to the Philippines as ransom until he got the trade terms he wanted. These did not include Truman's naturalization clause for Filipina/os. The archival record does not include extensive discussion of why Rep. Bell and other congressional lawmakers declined to include the Philippine naturalization clause. But a larger discussion surrounding the omission suggests that different understandings of Filipina/os' status under U.S. versus Philippine law played a role. Specifically, while Bell's camp generally saw the status of U.S. citizens under Philippine law as an economic and commercial matter, they regarded the status of Filipina/os under U.S. law as a social issue that did not belong in a trade bill. Ultimately, the omission was a testament to the power of Bell and a small handful of congressional lawmakers to fashion trade legislation in such a way to ensure that the United States' economic hegemony in the Philippines continued even after independence. In the words of one historian, the debates over the Bell Trade Act "demonstrated in crudest fashion America's continuing capacity for keeping the Filipinos in line." They were beholden to U.S. aid to rebuild their ruined economy and infrastructure, and U.S.-authored provisions in the trade act dictating quotas, tariffs, and currency policy meant that the Philippine economy would remain a "hostage" to American interests.[87]

Repeal and the Creation of a Philippine Client State

On April 23, 1946, the same day Roxas defeated Osmena by a wide margin to become the first president-elect of an independent Philippine Republic, the U.S. House passed both the Philippine Rehabilitation Act and the Bell Trade Act, absent the naturalization clause for Filipina/os. Truman signed them both into law one week later. The next step to secure approval by the Philippine legislature would require a whole new set of political machinations, but as one lawmaker put it matter-of-factly: "I vote yes because we are flat broke, hungry, homeless, and destitute."[88] Inasmuch as foregoing U.S. aid was not an option, choice was an illusion. Under the two laws, the Philippines would receive more than $600 million dollars in direct U.S. aid to rebuild its economy. But what the Philippines gave in return was arguably more valuable. As part of its independence negotiations, Manila was required to approve a series of agreements that undercut the Philippines' economic and military sovereignty: a parity clause required the Philippine government to treat Americans the same as Philippine citizens in economic matters; a general relations agreement gave the U.S. control over the islands' foreign policy; the Bell Trade Law granted Washington control of Philippine tariffs and currency; the Military Assistance Agreement retained U.S. control over the Philippine army; and the Military Bases Agreement allowed the U.S. to maintain military bases on the islands for ninety-nine years. Together they collectively laid the framework for a new client relationship to replace the old colonial one between Washington and Manila upon the official declaration of Philippine independence.

With the naturalization measure now back to a stand-alone proposal, proponents of the McGehee bill redoubled their efforts to compel a full vote in the U.S. Senate. They feared an even greater delay if they waited until after Philippine independence took effect. After months of pressure and petition, Senator Eastland, the chair of the immigration subcommittee charged with reporting on the measure, finally allowed a hearing. While it is unclear what finally secured Eastland's cooperation, his long-standing personal relationship with the bill's sponsor, Rep. McGehee, may have helped; the two men had served together in the Mississippi State House of Representatives before being elected to Congress. With Eastland on board, the bill passed the committee easily. Similar to the Indian bill, this was another case where the opposition of individual lawmakers delayed passage more than a general lack of support. In its final report, the Senate Immigration Committee described U.S. citizenship eligibility as a reward for Filipina/os' loyalty and "courageous" service against Japan in World War II. At the same time, it emphasized the limited number of beneficiaries whom the law would make eligible for U.S. citizenship since immigration from the Philippines remained highly restricted.

The Senate passed the Luce-Celler Act on June 14, 1946, and Truman signed it into law on July 2, the same day he issued an executive order increasing the Philippines' annual immigration quota from fifty to one hundred persons per year, effective immediately. Two days later, on July 4, the Philippines became independent after nearly half a century of U.S. rule, transforming the islands from a U.S. colony to a nominally independent client state. Truman's immigration quota was scarcely mitigating; neither was the fact that the quota was based on nationality, not race, meaning that Filipina/os born in other countries did not count against it. Designed in part to recognize the Philippines' special colonial history with the United States relative to other Asians, the distinction was still symbolic, since the nominal quota ensured that very few Filipina/os could immigrate to the United States and take advantage of their newly won right to naturalize.

Yet again lawmakers prioritized symbolism over substance and the appearance over the reality of change. Naturalization rights for Filipina/os symbolically supported the United States' colonial narrative of benevolent tutelage over the Philippines—a theme that was central to Washington's efforts to distinguish itself from the exploitation and violence associated with European imperialism.[89] They also upheld the fiction of Philippine sovereignty through their affirmation of the United States' commitment to racial liberalism. As such, the Filipina/o citizenship provisions of the Luce-Celler Act ultimately suggested the promise of a reciprocity and equality between the United States and its former colony that never materialized in reality.

Legacies of Luce-Celler

News of the naturalization bill's enactment prompted a flurry of discussion within the Filipina/o American community over who deserved credit for the legislative victory. Some accounts played up the role of individual activists. For example, the Washington, DC–based *Bataan* magazine ran a three-page feature profiling the efforts of Honolulu businessman Philip Gamponia as a member of the Hawaii Territorial Filipino Council delegation that came to Washington, DC, in July 1945 to lobby the cause in person.[90] Others applauded the work of Philippine officials such as Romulo, who received dozens of telegrams of gratitude from Filipina/os around the United States. Individual Filipina/o Americans may have played only a sporadic role in the wartime campaigns and lobbying, but no one welcomed the news with as much joy. Within hours of the bill's enactment, Juan de Abaya of Chicago became the first civilian naturalized under its provisions; as an interpreter and stenographer for the U.S. Immigration Service in Chicago, he had been one of the first community members to learn of the legislation and to begin the process.[91] By the fall of 1946, the demand for naturalization applications was so high that Filipina/o American community organizations began printing dedicated next steps pieces outlining and describing what information applicants needed to pass the citizenship examination.

The bill's success spurred lively conversations about the future of Filipino/a American communities' relationships with the Philippine government, particularly for those who decided to become U.S. citizens. A month after the McGehee bill's passage, delegates at the eighth annual Filipino Inter-Community Organization of the Western States (the conference first started by labor commissioner Francisco Varona in 1938) formally debated whether the organization should "retain [a] relationship with the Philippine Government or seek a different status." One attendee predicted that most Philippine Americans would "maintain a liaison with the government" in Manila even as they claimed U.S. citizenship.[92] It was unavoidable, he concluded, since the fates of Filipina/os on both sides of the Pacific were forever linked.

Not everyone felt the same. Like their more elite Indian counterparts, some Filipina/os continued to live in the United States but regarded themselves as citizens of the Philippines, and therefore as exiles rather than immigrants in the United States.[93] What their stories show us is that while the Philippine government sought to use the U.S. citizenship campaigns as a means to build affective ties to the Manila government that transcended formal citizenship, many Filipina/os themselves were less willing to abandon the distinctions. Poet and writer Jose Garcia Villa, for one, never naturalized. Despite spending the majority of his adult life in New York City, he famously described himself as a "'Filipino, but an American resident.'" Writer N. V. M. Gonzalez was similarly proud of his decision to remain a Philippine citizen while living in California for over twenty years. Writer Bienvenidos Santos and his wife found a middle ground. After independence, they maintained homes in both the United States and the Philippines for the next three decades, regularly sending money to the islands to support family members and household staff when they were stateside.[94] Like that of Indian nationalist Taraknath Das more than half a century earlier, their decision to become U.S. citizens in 1976 was a defensive one; the Santoses feared reprisal for their outspoken criticism of the Ferdinand Marcos regime, and U.S. citizenship promised to protect them. Even Carlos Romulo, who had gone to great lengths to claim credit for the Luce-Celler victory during his time as PRC, was quick to denounce anyone who accused him of becoming a U.S. citizen: in his words, Philippine citizenship was "the one proud possession and heritage" he wished to "bequeath" to his children "pure and undefiled."[95]

In the end, Manila's fears of insolvency and economic crisis following independence came true in spite of its efforts. Less than a year after the islands' change in status, a Joint Philippine-American Finance Commission reported that although many Filipina/os were "relatively well-off," the government in Manila was "destitute" not only as a result of wartime destruction but also due to "wealthy politicos . . . defrauding the government in large amounts." Over the next few years, the commission—whose creation had been a condition for a $75 million U.S. loan to the islands—oversaw the implementation of a protectionist and statist program that greatly expanded and centralized the Philippine government's control over the islands' economy: it included such measures as import controls to promote local industry, higher corporate taxes, currency reform, and the creation of a national bank in 1948. These measures violated the interests of Philippine elites, who opposed them vehemently, and the commission supported by Washington employed significant coercion to implement them.[96] One thing that remained constant was the favored status of U.S. investment in the islands; the Bell Trade Act of 1946 ensured that the interests of American business interests would remain protected. But the relationship between the central Manila government and longtime economic elites changed, as both constituencies targeted Washington as the main culprit behind their troubles.

The Philippine economy would survive and restabilize after 1946, and just as Philippine leaders including Quezon, Elizalde, and Romulo had predicted, remittances played an important role in not only sustaining but also expanding the islands' international and financial footprint. In subsequent decades, the efforts of the Philippine state to manage and maximize the benefit of what it came to call overseas Filipina/o workers (OFWs) quickly accelerated and globalized as Filipina/os seized labor opportunities in destinations other than the United States beginning in the 1960s. Nearly two decades into the twenty-first century, more than two million OFWs send the equivalent of $33 billion USD in remittances to the islands annually, comprising 10 percent of the country's overall gross domestic product.[97] The Philippine state has been central to the growth of overseas Philippine labor, sociologist Robyn Rodriguez argues, through its role as a "migrant labor broker" that exports its citizens and seeks to maintain relations while aggressively profiting from them. Situating this phenomenon historically reveals how the campaigns to pass the 1946 Luce-Celler Act fit within the longer history of Filipina/os' changing relationship to citizenship and national belonging.[98] It also suggests the wider impact of U.S. immigration and naturalization policies, and the lasting impact of U.S. colonialism beyond Philippine independence in 1946.

Conclusion

The World War II campaigns for a Philippine naturalization bill may have begun with the left-labor activism and economic struggles of Filipino workers in Depression-era California, but Philippine sources reveal how Commonwealth officials lobbied the legislation to passage in Washington, DC, as part of their preparations for Philippine independence. They foresaw how

Filipina/o American communities could play an important role in the nation- and state-building projects that followed independence, particularly through the remittances they sent back to the islands. Through championing the cause of Filipina/o naturalization rights in the United States, they sought to inculcate in diasporic communities a sense of loyalty and responsibility to the Manila government that transcended the ties of formal citizenship. Precisely because they tended to see national citizenship in pragmatic rather than ideological terms, they saw nothing incompatible or contradictory about Filipina/os becoming U.S. citizens while continuing to support the Philippines materially and otherwise. Indeed, they encouraged Filipina/os in the United States to maintain strong ties with the islands in line with their understanding of the diaspora as an extension of the Philippine nation. Centering the role of the Philippine Commonwealth government in this legislative victory thus complicates conventional understandings of wartime repeal measures as products wrought by grassroots activism undertaken by Filipina/o community members in the United States; it reveals instead how gains in the arena of naturalization and national citizenship were also the product of transpacific and colonial politics.

The Luce-Celler Act, like the Magnuson Act before it, was not designed or intended—at least by the majority of its congressional supporters—to result in meaningful change. This was evident in how the congressional campaign to extend naturalization to the small number of Filipina/os living in the United States coincided with efforts to restrict the benefits of U.S. citizenship already promised to hundreds of thousands of Filipino soldiers. Even as the McGehee bill was wending its way through the Senate in the fall of 1945, the Immigration and Naturalization Service began adding administrative requirements that made it more difficult for Filipino veterans to apply for naturalization.[99] Congressional lawmakers simultaneously began implementing changes that restricted access. For example, in a move that was not widely advertised, they set a one-year deadline on citizenship applications, after which time soldiers would no longer be permitted to apply. The impact was substantial. Of the estimated 270,000 Filipino veterans technically eligible to naturalize, only about 4 percent actually completed the process.[100] Making matters worse, in February 1946, Congress passed the First Rescission Act, which downgraded the administrative status of Filipino soldiers, making them ineligible for the "rights, privileges, or benefits" traditionally accorded to U.S. veterans. Three subsequent rescission acts reaffirmed Filipino veterans' disqualification; as Rick Baldoz writes, these actions were consistent with the U.S. state's long-standing practice of extracting maximum labor and military service from Filipinos at the lowest cost, as Washington sought to reframe the "obligations of the United States to Filipino veterans as a matter of charity rather than of civil rights or the imperial responsibility."[101] That even in the twenty-first century, some Philippine veterans of World War II continue to fight for retroactive citizenship and benefits is a testament to just how lasting the U.S. colonial legacy in the islands remains.[102]

CHAPTER FOUR

Testing the Limits of Postwar Reform

Japanese Americans, Afro-Caribbeans, and the
McCarran-Walter Act of 1952

In 1946, members of the Japanese American Citizens League (JACL) gathered in Denver, Colorado, to discuss their next steps now that World War II was over and the last of the incarceration camps had closed. The wartime roundup and years-long imprisonment of West Coast Japanese Americans had taken a heavy toll, leaving many uprooted and scrambling to rebuild their lives after the war's end. The JACL faced its own uphill road, as its leadership struggled to overcome the fallout of its cooperation with the U.S. government's incarceration policy and its championing of the War Department's decision to draft incarcerated nisei, or U.S.-born Japanese Americans, into the U.S. military. Such partnerships gave the league new prominence among U.S. officials who saw them as the voice of the Japanese American community. But they also invited the ire of many first-generation Japanese immigrants, or Issei, and second-generation Nisei, who rejected the JACL's claim to speak for them. With the league's membership at a record low, the national board decided to pursue U.S. citizenship eligibility for Issei—who comprised the majority of Asian immigrants in the United States still unable to naturalize—as a strategy to recapture community support. At a time when anti-Japanese sentiment remained strong and the Japanese American community was still reeling from the war's impact, it would not be an easy task.

Their association with a wartime enemy only recently defeated created a bumpy road to legal inclusion for Japanese Americans. JACL leaders had watched three previous repeal campaigns effectively play on the Allied status of China, India, and the Philippines to argue for exclusion repeal as a necessary act of solidarity or a reward for loyalty shown during war. But Japanese Americans had no such argument to make. Less than a decade after Japan's attack at Pearl Harbor, the JACL campaign's first task was to rehabilitate Japanese Americans in the public imagination: to prove that they were loyal patriots and not espionage agents. Scholars including Naoko Shibusawa have remarked on the speed with which Japanese and Japanese Americans were recast from wartime enemies to postwar friends, but in the late 1940s this was still a change in the making.[1] The JACL was a major agent of this transformation; its publicity campaigns advertising Japanese Americans' "110% Americanism" and the exemplary military service of nisei soldiers were all designed to promote a shift in public perception crucial to its future advocacy in the United States on behalf of its constituents.

This chapter charts the formal repeal of Asian exclusion from the vantage point of the JACL and of other Americans involved in the postwar campaigns that culminated in the 1952 McCarran-Walter Act. Commonly described as a Cold War measure, the law is best known for its most draconian attributes: national security codes strengthening the power of the federal government to detain, denaturalize, and deport individuals suspected of holding subversive views.[2] This discussion focuses on its lesser known provisions formally ending Asian exclusion as a feature of U.S. immigration and naturalization policy. As this chapter explores, the 1952 act's repeal clauses were a carryover from a stand-alone measure that Rep. Walter Judd, a veteran of the Citizens Committee responsible for the wartime repeal of Chinese exclusion, first drafted in 1943 and introduced to Congress in 1947.[3] The Judd bill proposed the Asia-Pacific Triangle system, which allotted race-based annual immigration quotas ranging from 100 to 185 to all Asian powers east of Iran and north of Australia. It also struck down all racial restrictions to naturalization, making Issei and other foreign-born Asians eligible for U.S. citizenship for the first time in history.[4] While applying to all of Asia in theory, its provisions promised to benefit Japanese the most. In the United States, Japanese immigrants composed 90 percent of the "ineligible aliens" who stood to gain U.S. citizenship, and the race-based immigration quota the new law gave to Japan was small but deeply symbolic, promising to end more than twenty years of Japanese exclusion.

The JACL's rehabilitation of Japanese Americans had two target audiences: the local and the international. Locally, the league sought to secure Issei rights to attract new members from the Japanese American community. Members of U.S. military and policy-making circles supported the JACL's efforts because they believed eliminating overt racism against Japanese Americans via formal repeal would serve U.S. interests in postwar Asia. A U.S.-led military government under the control of the Supreme Commander for the Allied Powers (SCAP), General Douglas MacArthur, was busily rebuilding a defeated Japan as an American-style democracy. Securing a modicum of cooperation from Japanese peoples in the reconstruction of Japan as an anticommunist ally was a way to reaffirm the imperial projects of the United States as inclusionary and consensual, rather than the actions of a white Western power imposed on Asian peoples.[5] The JACL was an ideal partner for U.S. state officials with these ambitions, both because of its cooperation with wartime incarceration and its policies trumpeting members' U.S. citizen status and Americanism.

Through their steadfast support for the U.S. state, JACL leaders certainly helped to reinforce notions of American greatness and liberal possibility. As the first half of this chapter describes, however, the league was not always a ready or straightforward instrument of U.S. empire building in Japan. As an organization that prided itself on its American identity, the JACL initially resisted any association with Japan and the U.S. occupation policies being implemented across the Pacific. Only after hitting a wall of opposition in Congress did JACL leaders strategically adopt the Cold War and other foreign policy arguments that white elites such as Judd had already been popularizing on Capitol Hill. When useful, they also embraced an association with Japan.

The encoding of Japanese Americans as indelibly foreign and tied to a Japanese homeland was not the only way the McCarran-Walter campaigns reflected the persistent racism and structural limits that continued to underwrite postwar race reform. Inroads Japanese Americans made through the law came at the expense of black immigrants. The second half of this chapter considers the conflict that erupted between JACL and black American activists over a "colonial quota" amendment to the Judd bill that, as part of the McCarran-Walter Act, closed the door on the black Caribbean even as it cracked open the door to Asia. The proposed restriction, dubbed an "empire quota" by critics, imposed a prohibitive immigration quota on the majority-black colonies of the Caribbean for the first time. News of its addition to what was generally considered an Asian immigration bill spurred protest by African and Afro-Caribbean American activists, who denounced it as an underhanded attempt by racist lawmakers to end black immigration. This little-known episode of black-Japanese conflict problematizes an easy analogy between postwar legislative gains for Asian Americans and those for black Americans as wholly complementary developments; to the contrary, it identifies the postwar immigration debates as a site of greater intergroup competition than collaboration. Negotiations between the two communities suggest the divergent possibilities as well as limitations the Cold War consensus created for differently racialized groups. At the same time, even as it affirms the importance of a crystallizing Cold War in shaping postwar immigration policy, this chapter also looks beyond a U.S. anticommunist lens to spotlight the continued importance of empire in the repeal movement.[6]

A Short History of Japanese Exclusion

Just as China's weakness on the international stage facilitated the initial passage and persistence of Chinese exclusion in the United States, Japan's status as a global power did the opposite, delaying the formal exclusion of Japanese for many years. Calls for Japanese exclusion had reached a fever pitch by the early 1900s with vehicles including the Japanese and Korean Exclusion League (later changed to the Asiatic Exclusion League), a San Francisco-based group founded by Euro-American labor leaders, agitating for complete Asian exclusion to ensure that the United States stayed a "white man's country." In 1907, a diplomatic agreement between Washington and Tokyo mollified exclusionists by restricting the entry of Japanese workers in practice, but without the stigma of formal exclusion. Even as the rest of Asia became subject to an immigration ban during World War I, congressional policies continued to exempt Japan. U.S. presidents from Theodore Roosevelt to Warren Harding persuaded Congress to keep Japan off the list of excluded Asian powers for fear of upsetting Tokyo; they saw good relations with the country as vital to U.S. interests in Asia, not least to discourage Japan's interference with its Philippine colony. Washington's policy of informal Japanese restriction ended with the 1924 Immigration Act's Japanese exclusion clause. Reports of its passage evoked sharp outcry across Japan, fueling criticism from Tokyo and anti-American protests among the Japanese public. The backlash was so strong, in fact, that U.S. and Japanese scholars alike widely cite the racial insult of exclusion as a major factor contributing to Japan's 1941 attack on Pearl Harbor.[7]

By 1924, efforts to secure Japanese eligibility for U.S. citizenship had developed down a distinct but parallel path toward exclusion. Despite historical restrictions limiting naturalization to "free white persons" and "persons of African descent," individual Japanese plaintiffs continued to seek U.S. citizenship in local courts and had some success. In light of Japan's rising status as a global imperial power, their petitions won support from several high-ranking U.S. officials, including President Theodore Roosevelt in 1906.[8] The case of World War I veteran Takao Ozawa ended any ambiguity, however. Upon returning from combat in Europe, Ozawa—born in Japan but a U.S. resident for twenty years—applied for American citizenship under a 1918 law allowing for the immediate naturalization of alien soldiers who had served in the war. The question arose: Could a foreign-born Japanese qualify? In *Ozawa v. U.S.* (1922), the Supreme Court denied his application and thus established beyond anyone's power to appeal that persons of Japanese descent were banned from naturalization as "aliens racially ineligible to citizenship."[9] This ruling hit Japanese immigrant farmers living along the West Coast particularly hard, leaving them vulnerable to state-level alien land laws that barred "aliens ineligible to citizenship" from owning (and in some cases, leasing) agricultural land. *U.S. v. Thind* (1923) solidified the racial bar preventing all Asians from becoming U.S. citizens the next year.

The United States' legal exclusion of Japanese did not go uncontested. Izumi Hirobe has described how, through the late 1920s and early 1930s, a diverse group of U.S. and Japanese nongovernmental actors—most notably, clergymen and missionaries such as Sidney Gulick, and businesses interested in trade with Japan—lobbied to overturn the Japanese exclusion clause of the 1924 Immigration Act by securing an annual immigration quota, however nominal, for Japan.[10] Deteriorating relations between Washington and Tokyo, along with the growing strength of exclusionists in Congress during a time of resurgent nativism and protectionism, doomed the effort. While the exclusion issue remained salient to government officials on both sides, neither was willing to take concrete action to redress it. Japanese foreign ministry officials strove to avoid even the appearance of interfering in U.S. domestic affairs, while U.S. State Department officials likewise refrained from getting too involved lest they infringe on Congress's jurisdiction over immigration matters.

Challenges to the bar on Japanese naturalization, led by a fledgling JACL, were more successful. U.S. citizenship was central to the JACL's identity and mission from its creation in 1930. While it maintained relationships with Issei organizations, the group notably restricted its membership to Nisei, who had citizenship due to their U.S. birth; this was a strategic move intended to bolster the organization's legitimacy through an embrace of Americanism. JACL leaders put their nationalist ideals to the test in one of the group's first forays into lobbying to pass a bill permitting the naturalization of Asian veterans. Working with a peculiar mix of anti-exclusion and traditionally exclusionist groups—including the American Legion and Veterans of Foreign Wars, both of whom set aside their racial concerns to support veterans' naturalization—the JACL helped win U.S. citizenship eligibility for approximately 500 foreign-born Asian veterans of World War I with passage of the Nye-Lea Act (1935).

In the words of Lucy Salyer, the success of the 1930s naturalization drive and the "odd allies it created" revealed the "continuing strength of the military service rationale for citizenship." At the same time, it remained a "precarious" basis for inclusion in that it did not displace "racialist citizenship ideals" that continued to brand whites as full U.S. citizens and nonwhites as foreigners, aliens, or second-class citizens.[11] The wartime incarceration of Japanese American veterans, including some naturalized under the Nye-Lea Act, just a few years later confirmed that legal citizenship was no guarantee of equality. The World War II evacuation and incarceration of 120,000 West Coast Japanese Americans, including more than 80,000 U.S.-born citizens, despite several Supreme Court challenges revealed the powerlessness of noncitizen Issei while exposing the second-class nature of Nisei's birthright citizenship during a time of national crisis.[12]

The JACL and Martial Patriotism

By the time JACL leaders gathered in Denver in November 1946 and adopted Issei naturalization as one of the league's primary goals, the organization was deep in the throes of a membership crisis created by its own wartime actions. While it had always attracted only a minority of Nisei within the community, the war years were dire; the league's membership dropped from upward of 8,000 before it began to 1,700 by war's end. Community researcher Tom Sasaki reported that disillusioned Japanese Americans were more inclined to denounce the group than to join it.[13] As one incarcerated Nisei told a reporter, the JACL's cooperation with U.S. government initiatives had clearly demonstrated its willingness to "sacrifice members of their national group to [its] own selfish interest."[14] Fewer members meant fewer dues, leaving the JACL in a constant state of financial precarity. After World War II, the organization only survived through the cultivation of two new revenue streams: wealthy Japanese Americans in Hawaii and Issei, whose dollars provided major funding even as they remained barred from joining the league. It was in fact Issei support that made it possible for JACL leaders to establish a national office in Washington, DC, from which the league's Washington spokesman, Mike Masaoka, championed its postwar legislative agenda as the head of the league's newly created Anti-Discrimination Committee (ADC).

The JACL's embrace of martial patriotism and generally assimilationist approach could promote U.S. imperial projects in Asia, whether intentionally or not. Juxtaposing the JACL's official recounting of its role in the wartime drafting of Nisei alongside Takashi Fujitani's of the internal mechanisms driving the War Department's 1943 decision to reverse a policy classifying Nisei as "enemy aliens" ineligible for service, suggests how this dynamic could work. According to JACL historian Bill Hosokawa, Masaoka was one of the first persons notified of the change, as was only "fitting" given his role in pushing for it.[15] He did so at some cost to the league's reputation, as reports of the JACL's role in lobbying the War Department to make the change angered many in the community. It was of a piece with disgust over the league's public relations campaigns celebrating Nisei wounded and killed in action, which some saw as the JACL again exploiting the community for self-interest.[16] However, Fujitani's research on the War Department suggests that angry Japanese Americans may have overestimated the JACL's role in the policy change, as certain Washington officials had been advocating for the U.S. military's use of Nisei for years as an effective propaganda tool to counter Japan's efforts to paint the Pacific war as a race war. Edwin Reischauer, then a recent PhD advising the State Department, suggested that Nisei soldiers fighting for the Allied cause would show that the United States was racially inclusive and that the war was about justice and freedom, not race. A consensus emerged that the symbolism of Japanese American involvement in the U.S. war effort could be useful after the war, when Japan might prove valuable, if subordinate, ally.[17] Masaoka was arguably ignorant of these expectations; from the vantage point of the JACL, Nisei military service provided an account of unflagging patriotism and loyalty under duress that fit neatly with the league's carefully constructed narratives. Their own postwar plans involved greater rights for Nisei, leveraged on such strategies.[18]

Masaoka led the effort to raise awareness of Japanese Americans and their postwar plight. Born in 1915, he was only twenty-five years old when the Japanese attacked Pearl Harbor and the mass evacuation and incarceration of Japanese Americans began along the West Coast. As national secretary for the JACL during the war, Masaoka was strongly associated with the league's most controversial policies. But the actions that infuriated Japanese Americans made Masaoka the community's most recognized and admired spokesperson on Capitol Hill both during and after the war. With the early help of Senator Elbert Thomas (R-UT), a former Mormon missionary to Japan and his politics professor at the University of Utah, Masaoka cultivated strong relationships with lawmakers including Nevada senator Patrick McCarran, who would go on to cosponsor the 1952 act.[19] In one of his earliest political coups, Masaoka's testimony before the President's Committee on Civil Rights helped bring national attention to the plight of

Mike Masaoka of the JACL addresses a congressional committee, 1943. Bettmann / Getty Images.

Japanese and other Asian Americans due to their historical ban from U.S. citizenship.[20] His participation not only challenged the government body to broaden its conception of what discriminations civil rights reform should address. It also prompted them to include Asian Americans among the racial minorities in need of state protection and redress. Because of Masaoka, the committee's final policy report contained references and solutions to grievances affecting Japanese Americans and Asian Americans in general. *To Secure These Rights* (1947) described the plight of "ineligible aliens" whose "race or national origin" permanently prevented them from pursuing U.S. citizenship; under naturalization laws that limited citizenship to persons of white and African descent, the term had historically applied to Asians alone. To redress these inequities, the committee recommended the repeal of state laws that discriminated against "aliens ineligible for citizenship" and, at the federal level, the restructuring of U.S. naturalization laws to "permit the granting of citizenship without regard to the race, color, or national origin of applicants."[21]

The Judd bill was born out of a partnership between the JACL and Rep. Walter Judd, whose involvement marked a point of continuity from previous repeal campaigns. As discussed in chapter 1, Judd had actually drafted an Asian immigration and naturalization bill in 1943 with the help of the Justice Department but scrapped the proposed legislation once the Citizens Committee's campaign for Chinese exclusion repeal gained momentum. At the time, congressional colleagues persuaded him that anti-Japanese sentiment made any broad-based measure for Asian immigration politically infeasible. After the success of the Magnuson Act, Judd continued to support repeal efforts from the sidelines of the Luce-Celler campaigns. But only in 1947 did he again become directly involved. He formally introduced his legislation to end wholesale Asian exclusion at the urging of JACL leaders, who gravitated toward him as someone widely respected for his expertise in Asian affairs.[22] Over the next two years, Judd reintroduced modified versions of the bill as congressional lawmakers and executive officials incorporated changes from various constituencies.[23] As JACL's full-time representative in Washington, Masaoka quickly earned a reputation as a masterful orator and tenacious lobbyist. Observers praised his novel style of "personal lobbying" and eloquent speeches before Congress as rhetorical "gems of clarity, logic, and delivery." Stories circulated of his dogged perseverance and remarkable success in winning over even the most reluctant lawmakers. Once, when unable to secure an appointment with Rep. John Robison of Kentucky, a powerful member of the House Judiciary Committee, Masaoka reportedly followed the lawmaker to the bathroom and "engaged him in conversation when he couldn't conveniently get away." According to one source, the result was that Robison soon became a "staunch supporter" of repeal.[24]

Masaoka looked to history for guidance on two counts. First, he studied carefully the Chinese, Philippine, and Indian repeal campaigns in search of effective strategies and other "clues as to what ought to be done."[25] It was no coincidence that the organizational structure set up by the JACL-ADC (Japanese American Citizens League–Anti-Discrimination Committee) so closely resembled that of the Citizens Committee to Repeal Chinese Exclusion, the catalytic pressure group responsible for the Magnuson Act during World War II. Citizens Committee members Richard Walsh and Pearl Buck were among those who joined the JACL-ADC's postwar fight. In early 1947, they created the Committee for Equality on Naturalization (CEN) as an all-white American partner group to the JACL. Edward Ennis, who served as CEN chairman, and John McCloy, one of its founding members, were former U.S. officials who had worked closely with Masaoka and the JACL while overseeing the community's wartime incarceration. As JACL's national board described it, much as the Citizens Committee had done as a white American lobbying vehicle during World War II, the CEN would serve as a "non-Japanese organ of distinguished Americans" pushing for general Asian exclusion repeal.[26] In reality, the CEN was an extension of the JACL-ADC; like the ADC, it worked under the aegis of the JACL's national board based in California and was also funded by Issei donors. But its creation suggests how both white and Asian advocates still believed white spokespersons were more effective than other Asians in winning over U.S. lawmakers to their cause.

Masaoka's second historical precedent was the JACL's successful campaign for the Nye-Lea Act (1935). Its passage had been quite a feat during a time of rising nativism and economic hardship in the United States, and deteriorating diplomatic relations between Washington and Tokyo overseas. The first lesson from the 1930s was that it was wise to separate the issue of naturalization from that of immigration, which tended to raise thorny questions regarding U.S. foreign relations. This separation had made it possible for Asian veterans to win the support of the American Legion, which in 1935 reaffirmed its opposition to Asian immigration even as it endorsed the naturalization of nonwhite veterans.[27] JACL representatives sought once again to distinguish naturalization from immigration demands, but the more sweeping nature of the Judd bill made it difficult to replicate this strategy without modification. League leaders briefly considered endorsing a naturalization-only measure, but many agreed that the dual structure of the 1924 Japanese exclusion clause, which made Asian immigration contingent on U.S. citizenship eligibility, necessitated broader legislation covering both arenas. The desire to adhere as closely as possible to the pattern of previous legislation already passed—both the Magnuson and Luce-Celler Acts included both immigration and naturalization provisions—also played a part.

Separating naturalization from immigration concerns was a messy business, but Masaoka did his best to distance the JACL from the Judd bill's immigration provisions however he could.[28] Lawmakers asked about his views on Asian immigration at an April 1948 hearing before a House immigration subcommittee. The bill's immigration and naturalization provisions, he responded in brief, reflected "two different problems." When pressed about the JACL's position on Asian immigration quotas specifically, he sidestepped the query, claiming that its stance was the "same as [that of] any other American."[29] Masaoka's vague responses likely did little to satisfy lawmakers, but they did accomplish the JACL's short-term goal of not riling up southern lawmakers already fearful that wholesale exclusion repeal would invite a flood of Asian immigrants. A surge in restrictionist sentiment immediately after the war made such machinations necessary. The influx of returning soldiers inundating the job market and straining housing and other public resources strengthened anti-immigrant sentiment; far from easing quotas, some lawmakers called for slashing them even further until equilibrium had been restored. Even Rep. Celler (D-NY), a longtime supporter of repeal and the cosponsor of the 1946 Luce-Celler Act, estimated that the Judd bill's immigration provisions were about "five years ahead of schedule" in terms of their ability to pass Congress.[30] Thus, Masaoka's early distancing efforts, together with the JACL's steadfastly patriotic approach, represented a strategic decision to maximize the campaign's odds of success.

Another important lesson from the Nye-Lea campaign was that an emphasis on martial patriotism—a loyalty to nation embodied by the bodily service and sacrifice of soldiers—offered a widely persuasive strategy to win congressional votes. Indeed, it was the only proven way foreign-born Asians had ever won naturalization rights under U.S. law.[31] In the 1930s, JACL spokespersons had successfully argued that Japanese veterans of World War I, among other foreign-born Asians, had purchased the right to U.S. citizenship with their bodies and blood. With this in mind, the JACL-ADC adopted a modified strategy of martial patriotism tailored to the postwar period.[32] Simply put, the league suggested, the bodily sacrifices of U.S.-born Nisei soldiers during World War II had earned their Issei parents and Issei more generally the right to U.S. citizenship. By downplaying differences of generation and citizenship to leverage the military service of Nisei as a justification for Issei rights, JACL affirmed its belief that the rights of immigrants were connected with those of citizens.[33] A special 1948 Christmas edition of the JACL newspaper *Pacific Citizen* typified this view. In a piece titled "Our Next Great Goal," the JACL's Masaoka described Issei naturalization as the long-cherished "dream of Japanese *and Japanese Americans*" alike.[34]

Speaking as the chair of the JACL-ADC, Masaoka proved to be one of the martial strategy's most skilled practitioners. At House and Senate subcommittee hearings on the Judd bill in 1948 and 1949, he made his mother the exemplary Issei whose sons' wartime sacrifices justified passage of the bill. All told, the Masaoka sons had earned more than thirty decorations and medals for their service; one died in battle and another experienced a crippling leg injury.[35] "German bullets did not swerve simply because we were Japanese Americans and our parents were ineligible to citizenship," Masaoka testified.

The "real conviction and faith in the American way" that these soldiers had demonstrated through their military service to were a credit to their first-generation immigrant parents: "Parents who can produce children like that, Mr. Chairman . . . are true Americans and naturalization should be granted them."[36] In statements and appeals before congressional audiences, Masaoka described with powerful rhetoric the patriotism and courage shown by Nisei soldiers who had volunteered to fight for the country that put them and their families "behind barbed wire" because they "believed fundamentally in the American way."[37] He cited intelligence estimates reporting that the military service of Japanese American troops in the Pacific had "shortened the war by months and saved thousands of American casualties."[38] Indeed, the scale of Japanese military participation and the meanings ascribed to their involvement in the war had changed radically between the two World Wars. In contrast to the World War I pool of Japanese and Asian soldiers, which was small and largely unknown, an estimated 33,000 Nisei fought for the United States during World War II in highly publicized fashion. Even today, the all-Nisei 442nd Regimental Combat Unit remains the most decorated military battalion in U.S. history.

References to the valor and service of Nisei proved effective in securing the JACL a series of legislative victories between 1947 and 1948. These included congressional passage of the Wartime Evacuation Claims Act—the federal government's first attempt to compensate losses suffered by incarcerated Japanese Americans during the war—and an amendment to the 1945 War Brides Act that allowed Japanese military brides to enter the United States as exceptions to the law's blanket exclusion of Japanese. In fact, Masaoka proved so capable that *The Sign*, a national Catholic magazine, declared him "Washington's Most Successful Lobbyist" on the basis of his legislative record alone.[39]

Masaoka's use of a martial patriotism strategy won over some critics of the Judd bill, including those from the South. Probably the most unlikely convert to the cause was southern Democrat Ed Gossett. Shortly after the war's end, Gossett famously proposed a measure to cut U.S. immigration quotas in half for five years until returning soldiers had been reincorporated into the workforce and their local communities.[40] But he agreed to meet with Masaoka after learning about the 442nd Regimental Combat Team's service record in Europe. A longtime Texan and military man, Gossett claimed to have been personally moved to support the Judd bill by the Nisei troop's daring rescue of the Lost Battalion, a group of soldiers from Texas trapped behind enemy lines in France. It is possible Gossett brought others to Masaoka's side by making this public statement.

But martial patriotism was not enough. By the time the Judd bill passed the House and moved to the Senate in the spring of 1949, Masaoka had begun calling for a reconsideration of the league's overall strategy based on his assessment of the political climate in Washington, DC, and his two years as a lobbyist on Capitol Hill. In light of "developments in the field of world politics and American foreign policy," he argued, the campaign would do better to move away from its current focus on "naturalization and domestic influence" and spotlight instead "immigration and its impact on the world situation," particularly "as it affects the struggle against the spread of communism." While he personally claimed to dislike such rhetorical pandering, Masaoka concluded that the JACL had little choice but to "stress this angle" lest the Judd bill get "lost" in the "legislative rush to do something about Russia."[41] The Cold War had begun in earnest, and the JACL had to shift its tactics accordingly.

Asian Decolonization and the Cold War Case for Repeal

JACL's embrace of a Cold War internationalist strategy was by no means novel on Capitol Hill. The NAACP and other prominent African American organizations had already begun using anticommunist arguments to make the case for civil rights reforms in both national and international forums.[42] Similarly, Asia-oriented internationalist policymakers such as Walter Judd had been refining a case for the wholesale repeal of the Asian exclusion laws for months, referencing the United States' imperative to court Asian allies as a way to contain communism's influence. Scholars have documented clearly the Cold War's animating yet narrowing effect on black Americans' legal gains.[43] In a parallel dynamic, the internationalist arguments advocates used for repeal facilitated U.S. empire-building projects abroad and the passage of immigration reform at home while constraining the scope of the legislation enacted. By and large, advocates continued to emphasize the Cold War imperative to contain the influence of Soviet communism in Asia. But as a 1948 House committee hearing on the Judd bill reflected, the fact that many of the Asian peoples were newly independent or in the process of seeking independence in the context of the emergent Cold War shaped the congressional debate over repeal in distinct ways.

State Department witness statements attest to how the Cold War was not yet an all-encompassing lens through which Washington policymakers viewed Asia; even as tensions between the United States and the Soviet Union crystallized, decolonization created overlapping yet distinct ripple effects and dilemmas. Surveying the aftermath of Philippine and Indian independence, State Department strategists offered suggestions for how the United States might best redefine its relationship with a postwar Asia made up increasingly of sovereign nation-states rather than dependent colonies. Lawmakers had called attention to this complication in relation to the Luce-Celler Act, which gave both India and Pakistan immigration quotas of 100, and asked whether other partitions might also necessitate the extension of additional ad hoc immigration quotas. With the status of so many colonies still in flux, on what basis should Congress count an Asian power as separate and sovereign? Watson Miller, commissioner of the INS, suggested as one possible solution U.S. immigration quotas based on U.N. membership; since only independent nation-states could be full-fledged members, this criterion presumably offered an easy way to determine status. Given southern lawmakers' general skepticism of the United Nations and other such international bodies, however, it is not surprising that the idea failed to gain traction.

Ultimately, the statements of Judd and Joseph Grew, a former U.S. ambassador to Japan, drew more of Congress's attention because of the clarity and specificity with which they articulated an early Cold War argument for Asian exclusion repeal. Both men were consummate anticommunists predisposed to see Asia through the lens of the emerging contest between the United States and the Soviet Union. Cognizant of previous repeal efforts, Judd adapted earlier arguments of wartime migration diplomacy to call for repeal as a matter of expediency and American self-interest. Just as the Magnuson Act had given China an "enormous lift" at a "dark hour in [its] struggle against Japan" five years earlier, Judd argued, his immigration bill promised to be a "powerful weapon" with "incalculable . . . benefits" to "tip" the "scale" for the "billion people in Asia" being presented with a choice between the United States and the "Soviet system." Japan's attacks on American racial hypocrisy during World War II still rang loud in their ears. In a modified version of the argument he had made in the Chinese campaign, Judd asserted that a bill repealing Japanese exclusion offered a low-cost, high-yield way to check growing Soviet influence in Asia; in his telling, immigration quotas for "citizens of Oriental countries" were a more effective way to "win the goodwill of Orientals by removing a stigma of inferiority" than military or foreign aid, which cost "hundreds of millions of American dollars" and proved "futile" in terms of fostering positive relationships.[44]

Rep. Walter H. Judd
of Minnesota, 1946.
Walter B. Lane /
Getty Images.

While Judd's statement concerned Asia more generally, Grew appealed directly to a foreign policy bloc in Washington committed to rebuilding a former Japanese enemy into the United States' "subordinate Cold War partner" and a counterweight to growing communist strength in the region.[45] While the U.S.-led SCAP Occupation initially implemented a liberal occupation policy focused on social reform, by the time of the Judd hearings, what scholars call the SCAP government's "reverse-course" toward a Cold War–centered program had already begun.[46] Grew was among the most influential figures calling on U.S. policymakers to remilitarize and rebuild Japan's economy under a conservative government likely to cooperate with U.S. containment goals after the occupation ended. His was arguably the most authoritative voice on Japan in postwar Washington, so his appearance at the hearing alone would have linked the Judd bill to U.S. Japan policy in lawmakers' minds.[47] Grew explained that its immigration provisions were particularly important for U.S. relations with occupied Japan, where "a new leadership" was "emerging under [U.S.] tutelage." This approach reflected a widely held understanding that the Judd bill's objective was the containment of communist influence and the promotion of Washington's postwar goals in Japan specifically. The 1924 Immigration Act had proven the power of racially discriminatory migration policies—and U.S. Asian exclusion laws in particular—to stoke international resentment and to contribute to war, he testified. At a time of "realignment" when Asian peoples were "choosing friends" and "everywhere there [was] receptivity to new ideas," Grew called on U.S. lawmakers to ensure that the "trend of friendship" continued even after the SCAP Occupation ended. Speaking in the language of consent and mutuality, he concluded, "if we want to hold our friends, we must support them."[48] Gen. Robert Eichelberger, who had served as a commanding officer in Japan from 1944 to 1948, echoed Grew's sentiment. The resentment felt by Japanese people over the insult of U.S. exclusion laws remained strong, he testified, making the Judd bill a welcome and much-needed salvo to the problem of anti-American sentiment in Japan both then and in the future.[49]

Multiple sources reflect how internationalist arguments emphasizing U.S. Cold War interests valued Asian Americans primarily as extensions of Asian audiences rather than as ethnic communities with interests of their own. If, as the President's Committee on Civil Rights had argued, the poor treatment of "hundreds of thousands . . . [of American] citizens of Oriental descent" had the potential to "outrage" "hundreds of millions" of their Asian "counterparts overseas," the implication was that Japanese and other Asians living in the United States were significant first and foremost as proxies for Asians living abroad, not as Americans in their own right.[50] Judd's sympathetic references to Asian peoples also tended to focus on Asians abroad rather than Asian Americans. During World War II, he critiqued the state's incarceration of Japanese Americans but confined his objection to the forced mixing of those Japanese Americans loyal to the United States with others more loyal to Japan.[51] Judd further emphasized that the size of the immigration quotas did not matter if Asians were the law's main audience. In other words, symbolic equality was not only sufficient; it was the goal. As he had done in the Chinese case, Judd stressed that the quota would admit "only an infinitesimal number" of Asian immigrants, thus enabling the United States to maximize the diplomatic value of repeal at minimum social cost.[52] Moreover, he offered no objection whatsoever when a critic proposed to halve the Asian immigration quotas from one hundred to fifty: "As long as [the quotas] are all alike," he maintained, "it is equality," conveniently eliding the fact that even the smallest European countries had larger quotas.[53] Thus, as with earlier campaigns, the Cold War strategy framed repeal as important primarily for its symbolic value and not as a way to create actual equality.

Concessions and creative proposals did little to assuage congressional critics of the Judd bill, who continued to protest that even nominal immigration from Asia could open the United States to an endless stream of migrants. Their warnings about how passing a repeal bill for one group could lay the path for others had proven prescient. According to a State Department witness, the problem now was one of principle: if racial restrictions on U.S. immigration were "not consistent" with the "sovereign dignity of independence," how else could Congress respond to decolonization but to give Asians immigration quotas similar to those given Europeans?[54]

A Cross Fire of Minorities

In March 1949, the House passed the Judd bill by a large majority following a discussion that one scholar described as "one of the most harmonious ever held on an immigration bill."[55] The expression of widespread agreement belied conflict brewing beneath the surface, however. Shortly before the House vote, eleventh-hour amendments to the legislation prompted the launch of two counter-campaigns seeking to remove provisions adding new restrictions on Chinese and black Americans. Members of both communities scrambled at the last minute to protest what they perceived as a direct attack. The first restriction proposed to reverse the hard-won gains of the Chinese Alien Wives Act of 1946 by ending the practice of allowing the alien Chinese wives of U.S. citizens to enter the country as nonquota immigrants. It was deleted shortly after the bill reached the Senate.[56] Judd had very reluctantly added it at the insistence of his fellow Republicans. Once the provision came under attack, he was quick to call for its removal.

The provenance of the second amendment, a colonial quota imposing a ceiling of 100 per year on migration from "colonies and other dependent areas" was less clear. Yet it remained a part of the Judd bill and was later incorporated and enacted as part of the McCarran-Walter Act. It was widely reported that House Judiciary Committee members had added the new restriction as a safeguard to prevent Asians in European colonies such as Hong Kong from flooding into the United States outside of the by-country Asian quotas. But it is hard to eliminate altogether the possibility of a targeted attempt to reduce migration from black colonies in the Caribbean—both in light of previous congressional efforts to reduce black migration and the dominance of segregationist southern Democrats on the Senate subcommittee overseeing immigration. Under a loophole in the 1924 National Origins Act, roughly two to three thousand black migrants entered the United States every year from the majority-black British, Dutch, and French Caribbean colonies of Jamaica, Trinidad and Tobago, Barbados, and British Guiana using the unfilled quota slots of their European colonizers.[57] Once enacted as part of the final McCarran-Walter legislation over the protests of African and Afro-Caribbean Americans and their allies, the colonial quota amendment slashed that number from tens of thousands to fewer than nine hundred migrants each year.[58] The question of why one effort for removal succeeded while the other failed is worth investigating, not least for what it reveals about how different groups benefited unevenly from Washington's empire-building imperatives.

The differences began with institutional support. Judd, the bill's sponsor, wholeheartedly endorsed the removal of the Chinese wives' amendment but was more supportive of the colonial quota. As discussed in chapter 1, the Minnesota congressman had opposed a similar wives' provision when it threatened Chinese exclusion repeal during the war. But half a decade later, he was reluctant to reverse gains Chinese Americans had already won and was concerned about what kind of message the amendment might send to Chinese overseas. Judd had much less invested in the colonial quota's main constituency. As a Minnesota Republican, Judd had little incentive to court black voters, few of whom lived in his district, and stood to lose little from upsetting them given that his reputation rested primarily on his expertise in Asian affairs. Like many lawmakers, he had experience working with the NAACP on local matters, but his larger legislative record bore little trace of support for black civil rights measures.[59] Like many conservative Republicans at the time, even as he acknowledged the harms of racial prejudice in the United States, he called first for education and other social strategies to address race problems, not "rules or regulations" in the form of congressional bills.[60]

Italian American Vito Marcantonio (D-NY) and African American Adam Clayton Powell Jr. (D-NY) formed the main congressional opposition to the colonial quota and generally lacked Judd's clout. Both had political and personal motives for speaking against passage. As House lawmakers representing Harlem districts with significant Afro-Caribbean populations, their advocacy served their constituents' interests; in Powell's district, for example, nearly one in five black residents had been born in the West Indies.

Powell's wife was herself from Jamaica and had family members on the islands.[61] Marcantonio's role was consistent with his championing of black civil rights and the rights of racial minorities in general. As a suspected communist, however, his prominent role in the counter-campaign may have harmed more than helped, enabling critics to paint it with a radical brush. At a March 1948 House subcommittee hearing, Powell and Marcantonio faced off against Walter Judd and Rep. Francis Walter (D-PA), the future cosponsor of the McCarran-Walter bill, in an hour-long debate. While Marcantonio cited principle, Powell, newly returned from Jamaica, argued against the quota on national security grounds. Just as the Judd bill's Asian immigration provisions promised to foster greater "goodwill with [America's] far-off neighbors in the Eastern Hemisphere," he warned that the colonial quota would alienate U.S. neighbors in the Caribbean; fueling anti-American sentiment in a "jumping-off place" only "2½ hours from Miami" was dangerous.[62] A heated exchange followed, with Judd defending the colonial quota as the price of "equality for all."[63] Calling this out as "extreme distortion," Powell lamented the "gross injustice" of "bring[ing] about equality for the Eastern Hemisphere by discriminating against the Western Hemisphere."[64] Ultimately, Powell and Marcantonio were Democrats trying to persuade a Republican-dominated House to delay passage of a Republican-sponsored measure. What is more, the House vote—19 to 118 against Powell's amendment, and 39 to 336 against Marcantonio's call for delay—revealed that not even all liberal Democrats agreed on the quota's fate.

The two amendments had disparate sources of support outside of Congress as well. While it is always difficult to determine what outside forces actually change the actions of lawmakers, the counter-protests of the CACA and the CCBA, the two Chinese American community organizations most active in securing passage of the 1946 Chinese Alien Wives Act, were impressive. Within weeks of learning about the Chinese wives amendment, CACA and CCBA leaders on both coasts recruited and dispatched a sixteen-member delegation to Washington to lobby members of Congress in person. Speaking at a Senate immigration subcommittee hearing on the Judd bill, CCBA and CACA witnesses deployed a modified strategy of martial patriotism centered around the military service and sacrifice of the more than 20,000 Chinese American soldiers who fought in World War II.[65] Repeating the arguments used in earlier campaigns, Edward Hong, speaking for the CCBA of New York and New England, argued that Chinese Americans' military service had earned them the "right of companionship." He took care to note that ethnic

Chinese soldiers had been "assigned to random units based upon their ability and capacity." The clarification suggested an awareness of how media and government attention to the exploits of Nisei military troops such as the 442nd and 110th had raised the profile of Japanese American soldiers in the minds of a wider American public. The implication was clear, even if his delivery was not: Chinese American soldiers had been no less courageous than Japanese Americans, even if their contributions were harder to isolate.[66]

Afro-Caribbean groups based in New York and Chicago were the most active opponents of the colonial quota, while the NAACP was among the few African American vehicles to get involved. NAACP leaders took greatest offense at the measure's zero-sum logic suggesting that gains for one group had to come at the expense of another.[67] Even as NAACP lawyer Charles Hamilton Houston affirmed his support for Japanese American rights, he denounced the bill's colonial quota as a "dirty sleeper" designed to target "colored peoples in the British Empire." The last thing we wan`t to do is "exchange a yellow discrimination for a black one," he maintained. "We want to eradicate both."[68] Houston's protégé, NAACP legal director Thurgood Marshall, likewise decried the "grim irony" in that the "House evidently believes that each step forward must be accompanied by a step backward."[69] Critics of the quota made their biggest showing at a Senate immigration subcommittee hearing in July 1949. Nine spokespersons representing African American and West Indian organizations from across the Northeast and Midwest spoke against the colonial quota on different grounds, but all condemned what they saw as the antiblack racist motives driving the bill. A. A. Austin of the United Caribbean American Council (UCAC) of New York, an umbrella group representing thirty organizations of native- and foreign-born U.S. citizens and residents of Caribbean origin, charged U.S. State Department officials with devising new strategies aimed at "discouraging and deterring peoples of African descent from entering the United States."[70] Echoing his critique from the earlier House debate, Rep. Powell bluntly denounced the amendment as "discrimination of the very rankest type."[71]

Adopting a diasporic strategy similar to that used by Indian repeal advocates, some Afro-Caribbean witnesses drew on their familial roots in and firsthand knowledge of their homelands to position themselves as unofficial spokespersons for the region's peoples. Austin of the UCAC emphasized that restriction would cause a "grave crisis" for Caribbean peoples, who had historically relied on immigration to the United States to escape the "poverty, malnutrition and high mortality" of the islands—either through firsthand migration or through the remittances of U.S.-based relatives sent to the families they had left behind. Two other speakers emphasized the critical labor of West Indians in the United States' construction of the Panama Canal several decades earlier; in their telling, the proposed quota made a mockery of Jamaican and Barbadian contributions to U.S. power and economic growth. Austin warned of the quota's promise to strain Washington's "good neighbor relations" with Caribbean peoples at a time when their support was more important than ever. He quoted directly from resolutions passed by the Barbados and Trinidad colonial legislatures denouncing the quota provisions of the Judd legislation as evidence that the diplomatic fallout had already begun. Still others objected to how the colonial quota singled out the Caribbean as an exception vis-a-vis its Latin American neighbors, who had long been exempt from immigration restrictions due to Washington's long-standing commitment to pan-Americanism and a hemispheric Good Neighbor policy. In the words of the UCAC's Hope Stevens, Afro-Caribbean peoples just want to be "treated as Latin Americans," with the same ability to migrate.[72]

The hearing's Afro-Caribbean witnesses also adapted the Luce-Celler campaign's focus on repeal as part of the U.S. response to anticolonial movements and the dismantling of formal empire.[73] In so doing they threw the dynamics of decolonization in Asia and the Caribbean—as well as the United States' different historical relationships with these regions—into sharp relief. Austin described the Judd bill as another prime opportunity for Washington to use its migration policy to demonstrate its commitment to self-determination and freedom for colonized peoples. European colonialism in the Caribbean would not last forever, he warned, and by inscribing "discrimination against colonial peoples" into official U.S. immigration policy, the quota sent a message that Washington sanctioned and reproduced colonial subjugation. His logic was sound, but by this time, U.S. policymakers were firm in their belief that Asia had more urgency as a site to expand the United States' postwar influence than the Caribbean. Decolonization was still unfolding fitfully across the southeastern part of Asia as wars raged between European colonial powers and formerly colonized peoples in French and Dutch Indochina and British Malaya. Farther north, U.S. military forces continued to occupy a defeated postwar Japan and parts of southern Korea, now under the U.S.-friendly dictatorship of anticommunist Syngman Rhee. Asia was also where Chiang Kai-shek's Nationalists, despite receiving millions of dollars in U.S. aid, were on the verge of losing to Mao Zedong's Communists in the decades-long Chinese civil war.

The United States had a very different history in the Caribbean as a peripheral power with deep economic ties but only an unofficial military and political role in the region. As several witness statements reflected, the Caribbean's significance to Washington lay primarily in its geographical proximity to the U.S. mainland: located squarely in the U.S. sphere of influence, the islands were unsurprisingly among the first places Washington sought to implement a policy of containment.[74] Still, despite its closeness, several factors diminished the Caribbean's significance in the minds of U.S. officials. First, because Britain and other European powers—not the United States—were the main imperial actors in the region, as one State Department consul reported, what little "colonial feeling" existed in the islands was generally "more anti-Britain" than "anti-American." Indeed, rather than inspiring further lenience, Indian independence in 1947 actually caused the British government to clamp down on its remaining colonial possessions, including in the Caribbean.[75] Second, as a 1949 CIA report concluded, because Soviet "capabilities in the area" were extremely "limited," any Cold War threat the region posed to the United States was similarly small.[76] Finally, lawmakers anticipated that independence for the Caribbean colonies was still a long way off. They were right; most would not gain their independence until the 1960s, and some remain colonies still.

As a minor power in the region, the United States once again found itself in the difficult position of balancing its responsibilities and commitments to colonized peoples—in this case, the Caribbean peoples who were part of an inter-American system—against those owed to their European colonizers. Washington could have applied lessons learned from the Indian case to avoid repeating similar errors in the Caribbean, but it did not. U.S. officials again chose to defer to the British, this time out of the belief that British control was the best way to contain Soviet influence in the region.[77] In another parallel with U.S. policy in India, this decision would eventually drive anti-American sentiment in the Caribbean to new heights by the 1960s. But in the late 1940s and early 1950s, that eventuality was far off, as unfolding crises compelled Washington policymakers to pivot away from Europe and toward Asia as the more urgent site of communist containment.

While diplomatic and geopolitical themes dominated the statements of witnesses opposing the colonial quota, several speakers also cited the growing political power of black voters in the United States as a reason lawmakers should think twice about passing an "anti-black" bill.[78] If Congress wished to avoid offending the "fifteen million Americans of African descent who constitute the largest single minority in this nation of minorities," one warned, it should take heed. The appeal was intended to resonate with liberal Democrats in the wake of the 1948 election, when the Democratic Party adopted a national civil rights plank for the first time in a targeted effort to court northern black voters. Nevertheless, so long as many northern Democrats remained reluctant to alienate southerners within their own party—many of whom had broken off to run a segregationist third-party candidate the previous year—these arguments carried limited power. This was particularly true in the Senate, which remained the "graveyard" of both immigration liberalization measures and civil rights bills throughout the late 1940s and 1950s.[79]

The standoff over the colonial quota put the JACL, which had at one time claimed to speak for all nonwhite minorities, in an awkward position. First, it came at a time when relations between the Japanese American and African American communities appeared stronger than ever. In California, the NAACP's West Coast branch and local JACL chapters were working toward shared goals including fair housing and nondiscrimination in hiring, and the JACL was collaborating with the NAACP's Legal Defense Fund on a series of civil rights cases.[80] After opening the JACL's national office in Washington, Masaoka had assiduously courted the NAACP and other civil rights organizations with a more established presence on Capitol Hill.[81] He successfully leveraged official remorse over Japanese Americans' wartime incarceration in testimony supporting antilynching legislation in 1948, when he testified alongside NAACP leaders. If such a bill had been in effect during the community's resettlement after incarceration, he argued, Japanese Americans would not have suffered so many burnings and armed attacks upon returning to their former homes and neighborhoods. As such, the bill was needed to protect all minority groups, not just black Americans, from violent expressions of racial hatred.[82] For their part, some black community leaders also saw value in working with the JACL. Both groups benefited by defining civil rights and racial discrimination as issues that affected more people than black Americans alone.[83] Trading on this history, Masaoka had successfully obtained a commitment from national African American and Jewish community leaders in New York not to block or hinder progress on Asian immigration and naturalization matters even as they continued to advance their own civil rights agendas.[84] But the two communities' clash over the Judd bill's colonial quota would ultimately imperil cooperation.

The JACL chose the side of expediency. Speaking at the 1949 Senate committee hearing Masaoka reiterated the JACL's desire to remain at peace with black activists but was unapologetic about the league's unwavering commitment to the bill and to Japanese American rights. "Certainly, we do not want either rights or privileges taken away from other minority groups," he explained in a report to the league's national board. "But, at the same time, we do believe that there should be equality in naturalization and immigration law" and "other sections, if necessary, should be sacrificed in order to gain the greater principle." Ultimately, then, objections by other groups should "not be permitted to cloud or confuse the issues."[85] This decision chilled relations between the JACL and the NAACP and the groups they represented, effectively foreclosing meaningful cooperation on immigration matters for years to come.

While the House passed the Judd bill with the colonial quota intact, high-ranking restrictionists derailed progress on the Judd bill in the Senate, tabling it in committee by early 1950. Most significant were the actions of Senator Patrick McCarran (D-NV), who used his position as the chairman of a Senate immigration subcommittee in charge of investigating the overall immigration system to put the legislation on hold. McCarran's near single-handed ability to stop the bill registered what political scientist Daniel Tichenor has called the overwhelming "power of committee barons," which grew even stronger with the consolidation of committee chairmanships during a 1946 reorganization of Congress.[86] Despite being himself the son of Irish immigrants, McCarran was a staunch restrictionist and ardent anticommunist. His position on the Senate Judiciary Committee in turn made him one of the most influential lawmakers in Congress after World War II. Like State Department officials and internationalists such as Rep. Judd, McCarran emphasized the need for immigration reform as a tool in the United States' battle against communism, but he was more interested in its domestic impact. The senator regularly expressed fears that an unmodified immigration policy would allow dangerous subversives to enter the country and thus jeopardize national security. Robert Divine has suggested that formal repeal could have been achieved several years earlier were it not for McCarran's intervention.[87] As it was, the Judd bill went no further.

JACL and the McCarran-Walter Act

In 1951, McCarran in the Senate and Rep. Francis Walter (D-PA) in the House incorporated the Judd bill's Asian immigration and naturalization provisions into their joint omnibus immigration legislation. As David Reimers has noted, the inclusion of the Asian repeal provisions was a strategic move. In the face of wide-ranging opposition and protest of their omnibus bills, the cosponsors hoped the "liberal tinge" and popularity of the Asian immigration and naturalization provisions would offset the legislation's more controversial sections strengthening the state's power over the detention and deportation of suspected subversives, the passing of which was actually their main priority.[88] Both men were staunch anticommunists, and the battle for national security at home indelibly framed their worldviews. Perhaps the greatest testament to Walter's anticommunism was that he spent the last nine years of his tenure in Congress on the House Committee on Un-American Activities, first as a member and later as chairman. Though widely seen as more flexible and open-minded than his Nevada counterpart, his voting record reflects how he was no less committed to restrictionism.

Over the following year, McCarran and Walter skillfully used their powers as committee chairmen to facilitate the passage of their omnibus bills. Opposition was widespread and strong: liberal, humanitarian, and religious groups denounced the legislation's retention of the much-maligned national origins quota system and provisions strengthening the government's powers to detain and deport as "un-American and undemocratic," "racist," and "draconian." Congressional critics turned the logic of migration diplomacy against passage, arguing that the legislation would actually "blacken the name of America all over the world" and thereby doom Washington's global efforts to win hearts and minds.[89] In the face of overwhelming criticism, the chairmen marginalized opponents by creating a joint hearings process that blunted dissenting voices. This allowed them to expedite passage, leaving little time for opponents to organize, and to pack the hearings with witnesses who supported their cause. McCarran and Walter also exercised their discretion to ensure that at least five other repeal bills died while their omnibus legislation progressed.

In addition to the power of its new sponsors, the McCarran-Walter bill benefited from a growing sense of urgency, which Judd conveyed in a lengthy statement before a joint House-Senate immigration subcommittee in the spring of 1951. Recent developments strengthening communist powers in the region made repeal more pressing than ever, he argued.[90] In short, the Chinese Communist victory had changed everything since the last congressional hearing on the Judd bill two years earlier. With war in Korea and the occupation of Japan poised to end with treaty negotiations already in progress, he called for the U.S. repeal of Asian exclusion to serve as a fulcrum that could shift the global "balance of power" in America's favor. The success of the Marshall Plan and other U.S. Cold War measures in Europe could only do so much to contain communism. Now it was up to the "700,000,000 people who live on the fringe of China . . . beginning with Korea, Japan, and then around clear to Iran" to decide what happened next. If allied with the United States, these 700 million Asians would tip the balance decisively in the United States' favor, Judd argued, but if they chose the Soviet Union—for whom he saw Communist China as a proxy—the United States would be forced to confront the "most difficult problem . . . in its history": a global race war it was unlikely to win.[91]

Even as the bill's cosponsors focused primarily on the legislation's domestic security impact, Masaoka joined Judd and other internationalists in framing the Asian immigration quotas as powerful tools of containment at the height of the U.S. Cold War in East Asia. Echoing the logic Joseph Grew had used, Masaoka cautioned that while congressional passage of the bill would surely build up Japan as the United States' "bulwark of democracy in the Orient," its defeat threatened to turn the Japanese people away from Washington—and, in his words, "further into the camp of the Soviet enemy."[92] This reframing had at least two additional benefits. First, it broadened the appeal of the naturalization campaign from a "special interest issue" specific to Japanese Americans to one that concerned all peace-loving Americans.[93] Second, it endeared the league to the legislation's cosponsors. Walter and McCarran were among the most powerful lawmakers in postwar Congress; their patronage would pay dividends for the JACL in subsequent immigration debates.

Along with the embrace of anticommunism, Masaoka's "strategic self-orientalizing" represented an about-face from the JACL's wartime policy of emphasizing Japanese Americans' identity as Americans first.[94] Now, for the first time before a congressional committee, Masaoka claimed to speak as a "member of the Japanese race" who understood "how the people of Japanese ancestry feel about America and her democratic ways."[95] In doing so, he claimed special insight into the mind of the Japanese people by dint of his Japanese heritage and positioned himself as an unofficial spokesman for Japanese interests in Washington. As a U.S. citizen born in central California and raised in Salt Lake City, he had never been to Japan or any other part of Asia. He had even joked about his inability to speak, read, or write the Japanese language in a wartime appearance before a congressional committee. Yet as white Americans' views of Japan and its people grew more positive after the war, Masaoka was quick to seize on any strategic advantage. As he later recounted about his time in the nation's capital, "I was the first *Nisei* that many of the legislators had ever seen, and I must have been something of a curiosity. But that was all right if being a curiosity helped the cause."[96]

Reports from the time reflected how Masaoka's Japanese heritage indelibly framed his reception on Capitol Hill.[97] Recalling one of his first congressional appearances after the war, ACLU staff member Mary Alice Baldinger recounted how news that a "Jap was making a good impression" had spread through the House offices, attracting a crowd to the congressional gallery until the "room was jammed full." Masaoka's enthusiastic reception so worried Harry Hayden Jr. of the American Legion that he rushed over to request the opportunity for a rebuttal.[98] At other times, the racial overtones were less overt and more paternalistic in nature, such as when a lawmaker called Masaoka a "little fellow" who could "lecture [Congress] on the meaning of democracy" surprisingly well. After seeing Masaoka speak, he began to "see the Japanese Americans for the first time, as people just like anyone else."[99] For at least one Washington observer, then, Masaoka's testimony evoked mixed feelings — it humanized him and other Japanese Americans even as it reinforced the apparent irony and sheer spectacle of a Japanese face preaching about the virtues of democracy to an audience of white American officials. Ellen D. Wu has problematized the JACL's use of a racialized strategy, noting how it rehabilitated Japanese Americans as loyal, patriotic Americans while reproducing their racial otherness by playing on their distinctive "Japanese-ness."[100] Ever the pragmatist, Masaoka was content to play along and leverage his perceived foreignness to the JACL's advantage whenever he could.

The JACL briefly joined a coalition of religious and ethnic groups opposing the McCarran-Walter bills in favor of a more liberal approach to immigration reform. As Maddalena Marinari describes, the opposition's need to present a united front meant that many groups "stopped short of attacking the national origins quota system itself" and instead rallied around broadly shared goals, such as the elimination of racial and gender restrictions in U.S. immigration policy; greater attention to refugee admissions; and more equitable policy and just treatment for eastern and southern European groups. Following in this vein, New York congressmen Emanuel Celler and Herbert Lehman introduced immigration measures proposing to ease, not replace, the oversubscribed quotas of eastern and southern European nations through redistribution.[101] These actions collectively reflected a consensus among opponents of McCarran-Walter that so long as restrictionists controlled the congressional committees in charge of immigration, the wholesale elimination of the national origins quota system was not politically feasible and more moderate reforms should be pursued.

Cooperation among the omnibus bill's critics proved short-lived, however. Marinari attributes fracturing by early 1952 to "political hurdles" and groups' "different positions of power" and "different priorities."[102] In one camp, the majority of Euro-American groups continued to call for a complete rejection of the legislation on principle. Advocates of this more liberal immigration agenda included spokespersons of the American Jewish Committee, the Congress of Industrial Organization (CIO) labor union, and the ACLU, among others. The JACL was in the other, much smaller camp, along with the National Catholic Welfare Council and a few others. This crowd expressed a willingness to work with McCarran and Walter to achieve their short-term goals, even at the cost of making enemies out of friends.[103] The JACL put this willingness to break rank into action during the final months of the campaign. Masaoka's statement at a spring 1952 hearing praising the Asian immigration quotas as an "important step toward strengthening U.S. relations with Asian powers" reportedly took Senator Lehman and other liberal advocates by surprise: coalition partners had generally opposed the race-based Asian quotas as a form of "disguised exclusion."[104] While it bore the brunt of liberals' ire, JACL was not the only Asian American organization to go on record as endorsing the McCarran-Walter bill. The JACL joined with the Los Angeles chapter of the CACA, the Korean National Association, and the Filipino Federation of America to create an umbrella group representing Asian American support for the legislation in May 1952.[105] The Four Nations Organization existed mainly on paper, but the coalition marked the first time members of all four communities collaborated on an immigration-related petition.

Representing more conservative elements within each community, the Four Nations Organization failed to recruit many like-minded members and thus remained a small minority. In general, critics of the McCarran-Walter Act far outnumbered supporters among Japanese and other Asian American communities.[106] The Nisei Progressives, an organization of leftist Japanese Americans numbering in the hundreds nationwide, was among the most outspoken opponents of McCarran-Walter. While it shared the JACL's desire for Issei citizenship and more equitable U.S. immigration quotas, the Progressives did not believe the legislation reflected the spirit of these goals.[107] Leaders of the group denounced the "reactionary" measure and its sponsors as selling "racism in the name of progress," offering Japanese "naturalization and immigration rights in exchange for discriminatory double standards for Negro and Oriental peoples." They also took issue with the bill's national security provisions providing for the deportation of any alien "who at any time after he was admitted to this country has been engaged in a Communist or totalitarian cause." They warned of the likely impact on Issei who were former members of Japanese organizations still on the attorney general's "subversive list."[108] A San Francisco committee claiming to speak for several "prominent Japanese-Americans" in the Bay Area sent telegrams to Congress opposing the omnibus measure and expressing support for the more liberal Lehman bill. Writing on behalf of Japanese Americans living in San Francisco and on the Berkeley campus, three Nisei students called for passage of Lehman's measure as the "better course for our democratic way of life."[109] Such statements exposed the limits of the JACL's claim to speak for other Japanese Americans, much less Asian Americans as a whole. At the same time, Chinese Americans in the New York City–based Fukien Benevolent Association of America and other New England community organizations were also petitioning Truman to veto the legislation, both in writing and in person. As discussed in the next chapter, these fissures would have an impact on relations between Japanese and Chinese American communities that extended well beyond 1952.

Continuing their work from the Judd campaign, African American and Afro-Caribbean groups simultaneously battled passage of the new omnibus bill, which retained the Judd bill's colonial quota intact. Speaking at the McCarran-Walter hearing in 1951, Bishop Reginald Barrow, representing the Brownsville Citizens Committee of 1000, described the bill as an "affront to all citizens of our country, especially the Negro people" and called on the president to veto it on those grounds.[110] Writing to the Truman White House, Felix A. Cummings, president of the British Guiana Development League of America, likewise denounced the quota as "reprehensible," condemning its "total disregard" for the many contributions West Indians had made to the United States.[111] Rep. Walter notably received the lion's share of correspondence from Afro-Caribbean groups, who erroneously saw him as a more sympathetic figure than McCarran. In a private letter to a colleague, Walter dismissed race-based criticisms of the colonial quota as communist "propaganda"; the quotas were about protecting labor and the livelihoods of American workers, he insisted, not race.[112]

The legislative battle reached a fever pitch in the spring of 1952. With the omnibus bill's successful passage through the House and then the Senate, the onus shifted to President Truman to block the legislation using a presidential veto. Reversing his previous opposition to black immigration from the

Caribbean, African American labor leader A. Philip Randolph of the Brotherhood of Sleeping Car Porters sent Truman a lengthy letter decrying the legislation's "sinister quota device" for imprinting a "stigma of inferiority based upon race and color to Negro peoples of African descent everywhere." Invoking the strength of black internationalist solidarities, he warned that enactment of the colonial quota would certainly "arouse and provoke resentment among Negroes throughout the United States, the West Indies and Africa." Finally, he likened the legislation to apartheid policies in South Africa that "decent, liberty-loving people" had "universally condemned."[113] The NAACP's Walter White requested a meeting to convey a similar message in person, but the White House denied the request, citing scheduling issues.

Even as the opposition sharpened, the JACL stayed the course, launching an eleventh-hour defense of the McCarran-Walter bills. In an April 1952 *New York Times* letter to the editor, Masaoka doubled down on the league's position. Despite its clear shortcomings, he wrote, the bill's "Asia-Pacific Triangle" formula represented a "long step forward . . . from absolute exclusion"; to "scrap improvements on the grounds of their not being ideal would frustrate the achievement of any gains whatsoever."[114] In other words, he contended, an imperfect or flawed bill was preferable to none at all. The league maintained this position two months later, when Truman's veto of the legislation forced a showdown in the Senate. JACL leaders were so confident of an ultimate victory that Masaoka preemptively wrote the White House requesting five commemorative pens from Truman's signing of the bill into law as keepsakes to distribute at the JACL's upcoming annual convention.[115]

Much to the JACL's chagrin, Truman vetoed the McCarran-Walter bill in a June 1952 message addressed to a transpacific audience of U.S. "residents of Japanese ancestry" and "friends throughout the Far East."[116] It was a remarkable statement. Expressing his desire that they understand "clearly" why he had chosen to veto a bill that promised to end Asians' decades-long exclusion from U.S. immigration and citizenship eligibility, the president explained that he could not in good conscience "strike down the bars that prejudice has erected against them" because in doing so he would also be "establishing new discriminations against the peoples of Asia and approving harsh and repressive measures directed at all who seek a new life within our boundaries." Truman concluded by expressing his belief that with a "little more time and a little more discussion," Congress would arrive at an immigration and naturalization policy "fair to all."[117] But Masaoka and the JACL were unwilling to wait. Upon returning to Capitol Hill, the JACL's Masaoka claimed to have personally persuaded nine liberal congressmen to absent themselves from the vote, thereby ensuring the bill's passage. On June 25, 1952, he was with his mother and another colleague in the congressional gallery when the Senate voted to override the White House veto by a margin of five votes. His mother was "jubilant" and Masaoka recounted "brushing back tears of happiness" at news that the McCarran–Walter bill had passed.[118]

The JACL would soon be called to account for its part in the legislation's success.[119] University of Chicago professor S. I. Hayakawa issued some of the harshest indictments in the *Chicago Shimpo*, the city's local Japanese American newspaper. A one-time donor to the league's Issei citizenship campaigns, Hayakawa declared that he would never contribute to the league again, having watched it "purchase the removal of one small discrimination at the cost of legalizing the continuance of many other forms." The 1952 law had changed the "meaning of naturalization" itself, he wrote, as provisions allowing for denaturalization ensured that the "naturalized citizen" would be a "second-class" one.[120] Asked to defend the league's controversial position at the President's Commission on Immigration hearings that fall, associate director of the JACL's Anti-Discrimination Committee Richard Akagi explained that the goal of Issei naturalization had been too urgent for the league to wait for a less controversial bill.[121] While "young people" might have had the choice to "stand on principle for another 10 to 15 years," aging first-generation immigrants "in the twilight of their lives" did not have that option. If the JACL had waited another "5 to 6 years," the fight would have become "meaningless" for those who stood to benefit most. In short, Akagi concluded, the ends justified the means, even if that meant the Issei's gain came at another community's loss and as part of a flawed legislative package.[122]

AS ADVERTISED BY its supporters, the 1952 McCarran–Walter Act ended Asian exclusion as a feature of U.S. immigration and naturalization law in the most symbolic manner possible. In this regard, its passage was a fitting complement to U.S. policies in Japan, where the SCAP Occupation led first by U.S. General Douglas MacArthur and later by General Matthew Ridgway ended that same year. Widely hailed in Washington as a success, over a period of seven years, the occupation government reconstructed a defeated Japanese enemy into what scholars have variously called a "subordinate Cold War partner," a "surrogate of U.S. power," and a "client state in all but name."[123] In addition to the San Francisco Treaty formally ending the occupation, the United States and Japan signed a Mutual Security Treaty whose terms were anything but mutual in practice. Together with Article Nine of the Japanese Constitution written by SCAP Occupation governors, the treaty effectively subordinated Japan to the United States in military matters and gave Washington free rein to uphold its strategic interests in the region without the threat of outside interference. Under its patently unequal terms, the United States maintained the right to station troops and operate military bases in Japan. Japanese critics protested that the treaty made a mockery of Japan's independence and sovereignty, but they also recognized that Tokyo had little choice but to approve it if they wanted the occupation to end. The persistence of U.S. military bases in Japan, more so than lingering discriminations in U.S. immigration and naturalization law, would focus anti-American ire in Japan in the decades that followed.[124]

The effects of the McCarran-Walter Act (1952) were the mixed bag that many had predicted. Reflecting the symbolic nature of Asians' admission to the national origins quota system, most Japanese who entered the United States after 1952 actually came in nonquota categories, including as military brides, adoptees, and students; the majority were women.[125] In addition to cutting black immigration from the Caribbean drastically, the law began crystallizing an immigration lobby among African and Afro-Caribbean Americans.[126] Black activists first mobilized in the Judd and McCarran-Walter campaigns remained active in the immigration arena as protests over civil rights legislation and desegregation efforts became front-page news.

By most accounts, the JACL got what it wanted. Its support for the McCarran-Walter Act helped the league grow its membership and financial base while cementing the organization's relationships with the law's powerful cosponsors, Patrick McCarran and Francis Walter; their patronage would prove valuable in future campaigns. Buoyed by JACL-sponsored citizenship drives, more than 60,000 Japanese issei naturalized between 1952 and 1965; now that they qualified as citizens, many joined the JACL, out of gratitude for the rights it secured on their behalf. It was on all these grounds that JACL historian Bill Hosokawa would later declare the 1952 act the league's "greatest legislative triumph."[127]

Within a few short years, however, the JACL would join the chorus of organizations calling for comprehensive reforms to the immigration system. This aligned the league with many of the same liberal groups that had condemned it for supporting the legislation in the first place. The challenges the JACL faced in the 1950s and early 1960s were different, as ethnic whites with roots in southern and eastern Europe came to dominate congressional immigration debates, and U.S. policymakers diverted their attention away from East Asia after a cease-fire in Korea restored a modicum of stability to the region. As U.S. goals in an Asia increasingly divided between communist and anticommunist blocs continued to shift and change, Chinese and Japanese American advocates and their allies would have to devise new ways to wield influence in their post-1952 fight to make repeal meaningful.

CHAPTER FIVE

Making Repeal Meaningful

*Asian Immigration Campaigns
during the Civil Rights Era*

On January 1, 1953, President Truman's Commission on Immigration and Naturalization issued its final report outlining a sweeping agenda for the liberal reform of U.S. immigration policy. Drawing on hearings in eleven cities nationwide and over 600 letters received from a broad public, *Whom Shall We Welcome* enumerated the many weaknesses of the national origins quota system as a primary basis for U.S. immigration policy, citing the "economic," "humanitarian," and "foreign policy" problems they caused. The document focused on European immigration; with regard to the entry of Asians, it had more to say about past progress than the possibility of—let alone a need for—future changes. Affirming the foreign policy logic that had underwritten previous repeal measures to date, the commission concluded that they had accomplished the intended goal by stanching foreign criticism of America's immigration and naturalization policies. It hailed the piecemeal acts repealing exclusions for Chinese (1943), Indians (1946), and now Japanese in the form of the 1952 McCarran-Walter Act as welcome proof of a "growing American realization that immigration policy can be a positive as well as a negative factor in foreign policy." But the task was not complete, commission members argued. Washington should continue to pursue equitable immigration as a moral obligation in keeping with its "position of leadership among the nations of the free world."[1] The commission's moral appeal suggested just how much some Americans' estimation of the United States' international status had risen from just a few years earlier, when Truman's Committee on Civil Rights warned that the country was "not so strong" that it could afford to ignore foreign powers; whether from a position of weakness or strength, however, the new logic pointed in the same, liberalizing direction.[2]

Whom Shall We Welcome would help guide and inspire critics calling for revisions to the McCarran-Walter Act for the next thirteen years. The report's blinkered attention to European immigration reflected just how quickly the urgency that had been driving U.S. immigration reform toward Asia dissipated after 1952. Certainly, the commissioners wrote, the United

States should address the continuing racial basis and the small size of the immigration quotas the 1952 law gave to Asia. But because postwar problems in Asia were "predominantly internal" and inseparable from the region's long history of overpopulation, they contended, Washington would do best to encourage economic development through foreign aid rather than reform its migration policies to help address Asia's challenges.[3] U.S. migration measures promised to be more effective in mitigating crises in Europe and thus Washington should return to its traditional focus on that continent. While its recommendations would remain more aspirational than real in terms of policy impact, the report's shift away from Asia reflected a broader turn in the official immigration debates that steadily depleted the power of arguments based on U.S. imperial interests and more immediate questions of migration diplomacy. Because foreign policy had historically dominated discussions of Asian immigration, the priority placed on domestic, partisan concerns on Capitol Hill undermined calls for changes to Asian immigration policy perhaps most severely.

This chapter explores how Asian American advocates negotiated the growing marginalization of Asians and Asia within the immigration debates between 1952 and 1965. If the McCarran-Walter campaign marked a peak in Asian Americans' influence amid unprecedented U.S. intervention in East Asia, the revision efforts that followed relegated Asians, and by extension Asian American lobbyists, to the periphery of the national conversation while calls to reform the national origins quota system's discriminations against southern and eastern Europeans took center stage. For decades, white ethnic voters in the United States had organized against the deeply biased system, which greatly favored northern and western European countries with large annual quotas while reserving only a pittance for countries such as Italy and Russia without Anglo-Saxon roots. By adopting immigration reform as a way to win white ethnic voters—that is, those of eastern and southern European descent—Republicans and Democrats alike sidelined internationalist arguments. They promoted instead an understanding of the national origins quotas as a proxy for the political status of Euro-Americans in the United States. Further undercutting the strength of a reform strategy rooted in U.S. imperatives abroad, the United States' changing Cold War in Asia created a more diffuse threat that many lawmakers doubted broad alterations in U.S. immigration policy could remedy. Over the decade following the Magnuson Act, various laws allowed for more women to enter the United States outside of restrictive quotas. Many were war brides. This small, if steadily growing, stream of Asian immigrants did little immediately to increase Asian Americans' electoral power relative to that of ethnic whites, but they did enable the growth of the U.S.-born Asian population in the decades to come.

Given their lack of electoral power and decentralized advocacy, it is not surprising, that Asian Americans' role in shaping immigration policy after 1952 was uneven. Yet their activism suggests how there were many ways to influence outcomes. The following discussion traces Asian American advocacy in three important efforts between 1952 and 1965. First, it considers the role that Chinese and Japanese Americans, in partnership with white allies, played in securing nonquota slots for a few thousand anticommunist Chinese and Japanese to enter the United States as refugees in the 1950s. Refugee admissions was the one arena of immigration policy where U.S. Asia policy remained formative,[4] and where white lawmakers and Asian American advocates actively continued to work together, even as long-time stalwarts such as Judd distanced themselves from the general immigration debates over quota reform. As white allies receded into the background or retired, lobbyists representing Chinese and Japanese American organizations looked for new strategies to wield influence.[5] The second part of the chapter examines their experimentation with interethnic solidarities in the 1955 campaigns renewing calls for quota reform. Through this departure from the largely single-group focus of earlier efforts, they sought to activate the pan-Asian racial category of "Asiatic" codified in the 1917 and 1924 Immigration Acts as a lobbying tool. Significant barriers continued to impede meaningful cooperation between groups, but at least in a rhetorical sense the post-1952 campaigns brought the story of exclusion and its repeal full circle, as advocates sought to deploy the racial categories the exclusion laws had themselves created as instruments of inclusion and equality.[6]

The final section assesses the significance of Hawaii's 1959 admission as the nation's fiftieth state in shaping the campaigns culminating in the 1965 Hart-Celler Act. Much as they had done when the United States granted Philippine independence in 1946, observers and politicians in 1959 widely hailed Congress's decision as evidence of the United States' racial inclusivity. Statehood proponents argued that Hawaii's greatest value was as an ideological and symbolic boon to the United States' fight to win Asian hearts and minds as decolonization continued and the Cold War intensified; in this view, Congress's legal embrace of the islands' majority Asian population was proof of the United States' capacity to not only tolerate but actually incorporate peoples of all races as political equals.[7] Challenging this rosy picture, scholars of empire and settler colonialism have recast statehood as Washington's rejection of Native Hawaiian demands for sovereignty, and as such an example of the failure—not the success—of decolonization and self-determination movements in the Pacific.[8] Framed in this light, it is perhaps fitting that Hawaiian statehood featured so prominently in the true end of Asian exclusion given the deep ambivalence that characterized both.

The election of the first U.S. congresspersons of Chinese and Japanese descent from the newly admitted state of Hawaii institutionalized Asian Americans' political voice in Washington and formed the main connection between Hawaiian statehood and the 1965 Hart-Celler Act. Having representatives on Capitol Hill gave Asian American advocates greater access in the congressional immigration debates even after infighting between lawmakers, rather than external pressures, became the most important factors shaping the final terms of the legislation. This was particularly important in the Senate, where the addition of two senators from a new state could make an appreciable difference in determining legislative outcomes. But the introduction of a majority Asian American delegation to Congress as part of Hawaii's political incorporation via statehood did not fulfill the racial promise many had predicted; in the case of the 1965 Act, it actually occasioned the exclusion of other groups. The liberal narrative surrounding statehood thus not only gave cover for the broken promises of self-determination in the Pacific; by connecting a liberal narrative of statehood to a liberal narrative of immigration reform, it also served to cloak the persistence of racism shaping U.S. immigration policy in facially nonracial terms.

The chapter ends with the passage of the 1965 Hart-Celler Act. Historians often group the Hart-Celler law with the 1964 Civil Rights Act and the 1965 Voting Rights Act as a "sibling" or even a third touchstone of the 1960s civil rights movement.[9] Such a characterization makes sense on several grounds. All three laws ostensibly sought to enshrine the principle of racial nondiscrimination within the law. Like Presidents Truman and even Eisenhower before them, John F. Kennedy, Lyndon B. Johnson, and their administration officials regularly framed civil rights and immigration reform as part of a common imperative to promote racial equality and civil rights at home and to safeguard the United States' democratic image abroad.[10] Even the timing supports this view. President Kennedy sent early drafts of both the Hart-Celler Act and the 1964 Civil Rights Act to Capitol Hill shortly before he was assassinated, and Johnson shepherded them both through Congress after his death. In terms of passage, the 1965 immigration law was sandwiched between the two major civil rights milestones of this period. Differences in the forces creating change at the time are equally revealing. The movement supporting the Civil Rights Act and the Voting Rights Act was bottom-up and protest-driven. By contrast immigration reform had become a largely internal conversation among U.S. lawmakers and officials themselves. Lawmakers passed the Civil Rights Act and the Voting Rights Act fully anticipating that they would alter conditions on the ground. They had no such expectations for immigration reform. The Hart-Celler Act was only supposed to tweak immigration to make it more receptive to U.S. labor needs, not change American society. Alterations to the racial demographics of the immigrant stream were an aftereffect, not part of the original intent. Yet placing it on equal footing with the Voting Rights Act and the Civil Rights Act rightly recognizes that these three laws transformed the complexion of the nation.

Whom Shall We Welcome?

After 1952, white ethnic reformers and their allies took center stage in organized campaigns to revise the McCarran-Walter Act. The backlash to the law was immediate and substantial, with critics sending a record number of protests and petitions for change. Japanese and Chinese Americans, including former supporters such as the JACL's Masaoka, were among them. But the greater share were white ethnic activists, or those with heritage tracing from the countries of eastern and southern Europe. From its inception in the 1920s, the quota system had disadvantaged these countries relative to those of northern and western Europe on the grounds that they had less to contribute to America's Anglo-Saxon traditions. Congress' postwar revisiting of the quota system had galvanized community groups, and many were still working for change by the 1950s in spite of many disappointments.[11]

Due to the quick work of Truman and other Democratic leaders, momentum to revise the law was strong. McCarran-Walter was enacted in late June. By the 1952 presidential election that November, national party leaders increasingly embraced immigration reform as an electoral strategy to win white ethnic voters, who were seen as important to winning critical swing districts in the Northeast and Midwest. Much of this was Truman's doing. Although he was not his party's nominee for president, he nonetheless took an active role, stumping across the country with speeches denouncing Republican support for the McCarran-Walter Act and its retention of national origins quotas as evidence of the party's isolationism, nativism, and general "moral blindness." Such qualities, he claimed, made Republican presidential candidate Dwight Eisenhower unfit to lead. According to political scientist Daniel Tichenor, these accusations effectively "goaded" the candidate and other Republicans to denounce the quota system.[12] By the time he won the election in November, Eisenhower had publicly pledged his support for an immigration policy consistent with both the United States' international obligations and its immigrant past. Through Truman's advocacy, the 1952 presidential campaigns thus made reform of the national origins quotas for Europeans a bipartisan commitment.

Meanwhile, white ethnic liberals rallied their coethnics to fight for changes to the national origins quotas. In a representative appeal published right after the McCarran-Walter bill passed in 1952, Harvard historian Oscar Handlin argued that the small quotas stigmatized southern and eastern Europeans. Now it was up to the descendants of the "millions of Poles and Italians and Jews," and the Greeks, Armenians, Magyars, and Slovaks who made up the "'riff-raff' of 1910"—a group that would have included his own Jewish parents—to press Congress for change as a matter of their own civil rights. As the "majority" of American voters, Handlin asserted, members of the ethnic white "minority groups" could shape the future of U.S. immigration policy. Nonwhite Americans, such as the "children of Japanese and Mexican immigrants," could also be good allies, but only ethnic whites could use their clout as part of the New Deal Coalition to persuade Congress to enact a "policy more in keeping with [the American] national character and aspirations."[13] The notion that the size of the immigration quotas was a proxy for political standing in the United States was not entirely new.[14] But it gained traction during this period. By pushing this notion, Handlin's writings, like those of many white liberals, marginalized Asian Americans in the revision campaigns; their advocacy was welcome, but it always remained secondary.

Changing conditions on the continent further sidelined Asian American advocates. The Asia-centered arguments that had been persuasive in the late 1940s and early 1950s had less power in response to different dangers and priorities, as the U.S. Cold War took new forms. The end of the SCAP Occupation of Japan in April 1952, the death of Soviet leader Joseph Stalin six months later, and a cease-fire in Korea in July 1953 restored a semblance of stability and gave U.S. lawmakers a sense of attenuated threat in East Asia. Increasingly, Washington officials turned their attention to Southeast Asia as the next major site for U.S. projects to contain communism; among these were the 1954 creation of the Southeast Asian Treaty Organization (SEATO), a mutual defense organization committed to stopping the spread of communism in the region, and the installation of anticommunist Ngo Dinh Diem as the leader of a South Vietnamese client state the following year.

Washington's pivot toward Southeast Asia also blunted the power of internationalist arguments in campaigns for the liberalization of immigration law, highlighting the different relationship of the region's peoples to U.S. histories of exclusion and to transpacific migration diplomacy in general. The United States historically played a very limited role in the region, and the Philippines was the only Southeast Asian country with a significant migration history to the United States. One consequence was that many Southeast Asians did not chafe at America's record of race-based exclusion with the same vitriol as the Chinese and Japanese. By extension, U.S. lawmakers saw liberalizing immigration policy towards them as less likely to confer diplomatic advantage. As France, Britain, and the Netherlands struggled to maintain their colonies in the region, Washington scrambled to prevent the spread of communism while retaining its reputation for supporting self-determination amid the instability that followed World War II. In a frantic effort to prevent the Vietnamese people from achieving independence under a communist regime, the United States supported France in the First Indochina War (1946–54). This choice complicated American efforts to distinguish itself from European imperial powers. Immigration policies seemed inadequate to counter such suspicions. In their stead, Washington instituted a combination of force and diplomacy to combat the United States' spiraling image problem in the region.

From Beyond the Bamboo Curtain:
The Fight for Asian Refugees

Diasporic Chinese living in Southeast Asia were a major source of U.S. concern about the spread of communism in the region. Members of Truman's Immigration Commission referenced these communities when they warned in 1953 that Chinese Communists would "exploit the antiforeignism latent in most of Southeastern Asia for decades" to undermine the United States' international image.[15] These "Overseas Chinese" living across East, South, and Southeast Asia became increasingly visible during the 1950s, as the governments of the United States and the anticommunist ROC vied against the communist PRC for their loyalties and, in the case of the two Chinas, their remittance dollars. As leaders hostile to Washington took charge of a nonaligned India and a communist North Vietnam, U.S. officials increasingly turned to these eleven million members of the Chinese diaspora as a key to preventing the entire region from falling to communism in a domino effect. In this context, the admission of Chinese refugees became one way the United States sought to counteract the PRC's appeal to Overseas Chinese.

Proposals to admit Chinese refugees again centered Asia in the U.S. immigration debates, but even this time advocates battled to overcome the dominance of Europe. In the words of Carl Bon Tempo, "refugee" continued to mean "anticommunist European" in the minds of Eisenhower and most members of Congress.[16] Indeed, the sentiment was global. Among the millions of Chinese displaced by the 1949 Chinese Communist Revolution, Hong Kong experienced one of the world's most severe population crises as Chinese fleeing the mainland nearly tripled the population of the small British colony. But international organizations such as the United Nations (UN) sought migration-related solutions to treat the situation in Europe first.[17] By the late 1940s, UN officials had declared the displaced population in Europe a humanitarian crisis and appealed to the international community to relieve these pressures by accepting refugees. They took a different approach to the situation in Asia, which they characterized as the result of a longer-term epidemic of overpopulation only exacerbated by recent events. Based on this understanding, they concluded that the European crisis might respond to migration measures, but in Asia, the situation called for economic development more than it did the willingness of other countries to receive Asian migrants.[18]

In focus as well as in impact, refugee admissions during the 1950s maintained a disproportionate emphasis on Europe. Among the 214,000 refugees admitted to the United States under the 1953 Refugee Relief Act (RRA), only a few thousand came from Asia; the overwhelming majority hailed from Italy, Greece, and other countries beyond the Iron Curtain. The 35,000 Hungarians who entered the United States under presidential parole authority after the 1956 Hungarian Revolution and the 1957 Refugee-Escapee Act reflected more of the same.[19] Within the minority of refugee admissions who were from Asia, Chinese refugees dominated, reflecting Washington's hope that their admission would aid in the containment of Communist China, which lawmakers saw as the main threat to the expansion of U.S. power in Asia after 1952. By then, a growing number of U.S. officials had begun accepting that the People's Republic of China (PRC) was here to stay. Rather than awaiting its downfall, they began devising ways to contain the new regime's influence, particularly among the Overseas Chinese in Southeast Asia. The governments of both the ROC and PRC sought the political and financial support of these communities during the Cold War. Scholars have described how Washington partnered with the ROC government in using migration policy to isolate the PRC, in part by discouraging Overseas Chinese from supporting its regime financially or otherwise.[20]

As in previous efforts, campaigns for the U.S. admission of Chinese refugees featured a mix of white and Asian advocates. Among the small handful of activists, Walter Judd, Minnesota congressman and veteran of the repeal movement, and Chinese American Ernest Moy were the most instrumental. As a longtime anticommunist with personal ties to Chiang Kai-shek even before the Cold War, Judd was one of Congress's most zealous anticommunist critics of Mao Zedong and an important figure in the pro-ROC Nationalist China Lobby.[21] Speaking at a 1953 congressional committee hearing, Judd called for the admission of Chinese refugees as a way to "contain the influence of the Kremlin" among Overseas Chinese "scattered across Malaya, Siam, the Philippine Islands, Indochina, Indonesia, Burma, and India as well as Hong Kong." He cautioned that U.S. policymakers were privileging Europe to America's detriment: leaving Asians and Arabs who "constitute half of the population of the world" out of the refugee act was downright dangerous, creating ready fodder for Soviet and other communist propagandists seeking to persuade the "enslaved and threatened peoples of Asia" that the "imperialist" Western powers were "abandoning" them because they did not "care about anything except for white people." Following this logic, he noted wryly, Asians and other nonwhite peoples might simply conclude that since "you cannot get into the western club . . . why not join [the] one that Joe Stalin [is] the head of?"[22] Just as he had assured his colleagues during the McCarran-Walter debates that a nominal quota would convince Asians that the United States was racially inclusive, he argued that admitting a small number of Chinese refugees was sufficient to send the message Washington wished to convey. To this end, he became a major supporter of the organization Ernest Moy founded in 1952, Aid to Refugee Chinese Intellectuals (ARCI).

Ernest Moy was a U.S. citizen of Chinese descent active in the New York City Chinese American community during World War II; he later developed close ties with the ROC government in ways that blurred the lines between ethnic and diasporic activism. Having witnessed firsthand the dire state of the Hong Kong refugee crisis, he sought to enlist Washington's help in ameliorating it. By the early 1950s, he worked less on behalf of local causes and primarily in service to the ROC government, exemplifying what Charlotte Brooks has described as the growing entanglement of New York City's Chinese American leaders with China politics.[23] Judd's partnership with Moy in

ARCI established the group's credibility in the eyes of U.S. officials.[24] For the next few years, ARCI worked to identify and resettle Chinese anticommunist intellectuals in the United States. While ostensibly a nongovernmental organization, it received more than 90 percent of its funding from the U.S. State Department and only admitted Chinese individuals with known anticommunist loyalties whom Washington deemed useful for American propaganda purposes. As such, scholars have concluded, ARCI largely operated as an arm of the U.S. state until the early 1960s, when U.S. officials redirected their financial support to other parts of the world and it went defunct.[25] While Moy's efforts to rally Chinese Americans to the refugee cause had only limited success, through his work on ARCI Moy played an important intermediary role.

Relative to advocates of Chinese refugee admissions, those seeking dedicated slots for Japanese had far less leverage available to them.[26] Six million returnees relocating from Japan's former colonies in the years after World War II created an overpopulation crisis in the islands; exacerbating matters, natural disasters such as the North Kyushu flood of 1953 left hundreds of thousands of Japanese homeless and seeking help. Comparing the effort to secure admission for Japanese alongside the Chinese case underscores just how unreliable and dynamic internationalist and imperial strategies could be. The United States, most officials in the Eisenhower administration believed, no longer needed to woo Japan or its people, having thoroughly secured its former wartime enemy as a subordinate Cold War partner and long-term host of U.S. military bases after 1952. The Korean War had marked the height of Japan's military significance to the United States as the islands became the center of U.S. military operations in the conflict. But with the end of the U.S. SCAP Occupation in 1952 and the cease-fire in Korea one year later, Washington officials, following the lead of the Eisenhower administration, were largely content to disregard Japan.[27] The United States' relationship with Tokyo showed growing signs of strain, but that was insufficient to pressure U.S. lawmakers to admit Japanese refugees.[28] The Chinese had Walter Judd and Ernest Moy, but Japan had no such similar spokesman with strong government ties; whatever informal Japan lobby had existed in Washington, DC, during the SCAP years had already disbanded.[29]

Into the void of leadership stepped the JACL's Mike Masaoka. The league's Washington spokesman was fresh off a series of victory tours in the wake of the McCarran-Walter Act. With the approval of the JACL's national board, he had even traveled to Japan as a guest of Tokyo—his first trip to

Asia—where, according to league reports, officials feted him as Washington's "most effective Japanese."[30] Upon his return to the United States, Masaoka drew on his time in Asia to petition for dedicated refugee slots for Japan; he described scenes of chaos and overcrowding that demanded international attention. Over the ensuing months, he skillfully leveraged the public profile he had built among lawmakers during the McCarran-Walter campaigns, as well as the personal relationships he and the JACL had cultivated with the 1952 law's cosponsors via the decision to endorse their controversial legislation. In the absence of Moy, who tended to work behind the scenes, Masaoka was the only person of Asian descent to speak at the 1953 congressional hearings on refugee admissions. When asked to explain who was a refugee, Masaoka offered a highly capacious definition very different from specific focus of the Chinese campaign on anticommunist elites with symbolic value to the U.S. Cold War.[31] While Judd and others focused on the plight of Chinese stranded in Hong Kong and across Southeast Asia, Masaoka was the lone witness among dozens to draw attention to the "thousands of American-educated Chinese and Koreans" still living in the United States and unable to return to Asia "because alien ideologies ha[d] taken over their respective countries."[32] He was also alone in citing the predicament of approximately three million South Koreans fleeing or displaced by "Soviet domination" stemming from the Korean War, and even prisoners of war from the communist camp refusing repatriation to the PRC and North Korea.[33]

In another striking reference, Masaoka was the only person to call on Congress to resolve the status of 1,800 Japanese Peruvians stranded in the United States since being forcibly relocated and incarcerated during World War II as part of a hemispheric roundup of persons of Japanese descent.[34] Denied the right to return to Peru, this remainder had somehow evaded deportation to Japan and stayed in the United States after the war, where they won a suspension of deportation, and in some cases, the opportunity to become legal resident aliens through a 1949 executive order.[35] Masaoka and the JACL were arguably more concerned that the legal adjustments would count against Japan's future immigration quotas and reduce the number of slots available to new applicants than they were with the plight of the Japanese Peruvians themselves. But no matter the motive, Masaoka strategically played on lawmakers' remorse over Japanese wartime incarceration to push for a resolution of their status.[36]

JACL leaders would ultimately succeed in their bid to win slots for Japanese refugees in an episode of creative policymaking that was at once a testament to Masaoka's savvy in the practice of political patronage and more proof that U.S. policymakers considered China a greater priority than Japan at this stage of the Cold War. Over the 1950s, several thousand Japanese entered the United States as refugees, but the mechanism was often indirect. The 1953 RRA was a case in point. At Masaoka's request, Francis Walter, the JACL's congressional ally, used his position as chair of the House Judiciary Committee to add a provision admitting "2,000 Japanese" to the House version of the bill. When the Senate committee deleted this allowance, Patrick McCarran personally assured Masaoka that the implementation of the law would include refugees from Japan. McCarran passed away one year later, but true to his word, the at-large visas allotted under the RRA's Cold War containment imperative were used to bring more than a thousand Japanese farmers to the United States as part of the Japanese Agricultural Workers Program (JAWP) between 1956 and 1965.[37]

JAWP exemplifies how the JACL's ties in California, where most growers were located, shaped Japanese refugee admissions in practice. Acting in a novel role as a liaison between the Japanese and U.S. governments, the JACL worked to uphold a positive narrative of JAWP as a valuable diplomatic bridge during the Cold War.[38] Speaking before a congressional committee in 1957, the league's Masaoka argued that participation in the JAWP would foster goodwill for the United States among the Japanese farmers who made up the "heart and soul of the Japanese nation" and thus serve the United States' "major national interest" in containing Soviet communism.[39] Masaoka even defended the program from reports of exploitation, reassuring lawmakers that he would never sanction a program that harmed his "fellow Japanese."[40]

It was no coincidence that the question had been raised, as accusations of exploitation—as well as rising undocumented migration and declining wages in the Southwest—were already imperiling the Mexican guest-worker program, which brought five million Mexicans to the United States as braceros, or temporary contract laborers, between 1942 and 1964. Indeed, U.S. growers, in consultation with the Japanese Embassy, had proposed the idea partly in response to declining support for the Bracero Program, which liberal activists and organized labor were already pressuring Congress not to reauthorize. The conversation reached a low point in the mid-1950s, when the Eisenhower administration deported 3.7 million undocumented Mexicans in a joint law enforcement initiative called "Operation Wetback."[41] The Bracero Program would continue through the early 1960s, but the threat of its discontinuation caused anxious U.S. growers to explore the use of Japanese, Filipina/os, and other international workers as less controversial sources of foreign labor. Given the temporary design of the program, most JAWP participants eventually returned to Japan, and their numbers came nowhere close to the number of refugees from similarly sized European countries who entered the United States during the same period. Yet, as Masaoka himself emphasized more than once, the size of the group was significant when considered in context; a few thousand total JAWP beneficiaries over roughly a decade was "the equivalent of more than sixteen years of quota immigration" from Japan under the 1952 McCarran-Walter Act.[42]

The admission of Asian refugees epitomized how small numbers could nonetheless advance the narratives Washington wished to convey. As Cold War symbols, Chinese and Japanese refugees became part of a global story of anticommunism that Washington wanted to disseminate about the world's many peoples who rejected communism by leaving their homelands. At the same time, differences between the Chinese and Japanese cases—evident even in relation to such small numbers—show how U.S. lawmakers continued to draw sharp lines between Asian peoples based on Washington's ever-shifting hierarchy of priorities in the region.

Lobbying from the Margins

While the passage of refugee legislation helped subdue calls for a complete immigration overhaul, they did not fully mollify advocates calling for revision, and even elimination, of the national origins quota system that the McCarran-Walter Act had upheld in 1952. Three years later, liberal Democratic senators Hubert Humphrey of Minnesota and Herbert Lehman of New York, in the last term before his retirement, successfully pushed for a congressional hearing on their newly reintroduced comprehensive immigration reform bills.[43] A confluence of factors made the timing opportune. Key among these were Senator Patrick McCarran's death in 1954 and organized labor's decision to embrace liberal immigration reform, both of which strengthened a growing consensus in favor of revision.[44] As a modified version of the legislation first offered as alternatives to McCarran-Walter in 1952, the Humphrey-Lehman bill provided for larger Asian immigration quotas and included a mechanism for pooling and redistributing unused quota slots to benefit immigrants from southern and eastern Europe. Given that it proposed to rework rather than replace the national origins quota system, the bill was far from the most radical proposal before the

Senate.[45] But its moderate provisions enabled it to capture bipartisan support at a time when both Democrats and Republicans were honing their use of immigration reform as a strategy to win white ethnic voters in the 1956 presidential and congressional elections.[46]

White ethnic reformers and their allies dominated the roster of the 1955 hearing before a Senate immigration subcommittee, but the JACL's Masaoka and six Chinese American witnesses representing far-flung communities kept Asian immigration part of the official conversation. Their testimony collectively registered the persistence of inequality in the law's treatment of Asians and Europeans even after the 1952 McCarran-Walter Act formally repealed Asian exclusion. The main grievance concerned the race-based quotas the 1952 act's Asia Pacific Triangle had granted to Asians. That quotas operated on the basis of nationality for Europeans but race for Asians demonstrated their discriminatory intent, witnesses argued. Formal repeal would not address the wrong; citing their rights as American citizens, they demanded more meaningful change.

Chinese Americans increasingly used the language of citizenship in this period, much as the JACL had been doing since its creation. The U.S. State Department's scrutiny of Chinese seeking to enter the United States under special exempt classes and family reunification allowances had increased dramatically after the 1949 Chinese Communist Revolution, resulting in the exclusion of millions of Chinese displaced by the conflict. Quota and nonquota immigrants faced far greater documentation requirements. The result was a labyrinthine process that virtually closed consular action as a viable pathway, even as Chinese flooded the U.S. Embassy in Hong Kong with requests to immigrate to America. Many Chinese Americans complained that a few thousand refugee slots for Chinese refugees were scarcely adequate to ameliorate the problem. Witnesses at the hearing took special issue with the absolute power and rampant abuses of U.S. consular officials in Hong Kong, whose arbitrary decisions separated families and, after changes in the law, could not be appealed.[47] The McCarran-Walter Act had ended the specific practice of *diaozhi*, by which migrants could move their cases from the Hong Kong consulate to U.S. courts and remain in the United States during the review of their cases. Closing the loophole allowing for judicial review of immigration cases left hundreds of applicants stranded in Hong Kong with little recourse and few options.[48]

Statements by the six Chinese American witnesses reflected clear differences between East and West Coast Chinese communities and their reaction to the crisis. West Coast organizations tended to emphasize their American identity and to be more circumspect so as to maintain their close ties with U.S. elected officials, as exemplified by the California-based CACA. Grand Lodge president Y. C. Hong, a veteran of the Chinese wives campaigns, treaded lightly in his critiques of U.S. policy. Emphasizing that CACA only admitted citizens, he claimed to speak based on the right of the group's members to "receive equal privilege and equal treatment" under the law. If witnesses of southern and eastern European descent could demand reform by invoking their own civil rights as Americans, he suggested, Chinese American citizens should be able to do the same. George Y. Chinn of the San Francisco Six Companies (the local chapter of the Chinese Consolidated Benevolent Association, or CCBA) was more blunt, stating frankly his view that the 1952 law's "bad features outweigh the good."[49] Even so, he reaffirmed his anticommunism and positioned himself squarely within the Cold War consensus.[50] East Coast Chinese Americans had fewer ties to U.S. electoral politics and could therefore operate more freely due to their outsider position; they were also more entangled in Chinese politics. It was not surprising that the CCBA's representative from Boston, Dr. Stanley Chin, was the only speaker to address the deportation threat facing scores of Chinese Americans suspected of harboring procommunist sympathies or having ties with the PRC government. He claimed to speak for the "entire Chinese population of the New England states" when he insisted that they were actually "anti-Communist" and would be likely to suffer "imprisonment, death or persecution" if deported.[51] It was an argument representatives of the CACA as well as the JACL knew better than to make, since defending those suspected of having communist ties could easily bring one's own loyalties under scrutiny in the prevailing climate.[52]

Masaoka was the hearing's lone Japanese American. Unlike Chinese American witnesses' focus on administrative reforms, he singled out for critique the Eisenhower administration's disregard for Asia. The Humphrey-Lehman bill's overwhelming focus on European immigration pointed to a major failing in U.S. diplomacy, he argued.[53] Americans were "overlooking the Orient" and its peoples at their own peril. Since "three-fifths of the world population" lived in Asia, it behooved the United States to give "due consideration and fair treatment" to its peoples, out of its own self-interest, if not for the sake of justice.[54] This sentiment was not original: Masaoka's logic echoed that of Judd and other so-called Asia-First conservatives who emphasized the importance of Asia—and particularly, Washington's continued support for Chiang Kai-shek's Nationalist government—to secure the United States' future in the region.[55] Compared to the majority focused on

China, however, Masaoka was one of the much smaller group of witnesses to spotlight Japan.

The JACL had built its postwar record of success by describing how its agenda upheld U.S. goals in the reconstruction of the island nation. With the SCAP Occupation now over, league leaders grieved Japan's loss of priority and sought to shore up the JACL's influence by widening its footprint as an American lobbying vehicle. First, the league joined with white ethnic reformers to campaign for revisions to the 1952 McCarran-Walter Act. Less than three years after the JACL broke ranks with a majority of liberal and white ethnic groups to support the controversial law, Masaoka surprised many of those present at the Senate subcommittee hearing by calling for modifications to it. One congressman even challenged his change of heart, but Masaoka's response was conciliatory but firm. Of course the JACL stood by its earlier endorsement of the 1952 law, he testified, but it also wanted "remedies" and "improvements" to make it "even more perfect." If the old law was a "1950 car" with "a lot of defects" as well as "a lot of good things," the proposed revision bill was an improved "1955 model."[56] Second, the JACL tried to rebrand itself as an "Asian American" organization that spoke for more than Japanese alone. In a novel turn, Masaoka described the JACL as the "only" "national association of Americans of Asian ancestry" in existence[57] and included Chinese and Koreans, along with Japanese, in his public appeals for greater Asian immigration, citing their common "courage in battling communism." What Japanese Americans alone could not accomplish, his pan-Asian statements intimated, perhaps Asian Americans collectively could.

The JACL's emphasis on strength through numbers redirected its focus and led it to adopt some new arguments. For the first time in his more than thirty official statements on Capitol Hill, Masaoka expressed hope that legal changes to immigration would meaningfully increase the "Asian American" population in ways that were not just symbolic but could materially boost their political power. In an allusion to Japanese Americans' wartime incarceration, he lamented how Asians' lack of political influence had historically made them vulnerable to being scapegoated or oppressed during times of national crisis. "When the stakes are down we take a licking," he bemoaned, but having some political power would help ensure Asian Americans had "certain minimum guarantees . . . regardless of the temper of the time."[58] As such, the JACL's attempt at rebranding can be seen as both a means to bolster their voice in the short term and a defensive act intended to safeguard Asian American rights in the long term.

The JACL's pan-Asian language may have suggested an appetite for alliance, but partnerships between communities remained more rhetorical than real. To be sure, there was precedent for cooperation across ethnic lines: as discussed in chapter 4, just a few years earlier, the JACL had joined with the CACA, the Korean National Association, and the Filipino Federation of America to issue a collective endorsement of McCarran-Walter as part of the "Four Nations Organization." Although the alliance existed primarily on paper, the interethnic solidarity it suggested was still noteworthy. Other JACL leaders made similar gestures: perhaps most notably, Larry Tajiri, editor of the league's newspaper *Pacific Citizen*, penned editorials expressing sympathy for Chinese and Korean Americans subject to red-baiting by the U.S. government at the height of the McCarthy era.[59] Nevertheless, multiple historical and structural factors made cooperation challenging. Animosities established over decades of Japanese aggression and sharpened by Japan's expansion into the Chinese mainland during the 1930s and World War II did not dissipate quickly.[60] The rise of anti-Japanese sentiment after Pearl Harbor and the decision of some Chinese Americans to join in the public vilification of Japanese increased tensions within the United States as well.[61] The postwar rehabilitation of the Japanese American community in the eyes of white officials ended that practice, but resentments between the two communities remained.[62] The JACL and the CACA formed a temporary partnership to support McCarran-Walter, but the league's perceived success later provoked sharp pushback from other Chinese Americans wary of being overshadowed.

Internal challenges also prompted the leadership of both communities to turn inward. The question of how closely Japanese Americans should align themselves with Japan and engage in matters of U.S. foreign relations was an ongoing source of internal conflict for the JACL,[63] and a more sweeping and catastrophic crisis preoccupied the CACA. Less than two weeks after the Humphrey-Lehman bill hearing in the Senate, a U.S. consul in Hong Kong named Everett Drumright issued a report describing a "criminal conspiracy" turned industry in which Chinese applicants gained entry to the United States by claiming to be the child of a U.S. citizen or another exempt status. All told, Drumright estimated that 84 percent of Chinese applying on these grounds were "fraudulent," part of a highly profitable business that had come to involve citizenship brokers, Chinese and U.S. officials, and a vast network of middlemen who made the deception possible.[64] The fallout was swift and harsh. Within months, the Justice Department subpoenaed Chinese across San Francisco and New York. Panicked community leaders turned to Chinese consuls for help, but the ROC's efforts backfired when U.S. officials condemned its attempts to meddle in a "wholly domestic" matter. The episode helps explain both the ROC government's reluctance to intervene in immigration debates and Chinese Americans' hesitation to ask the regime for help.[65] The furor over the so-called paper son system gave rise to the Chinese Confession Program; for the next decade the Justice Department offered a potential adjustment of status to Chinese who voluntarily "confessed" their lies and detailed the fraudulent means they used to enter the country and others implicated in the process. The crisis monopolized leaders' attention at a time when they might have been reaching out to the JACL and other community vehicles more aggressively.

By the time Chinese American groups were once again in a position to seek closer ties with the JACL, they had little incentive to do so. Writing to a San Francisco colleague in 1957, Y. C. Hong suggested that the CACA could learn from the JACL's tactic of soliciting endorsements—or "get[ting] other people to praise you"—to build a national reputation.[66] Hong and several other CACA chapter heads went on to ask the JACL's national leadership to train them in how to cultivate a bigger profile; it was at once part of an effort to rehabilitate the CACA's sullied image and to secure greater protection by building political leverage for the future. At Masaoka's urging, the JACL board declined. In light of the "forgery" and "smuggling" associated with the Chinese American community, the league spokesman argued, the JACL could not "afford to get involved or mixed up with Chinese groups if we are to keep our own skirts clean."[67] JACL leaders showed similar reluctance the following year when a group called the Chinese American Civic Association began "making overtures" to "establish closer contacts"; according to one observer, the Chinese group had been studying the JACL in an effort to "ascertain [its] modus operandi" and copy it. Harold Gordon, the league's sometime legal advisor, advised Masaoka to "steer clear" of the group, which he described as "pathetic without strong Washington representation," since it was unclear what impact the association could have on the JACL's own legislative agenda.[68] While the 1950s undeniably saw Chinese and Japanese Americans express a growing sense of "Oriental" racial solidarity, then, pragmatism still trumped partnership for an established group such as the JACL. Particularly in the absence of a pending bill or larger crisis, leaders saw little reason to extend themselves in ways that could potentially undermine their organization's own credibility.

That said, the JACL was willing to partner with other groups when it promised to serve their interests. In the last three months of the Humphrey-

Lehman campaign in the Senate, for example, the JACL joined the National Committee on Immigration and Citizenship (NCIC), a coalition comprising many of the Euro-American organizations most active in fighting for immigration reform during the late 1950s.[69] The NCIC included many of the groups the JACL had broken with in 1952 to support McCarran-Walter, suggesting a reconciliation of sorts. They collectively celebrated when the Humphrey-Lehman bill passed the Senate with bipartisan support in July 1956[70] and mourned together shortly thereafter, when Francis Walter, a ranking member of the House Judiciary Committee, buried the bill as other restrictionist "committee barons" had done before him.[71] Building on the Four Nation Organization of the McCarran-Walter campaign, these gestures at solidarity may have planted another seed for interethnic partnership and cooperation, but it would not bear fruit for many more years.

Hart-Celler, Hawaii, and the Limits of Racial Liberalism

Eight years after the Senate subcommittee hearing on Humphrey-Lehman failed to bring change, the Asian immigration campaigns reignited in the shadow of contests over black civil rights.[72] The African American civil rights movement was capturing national and even international attention, as the people of Birmingham, Alabama, marched and suffered violence to integrate their city. On June 11, 1963, the same day that Alabama governor George Wallace fulfilled his promise to "stand in the schoolhouse door" to defend segregation, President John F. Kennedy delivered his historic civil rights address to a television audience of millions. As pledged, within weeks his administration sent a civil rights bill to Congress, where it languished in committee, stymied by southern Democrats committed to protecting Jim Crow. One month later, the administration sent a comprehensive immigration reform bill to Capitol Hill, where it met the same fate.[73]

Forming the basis of what would ultimately become the Hart-Celler Act, Kennedy's immigration bill included many of the features that immigration reformers had been pushing for years. It would phase out the national origins quota system over five years and replace it with a preference system based on job skills and family relationships. Most important for advocates of Asian immigration, it proposed to eliminate the Asia-Pacific Triangle and its race-based immigration quotas for Asia once and for all. As Maddalena Marinari has noted, despite the important role of activists and other nonstate actors in keeping the flaws of the national origins system part of the conversation, backroom negotiations among political elites, more than pressures from any external group, would shape the final version of the law.[74] The 1963 death of Rep. Francis Walter was crucial; the absence of the 1952 McCarran-Walter Act's remaining sponsor removed a powerful barrier to reform.

For the first time there were Asian American lawmakers in Congress representing the new state of Hawaii.[75] Fresh off their electoral victories, Hawaii's House representatives and senators eagerly embraced the narrative of their election as proof of the United States' commitment to racial liberalism and racial progress to bolster their own standing in Washington. When it came to advocating for legislation related to Asian immigration, they eagerly drew on their Asian heritage and on Hawaii's strategic location in the Pacific to amplify their voices on Capitol Hill. But their presence created an unprecedented dynamic, as Asian American immigration reformers and black American activists clashed in matters of race reform.

Hiram Fong embodied this ambivalence perhaps most keenly. Elected in 1959, he was one of Hawaii's first two U.S. senators as well as the state delegation's lone Republican and lone Chinese American. Born the seventh child of poor plantation workers, he was a self-made millionaire dubbed the "Hawaiian Horatio Alger" by local media.[76] After working his way through the University of Hawaii and Harvard Law School, Fong returned to the islands, where he spent the next two decades as a government lawyer, local politician, and entrepreneur running businesses that amassed him a fortune. Upon his election to the U.S. Senate, Fong quickly earned a reputation as an outspoken and committed champion of immigration liberalization for Asians and Pacific Islanders. One of his first acts was to propose an amendment to the bill that became the 1960 Fair Share Refugee Relief Act. He took issue with the legislation's exclusion of displaced persons in the Middle East and Far East, including Hong Kong and his parents' native China, and proposed granting the executive limited parole authority to admit from these regions as well.[77] Fong continued to advocate for refugees, calling on the United States to live up to its "tradition of leadership in world affairs" by opening its borders further still.[78] The appeals failed to result in legislation, but his impassioned stand on the Senate floor caught the attention of lawmakers across the aisle. Senator Philip Hart (D-MI), the chair of the Senate subcommittee on refugee policy who would go on to cosponsor the 1965 Hart-Celler law, commended Fong for his "dramatic demonstration," saying it proved that the "old hands" overseeing immigration policy were "not always right." Reflecting the strong historical ties Hawaii shared with other Pacific islands, Fong also introduced bills granting the

Senator Hiram L. Fong of Hawaii, undated. Bettmann / Getty Images.

Ryukyus (including Okinawa) and Tonga separate immigration quotas of 100 per year as part of the Asia-Pacific Triangle.[79] Even if these did not reform the system, they proposed to expand its reach.

Even as Fong earned applause for his advocacy on Asian immigration, a controversy from his first month in office drew the ire of black Americans and undermined his claims to support racial equality. Following his 1959 election, Fong had been in Washington, DC, for only a week when one of his statements ignited a firestorm in the black press. During a televised interview with a Republican colleague in the Senate, Fong suggested that Congress should be "very careful" about "rushing" the passage of civil rights legislation given that Jim Crow had been a "way of living in the South" for a "long, long time." Echoing a sentiment popular among conservatives and segregationists at the time, he intimated that federal laws might not be the best solution to the southern race dilemma. "It is difficult to legislate a mode of life," Fong was quoted as saying. "I think this is an emotional problem that will be cured by time."[80] For many black Americans who had welcomed his election with high hopes, the Chinese American senator's words evoked a deep sense of betrayal at the hands of a fellow racial minority. Recounting an earlier interview of Fong for his weekly newspaper column, A. S. "Doc" Young of the *Los Angeles Sentinel* warned readers not to "believe those false reports about the tremendous liberality rampant in Hawaii." "Maybe after some Dixiecrat calls him 'coolie,' he'll change his mind fast," Young quipped.[81] Black newspaperman P. L. Prattis of the *New Pittsburgh Courier* used Fong's statement to issue a warning about "Orientals" in general.

> We Negroes must often wonder about these transplanted (or home-grown) Orientals. Almost the first gesture the distinguished Senator from Hawaii made in the Senate was in the nature of a kow-tow to the South. He smiled upon his Southern colleagues as brothers, completely forgetting that they were the rascals who had kept him out so long. The Southern oligarchy in the House and Senate did not want Hawaii as a state because they were against any Oriental infusion. But you watch Mr. Fong. He will play being white, you can bet your life. He'll try to play the game and delude himself into believing that he is accepted. At this point, I would not bet two cents that he will be for any civil rights bill, strong or diluted.[82]

As Prattis suggested, many southern lawmakers had opposed Hawaiian statehood for decades precisely because they expected Hawaiian lawmakers to support civil rights, and many African Americans had welcomed statehood for the same reason.[83]

The fact that the debate over Hawaiian statehood had become so closely entangled with congressional views on black civil rights intensified black Americans' disappointment in Fong. As Ann Ziker writes, southern votes opposing the 1957 civil rights bills "aligned almost perfectly" with those cast against Hawaiian statehood.[84] This association was the product of a long history. In the 1890s, white southern Democrats had been the strongest opponents of annexing Hawaii, along with the Philippines and Puerto Rico, on the grounds that its residents were not white and were therefore a threat to an Anglo-Saxon America.[85] More than half a century later, with the revival of calls for Hawaiian statehood after World War II, southern lawmakers again rallied against the evils of admitting a majority "Oriental" territory to join the nation. A 1953 statement by Mississippi senator James Eastland decrying Hawaiian statehood for its promise to destroy the United States' "social institutions and harmonious racial relations" was representative for this bloc. Of particular alarm was the potential for two new senators from Hawaii to undermine the southern bloc's ability to obstruct civil rights legislation through filibuster and the other procedural mechanisms they had used for years to prevent civil rights bills from coming to a full floor vote. In his telling, not only would nonwhite lawmakers threaten the integrity of American self-government; the Hawaiian senators' "two votes against all racial segregation and two votes against the South on all social matters" could also give the pro–civil rights factions a majority in the Senate, which historically functioned as the legislative check on civil rights bills.[86]

Before Fong, black Americans expressed hope that Eastland's prediction would come true. For example, shortly before the 1959 Hawaiian elections, a writer in the *Chicago Defender* newspaper called on Hawaii voters on behalf of its black readership to take seriously their "mission" to "bring down the walls of American racial prejudice" by choosing lawmakers who would challenge the power of southerners in Congress.[87] Indeed, Fong's own statements before the 1959 election had encouraged black Americans to hope. As the "only non-caucasian senator . . . coming from a state which lives the principle of democracy," he told Memphis's black newspaper on the eve of his election, it was only "natural to assume that I will fight anything that interferes with civil rights."[88] Partisanship was certainly a factor: as Hawaii's only congressional Republican, Fong faced different pressures from the rest of the state's delegation, who, as liberal Democrats, were strongly encouraged to support federal civil rights legislation as part of the northern contingent's national agenda. Republicans were more mixed on the issue. Whatever his motives, Fong's words caused many black Americans to question whether Hawaii's unique demographics—African Americans made up less than 1 percent of the islands' population in 1960—limited the ability of Asian American lawmakers from the state to understand the black-white racial dynamic that structured race relations and politics in the American South.[89] Like many Republicans, Fong would eventually vote for the Civil Rights Act five years later, but the black community's goodwill once lost was not easily regained.

In recognition of his value to the GOP, the party leadership gave Fong a seat on the powerful Senate Judiciary Committee after the 1964 elections; as one of nine members of a Judiciary Subcommittee on Immigration, he had a decisive vote on all subsequent immigration bills. Specifically, he was responsible for deciding which version of the Hart-Celler legislation to forward to the full Senate. In that capacity, Fong helped shape its final form in ways that reveal other limits on his commitments to national inclusion. Perhaps most notably, his vote was decisive to the law's incorporation of the McGregor Amendment, which put numerical limits on immigration from the Western Hemisphere for the first time.[90] Congressional restrictionists, it was widely understood, had introduced the amendment in an eleventh-hour effort to limit permanent immigration from Mexico and Latin America. Scholars have singled out the importance of powerful senators and members of the Senate Judiciary Committee Sam Ervin (D-NC) and Everett Dirksen (R-IL) in persuading the Johnson administration to accept the ceiling as the price of immigration reform.[91] But without Fong's support in a five-to-three vote, the amended bill would never have reached the Senate Judiciary Committee or the full Senate for passage. Senator Edward ("Ted") Kennedy (D-MA), the immigration subcommittee chairman, recognized Fong's pivotal role; hoping to make him a swing vote, the Massachusetts lawmaker enlisted the JACL's Masaoka to use his personal relationship with the Hawaiian senator to change his mind, but the plan proved unsuccessful.[92] Fong's vote was critical to passing a version of the legislation that liberalized entry for some—namely, Asians and Europeans—at the expense of Latina/os. Within a few years, the McGregor Amendment's new restrictions would help set off a chain of events that transformed the national conversation about Mexican immigration from one of outcry over the exploitation of Mexican workers to one focused on the problem of "illegal" migration.[93]

Spark "Sparky" Matsunaga, another Hawaii legislator at this time, also made Asian immigration causes central to his political record. He and Fong were in many ways a study in contrasts. Both were born in Hawaii to Asian immigrants and attended Harvard Law School. But Matsunaga was Japanese American and a member of the Democratic Party while Fong was a Chinese American Republican. Matsunaga was a decade younger than his Senate counterpart and a World War II veteran who had served in an all-Nisei military unit.[94] On immigration matters, he sponsored legislation that appealed to a cross-section of his heavily Asian American and Pacific Islander constituency. One of the best known was a symbolic measure to repeal the Coolie Trade law, which Congress had passed in 1862 to reduce the entry of Chinese contract workers into the United States. Echoing many of the arguments used in previous campaigns for exclusion repeal, Matsunaga described his measure as a low-cost tool of migration diplomacy that would "help the United States in its relations with Asia by removing from our books what is regarded as an expression of racial prejudice."[95] He also departed from Fong in his willingness to speak out against the deportation of Asian Americans, an issue that generally involved individuals suspected of communist sympathies or subversion. One of Matsunaga's failed attempts was a bill placing a five-year statute of limitations on deportation and denaturalization proceedings by the U.S. state, a change that promised to reduce the number of foreign-born Asians affected.[96] In 1964, Matsunaga was one of several Democrats in the House to cosponsor the legislation that ultimately became the Hart-Celler Act.

For all their differences, Fong and Matsunaga practiced many of the same strategies to make themselves legible to a Washington audience. Their speeches on Capitol Hill consistently affirmed Hawaiian statehood as evidence of American national greatness. Describing Hawaii as a link between the United States and Asia, both lawmakers claimed a unique authority and expertise on matters related to Asia and U.S.-Asia diplomacy.[97] Fong, who twice campaigned as a "Man of the Pacific," described Asian Americans like himself as "bridges of understanding" who could win the "peoples of the Triangle area with their messages of goodwill, democratic freedom and individual dignity." In a speech about the Hart-Celler bill, he recounted meeting many Asians who claimed to feel the "sting of discriminatory treatment" by U.S. immigration policies, which, in turn, increased the allure of communism on the continent.[98] Using similar language, Matsunaga often described Hawaii as a "showcase of American democracy."[99] Speaking at House committee hearings on Hart-Celler, he declared the United States "at the crossroads of destiny" in Asia, referencing the communist threat and the American blood and dollars at risk in Vietnam, Korea, and India. The conflict in Vietnam was months away from escalation, but lawmakers were aware of the growing American investment there, and Matsunaga's assertion that the Asia-Pacific Triangle threatened Asian sympathies likely resonated.[100] Such statements positioned both Matsunaga and Fong as vanguards of U.S. imperial power in the Pacific. Even as their advocacy for greater immigration and refugee admissions challenged the status quo, it simultaneously supported the reach of U.S. power by reaffirming America's image as a desirable and racially inclusive destination suitable for all the world's peoples. Both men would go on to support the U.S. ground war in Vietnam, in spite of widespread criticism describing it as a power grab by Washington.[101]

President Lyndon B. Johnson did not directly address the law's implications for the U.S. relationship to Asia as he signed the Hart-Celler Act into law under the shadow of New York Harbor's Statue of Liberty. Even as he declared it "one of the most important acts" the eighty-ninth Congress and his

U.S. president Lyndon B. Johnson signs the 1965 Immigration Act; to Johnson's left is vice president and former U.S. senator Hubert Humphrey; Senator Edward ("Ted") Kennedy is third from the right. Courtesy of the Lyndon B. Johnson Presidential Library and Museum.

administration could take to repair a "deep and painful flaw in the fabric of American justice," he simultaneously reassured the law's critics that it was not expected to result in any measurable change, whether at home or abroad: "It will not reshape the structure of our daily lives, or really add importantly to either our wealth or our power."[102]

The legislative process behind the Hart-Celler campaigns, with all its modifications and backroom dealings, betrayed a similar ambivalence. The 1965 act, both at the time and in retrospect, has been widely hailed as a liberal achievement. But its path to passage is a lesson in political accommodation within a legislative system structured to serve the interests of the powerful. Viewed through this lens, the 1965 Hart-Celler law emerges less as an embodiment of the United States' commitment to racial liberalism and more so as a measure designed to support American power and prestige in the world while maintaining white dominance at home.[103]

Asian America under Hart-Celler

Widely seen as a corrective to the 1952 McCarran-Walter Act, the Immigration Act or Hart-Celler Act of 1965 replaced national origins quotas with a system of preferences that emphasized would-be immigrants' job skills relative to the nation's labor needs and their family relationships with citizens and permanent residents already living in the United States. Asians would be among the main beneficiaries of the law's heavy emphasis on family relationships within the preference categories for entry, but few predicted this outcome, including Asian Americans themselves. Indeed, during the final negotiations, Asian American lawmakers and community representatives were some of the loudest voices opposing the reshuffling of the system to favor family preference categories over those emphasizing skills, talents, and occupation. They correctly saw the preference system as a restrictionist strategy designed to preserve the status quo by privileging those with a more robust history of immigration. As one American Legion spokesman explained it, weighing family preference more heavily than other categories would mean that "Asiatics . . . would automatically arrive in far fewer numbers than Italians, Greeks, and other southern European stock" since they generally had "fewer immediate family members now in the United States than southern Europeans." But, significantly, the law would contain "no sting . . . to offend Asian nations": Asians would "qualify on the same basis as others, though far fewer of them will be able to do so."[104] Yet again, an advocate for reform claimed that the symbolism was more important and would make it easier to prevent practical change.

As they had done in the past, Asian American observers were quick to decry what they feared would be yet another purely symbolic reform bill that did little to address their concerns. Hart-Celler might claim to "eliminate race as a matter of principle," the JACL's Mike Masaoka complained to a congressional committee in 1965, but "in actual operation" its provisions ensured that "the now discredited national origins system" would still shape immigration.[105] Using similar logic, Hawaii's Matsunaga lamented that the bill would be "less revolutionary as some have claimed or believe it to be." It might "eliminate the discriminatory basis of apportioning immigration" in theory, but he predicted that it would do little to change the large disparity between European and Asian immigration in practice.[106] In a statement sent to the immigration subcommittees of both the House and Senate, JACL leadership concluded that the bill was unlikely to "disturb the cultural and ethnic composition of our country."[107] As evidence they cited Justice Department estimates predicting that between 5,000 and 7,000 Asians would immigrate to the United States during the first year of the new system, with numbers falling off quickly thereafter. Under the new system, they concluded, "the general pattern of immigration which exists today will continue for many years to come."[108]

Time would prove them all wrong. Although they did not know it in 1965, by creating a preference system that prioritized family relationships, U.S. lawmakers opened the floodgates to Asian immigration in ways that would transform the American nation. By the early 1970s, the number of Asians immigrating to the United States per year had more than quadrupled compared with the period before Hart-Celler. By the 1980s, Asian immigration had increased tenfold, and Asians grew from 7 percent of the overall immigrant stream in the 1960s to more than 40 percent.[109] As of 2012, Asia has surpassed Latin America as the main source of immigration to the United States. It remains to be seen whether this trend that began with the passage of Hart-Celler will continue.[110]

Conclusion

Throughout the 1950s and early 1960s, Asian American reformers seeking more meaningful changes to U.S. immigration policies and practices found themselves increasingly marginalized within revision campaigns that centered on the McCarran-Walter Act's discriminations against southern and eastern Europeans. In the meantime, changes to the form and focus of U.S. empire building in Asia weakened the link between U.S. immigration policies and Washington's projects in the region, undercutting the strength of arguments centering U.S. power that had helped drive earlier repeal campaigns. With the exception of the refugee debates, which continued to focus on U.S. state projects in Asia, Asian American advocates adapted to Asians' marginalization within the immigration debates after 1952 by turning inward as well. Both in speeches at congressional hearings and written petitions, they appealed to their rights as U.S. citizens and to their identity as Americans to argue for additional immigration reforms. The institutionalization of Asian American political power made possible by the election of Chinese and Japanese American lawmakers from the new state of Hawaii cemented this shift in political lobbying strategies and signaled a new chapter in Asian American politics.

Ultimately, post-1952 Asian immigration reform was a story of incidental and unintentional change. Far from reflecting a depth of commitment to racial liberalism, this chapter has unmasked the 1965 Hart-Celler Act as a highly conservative measure consistent with the repeal movement's longer tradition of symbolic measures that did little to alter the status quo.[111] That it occurred in a context where tensions between Asian Americans and other nonwhite communities over race reform continued underscores how limited opportunities for reform inhibited meaningful cooperation, even at a height in civil rights activism.

Nonetheless, the 1965 Hart-Celler Act failed to conserve the whiteness of the nation. While designed to prevent changes to the United States' majority-European immigrant stream, it did precisely the opposite, opening the nation's borders to unprecedented numbers of migrants from Asia and other nonwhite parts of the world. Over the next decades, these new arrivals would transform the nation.

Epilogue

The bill that we sign today is not a revolutionary bill.
It does not affect the lives of millions.

—LYNDON B. JOHNSON

It was with these words that the movement to repeal Asian exclusion—a movement more than two decades in the making—came to an end. The formal ceremony for the 1965 Hart-Celler Act conveyed the pomp the Johnson administration desired. But the president's statement in honor of the bill, while expressing the sentiments of many who had advocated for it, undercut the dramatic effect.

Given the largely symbolic intent of the 1965 law, many supporters were shocked when its provisions began increasing the share of immigration from Asia and Latin America relative to Europe, growing it from single- to double-digit percentages by the mid-1970s.[1] Some of the congressional lawmakers who had opposed its passage spoke out, trying to raise public awareness of how the law designed to make the U.S. immigration system nondiscriminatory in principle was bringing real change, just as they had warned it would. But their protest was to no avail. Congress had little political appetite for further immigration reform, particularly as it confronted other crises in confidence stemming from the Vietnam War. For decades, the Hart-Celler Act would stand largely unchanged as one of the twentieth century's best examples of unintended policy outcomes.

With the benefit of hindsight, we now understand the importance of multiple ancillary factors that lawmakers at the time overlooked or underestimated. Key among these were events happening in Asia that acted as push factors, or local circumstances compelling Asians to emigrate. In Southeast Asia, these were largely of the United States' own making: the final year of the Hart-Celler debate marked the first year that U.S. ground troops in Vietnam exceeded 100,000. Within a decade, a U.S. military presence had expanded across the region, stretching from southern Vietnam to Cambodia and the hills of Laos. As the Korean War had done on a smaller scale, U.S. wars in Southeast Asia gave rise to new migrations of military brides and the children of American soldiers, as well as the vast displacement of hundreds of thousands of Southeast Asians who would later come to the United States as refugees in the 1970s and beyond. All told, by 2015, over one million of the two million–plus persons who fled Vietnam, Cambodia, and Laos had been resettled in the United States under a series of refugee laws that provided for their entry; most other Asians came as nonquota migrants under the family reunification provisions of the Hart-Celler Act. This was just one illustration of how prioritizing family relationships backfired in a snowball effect. Indeed, far from keeping the immigrant stream predominantly European, the law's family-based provisions have accounted for the majority of Asian immigration to the United States in all decades since 1970.[2]

The 1965 Act's impact on Latina/o immigration was similarly unexpected and misunderstood. In capping Mexican and other Latina/o immigration from the Western Hemisphere for the first time, U.S. lawmakers had not considered how the change would affect labor flows. Congress passed the Hart-Celler law one year after terminating the Bracero Program due to reports of U.S. employers abusing and exploiting workers and under pressure by organized workers. The government guest worker program had permitted millions of Mexicans to work legally in the United States since the 1940s. As sociologists Douglas Massey and Karen Pren have shown, Mexican migration flows that had developed over previous decades continued largely apace after 1968, when both the Hart-Celler cap and bracero termination took effect. Employers across the Southwest and West continued to rely on Mexican laborers, who now came outside of state-sanctioned channels.[3] State figures and media observers raised growing alarm over the threats these undocumented migrants posed, politicizing Mexican immigration in new ways.

Ultimately, the Hart-Celler Act did more than change the nation's racial demographics. It also shifted the terms of the immigration debates in ways that would resonate more than half a century later. Thus, even in areas that its supporters and least of all President Johnson seemed to expect, the 1965 act would eventually become as one pundit wrote in 2008, the "most important piece of legislation that no one's ever heard of."[4]

The United States and the Brain Drain

By the time the Hart-Celler bill passed Congress in June 1965, the international conversation about Asian immigration in forums such as the U.N. General Assembly had shifted from protests against discriminatory immigration policies to alarm over an international brain drain. Skilled migrants from Asia, Africa, and Latin America were leaving their homelands en masse to settle in the United States and other Western countries with more advanced economies. In 1964, a delegation of leaders from the developing world delivered an impassioned appeal to the U.N. secretary-general requesting that the international body take action on the problem which they believed to be one of the greatest threats to their nations' futures. He consented, and for the next four years, the U.N. Educational, Social, and Cultural Organization (UNESCO) enlisted social scientists and experts from across the world in a systematic study of the brain drain phenomenon, its effects, and its likely causes. The work of economists Theodore Schultz and Gary Becker, among other pioneers of human capital theory, had drawn international attention to the importance of an educated workforce to drive a nation's economic development.[5] Citing this research, state officials representing Nigeria, India, Brazil, and other post-colonial economies decried the outmigration of their nations' skilled workers as a zero-sum game that reinforced global economic inequality by ensuring that the developed world profited and the developing world could never catch up.[6]

The United States featured centrally in both national and international discussions of the brain drain. U.S. government reports showed that Asians comprised an outsized percentage of the educated migrants settling in the United States.[7] Similarly, Indian sociologist Man Singh Das found that even though students from Asia, Latin America, and Africa came to the United States to study in comparable numbers, Asians were the most likely to express a desire to settle in the country.[8] In his telling, skilled migrants from Asia comprised doctors, nurses, scientists, engineers, and other professionals whose talents their homelands desperately needed but who were enriching the United States instead. The outmigration of medical health professionals from the developing world elicited special concern. Not only did their leaving impact local economies. It also left a shrinking number of doctors to care for a rapidly expanding population. At a 1967 Senate subcommittee hearing, Senator Edward ("Ted") Kennedy (D-MA) used the example of South Vietnam, where 700 doctors served a population of over 16 million people, to illustrate the magnitude of the problem.[9]

Flush off his battle to pass the Hart-Celler Act, Ted Kennedy convened a Senate immigration subcommittee hearing to study the issue in response to U.N. resolutions calling for coordinated international action on the matter. Suggesting the lack of wider congressional interest in the issue, only two of its eight members attended: Kennedy and Hiram Fong of Hawaii. The hearing's stated goal was to ascertain whether a brain drain was indeed happening, and if so, to calculate both its severity and its impact on the

United States' diplomatic relations with the developing world. A panel of social scientists and government experts addressed the question of liability. Did the United States have an obligation to ameliorate the situation, and if so, how?

Witness statements reflected how much modernization theory had infused the language used to discuss international migration in Washington. The ideology described the economic development, or modernization, of newly decolonized nations as an imperative of U.S. security interests and framed U.S. foreign aid as a prime vehicle toward that end. It was one of the central paradigms through which U.S. officials constructed 1960s foreign policy toward the developing world.[10] Its tenets first gained prominence during the Kennedy administration, resulting in the creation of the U.S. Agency for International Development in 1961 and the Peace Corps in 1962, and they remained the major frameworks through which U.S. policymakers viewed the Third World and their responsibilities to it in the ensuing decades. Many factors contributed to the popularity of modernization theory. Like geopolitics before it, the race-neutral language of development made it possible to speak about difference in nonracial terms. Modernization theory also fit well with anticommunism. Using this paradigm, policymakers began to frame immigrants as assets whose brainpower secured the United States an advantage in its Cold War contest with the Soviet Union, rather than as unskilled workers pushing down wages and taking jobs. Mounting anxiety about the United States' technological advancement, spurred in part by the specific pressures of the Cold War space race, also explains Americans' receptivity to this view. This shift should not be overstated—anti-immigrant and anti-Asian sentiment remained strong in many circles—but the reframing of migration could encourage resistant lawmakers to accept higher levels of nonwhite migration as expedient to the maintenance of the United States' global power.

Some U.S. officials cautioned that ignoring the brain drain raised a potentially serious image problem. At the hearing Kennedy had convened, a State Department official warned that people across the developing world were already complaining that the "richest country in the world" was "skimming the cream of their potential leadership" and acting to "enhance its position" at the expense of their economies.[11] Yet he and other officials expressed uncertainty as to what the United States could or should do. For example, a special advisor to President Johnson, while acknowledging the United States' special "responsibility to the entire world" as its "richest and most developed country," claimed that brain drain was not a "particularly . . . American problem." The sending countries had "primary responsibility." All the United States could do was send aid and other assistance to promote development, but the homelands must address the problem.[12]

Even those U.S. state figures most committed to investigating brain drain were ultimately reluctant to offer any prescriptions based on what they found. Perhaps mindful of his brother's legacy as the president who created the U.S. Agency for International Development (USAID), Kennedy was interested in whether the brain drain phenomenon was undercutting the desired effect of U.S. foreign aid and educational exchange programs in the developing world. The Massachusetts senator also wanted to know how the Hart-Celler Act, a law he had personally shepherded through the Senate, might have affected the issue. But most of the law's provisions had not yet taken effect. Fong's statement emphasized the potential harm as well, but State Department witnesses were quick to caution against making any drastic changes to U.S. immigration policy without more information; there was no way to know how Hart-Celler would ultimately impact the brain drain, they noted. UNESCO's final report in 1968 likewise expressed concern about the problem of brain drain without issuing policy recommendations to resolve it. The "root cause" of brain drain, it claimed, was the "receiving countries' wish to acquire productive intellectual capital as quickly and as cheaply as possible." Developed countries, it charged, had "encourage[d] selective immigration in various ways," with severe consequences for developing countries, including "additional obstacles to progress towards national economic independence" and "tensions and conflict between the loser and winner countries."[13] The United Nations was financially dependent on U.S. funds for its survival, meaning that official UN-issued reports of the time tended to treat Washington gingerly. While the logic of the report suggested that as the main receiving country of the world's skilled migrants, the United States bore some responsibility for the problem, it limited its recommendations to calling on developed countries to provide the UN and other relevant international organizations with accurate and updated statistics so they could conduct a systematic and scientific study of the issue.

The discussion of the brain drain that began with an impassioned meeting at the U.N. secretary-general's office in 1964 thus ended with a whimper. Congress would take no specific actions to restrict skilled migration until 1976, and that was only in relation to the medical professions.[14] George B. Baldwin, an economic advisor at the World Bank, encapsulated the brain drain concern and the United States' response to it in a piece in *Foreign Affairs* magazine in 1970. After recounting the "emotional debate" that had launched UN investigations into the phenomenon, he closed the piece by stating that nothing could be done about the problem since there was no clear agreement on its main causes. And so it was, Baldwin wrote, that "half a decade of concern" about the brain drain ended "not with a series of proposals for reform" but with a "'decision by default'" to enter the next decade with the international "ground rules on migration left essentially unchanged."[15]

Revisiting Migration and Empire

While restrictionists in Congress continued to raise similar objections in domestic discussions of immigration, international conversations about migration had changed significantly by the 1960s. The imperial and internationalist rationale underwriting the repeal movement had rested squarely on the politics of symbolism. The "brain drain" now described a material change in which the movement of human capital threatened concrete and quantifiable harm on a less developed economy. In Washington, the influence of the international brain drain debate began shifting the main logics framing official discussions of Asian immigration from the abstract to dollars and cents. The change also benefited from the Kennedy and Johnson administrations' emphasis on foreign aid and development as the tools of choice for U.S. engagement with the developing world.

A closer examination of the brain drain discussion suggests how the relationship between U.S. empire and Asian migration had likewise changed. By the 1960s, foreign critics looking to undermine the United States' international legitimacy were more likely to call out the lynchings and racial violence suffered by black Americans or U.S. soldiers' murder of Asian civilians in the name of American anticommunism than they were to single out an immigration law. For many, the scale and brutality of the U.S. war in Vietnam shattered any pretense that Washington supported Vietnamese self-determination. With the onset of a full-scale U.S. war in Southeast Asia, the postwar logics of consent and reciprocity that had made repeal such an attractive tool of empire no longer seemed to apply.

Even if the exigencies of empire no longer shaped the letter of U.S. immigration policy as directly as they once did, the influx of migrants from Southeast Asia reflected how the United States' imperial activities themselves produced more actual migration than ever before. After 1965, Asians came to the United States in two major streams that later converged. The displacements and disruptions of the U.S. Vietnam War brought waves of refugees and other migrants from across Southeast Asia at the same time that the 1965 Hart-Celler Act's family and jobs provisions opened the doors for medical professionals, scientists, engineers, and other skilled migrants and their families to settle in the United States in historic numbers.

But as we have seen, the liberalization of U.S. immigration law by no means assured Asian immigrants welcome. The arrival of millions of Southeast Asians in the late 1970s and 1980s met strong opposition; polls taken from 1975, when the northern Vietnamese finally won the war, through the 1980s, consistently showed a majority of Americans opposed to the admission of refugees from Vietnam, Cambodia, and Laos.[16] Whether primarily a function of racism or the unpopularity of the war itself, these findings were strikingly consistent with the United States' long history of resistance to refugees and nonwhite immigration in general.

The ambivalence and resistance that characterized the story of repeal were no aberration in U.S. history; migration's special connection to Asia and American power affected the shape, not the substance, of the repeal battle and the laws it produced. Soaring rhetoric about a nation of immigrants and the huddled masses yearning to breathe free notwithstanding, immigrants seeking a better life in the United States have always been imperiled by the country's complex relationship to the wider world.

Acknowledgments

Writing a book is an incredible undertaking. I am grateful for the many people who made the process a little easier, and even enjoyable at times.

First, I thank Erez Manela, whose avuncular and unflagging support made my Harvard experience a positive one. He was steadfastly humane and, as a graduate advisor, never failed to prioritize the whole person. Thanks to Lizabeth Cohen for her incisive questions and wise counsel. Liz's twentieth-century U.S. writing group provided a great forum to share work in progress. It also gave me the chance to read early drafts of some of the most cutting-edge books out there today. I met David K. Yoo while I was a PhD candidate researching in Los Angeles, and he graciously agreed to advise an East Coast transplant. I count myself fortunate to enjoy his continued mentorship and friendship. All that I learned as a teaching assistant for S. Deborah Kang's immigration history course at Harvard continues to shape the way I think about the subject more than a decade later. Naoko Shibusawa's courses during my brief time at Brown influenced my understanding of U.S. foreign relations in similarly formative ways. I would not be a historian today without the example and encouragement of Mary Lui, who cultivated my interest in Asian American history while I was an undergraduate at Yale, and of Dr. Edward Michels, whose infamous AP classes instilled in me a deep love of history during high school.

Funding from a wide range of sources made research for this book possible. At Harvard, the South Asia Initiative, Korea Institute, Weatherhead Center for International Affairs, Harvard History Department, and Charles Warren Center for American History provided the grants and travel funds that enabled me to spend time in Delhi, Seoul, Washington, DC, Michigan, California, Utah, Washington, and Hawaii. During my brief but happy year at Seton Hall, junior faculty start-up funds supported research trips to Pennsylvania and Washington, DC. At Occidental, faculty travel and development funds allowed me to do archival work in the Philippines, Washington, DC, and Korea. Sadly, my Korea chapters did not make it into this book, but I hope to find other venues for that work. In the final days, Dean Wendy Sternberg of the Occidental College provided a timely subvention for which I am thankful.

Supportive colleagues and friends facilitated the writing and revision process. Special thanks belong to Kornel Chang, Dorothy Fujita-Rony, Justin Hart, Torrie Hester, Erez Manela, Isabela Quintana, Maria Su Wang, and Susie Woo for their close readings of various chapter drafts. Cindy I-Fen Cheng deserves a separate shout-out for reading multiple drafts of multiple sections. The incomparable Dan Horowitz generously read the whole manuscript late in the process. I thank anonymous readers at the University of North Carolina Press, as well as at the *Journal of American Ethnic History* and the *Pacific Historical Review*, which published early pieces of chapters 3 and 4, respectively. Your comments and suggestions have all made the book better. Any and all errors are, of course, my own.

Here in Los Angeles, I am fortunate to belong to several writing and accountability groups, whose support and feedback have been invaluable. Thank you to the Asian American Women Historians' writing group: Kelly Fong, Dorothy Fujita-Rony, Adria Imada, Karen Leong, Valerie Matsumoto, Isabela Quintana, Susie Woo, and the superb leadership of Judy Tzu-Chun Wu. In addition to sharing pieces of the book at multiple conferences, I presented a very early version of chapter 3 to the Asian American Pacific Islander History group at the Huntington Library, organized by Constance Chen, Lon Kurashige, and David K. Yoo. Thank you to guest commenter Kelly Lytle Hernandez for pushing me to be bolder in my arguments. I also received welcome encouragement from the UCLA Speaker Series on International Migration, organized by Roger Waldinger. In addition, I wish to thank David Atkinson, Charlotte Brooks, Gordon Chang, Genevieve Clutario, Roger Daniels, Madeline Hsu, Nick Kapur, Paul Kramer, Lon Kurashige, Heather Lee, Shelley Lee, Maddalena Marinari, Grainne McEvoy, Greg Robinson, Rachel St. John, Duncan Williams, Ellen D. Wu, and the late Marilyn Young, for answering queries, recommending sources, and for offering valuable advice, whether they were aware of what they were doing or not.

Occidental College has been a wonderful place to work. Junior faculty writing and research groups organized by Krystale Littlejohn and James Ford provided collegial spaces to write and share work in progress. Thanks to Krystale, James, J. Mijin Cha, Ross Lerner, Ainsley Lesure, and Kelema Moses for being a valuable source of encouragement on campus. On that note, I still miss Donna Maeda. Patty Micciche and Kathy Izumi are the greatest administrators a department could ask for. Laura Chun, history major extraordinaire, provided much appreciated assistance. Last but not least, I belong to a truly outstanding history department. Many thanks to Jenn Axelrod, Sasha Day, Sharla Fett, Michael Gasper, Nina Gelbart, Maryanne Horowitz, Alexandra Puerto, Lisa Sousa, and Marla Stone. You all set a high bar for excellence in every arena.

Writing can often be a lonely endeavor, but I found a great community that sustained me in ways big and small. My online writing partners, Esther Chung-Kim and Nancy Wang Yuen, helped keep me on track in the day to day. Cindy I-Fen Cheng, Maria Su Wang, and other friends who have passed through the Huntington Library made long days of writing and revision more bearable; I look forward to more walks and talks in the gardens. The presence of Sarkis Badalyan, Joe Bondy, Marco Perez, and Jim Smith made the Huntington a welcoming space, and it was also where I met Rebecca Shea and Li-Wei Yang. I will always treasure my long afternoons with Janna Louie. Kate Epstein is among the most talented and humane editors I have ever met. Thank you to Li-Wei for his assistance with images, and to Baldwin Chiu and Larissa Lam for sharing their family's story with me. SueJeanne Koh provided last-minute help at a busy time. Finally, I thank my editor at the University of North Carolina Press, Brandon Proia, for his exceedingly quick response times and his unfailing support through this process.

Friends from different seasons of life have encouraged me through the years. Maria Ham Kowzun, Jee-Yeon Kim Lehmann, Antonia Chen, Patty Cho Hwang, Christen Lee, Emily Lee, Ellen Huang, and (Rep.) Aaron Johanson are just a few of the

Yalies for whom I am and will always be grateful. Sung Hee Jang and Nayoung Kim are two reasons I miss New Jersey. Javier Cha, Cindy I-Fen Cheng, Bryant Etheridge, and Lori Flores make the academy a better place. Among those who have made West Coast life more fun are J. Mijin Cha, Christine Chow, Peaches Da-In Chung, Mike Karim, Joy Kwong and Tim Olshefski, Liz Marino, Diana Lee Ngo, Ji Son, Diane Yoon, and Nancy Wang Yuen. I have loved doing life with Janna Louie, Christine Brinn, Mary Duong, Krystina Daniels, Pamela Lee, Lynn Mayer, and Avril Speaks. I would be remiss not to acknowledge the Faculty Women of Color group Janna leads under the umbrella of InterVarsity, which eased my transition back to Los Angeles and gave me the chance to meet many incredible and like-minded women of color scholars.

Finally, I thank my family. In New Jersey, I am enormously grateful to Anna and my "hb" Won-Kang Huh, and to Maya, Charlotte, and Harris, for loving *emo* Jane so unconditionally. In Los Angeles, I thank Cliff and Heejin Baek Hong, my in-laws Young Joong and Sung Keun Lee, David and Celina Lee Chao, and their daughters Marlowe and Penelope, for making California feel a little more like home. To my extended family scattered across New York, New Jersey, Chicago, and Seoul, thank you. My mother, Susie Sook-Hi Min, deserves more of my gratitude and more credit than I can ever give her. An immigrant who later became a widow, she raised three children as a single parent in a community where that is by no means the norm. *Umma*, you are very strong. Many thank-yous belong to my husband, James Kyung-Ho Lee, who more than anyone has walked with me through this process. I love the life we are building together, and I love you.

I dedicate this book to my paternal grandparents, Hong Il Sun and Min Ae Ki, who passed away in 2007 and 2017, respectively. Before he died, I recorded an oral history of my grandfather's life. It was then that I learned in great detail how he spent the first half of his life following the circuits of Japanese empire, from growing up in Korea's Gyeonggi Province, to becoming a student in Japan, an airplane factory worker in Manchuria, and finally, a school principal in Anseong, Korea. Thanks to my mother's nursing degree and the family reunification provisions of the 1965 Immigration Act, he and my grandmother spent the last decades of their lives in New York City, circulating between their children's homes in Queens and the Bronx, the family store in Brooklyn Heights, and their apartment at 106th and Amsterdam. Well into their eighties, they made the city their home, taking long walks in Central Park and furtively gathering acorns from its trees every fall to make *muk*. From Anseong to the Upper West Side, theirs are the transpacific histories I cherish the most. I love you, and I miss you, *harabeoji* and *halmeoni*. This book is for you.

APPENDIX A

Select U.S. Immigration and Naturalization Laws
Pertaining to the Repeal of Asian Exclusion, 1943–1965

1943   *Magnuson Act, Public Law 78-199 (57 Stat. 600)*
Repealed the Chinese Exclusion Act, established an annual immigration (race-based) quota of 105 for Chinese, and made Chinese eligible for U.S. citizenship.

1946   *Luce-Celler Act, 8 U.S.C.A. 703 (60 Stat. 416)*
Provided annual immigration (race-based) quota of Indians and made both groups eligible for U.S. citizenship.

1946   *Chinese Alien Wives of American Citizens Act, Public Law 79-713 (60 Stat. 975)*
Permitted Chinese alien wives of U.S. citizens to enter the United States as nonquota immigrants.

1947   *Alien Fiancés and Fiancées Act, or Soldier Bride Act, Public Law 213-289*
(80 Stat. 190)
Amended War Brides Act of 1945 to allow Asian wives of U.S. GIs to enter the United States despite the general restriction on Asian immigration under the 1924 Immigration Act.

1952   *McCarran-Walter (Immigration and Nationality) Act, Public Law 82-414*
(66 Stat. 163)
Created the Asia-Pacific Triangle to replace the Asiatic Barred Zone, granting all Asian powers annual (race-based) immigration quotas (ranging from 100 to 185) with an overall ceiling of 2,000 immigrants from Asia; struck down all racial restrictions to U.S. citizenship; and strengthened the power of the federal government to deport and denaturalize suspected subversives.

1953   *Refugee Relief Act, Public Law 203 (67 Stat. 400)*
Allocated 214,000 nonquota refugee visas, including 2,000 to Chinese, and enabled several thousand Chinese living in the United States to adjust their status to permanent residence and citizenship. In total, 2,777 Chinese refugees entered the United States under this act.

1965   *Immigration and Nationality (Hart-Celler) Act, Public Law 89-236*
(79 Stat. 911)
Abolished the national origins quota system and replaced it with a series of preferences based on immigrants' skills and family reunification; under the revised system, Asians have comprised 40 percent of all legal immigrants to the United States since the early 1970s.

APPENDIX B

Population and Immigration Tables, 1900–2010

Chinese American population with immigration by decade and the
immigration law in effect, 1900–2010

Decade ending	Population	Immigration over prior decade	Law in effect during prior decade
1900	118,746	14,799	Chinese Exclusion Act
1910	94,414	20,605	Chinese Exclusion Act
1920	85,202	21,278	Chinese Exclusion Act
1930	102,159	29,907	Chinese Exclusion Act and 1924 act
1940	106,334	4,928	Chinese Exclusion Act and 1924 act
1950	150,005	16,709	1924 act until Magnuson Act in 1943
1960	237,292	25,201	Magnuson Act, then 1952 act
1970	436,062	109,771	1952 act until 1965 amendments
1980	812,178	237,793	1965 amendments
1990	1,645,472	446,000	1965 amendments
2000	2,564,190	528,893	1965 amendments
2010	3,535,382	819,633	1965 amendments

Note: These numbers include mainland China, Taiwan, and Hong Kong.

Source: Bill Ong Hing, *Making and Remaking Asian America through Immigration Policy,
1850–1990* (Stanford, CA: Stanford University Press, 1993), 48; *INS Annual Reports and
Statistical Yearbooks*.

Asian Indian population with immigration by decade and the
immigration law in effect, 1900–2010

Decade ending	Population	Immigration over prior decade	Law in effect during prior decade
1900		68	Open immigration
1910	5,424	4,713	Open immigration
1920		2,082	Open, then Asiatic Barred Zone of 1917 act
1930	3,130	1,886	1924 act
1940	2,405	496	1924 act
1950		1,761	1924 act, then Luce-Celler quota in 1946
1960	12,296	1,973	1946 quota, then 1952 act
1970	72,500	27,189	1952 act until 1965 amendments
1980	387,223	164,134	1965 amendments
1990	815,447	147,900	1965 amendments
2000	1,930,311	363,060	1965 amendments
2010	3,443,881	656,649	1965 amendments

Note: The term "Asian Indian" includes natives of India, Pakistan (after its creation in 1947), and Bangladesh (after its creation in 1971).

Source: Bill Ong Hing, *Making and Remaking Asian America through Immigration Policy, 1850–1990* (Stanford, CA: Stanford University Press, 1993), 70; *INS Annual Reports and Statistical Yearbooks*.

Filipina/o population with immigration by decade and the
immigration law in effect, 1900–2010

Decade ending	Population	Immigration over prior decade	Law in effect during prior decade
1900			
1910	5,008		Open until Gentleman's Agreement (1907)
1920	6,181		Gentleman's Agreement (1907)
1930	8,332		Gentleman's Agreement (1907) until 1924 act
1940	8,568		1924 act
1950	7,030		1924 act
1960	11,000	7,025	1924 act until 1952 act
1970	69,150	34,526	1952 act until 1965 amendments
1980	357,393	267,638	1965 amendments
1990	798,849	336,000	1965 amendments
2000	1,908,125	503,945	1965 amendments
2010	2,649,973	601,862	1965 amendments

Source: Adapted from Bill Ong Hing, *Making and Remaking Asian America through Immigration Policy, 1850–1990* (Stanford, CA: Stanford University Press, 1993), 61; *INS Annual Reports and Statistical Yearbooks*.

Japanese American population with immigration by decade and the
immigration law in effect, 1900–2010

Decade ending	Population	Immigration over prior decade	Law in effect during prior decade
1900	85,716	25,942	Open immigration
1910	152,745	129,797	Open immigration until Gentleman's Agreement (1907)
1920	220,596	83,837	Gentleman's Agreement (1907)
1930	278,743	33,462	Gentleman's Agreement (1907) until 1924 Act
1940	285,115	1,948	1924 act
1950	326,379	1,555	1924 act
1960	464,332	46,250	1924 act until 1952 act
1970	591,290	39,988	1952 act until 1965 amendments
1980	716,331	49,775	1965 amendments
1990	847,562	44,800	1965 amendments
2000	852,237	67,942	1965 amendments
2010	841,824	91,652	1965 amendments

Source: Adapted from Bill Ong Hing, *Making and Remaking Asian America through Immigration Policy, 1850–1990* (Stanford, CA: Stanford University Press, 1993), 54; *INS Annual Reports and Statistical Yearbooks*.

Notes

Introduction

1. *U.S. v. Bhagat Singh Thind*, 261 U.S. 204 (1923).

2. These calculations use the Page Law of 1875, not the 1882 Chinese Exclusion Act, as the beginning of federal immigration restrictions targeting Asians. For more on the Page Law, see chapter 1.

3. The 1917 Immigration Act excluded Indians as part of the Asiatic Barred Zone, a geographical designation that prohibited the immigration of all Asians from as far north as China to as far west as present-day Iran. Japan was not included. As a U.S. colony, the Philippines was also exempt; it came under restriction in 1934. See chapter 3.

4. The "free white persons" clause can be found in the 1790 Naturalization Act; "persons of African descent" were added by the Fourteenth Amendment (1868) to the Constitution. Before the 1920s, dozens of Indians exploited racial ambiguities surrounding whiteness to claim U.S. citizenship. See Ian Haney Lopez, *White by Law: The Legal Construction of Race* (New York: New York University Press, 1997), 38–39, 56–77.

5. U.S. House Committee on Immigration and Naturalization, *Repeal of the Chinese Exclusion Acts: Hearings on H.R. 1882 and H.R. 2309*, 78th Cong., 1st sess. (1943), 31, 35, 40–41.

6. I use the terms U.S. empire and empire building to encompass the diverse and largely informal methods and tactics Washington used to exert its influence globally after World War II. In general, I prefer "empire building" over "empire" because the former suggests a dynamic process or project rather than a static object or thing. That said, I use both terms throughout the book. For a good discussion of terminology, see Julian Go, *Patterns of Empire: The British and American Empires, 1688 to the Present* (New York: Cambridge University Press, 2011).

7. There is a long relationship between U.S. expansion and Asian exclusion in the United States. In her pioneering study of Indian immigrants in North America, historian Joan Jensen observed that Indians' "struggle for equality in North America remained linked to the larger issue of political independence for India." Joan M. Jensen, *Passage from India: Asian Indian Immigrants in North America* (New Haven, CT: Yale University Press, 1988), 272. See also Premdatta Varma, *Indian Immigrants in USA: Struggle for Equality* (Ann Arbor, MI: Heritage, 1995); Kornel S. Chang, *Pacific Connections: The Making of the US-Canadian Borderlands* (Berkeley: University of California Press, 2012); Seema Sohi, *Echoes of Mutiny: Race, Empire, and Indian Anticolonialism in North America* (New York: Oxford University Press, 2014).

8. The debate over whether the United States is (or ever was) an empire and, if so, what kind, remains one of the most contentious and enduring, including among

scholars of U.S. diplomatic history. For a good overview, see Dane Kennedy, "Essay and Reflection: On the American Empire from a British Imperial Perspective," *International History Review* 29, no. 1 (2007): 83–108.

9. According to Paul Kramer, the class-based loopholes and exemptions—or "imperial openings"—built into the Chinese Exclusion Act of 1882 exemplified the "politics of imperial anti-exclusion," or the "selective and hierarchical incorporation of foreign populations as a function of state and corporate efforts to project global power." See Paul A. Kramer, "Imperial Openings: Civilization, Exemption, and the Geopolitics of Mobility in the History of Chinese Exclusion, 1868–1910," *Journal of the Gilded Age and Progressive Era* 14, no. 3 (2015): 320.

10. For more on the shift from formal to informal empire, see Kwame Nkrumah, *Neo-Colonialism: The Last Stage of Imperialism*, 1965 (New York: International Publishers, 1966), 1; Simeon Man, *Soldiering through Empire: Race and the Making of the Decolonizing Pacific* (Berkeley, CA: University of California Press, 2018), 4–10, especially 6–9; Takashi Fujitani, *Race for Empire: Koreans as Japanese and Japanese as Americans during World War II* (Berkeley, CA: University of California Press, 2011).

11. For more on this idea, see Yukiko Koshiro, *Trans-Pacific Racisms and the U.S. Occupation of Japan* (New York: Columbia University Press, 1999); Fujitani, *Race for Empire*; Man, *Soldiering through Empire*.

12. Fujitani, in turn, drew upon the work of Etienne Balibar. Unlike more "vulgar" forms of racism, "polite racism" allowed for the possibility of assimilation and acknowledged, at least to an extent, the volition of racialized subjects within imperial systems of power. In Fujitani's telling, the Japanese empire adopted a similar racial project. Fujitani, *Race for Empire*, 38–39.

13. I employ the term "Asian American" expansively to refer to all persons of Asian descent living in the United States—foreign- and native-born, U.S. citizens and noncitizens.

14. For more on the term "transpacific" and its uses across disciplines, see the introduction in *Transpacific Studies: Framing an Emerging Field*, ed. Janet Hoskins and Viet Thanh Nguyen (Honolulu: University of Hawai'i Press, 2014), 1–38.

15. One need only recall the cautionary tale about how Japan's perceived meddling in U.S. congressional debates about Japanese exclusion leading to the 1924 Johnson-Reed Act actually strengthened U.S. lawmakers' support for full Asian exclusion to see this assumption in action. Asian governments were by no means the only foreign entities that tried to influence U.S. immigration policy. For example, from the late nineteenth century through the Cold War, the Italian government sought to shape U.S. laws governing Italian migration to the United States in various ways. Danielle Battisti, *Whom We Shall Welcome: Italian Americans and Immigration Reform, 1945–1965* (New York: Fordham University Press, 2019).

16. Oscar V. Campomanes, "New Formations of Asian American Studies and the Question of U.S. Imperialism," *Positions* 5, no. 2 (1997): 533. Paul Kramer has remarked on an absence of attention to empire in U.S. immigration scholarship. See Paul A. Kramer, "Power and Connection: Imperial Histories of the United States in the World," *American Historical Review* 116, no. 5 (2011): 1349. See also Kramer, "Imperial Openings," 317–18. Of notable exception are historians of Asian immigration,

who have centered empire in their analyses for years. See, for example, Jensen, *Passage from India*; Lili Kim, "The Limits of Americanism and Democracy: Korean Americans, Transnational Allegiance, and the Question of Loyalty on the Homefront during World War II," *Amerasia Journal* 29, no. 3 (2003): 79–96; Eiichiro Azuma, *Between Two Empires: Race, History, and Transnationalism in Japanese America* (New York: Oxford University Press, 2005); Augusto Espiritu, *Five Faces of Exile: The Nation and Filipino American Intellectuals* (Palo Alto, CA: Stanford University Press, 2005); Richard S. Kim, *The Quest for Statehood: Korean Immigrant Nationalism and US Sovereignty, 1905–1945* (New York: Oxford University Press, 2011).

17. Here I build on the work of scholars linking African and African American movements for freedom. See Brenda Gayle Plummer, *In Search of Power: African Americans in the Era of Decolonization, 1956–1974* (New York: Cambridge University Press, 2013); Thomas Borstelmann, *The Cold War and the Color Line: American Race Relations in the Global Arena* (Cambridge, MA: Harvard University Press, 2001).

18. See footnote 7 for some notable exceptions.

19. Sau-ling C. Wong, "Denationalization Reconsidered: Asian American Cultural Criticism at a Theoretical Crossroads," *Amerasia Journal* 21, no. 1/2 (1995): 3.

20. For more discussion of this political challenge, see Kim, *The Quest for Statehood*.

21. Lisa Levenstein, *A Movement without Marches: African American Women and the Politics of Poverty in Postwar Philadelphia* (Chapel Hill: University of North Carolina Press, 2009), 4.

22. In this I embrace the more critical view of law professor Lani Guinier and depart from the more capacious characterizations of racial liberalism offered by historians including Gary Gerstle and Mark Brilliant. Lani Guinier, "From Racial Liberalism to Racial Literacy: Brown v. Board of Education and the Interest-Divergence Dilemma," *Journal of American History* 91, no. 1 (June 2004): 92–118. For a brief discussion of these two schools, see Mark Brilliant, *The Color of America Has Changed: How Racial Diversity Shaped Civil Rights Reform in California, 1941–1978* (Oxford University Press, 2010), 271n24; Gary Gerstle, "Crucial Decade: The 1940s and Beyond," *Journal of American History* 92, no. 4 (2006): 1292–99. The literature addressing this tactic is extensive and crosses disciplinary boundaries. Historians including Mary Dudziak and Brenda Gayle Plummer have demonstrated how the United States' Cold War imperative to rehabilitate its tarnished domestic record on race and to counter international charges of American racial hypocrisy both facilitated and constrained legal gains for African Americans at home. These scholars' work built, in part, on the interest-convergence theory first described by law professor Derrick Bell and the social movement theories of sociologist Douglas McAdam. Brenda Gayle Plummer, *Rising Wind: Black Americans and US Foreign Affairs, 1935–1960* (Chapel Hill: University of North Carolina Press, 1996); Mary Dudziak, *Cold War Civil Rights: Race and the Image of American Democracy* (Princeton, NJ: Princeton University Press, 2000); Borstelmann, *The Cold War and the Color Line*; Derrick A. Bell Jr., "Brown v. Board of Education and the Interest-Convergence Dilemma," *Harvard Law Review* 93, no. 3 (1980): 518–33; Douglas McAdam, "On the International Origins of Domestic Political Opportunities," in *Social Movements and American Political Institutions*, ed. Anne Costain and Andrew McFarland (Totowa, NJ: Rowman and Littlefield, 1998), 251–67.

23. A broad consensus dates the shift to the 1930s, in response to Japanese expansionism and wide-scale devastation in China, but it was not until World War II that U.S. policymakers first saw their own fate as dependent on the loyalties and goodwill of Asian peoples. See Warren I. Cohen, "American Leaders and East Asia, 1931–1938," in *American, Chinese and Japanese Perspectives on Wartime Asia, 1931–1939*, ed. Akira Iriye and Warren Cohen (Wilmington, DE: Scholarly Resources, 1990), 2, 25. For a longer discussion, see Waldo Heinrichs, "The Middle Years, 1900–1945, and the Question of a Large U.S. Policy for East Asia," in *New Frontiers in American-East Asian Relations: Essays Presented to Dorothy Borg*, ed. Warren I. Cohen (New York: Columbia University Press, 1983), 98–100.

24. Taken from "May 25, 1943: Tokyo Domei in English to the Pacific Zone," U.S. House Committee on Immigration and Naturalization, *Samples of Japanese-Controlled Radio Comments on America's Exclusion Act*, 78th Cong., 1st sess. (1943) (Washington, DC: Government Printing Office, 1943), 6.

25. On this point, I find useful Jason Parker's definition of the Cold War as a "protean conflict whose fluctuating 'East-West' dynamics slowed, stalled, and then sped the 'North-South' decolonization and race revolutions." Along similar lines, Parker argues that it is problematic to talk about the conflict as one "broadly unified" idea or concept spanning decades of international history; I especially appreciate his division of the postwar period into "at least two 'Cold Wars': an early one characterized by Race repression, which gave way to a second one of Race liberation." See Jason C. Parker, "Cold War II: The Eisenhower Administration, the Bandung Conference, and the Re-periodization of the Postwar Era," *Diplomatic History* 30, no. 5 (2006): 869–70, 873.

26. Man, *Soldiering through Empire*, 8.

27. See, for example, Alexander Saxton, *The Indispensable Enemy: Labor and the Anti-Chinese Movement in California* (Berkeley: University of California Press, 1975); Elmer Clarence Sandmeyer, *The Anti-Chinese Movement in California* (Urbana: University of Illinois Press, 1991); Andrew Gyory, *Closing the Gate: Race, Politics, and the Chinese Exclusion Act* (Chapel Hill: University of North Carolina Press, 1998); Sucheng Chan, "The Exclusion of Chinese Women," in *Entry Denied: Exclusion and the Chinese Community in America* (Philadelphia: Temple University Press, 1991), 94–146; Sucheng Chan, *This Bittersweet Soil: The Chinese in California Agriculture, 1860–1910* (Berkeley: University of California Press, 1989); Gordon H. Chang, "China and the Pursuit of America's Destiny: Nineteenth-Century Imagining and Why Immigration Restriction Took So Long," *Journal of Asian American Studies* 15, no. 2 (2012): 145–69.

28. Yuji Ichioka, *The Issei: The World of the First-Generation Japanese Immigrants, 1885–1924* (New York: Free Press, 1988).

29. Gary R. Hess, "The 'Hindu' in America: Immigration and Naturalization Policies and India, 1917–1946," *Pacific Historical Review* 38, no. 1 (1969): 59–79; Seema Sohi, *Echoes of Mutiny: Race, Empire, and Indian Anticolonialism in North America* (New York: Oxford University Press, 2014).

30. Mae M. Ngai, *Impossible Subjects: Illegal Aliens and the Making of Modern America* (Princeton, NJ: Princeton University Press, 2004); Desmond King, *Making Americans: Immigration, Race, and the Origins of the Diverse Democracy* (Cambridge, MA: Harvard University Press, 2000).

31. See, for example, Delber L. McKee, "The Chinese Boycott of 1905–1906 Reconsidered: The Role of Chinese Americans," *Pacific Historical Review* 55, no. 2 (1986): 165–91; Michael H. Hunt, *The Making of a Special Relationship: The United States and China to 1914* (New York: Columbia University Press, 1983); Izumi Hirobe, *Japanese Pride, American Prejudice: Modifying the Exclusion Clause of the 1924 Immigration Act* (Palo Alto, CA: Stanford University Press, 2001); Jennifer Snow, *Protestant Missionaries, Asian Immigrants, and Ideologies of Race in America, 1850–1924* (New York: Routledge, 2006); Lon Kurashige, *Two Faces of Exclusion: The Untold History of Anti-Asian Racism in the United States* (Chapel Hill: University of North Carolina Press, 2016).

32. Japan's example makes clear the critical importance of power and status in shaping the history of international migration policy: the more a country possessed, the less likely it was to be subjected to restriction by others. Indeed, this was some of the main logic underpinning the Japanese government's objections to U.S. exclusion laws, which Tokyo officials protested as a symbol of Japan's weakness on the international stage.

33. Due to the sheer volume of titles, specific citations appear in individual chapters. Studies tend to emphasize the work of four distinct but overlapping groups in overturning legal exclusion: U.S. foreign policy officials, racial liberals in Congress, a timely confluence of white elites and immigration reformers, and Asian American communities.

34. These notable exceptions include Neil Gotanda, "Exclusion and Inclusion: Immigration and American Orientalism," in *Across the Pacific: Asian Americans and Globalization*, ed. Evelyn Hu-Dehart (Philadelphia: Temple University Press, 1999), 129–51; Kurashige, *Two Faces of Exclusion*.

35. Legal scholars, or specifically critical race theorists, were among the first to talk about successive repeal campaigns as part of a longer, coherent movement. Consistent with their interest in the law's role in racial formation, their analyses focus primarily on repeal's consequences for domestic U.S. racial categories and attitudes. See, for example, Neil Gotanda, "Exclusion and Inclusion: Immigration and American Orientalism," in *Across the Pacific: Asian Americans and Globalization*, ed. Evelyn Hu-Dehart (Philadelphia: Temple University Press, 1999), 129–51. Among historians, David Reimers provided a brief overview of the repeal acts as part of a larger study on "Third World" immigration to the United States. See David M. Reimers, *Still the Golden Door: The Third World Comes to America* (New York: Columbia University Press, 1992), 11–31. More recently, Madeline Y. Hsu and Ellen D. Wu used "minor reforms" in pre-1965 Asian immigration to illustrate Asian Americans' "conditional inclusion," a "delimited integration" that enacted "new modes of inequality." Madeline Y. Hsu and Ellen D. Wu, "'Smoke and Mirrors': Conditional Inclusion, Model Minorities, and the Pre-1965 Dismantling of Asian Exclusion," *Journal of American Ethnic History* 34, no. 4 (2015): 47–48.

36. Sean Brawley, *The White Peril: Foreign Relations and Asian Immigration to Australasia and North America, 1919–1978* (Sydney, Australia: University of New South Wales, 1995); Marilyn Lake and Henry Reynolds, *Drawing the Global Colour Line: White Men's Countries and the International Challenge of Racial Equality* (London: Cambridge University Press, 2008); Chang, *Pacific Connections*; David Atkinson, *The Burden of*

White Supremacy: Containing Asian Migration in the British Empire and the United States (Chapel Hill: University of North Carolina Press, 2017).

37. Erez Manela, *The Wilsonian Moment: Self-Determination and the International Origins of Anticolonial Nationalism* (New York: Oxford University Press, 2007).

38. On this point, I find useful Jason Parker's definition of the Cold War as a "protean conflict whose fluctuating 'East-West' dynamics slowed, stalled, and then sped the 'North-South' decolonization and race revolutions." I also appreciate his division of the postwar period into "at least two 'Cold Wars': an early one characterized by Race repression, which gave way to a second one of Race liberation." See Jason C. Parker, "Cold War II: The Eisenhower Administration, the Bandung Conference, and the Reperiodization of the Postwar Era," *Diplomatic History* 30, no. 5 (2006): 869–70, 873. For a good critique of totalizing Cold War lenses, see Matthew Connelly, "Taking Off the Cold War Lens: Visions of North-South Conflict during the Algerian War for Independence," *American Historical Review* 105, no. 3 (2000): 739–69.

39. David M. Reimers, "An Unintended Reform: The 1965 Immigration Act and Third World Immigration to the United States," *Journal of American Ethnic History* 3, no. 1 (1983): 9–28.

40. Recent work has illuminated the settler roots of Asian migrations, including to the United States. See, for example, Dean Saranillio, *Unsustainable Empire: Alternative Histories of Hawai'i Statehood* (Durham, NC: Duke University Press, 2018) and Eiichiro Azuma, *In Search of Our Frontier: Japanese America and Settler Colonialism in the Construction of Japan's Borderless Empire* (Berkeley, CA: University of California Press, 2019).

41. Canada acted next, repealing its 1923 Chinese Exclusion Act in 1947. See Kenneth M. Holland, "A History of Chinese Immigration in the United States and Canada," *American Review of Canadian Studies* 37, no. 2 (2007): 150–60; Stephanie D. Bangarth, "'We are not asking you to open wide the gates for Chinese immigration': The Committee for the Repeal of the Chinese Immigration Act and Early Human Rights Activism in Canada," *Canadian Historical Review* 84, no. 3 (2003): 395–422.

42. As historians Marilyn Lake and Henry Reynolds have described, Australian governments moved to exclude Chinese migrants as early as the 1870s and more fully with the passage of the White Australia policy in 1903. In contrast, Washington passed the first Chinese Exclusion Acts during the 1880s and would not codify wholesale Asian exclusion until 1924. Marilyn Lake and Henry Reynolds, *Drawing the Global Colour Line: White Men's Countries and the International Challenge of Racial Equality* (London: Cambridge University Press, 2008), 17–30, 152–62. Scholars have similarly highlighted the wide scale of white supremacy and anti-Asian movements as global and hemispheric rather than national histories in ways that this study appreciates. See Erika Lee, "Orientalisms in the Americas: A Hemispheric Approach to Asian American History," *Journal of Asian American Studies* 8, no. 3 (2005): 235–56; Chang, *Pacific Connections*; Mae M. Ngai, "Chinese Gold Miners and the 'Chinese Question' in Nineteenth-Century California and Victoria," *Journal of American History* 101, no. 4 (2015): 1082–1105. In similar fashion, David Atkinson has shown how U.S. restrictions against Japanese and South Asians fit within a longer history of efforts by British Dominion governments to contain Asian migration. Compared with Lake and Reynolds,

however, he sees more disconnect and disruption than solidarity among white settler powers. See Atkinson, *The Burden of White Supremacy*, 5.

43. For example, as one of the few scholars to consider the dismantling of the United States' Asian exclusion regime in a global context, historian Sean Brawley credited foreign policy and diplomatic pressures on national governments with helping drive the repeal of Asian exclusion laws in the United States, Canada, New Zealand, and Australia after World War II; in his words, "internationalism" became "immigration exclusionists' greatest enemy." Brawley's discussion, however, says little about the unevenness in status and power among the four countries and the major differences distinguishing each nation's relationship with Asian powers and its specific interests in the Pacific region. See Sean Brawley, *The White Peril: Foreign Relations and Asian Immigration to Australasia and North America, 1919–1978* (Sydney, Australia: University of New South Wales, 1995), 199.

44. Marilyn B. Young, "The Age of Global Power," *Rethinking American History in a Global Age*, ed. Thomas Bender (Berkeley: University of California Press, 2002), 271, 295.

45. The other three powers also shared close ties with Great Britain: Australia became a Commonwealth nation in 1901; Canada became a self-governing dominion of the British empire in 1867 and gained formal independence in 1931; New Zealand did so in 1907 and 1947, respectively.

46. Along similar lines, historian Meredith Oyen observes that the United States "appeared as a leader—the first to enact formal exclusion laws . . . and the first to repeal them." Meredith Oyen, *The Diplomacy of Migration: Transnational Lives and the Making of U.S.-Chinese Relations in the Cold War* (Ithaca, NY: Cornell University Press, 2015), 48.

47. For more on U.S. interimperial relations, see Eiichiro Azuma, *Between Two Empires: Race, History, and Transnationalism in Japanese America* (New York: Oxford University Press, 2005); Chang, *Pacific Connections*.

48. Melvyn Leffler, *A Preponderance of Power: National Security, the Truman Administration, and the Cold War* (Palo Alto, CA: Stanford University Press, 1992). Scholars continue to debate when the United States became a world power. I date the United States' initial rise to global supremacy to what historian Brian McKercher calls the "transition of power" from British to U.S. dominance between 1930 and 1945. This is later than other scholars who cite the United States' economic strength to suggest that it was "indisputably the strongest Power in the world" by the end of World War I. Brian McKercher, *Transition of Power: Britain's Loss of Global Pre-Eminence to the United States, 1930–1945* (New York: Cambridge University Press, 1999), 154; Paul Kennedy, *The Rise and Fall of the Great Powers: Economic Change and Military Conflict from 1500 to 2000* (New York: Random House, 1987), xix, 274–343.

49. Augusto Espiritu, "Inter-Imperial Relations, the Pacific, and Asian American History," *Pacific Historical Review* 83, no. 2 (2014): 240–41.

50. Legal scholars were the first to elaborate on the importance of this coupling. For more on the debate that led to inclusion of the term "aliens ineligible to citizenship" in the 1924 Immigration Act, see Deenesh Sohoni, "Unsuitable Suitors: Anti-Miscegenation Laws, Naturalization Laws, and the Construction of Asian Identities," *Law & Society Review* 41, no. 3 (2007): 602–8; Ngai, *Impossible Subjects*, 37–50.

51. Scholars of postwar California have identified moments of cooperation and coalition between Asian Americans and other nonwhite communities around issues of common concern, including discrimination in housing, employment, and access to public facilities. Select titles in this still-growing literature include Shana Bernstein, *Bridges of Reform: Interracial Civil Rights Activism in Twentieth-Century Los Angeles* (New York: Oxford University Press, 2010); Brilliant, *The Color of America Has Changed*; Charlotte Brooks, *Alien Neighbors, Foreign Friends: Asian Americans, Housing, and the Transformation of Urban California* (Chicago: University of Chicago Press, 2009); Lon Kurashige, *Japanese American Celebration and Conflict: A History of Ethnic Identity and Festival, 1934–1990* (Berkeley: University of California Press, 2002); Scott Kurashige, *The Shifting Grounds of Race: Black and Japanese Americans in the Making of Multiethnic Los Angeles* (Princeton, NJ: Princeton University Press, 2008); and Greg Robinson, *After Camp: Portraits in Midcentury Japanese American Life and Politics* (Berkeley: University of California Press, 2012).

52. David M. Reimers, "An Unintended Reform: The 1965 Immigration Act and Third World Immigration to the United States," *Journal of American Ethnic History* 3, no. 1 (1983): 9–28.

53. Fred Riggs, *Pressures on Congress: A Study of the Repeal of Chinese Exclusion* (New York: King's Crown Press, 1950), 41.

54. Sau-ling C. Wong, "Denationalization Reconsidered: Asian American Cultural Criticism at a Theoretical Crossroads," *Amerasia Journal* 21, no. 1/2 (1995): 3.

55. Figures taken from Jie Zong and Jeanne Batalova, "Asian Immigrants in the United States," *Migration Information Source*, January 6, 2016, https://www.migrationpolicy.org/article/asian-immigrants-united-states, accessed April 15, 2019.

56. Lisa Lowe, *Immigrant Acts: On Asian American Cultural Politics* (Durham, NC: Duke University Press, 1996), 16–17.

57. For more on this idea, see Gary Y. Okihiro, *Margins and Mainstreams: Asians in American History and Culture* (Seattle: University of Washington Press, 1994), 28–29 and Gary Y. Okihiro, *American History Unbound: Asians and Pacific Islanders* (Berkeley: University of California Press, 2015), 9.

Chapter One

1. I thank Baldwin Chiu for sharing his family's story with me. Chiu and his wife, Larissa Lam, have made a documentary that uses his family's story as a window into the history of early Chinese immigrants in the Mississippi Delta. See *Finding Cleveland*, directed by Larissa Lam (Los Angeles: 2015).

2. Private Bill 918, July 15, 1952.

3. K. C. Lou's son eventually came to the United States in 1952, using the papers that his grandfather Charlie had begun filing years earlier. Lou built a life in southern California, where his children and grandchildren still live today. His sister and mother ultimately died in China. For more on Chinese exclusion's impact, see Haiming Liu, "The Trans-Pacific Family: A Case Study of Sam Chang's Family History," *Amerasia Journal* 18, no. 2 (1992): 1–34.

4. While the history of Chinese exclusion has been well studied, the broader impact of the law's family-related loopholes is lesser known. Over the last two decades, scholars have shone a brighter spotlight on these legal exemptions, their significance, and their consequences. In chronological order, see Xiaojian Zhao, *Remaking Chinese America: Immigration, Family, and Community, 1940-1965* (New Brunswick, NJ: Rutgers University Press, 2002); Adam McKeown, "Transnational Chinese Families and Chinese Exclusion, 1875-1943," *Journal of American Ethnic History* (1999): 73-110; Gordon H. Chang, "China and the Pursuit of America's Destiny: Nineteenth-Century Imagining and Why Immigration Restriction Took So Long," *Journal of Asian American Studies* 15, no. 2 (2012): 145-69; Beth Lew-Williams, "Before Restriction Became Exclusion," *Pacific Historical Review* 83, no. 1 (2014): 24-56; Paul Kramer, "Imperial Openings: Civilization, Exemption, and the Geopolitics of Mobility in the History of Chinese Exclusion, 1868-1910," *Journal of the Gilded Age and Progressive Era* 14, no. 3 (July 2015): 317-47.

5. See, for example, Fred Riggs, *Pressures on Congress: A Study of the Repeal of Chinese Exclusion* (New York: King's Crown Press, 1950); Ling-chi L. Wang, "Politics of the Repeal of the Chinese Exclusion Laws," in *Remembering 1882: Fighting for Civil Rights in the Shadow of the Chinese Exclusion Act* (San Francisco: Chinese Historical Society of America, 1993); Madeline Y. Hsu, *The Good Immigrants: How the Yellow Peril Became the Model Minority* (Princeton, NJ: Princeton University Press, 2015), 91-103; Meredith Oyen, *The Diplomacy of Migration: Transnational Lives and the Making of U.S.-Chinese Relations in the Cold War* (Ithaca, NY: Cornell University Press, 2015), 24-41.

6. Soong's exact words were that the "prevailing opinion seems to consider the defeat of the Japanese as of relative unimportance and that Hitler is our first concern. This is not borne out by actual facts, nor is it to the interests of the United Nations as a whole to allow Japan to continue, not only as a vital potential threat but as a waiting sword of Damocles, ready to descend at a moment's notice." Reprinted in "Speech to Congress," *Life Magazine*, March 1, 1943.

7. For more on American media coverage of the visit, see Lorraine Dong, "Song Meiling in America 1943," in *The Repeal and Its Legacy: Proceedings of the Conference on the 50th Anniversary of the Repeal of the Exclusion Acts* (San Francisco: Chinese Historical Society of America, 1994), 39-46.

8. Here I build on the work of other historians who have written about the problem of Chinese wives, including in the context of the larger Chinese exclusion repeal campaign. Xiaojian Zhao, *Remaking Chinese America: Immigration, Family, and Community, 1940-1965* (New Brunswick, NJ: Rutgers University Press, 2002), 24-27; Oyen, *Diplomacy of Migration*, 25-26, 79-82.

9. Historian Xiaojian Zhao has suggested that the Magnuson Act's quota of 105 probably reduced the number of Chinese coming to the United States by closing loopholes in a 1930 law that had allowed the Chinese children and wives of U.S. citizens married before the 1924 Immigration Act to enter the United States outside of any quota limit. Under the Magnuson Act, even these individuals were subject to the restrictive annual quota. See Zhao, *Remaking Chinese America*, 24. This is discussed in the last part of the chapter.

10. Sucheng Chan, *Asian Americans: An Interpretive History* (Boston: Twayne, 1991), 105–6.

11. Sucheng Chan argued that U.S. state efforts at restricting Chinese women were a "more significant factor" than cultural and economic explanations in explaining the skewed gender dynamics of the Chinese American community from the late nineteenth century onward. See Sucheng Chan, "The Exclusion of Chinese Women, 1870–1943," in *Entry Denied: Exclusion and the Chinese American Community, 1882–1943*, ed. Sucheng Chan (Philadelphia: Temple University Press, 1991), 94–95; Zhao, *Remaking Chinese America*.

12. *Tsoi Sim v. United States*, 116 F. 920, 925 (9th Cir. 1902). Based on the legal logic of coverture, the case established a judicial policy whereby Chinese alien wives could enter the United States on the basis of the rights enjoyed by their U.S. citizen husbands, who served as sponsors. Judges could be inconsistent in how they interpreted the exclusion laws to apply to Chinese wives, however. Chinese seeking admission fought these battles on an individual basis through the early 1920s. See Chan, "The Exclusion of Asian Women," 118.

13. These figures were taken from Chan, "The Exclusion of Chinese Women," 95. The U.S. population of Chinese women never exceeded 5,000 before 1900. See Chan, *Asian Americans*, 104–5.

14. Charles J. McClain, *In Search of Equality: The Chinese Struggle against Discrimination in Nineteenth-Century America* (Berkeley: University of California Press, 1994).

15. Yong Chen, *Chinese San Francisco, 1850–1943: A Trans-Pacific Community* (Palo Alto, CA: Stanford University Press, 2000), 148–61.

16. Lucy Salyer, *Laws Harsh as Tigers: Chinese Immigrants and the Shaping of Modern Immigration Law* (Chapel Hill: University of North Carolina Press, 1995); Charles McClain, *In Search of Equality: The Chinese Struggle against Discrimination in Nineteenth-Century America* (Berkeley: University of California Press, 1994); Erika Lee, *At America's Gates: Chinese Immigration during the Exclusion Era, 1882–1943* (Chapel Hill: University of North Carolina Press, 2003), 111–46.

17. Washington's traditional emphasis on diplomacy with Europe meant that nonstate or private actors historically exercised a disproportionate influence in U.S.– East Asia affairs. In the absence of strong interest by Washington, the task of challenging Chinese exclusion fell largely to Americans outside of government. See Izumi Hirobe, *Japanese Pride, American Prejudice: Modifying the Exclusion Clause of the 1924 Immigration Act* (Palo Alto, CA: Stanford University Press, 2001), 1–20.

18. Jennifer C. Snow, *Protestant Missionaries, Asian Immigrants, and Ideologies of Race in America, 1850–1924* (New York: Routledge, 2007), xv, 55–88; James J. Lorence, "Business and Reform: The American Asiatic Association and the Exclusion Laws, 1905–1907," *Pacific Historical Review* 39 (November 1970): 421–38. For more on perceptions of the possibilities of the China market, see Paul A. Varg, "The Myth of the China Market," in *The Making of a Myth: The United States and China, 1897–1912* (East Lansing: Michigan State University Press, 1968); Marilyn B. Young, *The Rhetoric of Empire: American China Policy, 1895–1901* (Cambridge, MA: Harvard University Press, 1968); Michael H. Hunt, "Americans in the China Market: Economic Opportunities and Economic Nationalism, 1890s–1931," *Business History Review* 51, no. 3 (Autumn 1977): 277–307.

19. See, for example, James J. Lorence, *Organized Business and the Myth of the China Market: The American Asiatic Association, 1898–1937* (Philadelphia: The American Philosophical Society, 1981).

20. Oyen, *Diplomacy of Migration*, 13–51.

21. Protestant and Catholic organizations were historically strong advocates of migration policies supporting family reunification. See, for example, Gráinne McEvoy, "Justice and Order: American Catholic Social Thought and the Immigration Question in the Restriction Era, 1917–1965" (PhD diss., Boston College, 2014).

22. American Board of Commissioners for Foreign Missions to Van Kirk, September 2, 1941, Box 34, Federal Council of Churches (FCC) Papers, Presbyterian Historical Society (PHS), Philadelphia.

23. *Cheung Sum Shee v. Nagle*, 268 U.S. 336 (1925); *Chang Chan et al. v. John Nagle*, 268 U.S. 346 (1925).

24. For more on the history of the CACA, see Sue Fawn Chung, "Fighting for Their American Rights: A History of the Chinese American Citizens Alliance," in *Claiming America: Constructing Chinese American Identities during the Exclusion Era*, ed. K. Scott Wong and Sucheng Chan (Philadelphia: Temple University Press, 1998), 98–126, especially 118–19.

25. Y. C. Hong, *A Plea for Relief*, Box 1, Hong Family Papers, Huntington Library, San Marino, CA.

26. In the 69th Congress (1926), S. 2358 was sponsored by Senator Willian H. King (D-UT), and H.R. 6544 by Rep. Leonidas C. Dyer (R-MO). In the 70th Congress (1928), the two lawmakers reintroduced their legislation (S. 2271, H.R. 6974).

27. Zhao, *Remaking Chinese America*, 20. In the 75th Congress (1929–1930), these bills were S. 2826, introduced by Senator Bingham, H.R. 5654 introduced by Hawaii Territorial Delegate Houston, and H.R. 12379 sponsored by Rep. Dyer.

28. Zhao, *Remaking Chinese America*, 21. Attempts in 1935 and 1937 to expand the law to allow wives of all races ineligible for citizenship to enter the United States passed the House only to be blocked in the Senate. These bills would have expanded nonquota admission to the foreign-born Asian wives of white American soldiers and veterans.

29. State-sponsored repatriation and deportation programs targeting Mexicans and Filipina/os were two notable examples.

30. Three of the hearing's six witnesses were clergy, while a fourth witness, Ernest Hocking, a philosophy professor at Harvard University, had worked closely with Pearl Buck and other American missionaries in Asia to author a 1932 study that called for fundamental changes to the U.S. missionary project overseas.

31. David A. Hollinger, *Protestants Abroad: How Missionaries Tried to Change the World but Changed America* (Princeton, NJ: Princeton University Press, 2017), 24–48.

32. Sheryll Cashin, *Loving: Interracial Intimacy in America and the Threat to White Supremacy* (New York: Beacon Press, 2017).

33. U.S. House Committee on Immigration and Naturalization, *To Provide for the Admission to the U.S. of Alien Chinese Wives of American Citizens*, 78th Cong., 1st sess. (March 1943), 14b.

34. Tichenor, *Dividing Lines: The Politics of Immigration Control in America* (Princeton, NJ: Princeton University Press, 2002), 163–65.

35. Dickstein was a strategic presence. As discussed in chapters 2 and 3, it was because of his position as the House Immigration Committee chairman that Indian and Filipino American activists had their citizenship bills heard as early as 1939. See Chin Jou, "Contesting Nativism: The New York Congressional Delegation's Case against the Immigration Act of 1924," *Federal History* 3 (2011): 66–79.

36. U.S. House Committee on Immigration and Naturalization, *To Provide for the Admission to the U.S. of Alien Chinese Wives of American Citizens*, 37–38.

37. While he styled himself as a friend to immigrants, Dickstein also allegedly used his position as House Immigration Committee chairman to profit off the selling of U.S. passports and citizenship. See Allen Weinstein, Alexander Vassiliev, and Bill Wallace, *The Haunted Wood: Soviet Espionage in America—the Stalin Era* (New York: Random House, 1999), 140.

38. Of course, this is not to suggest that Dickstein did not care about U.S. foreign affairs. In a strange addendum, he is the only U.S. lawmaker in history known to have served as a secret agent for a foreign power (in this case, the Soviet Union), although his actions did not become known until long after his death in 1954. Not without irony, his Soviet code name was "Crook." Weinstein, Vassiliev, and Wallace, *The Haunted Wood*, 140.

39. Gary Gerstle, *American Crucible: Race and Nation in the Twentieth Century* (Princeton, NJ: Princeton University Press, 2001), 196; Walter Judd to Raymond Buell Goodwood, of Richmond, MA, June 26, 1943, Box 71, Walter H. Judd Papers, Hoover Institution, Stanford University, Stanford, CA.

40. One of the great ironies of Dickstein's career was that, under later conservative leadership, the same committees he had helped found to stamp out racism and anti-Semitism became state vehicles used to suppress leftists and liberals during the Cold War. The House Committee on Un-American Activities (HUAC) was a prime example; he was in fact excluded from serving on the committee after founding it. See Ted Morgan, *Reds: McCarthyism in Twentieth-Century America* (New York: Random House, 2004), 187; Walter Goodman, *The Committee: The Extraordinary Career of the House Committee on Un-American Activities* (New York: Farrar, Straus, and Giroux, 1968), 44.

41. U.S. House Committee on Immigration and Naturalization, *To Provide for the Admission to the U.S. of Alien Chinese Wives of American Citizens*, 8–9.

42. Zhao, *Remaking Chinese America*, 22.

43. Renqiu Yu, "Little Heard Voices: The Chinese Hand Laundry Alliance and the *China Daily News*' Appeal for Repeal of the Chinese Exclusion Act in 1943," *Chinese America: History & Perspectives* (1990): 21–35.

44. Riggs, *Pressures on Congress*, 112. See chapter 5 for more on Hawaii's role in a later stage of the repeal movement.

45. Zhao, *Remaking Chinese America*, 24.

46. This is largely due to the work of political scientist Fred Riggs, who studied the Citizens Committee campaign in real time. Riggs, *Pressures on Congress*.

47. Riggs, 48–50.

48. "Repeal Chinese Exclusion," *Asia and the Americas* 42 (February 1942): 92–94. It was followed by a similar piece in another China-centered journal, *Contemporary*

China. See "Exclusion and Extraterritoriality," *Contemporary China* 1, no. 26 (May 18, 1942).

49. Riggs, *Pressures on Congress*, 135.

50. Roger Daniels, *Prisoners without Trial: Japanese Americans in World War II* (New York: Hill and Wang, 1993), 22–48.

51. Riggs, *Pressures on Congress*, 53–54.

52. As historian Andrew Preston has described it, with "millions of members on its rolls" as well as "clergy who could repeat policy platforms from the pulpit Sunday after Sunday," the FCC in the 1940s wielded "significant, if sometimes imprecise and unwieldly, political authority." See Andrew Preston, "Peripheral Visions: American Mainline Protestants and the Global Cold War," *Cold War History* 13, no. 1 (2013): 117.

53. Quoted in Riggs, *Pressures on Congress*, 97.

54. White American missionaries are widely recognized as one of the main constituencies that historically supported immigration and other rights for Asian peoples and for Chinese in particular. See Jennifer Snow, *Protestant Missionaries, Asian Immigrants, and Ideologies of Race in America, 1850-1924* (New York: Routledge, 2006); Izumi Hirobe, *Japanese Pride, American Prejudice*; Lon Kurashige, *Two Faces of Exclusion: The Untold History of Anti-Asian Racism in the United States* (Chapel Hill: University of North Carolina Press, 2016). Michael Hunt has stressed the importance of American missionaries as part of what he called the "Open Door constituency." See Michael H. Hunt, *The Making of a Special Relationship: The United States and China to 1914* (New York: Columbia University Press, 1983), xi.

55. Harold R. Isaacs, *Scratches on Our Minds: American Images of China and India* (New York: John Day, 1958), 155–59.

56. Hollinger, *Protestants Abroad*, 1–3, 12.

57. John R. Mott, "New Forces Released by Cooperation," in *The Foreign Missions Convention at Washington, 1925*, ed. Fennell P. Turner and Frank Knight Sanders (New York: Foreign Missions Conference of North America, 1925), 209.

58. Tony Ladd, "Mission to Capitol Hill: A Study of the Impact of Missionary Idealism on the Congressional Career of Walter H. Judd," in *United States Attitudes and Policies Toward China: The Impact of American Missionaries*, ed. Patricia Neils (Armonk, NY: M.E. Sharpe, 1990), 271.

59. March 27, 1943, Box 25, Walter H. Judd Papers, Minnesota History Center, St. Paul, MN.

60. Hollinger describes World War II as a time when "missionary expertise was much in demand." See Hollinger, *Protestants Abroad*, 8.

61. Quoted in Tony Ladd, "Mission to Capitol Hill," 272–74.

62. Richard H. Rovere, "Eight Hopeful Congressmen," *Nation* 156, no. 9 (February 27, 1943): 294–97. Yet even in this brief piece, Rovere arguably gave fodder to Judd's more nationalistic critics, citing the Minnesotan's desire to "do all I can for China."

63. Riggs, *Pressures on Congress*, 135.

64. Judd to J. W. Dyson, February 26, 1943, Box 25, Judd Papers.

65. Robert E. Herzstein, *Henry R. Luce, Time, and the American Crusade in Asia* (New York: Cambridge University Press, 2005), i, iv, 20.

66. Crossley, Inc., *National Study of Magazine Audiences 1952* (Cowles Magazines: 1952). Herzstein, *Henry R. Luce*, i, iv, 20, 136.

67. With roots dating to World War II, the China Lobby, comprising former missionaries, state officials, journalists, and other white elites, emerged in force during the early 1950s, when its demonization of Chinese Communism and adulation of anticommunist Nationalist leader Chiang Kai-shek dovetailed neatly with the virulent anticommunism pervading foreign policy circles in Washington. See Ross Y. Koen, *The China Lobby in American Politics* (New York: Harper Collins, 1974); D. Bachrack Stanley, *The Committee of One Million: "China Lobby" Politics, 1953-1971* (New York: Columbia University Press, 1976).

68. Peter J. Conn, *Pearl S. Buck: A Cultural Biography* (New York: Cambridge University Press, 1998), 324 and 324–26 more generally.

69. In turn, Buck's 1951 novel *God's Men* is widely believed to satirize Luce, who served as the model for one of its main characters: a former missionary kid turned overbearing and sanctimonious publisher. For more, see Vanessa Künnemann, *Middlebrow Mission: Pearl S. Buck's American China* (London: Transcript Verlag, 2015), 235–40.

70. Quoted in Riggs, *Pressures on Congress*, 243. See also Riggs, 56–59.

71. Wang, "Politics of the Repeal," 79–80.

72. This figure is taken from the 1940 U.S. Census and excludes the territory of Hawaii.

73. U.S. House Committee on Immigration and Naturalization, *Repeal of the Chinese Exclusion Acts: Hearings on H.R. 1882 and H.R. 2309*, 78th Cong., 1st sess. (1943), 204, 209.

74. Riggs, *Pressures on Congress*, 127–28, 133.

75. U.S. House Committee on Immigration and Naturalization, *Repeal of the Chinese Exclusion Acts*, 215.

76. Indeed, Rep. Elmer (R-MO) accused the FCC's Van Kirk of using geopolitics precisely to dodge the "racial question inside the United States." U.S. House Committee on Immigration and Naturalization, *Repeal of the Chinese Exclusion Acts*, 121.

77. Quoted in Riggs, *Pressures on Congress*, 236; U.S. House Committee on Immigration and Naturalization, *Repeal of the Chinese Exclusion Acts*, 72–73.

78. U.S. House Committee on Immigration and Naturalization, *Repeal of Chinese Exclusion Acts*, 65 (emphasis added).

79. For an example that references southerners' opposition to an anti–poll tax, see U.S. House Committee on Immigration and Naturalization, *Repeal of the Chinese Exclusion Acts*, 64–65.

80. Moon-Ho Jung, *Coolies and Cane: Race, Labor, and Sugar in the Age of Emancipation* (Baltimore, MD: Johns Hopkins University Press, 2006).

81. U.S. House Committee on Immigration and Naturalization, *Repeal of Chinese Exclusion Acts*, 21, 26, 72.

82. U.S. House Committee on Immigration and Naturalization, *Repeal of Chinese Exclusion Acts*, 133, 136, 140.

83. Kilsoo Haan to Warren Magnuson, April 30, 1943, Box 1, Folder 33, Kilsoo Haan Papers, University of California, Santa Cruz, Santa Cruz, CA. The Sino-Korean military partnership to which Haan alluded was real, but cooperation was informal and

limited. Relative to the central role played by the Chinese military, which bore the brunt of Allied casualties on the Pacific front, U.S. policymakers estimated Korea's military value to the war as minimal at best. Korea's status as a Japanese colony further complicated matters. See Timothy L. Savage, "The American Response to the Korean Independence Movement, 1910–1945," *Korean Studies* 20/21 (1996): 215–16.

84. U.S. House Committee on Immigration and Naturalization, *Repeal of Chinese Exclusion Acts*, 40–41.

85. Riggs, *Pressures on Congress*, 177–80.

86. Franklin D. Roosevelt, "Message from the President of the United States Favoring Repeal of the Chinese Exclusion Laws," October 11, 1943.

87. Riggs, *Pressures on Congress*, 180–82.

88. Franklin D. Roosevelt, "Statement by the President on the Repeal of the Chinese Exclusion Laws," December 17, 1943.

89. Quoted in Riggs, *Pressures on Congress*, 235n24.

90. Political scientist Fred Riggs erroneously credited the omission of the wives provision in the Magnuson bill "primarily to a technicality of drafting" and suggested that had the wives provision been incorporated earlier, it "might have gone through without debate." Quoted in Riggs, *Pressures on Congress*, 235n24, 125–26.

91. Quoted in Riggs, *Pressures on Congress*, 235n24.

92. Quoted in Riggs, 62–63.

93. Oyen, *Diplomacy of Migration*, 32.

94. The law had a lesser impact on Chinese merchants' wives, who remained exempt from the new quota restriction.

95. Until his retirement from the U.S. Senate in 1950, Sheridan Downey was one of the Chinese American community's most powerful political patrons in the state. See Charlotte Brooks, *Between Mao and McCarthy: Chinese American Politics in the Cold War Years* (Chicago: University of Chicago Press, 2015), 71–74.

96. Zhao, *Remaking Chinese America*, 197n87.

Chapter Two

1. *New York Times*, February 8, 1944.

2. The letter is reprinted in *India News Bulletin*, December 1943, 1.

3. Agent-General Bajpai to O.K. Caroe, Department Secretary, June 10, 1943, External Affairs Department, File 379-X/43, Indian National Archives (INA), Delhi, India.

4. In this regard, U.S. India policy during World War II was consistent with the United States' longer history of ambivalence about independence movements. See Kenton J. Clymer, *Quest for Freedom: The United States and India's Independence* (New York: Columbia Univerty Press, 2010); Sarah Ellen Graham, "American Propaganda, the Anglo-American Alliance, and the 'Delicate Question' of Indian Self-Determination," *Diplomatic History* 33, no. 2 (2009): 223–59.

5. Gary R. Hess, "The 'Hindu' in America: Immigration and Naturalization Policies and India, 1917–1946," *Pacific Historical Review* 38 (1969): 71–77; Premdatta Varma, *Indian Immigrants in USA: Struggle for Equality* (New Delhi: Heritage, 1995), 270–370; R. Narayanan, "Indian Immigration and the India League of America," *Indian Journal*

of American Studies 2, no. 1 (1969): 1–29. For a general interest study, see Harold Gould, *Sikhs, Swamis, Students, and Spies: The India Lobby in the United States, 1900–1946* (New Delhi, India: Sage, 2006), 261–326.

6. Within the very sparse literature on Indian exclusion repeal, Dr. Premdatta Varma, who studied under historian Roger Daniels at the University of Cincinnati, is the only scholar I know of whose research addresses this. See Varma, *Indian Immigrants in USA*.

7. The few existing accounts of the campaign have generally disregarded the role of Indian officials in the effort. Varma's *Indian Immigrants in USA* is a notable exception. Others note links between Indian American campaigns and the Indian independence struggle without examining the relationship in any depth. See H. Brett Melendy, *Asians in America: Filipinos, Koreans, and East Indians* (Boston: Twayne, 1977).

8. For more on this idea, see Paul Kramer, "Geopolitics of Mobility: Immigration Policy and American Global Power in the Long Twentieth Century," *American Historical Review* 123, no. 1 (April 2018): 393–438.

9. Melvyn P. Leffler, *A Preponderance of Power: National Security, the Truman Administration, and the Cold War* (Palo Alto, CA: Stanford University Press, 1992).

10. The restrictions on Chinese and Japanese immigration were due to the Chinese Exclusion Act of 1882 and the Gentleman's Agreement of 1907, respectively.

11. For a more detailed history of Indians' early history in the United States, see Joan M. Jensen, *Passage from India: Asian Indian Immigrants in North America* (New Haven, CT: Yale University Press, 1988), 24–138.

12. Quoted in Arthur W. Helweg, "The Immigration Act of 1917: The Asian Indian Exclusion Act," in *Asian Americans and Congress: A Documentary History*, ed. Hyung-Chan Kim (Westport, CT: Greenwood Press, 1996), 157.

13. The World War I years were a pivotal time in the history of Indian struggles for independence from Great Britain. Erez Manela argues that the failure of Indian appeals to the United States' Woodrow Wilson helped radicalize Indian activists such as Mahatma Gandhi to seek greater autonomy and, eventually, independence for India beginning in the 1920s. See Erez Manela, *The Wilsonian Moment: Self-Determination and the International Origins of Anticolonial Nationalism* (New York: Oxford University Press, 2007).

14. Ronald Takaki, *Strangers from a Different Shore: A History of Asian Americans* (Boston: Little, Brown, 1989), 8.

15. Japan and the Philippines were exempt. See Helweg, "The Immigration Act of 1917."

16. Seema Sohi, *Echoes of Mutiny: Race, Surveillance, and Indian Anticolonialism in North America* (New York: Oxford University Press, 2014), 3, 8.

17. Before 1924, the two categories of people eligible for U.S. citizenship were "free white persons" and "persons of African descent."

18. Ian Haney Lopez, *White by Law: The Legal Construction of Race* (New York: New York University Press, 1997), 61–65.

19. The defendant Bhagat Singh Thind was a World War I veteran who had been granted citizenship by a federal court in Oregon. The case was not free of anticolonial

politics: Thind was a known advocate of Indian independence with personal ties to some of the "Hindus" implicated in the World War I Ghadar movement, while Supreme Court justice George Sutherland, who wrote the court's decision, had been born in Great Britain.

20. "America Takes Notice of Indian Legislature," *Modern Review* 37 (1925): 475–76.

21. Mark Juergensmeyer, "The Ghadar Syndrome: Nationalism in an Immigrant Community," *Punjab Journal of Politics* 1, no. 1 (1977): 8.

22. By his own account, Khan arrived in the United States after spending World War I as a German prisoner of war. On October 15, 1920, he arrived in New York as a "seaman" after the home secretary for India in London refused to issue him a passport for the United States File on S. 236, 79th Cong., 2nd sess. (1946), Legislative Records Office (National Archives [NARA] I), Washington, DC.

23. Vivek Bald, "Desertion and Sedition: Indian Seamen, Onshore Labor, and Expatriate Radicalism in New York and Detroit, 1914–1930," in *The Sun Never Sets: South Asian Migrants in an Age of U.S. Power*, ed. Vivek Bald, Miabi Chatterji, Sujani Reddy, and Manu Vimalassery (New York: New York University Press, 2013), 80 and 75–102 in general.

24. One Indian government report described the IWL's membership as comprising "seamen, laborers, and poor Indians." Report on India League, File 379-X/43 (1943), 57, INA, Delhi, India.

25. Haridas Muzumdar, *America's Contribution to India's Freedom* (Allahabad, India: Central Book Depot, 1962), 36.

26. Other related measures introduced during this period included H.R. 10736 (1938), H.R. 6798, and H.R. 4996 sponsored by Rep. Rudolph G. Tenerowicz (D-MI) in 1939, and H.R. 7110 (1939) sponsored by Rep. John Lesinski (D-MI).

27. U.S. House Committee on Immigration and Naturalization, *Naturalization of India-Born Immigrants: Hearing on H.R. 7110*, 76th Cong., 3rd sess. (1940).

28. U.S. House Committee on Immigration and Naturalization, *India-Born Residents of the U.S. Request for Naturalization*, 76th Cong., 1st sess. (1939), 15–19, 34–36.

29. Khan to Richard Russell, April 17, 1946, Senate Immigration Committee, file on S. 236, 79th Cong., 2nd sess. (1946) (NARA I), Washington, DC.

30. It was signed by fifty-seven prominent Americans. *New York Times*, September 28, 1942; reprinted in *India Today*, September 1942, 1.

31. This was ironic, since Singh frequently complained about the condescending attitudes of the ILA's more elite Indian members toward him for being a merchant without a graduate degree. Within what he called the "Indian brain trust," Singh often joked that he was the least educated among them, a "lowly merchant rather than a PhD." Levity aside, tensions between J. J. Singh and Indian elites within the ILA eventually became so bad that several left the group and formed an Indian independence organization of their own called the National Committee for India's Freedom. Members included Krishnanal Shridlani, a sociologist; Haridas Muzumdar; and Anup Singh. For more on interpersonal tensions, see J. J. Singh's 1951 *New Yorker* profile. Robert Shaplen, "One-Man Lobby," *New Yorker* 24 (1951): 35–55; Varma, *Indian Immigrants in USA*, 285–90.

32. Varma, 294.

33. Fred Riggs, *Pressures on Congress: A Study of the Repeal of Chinese Exclusion* (New York: King's Crown Press, 1950), 24.

34. Varma, *Indian Immigrants in USA*, 303. Although that was certainly an exaggeration, Singh's reach was undoubtedly wide; through years of hobnobbing with New York City's elite, he had cultivated a broad network of influential white contacts and allies whose influence reached to Washington, DC. For more on Singh, see Robert Shaplen's 1951 profile of Singh. Shaplen, "One-Man Lobby."

35. *Los Angeles Times*, March 21, 1944; *Asia and the Americas*, July 1944, 324.

36. In part at Singh's urging, the *New York Times* editorialized in favor of a broad Indian immigration and naturalization bill one full month before the Luce-Celler measure was formally introduced to Congress. *New York Times*, February 8, 1944.

37. "1944 Motilal Statement on Proposed Indian Immigration Bills," File 776(3)-X (1944), Indian National Archives (INA), Delhi, India; "India Bids America Naturalize People," *New York Times*, April 3, 1944, 11.

38. *New York Times*, April 3, 1944, 11.

39. White accepted a position on the ILA's National Advisory Board later that year. Historian Nico Slate cites White's relationship with Singh as a major reason that the NAACP leader's "knowledge of India and his connections with powerful Indians grew rapidly during the 1940s." Nico Slate, *Colored Cosmopolitanism: The Shared Struggle for Freedom in the United States and India* (Cambridge, MA: Harvard University Press, 2012), 170.

40. Gerald Horne, *The End of Empires: African Americans and India* (Philadelphia: Temple University Press, 2009); Slate, *Colored Cosmopolitanism*.

41. This sense of solidarity was not limited to elite circles; an October 1942 poll of 10,000 black Americans found that more than 87 percent believed India should demand immediate independence from Britain. Slate, *Colored Cosmopolitanism*, 144; Horne, *The End of Empires*, 179–81.

42. Slate, *Colored Cosmopolitanism*, 127; Horne, *The End of Empires*. The NAACP connected the Indian independence movement to black civil rights struggles in the United States, as well as to the Allied fight against Nazism. To support this point, black leaders regularly cited the Indian media's close coverage of U.S. race relations and the nation's "Negro problem."

43. Michael L. Krenn, *Race and U.S. Foreign Policy during the Cold War* (New York: Taylor & Francis, 1998), 141. The sense of solidarity should not be overstated, however. Particularly in his private actions, Nehru proved just as willing to distance the Indian cause from black American struggles when he saw fit. See, for example, Slate, *Colored Cosmopolitanism*, 172.

44. *The New India*, February 1945, 2.

45. In general, this would not significantly change until the Vietnam War.

46. Charles Colby, of University of Chicago, to Richard Russell, June 7, 1944, Senate Immigration Committee, *File on S. 1595*, 78th Cong., 2nd sess. (1944), Box 57, Record Group (RG) 46, Legislative Records Office (NARA I), Washington, DC.

47. "1944 Council of State Statement on Proposed Indian Immigration Bills," Office of External Affairs, 776(3)-X (1944), INA, Delhi, India. Indian media commenters had done similarly after Chinese exclusion repeal, citing its success to argue that other

nations—Canada, Australia, New Zealand, and South Africa—should "take lessons" from the U.S. example and do the same. Quoted in Sean Brawley, *The White Peril: Foreign Relations and Asian Immigration to Australasia and North America, 1919–78* (Sydney: University of New South Wales Press, 1995), 198.

48. This tendency was not unique to Indians; some Korean Americans during this same period sought an immigration and naturalization bill in similar hopes of bolstering Koreans' standing as an internationally recognized people and thereby advancing the cause of Korea's independence from imperial Japan. They were not successful. Among other factors, the Korean case was more complicated because to many white Americans, Koreans and Japanese were too racially and culturally similar to separate easily. Further complicating matters was U.S. officials' deep ambivalence toward the Korean independence movement. See Timothy L. Savage, "The American Response to the Korean Independence Movement, 1910–1945," *Korean Studies* 20/21 (1996): 189–231; Richard S. Kim, *The Quest for Statehood: Korean Immigrant Nationalism and U.S. Sovereignty, 1905–1945* (New York: Oxford University Press, 2011), 135–57.

49. Varma, *Indian Immigrants in USA*, 272–73.

50. Das came to the United States as a student in 1907 and had to battle the interference of British censors in his attempts to naturalize. They sought to suppress his revolutionary activities and silence his anti-British statements for years before he finally became a U.S. citizen in 1914. During World War I, Das's American citizenship enabled him to travel undeterred to Tokyo on a mission to recruit Japanese help in the planned rebellion to liberate India from British rule. For more on Das, see Jensen, *Passage from India*, 165, 173–75; Sohi, *Echoes of Mutiny*, 88–89.

51. "Mr. Singh Goes to Washington," *Time*, February 28, 1944, 19.

52. Dr. Dalip Saund, who later naturalized and, in 1956, became the first person of Indian descent elected to U.S. Congress, was one of the first to frame the distinction in these terms, citing the "big difference between becoming a citizen and having the right to become a citizen." See Varma, *Indian Immigrants in USA*, 343n7.

53. Mumtaz Kitchlew and Dr. Tarani Sinha to J. J. Singh, March 9, 1944; quoted in Varma, *Indian Immigrants in USA*, 272.

54. See, for example, Karen Leonard, *Making Ethnic Choices: California's Punjabi Mexican Americans* (Philadelphia: Temple University Press, 2010).

55. Krishnanal Shridlani and Anup Singh formally appeared as spokespersons for the National Association for India's Freedom, which was an offshoot of the ILA. Due to power struggles among the ILA's Indian members, they left the organization in 1944 and started the National Association as an all-Indian voice for Indian independence in the United States.

56. U.S. Senate Committee on Immigration and Naturalization, *To Permit the Naturalization of Approximately Three Thousand Natives of India*, 78th Cong., 2nd sess. (1944), 52–53.

57. U.S. Senate Committee on Immigration and Naturalization, *To Permit the Naturalization of Approximately Three Thousand Natives of India*, 45, 51.

58. Varma, *Indian Immigrants in USA*, 180.

59. Gary R. Hess, *America Encounters India, 1941–1947* (Baltimore: Johns Hopkins Press, 1971), 149.

60. This was not the first time Khan corresponded with Jinnah. Jinnah to Khan, August 27, 1941, Senate Immigration Committee, file on S. 1595, Box 22, RG 46, NARA I.

61. Reprinted in the *New India Bulletin*, November 1944, 3–4.

62. In a brief discussion of the 1944 Senate committee hearing, scholar Vivek Bald argued that class, rather than sectarian differences of nation or religion, was the "most significant division" between the constituencies these two groups represented. While this may have been the case initially, I would argue that Bald downplays the extent to which the two Leagues' divergent diasporic loyalties shaped the identities of these organizations from their beginning and how these divergent diasporic identifications—and their connection to the Indian independence movement—came to serve as tools, rhetorical and otherwise, that the two Leagues wielded to further their legislative agenda in Washington. See Vivek Bald, *Bengali Harlem and the Lost Histories of South Asian America* (Cambridge, MA: Harvard University Press, 2013), 184.

63. Singh made the decision to discard his distinctive Sikh turban, beard, and long hair usually worn by Sikh males soon after arriving in New York City. He described the move as practical, citing the "awful mental strain" he experienced as a "6-ft. Sikh . . . stopping traffic at every corner" as a "cynosure of all eyes." See Robert Shaplen, "One-Man Lobby," 38, 40.

64. Varma, *Indian Immigrants in USA*, 289.

65. File on S. 236, NARA I, Washington, DC.

66. U.S. Senate Committee on Immigration and Naturalization, *To Permit the Naturalization of Approximately Three Thousand Natives of India*, 19–20, 26.

67. Reprinted in *India Today*, March 1945, 2.

68. The bill was also endorsed by the Federal Council of the Churches of Christ, the Foreign Missions Conference, which represented over a hundred foreign missions boards and organizations, and the International Ladies' Garment Workers Union.

69. Changing attitudes among organized labor were a crucial factor in the postwar liberalization of immigration policy. See Daniel J. Tichenor, *Dividing Lines: The Politics of Immigration Control in America* (Princeton, NJ: Princeton University Press, 2002), 40.

70. U.S. House Committee on Immigration and Naturalization, *File on H.R. 1624*, 79th Cong., 1st sess. (1945), Box 100, RG 46, NARA I, Washington, DC.

71. U.S. House Committee on Immigration and Naturalization, *To Grant a Quota to Eastern Hemisphere Indians and to Make Them Racially Eligible for Naturalization: Hearings on H. R. 173*, 79th Cong., 1st sess. (1945), 82–86.

72. Nehru was released from prison in June 1945.

73. U.S. House Committee on Immigration and Naturalization, *To Grant a Quota to Eastern Hemisphere Indians*, 85–86, 89.

74. Mahatma Gandhi cofounded the *Hindustan Times* in 1924. It remained a proindependence vehicle for the next two decades and was one of the newspapers that stopped printing in the early 1940s to protest increased British censorship following the launch of the Quit India Movement. Singh penned pieces that kept the newspaper's pro–Indian National Congress readers apprised of Madame Pandit's efforts on their behalf; these included reports on alleged efforts by the British-appointed delegation to interfere with her public speeches, including the planting of a heckler to disrupt one of her press conferences. "BBC Silent over San Francisco," *Hindustan*

Times, May 2, 1945; "How Indian Press Is Fed by British Agency," *Hindustan Times*, May 5, 1945, 3; J. J. Singh, "The Stooge Who Heckled Mrs. Pandit," April 30, 1945, 1.

75. U.S. House Committee on Immigration and Naturalization, *To Grant a Quota to Eastern Hemisphere Indians*, 85–86.

76. Brian McKercher, *Transition of Power: Britain's Loss of Global Pre-Eminence to the United States, 1930-1945* (New York: Cambridge University Press, 1999).

77. Quoted in Varma, *Indian Immigrants in USA*, 323.

78. On hearing the news, members of the External Affairs Department in Delhi cited a combination of anti-Semitism directed at the bill's cosponsor Emanuel Celler, infighting among U.S. Indian constituencies, and above all, the lack of endorsement from the British government for the negative outcome. See Varma, *Indian Immigrants in USA*, 320–21.

79. Varma, 321.

80. *Hindustan Times*, March 27, 1945.

81. Hugh Tinker, *Separate and Unequal: India and the Indians in the British Commonwealth, 1920-1950* (Vancouver, B.C.: University of British Columbia Press, 1976), 43–77.

82. Quoted in Tinker, 154, 221.

83. It was a continuation of efforts that were part of Britain's general policy of scaling back central control of its colonies during the interwar years, an effort that included the 1935 Government of India Act.

84. *India Today*, August 1941, 1.

85. J. J. Singh to Jawaharlal Nehru, April 10, 1942, J. J. Singh Papers, Nehru Memorial Museum & Library, New Delhi, India; *India Today*, August 1941, 1.

86. Agent General (Sir Girja) Bajpai's report for July/September 1944, File 205(2)-X, Office of External Affairs, INA.

87. File 205(2)-X: Agent General Bajpai's Report for February 1944, 38, INA, Delhi, India. Bajpai hastened to add that Emanuel Celler (D-NY) was controversial in his own right as a "left-wing and extremely Zionist . . . supporter of freer immigration generally." "Resolution regarding Citizenship for Indians in US," Indian Agent-General Bajpai to Sir Olaf Caroe, Secretary of External Affairs, Delhi, March 18, 1944, File 776(3) X (1944), INA.

88. Varma, *Indian Immigrants in USA*, 274.

89. Agent-General to Delhi, Report for January, January 1944, 11, File 205(2)-X (1944), INA.

90. "Drama in Atlantic City," *Time*, December 6, 1943. Indian government reports similarly emphasized Singh's personal charisma to explain his success. According to one official Indian observer, what Singh lacked in formal qualifications of education or caste, he had made up for through "sheer hard work, guts, and the almost callous effrontery with which he asserts himself and brushes aside all opposition." Such were his skills that he could "inspire missionaries and other American pacifists to go on fast in sympathy with Gandhi and picket the British Embassy on Independence Day." Shah to Office of External Affairs, Report on India League, July 1943, File 379-X/43 (1943), 48, 50, INA.

91. G. C. Ryan, "Visit of the Agent-General to the Sikh Temple at Stockton," March 24, 1944, File 271-X/44, Office of External Affairs, INA. "Mr. Singh Goes to Washington," *Time*, February 28, 1944.

92. Major Shah to Publicity and Information Department, June 22, 1943, 379-X/43, 3–4, INA.

93. Christopher Thorne, *Allies of a Kind: The United States, Britain, and the War against Japan, 1941–1945* (New York: Oxford University Press, 1978), 238–39; Clymer, *Quest for Freedom*, 48; Dennis Kux, *India and the United States: Estranged Democracies, 1941–1991* (Thousand Oaks, CA: Sage, 1994), 39n12.

94. Shah to Office of External Affairs, Report on India League, July 1943, File 379-X/43 (1943), 42–71, especially 45, INA.

95. "Report on the India League of America, June 1943," Office of External Affairs, 379-X/43 (1943), INA.

96. Ryan to Shah, July 13, 1943, 379-X/43, 3–4, INA.

97. On the day of the hearing, Bajpai was supposed to be in India on an earned sabbatical, but he forewent his trip to see the legislation through. "Should [the] bill fail here during my absence, both the Government of India and I might come in for criticism in India for my absence," he wrote to Delhi. Varma, *Indian Immigrants in USA*, 320.

98. Telegram 73, May 3, 1945, File 256-F.E./45 (1945), INA. Ironically, before he was British ambassador to the United States, Lord Halifax served as the viceroy of India, a fact that led historian Varma to note how, for Singh, "it must have seemed like a national insult" that the "key" to winning passage of the Luce-Celler bill came from a "hated former Viceroy." At the time, it seems Singh was unaware of Bajpai's primary role in securing the endorsement letter. According to Varma, Singh "probably would have been embarrassed" by this turn of events. Varma, *Indian Immigrants in USA*, 324.

99. Celler to Truman, April 25, 1945, Box 682, White House Central File: Office Files 133, Truman Papers, Truman Library.

100. The statement echoed the pan-Asianist warnings President Roosevelt had sounded before his death. Thorne, *Allies of a Kind*.

101. U.S. House Committee on Immigration and Naturalization, *To Allow Greater Immigration from India: Hearings on H. R. 2609*, 79th Cong., 1st sess. (1945), 10, 27.

102. The vote was 9 to 6, in favor. Five of the opposing members wrote a minority report that recapitulated many of the southern Democrats' major arguments against passage.

103. A lengthier *Time* cover story and profile piece on Jinnah the following year would prove far less flattering, depicting an icy and urbane sophisticate "lax in his religious observances" who wore his Muslim faith as one did a change of clothing. "Long Shadow," *Time*, April 22, 1946. The *Time* profile was consistent with the Jinnah described in Bose and Jalal's *Modern South Asia* (1997) as someone whose use of religion was a "political tactic, not an ideology to which he was even committed." Sugata Bose and Ayesha Jalal, *Modern South Asia: History, Culture, and Political Economy*, 2nd ed. (New York: Routledge, 1997), 159.

104. *Congressional Record*, October 10, 1945, 9526–27.

105. Rep. Walter Judd, quoted in Varma, *Indian Immigrants in USA*, 332.

106. There has been a long-standing tendency by scholars to overemphasize the importance of the Cold War in American thinking about India during the years immedi-

ately after World War II. In fact, a more straightforward Cold War lens did not take hold of U.S. India policy until the Communist Chinese victory in 1949 and the start of the Korean War one year later. See Clymer, *Quest for Freedom*, 291; H. W. Brands, "The Trouble with US-Third World Studies," *Diplomatic History* 20, no. 3 (1996): 502.

107. Rep. Allen, quoted in *India Today*, October 1945, 1.

108. A decade later, Russell would coauthor the Southern Manifesto with House colleague Strom Thurmond. See Fite, *Richard B. Russell, Jr., Senator from Georgia* (Chapel Hill: University of North Carolina Press, 2002), 220–21, 500.

109. Russell, quoted in Fite, *Richard B. Russell, Jr.*, 220.

110. Roosevelt had relied on southern Democrats' support at key moments, including the votes ushering U.S. formal entry into World War II and approving participation in the United Nations. See William J. Cooper Jr and Thomas E. Terrill, *The American South: A History* (Lanham, MD: Rowman & Littlefield Publishers, 2009), 728.

111. Various scholars have described Russell as an isolationist—and certainly he also described himself in these terms—but I would argue that he was more of a conservative internationalist. Quoted in Fite, *Richard B. Russell, Jr.*, 175.

112. Historian Premdatta Varma has weighed the various factors that may have led Russell to relent on Luce-Celler, but because Russell never explained his decision firsthand, it remains speculative. See Varma, *Indian Immigrants in USA*, 334–37.

113. Fite, *Richard B. Russell, Jr.*, 188–95.

114. The U.S. Congress quietly extended natives of Pakistan the same eligibility to immigrate and naturalize upon the nation's creation in 1947.

115. Fern Marja, "India's One-Man Lobby," *New York Post*, July 31, 1946; Varma, *Indian Immigrants in USA*, 299, 340–41, 370n217–19, 399nn1–5.

116. "100 Indians," *Time*, June 17, 1946. In the fall of 1946, Singh applied to become the first Indian to be naturalized under the new law, but after a series of frustrated inquiries with U.S. immigration officials he abandoned the idea.

117. For the rest of his life, Khan continued to take credit for Indians' legal gains. For example, in a letter to Truman written during the president's stop in Phoenix during the 1948 presidential campaign, Khan claimed a major role in the Luce-Celler bill's passage. He referenced the brief meeting he had had with Truman at the White House two years earlier and expressed gratitude for the president's pledge at the time to "do everything" he could to make U.S. citizenship eligibility for Indians a reality. Khan to Truman, September 24, 1948, Box 682, WHCF: OF 133, Truman Papers, Truman Library.

118. J. J. Singh, "Why I Came Back to India," *Times of India*, January 26, 1959, 5.

119. The Muslim League's emphasis shifted over time from a focus on Muslims' minority rights to a pan-Muslim imperative to foster unity among Muslims internationally. See Montague A. Machell, *Muslim Valley Forge: An Introduction to Mubarek Ali Khan* (1949), 13–15. See also Bald, *Bengali Harlem*, 184–88.

120. Madame Shah Nawaz of the Punjab Legislative Assembly and Mr. M. A. H. Ispahani of the Bengal Legislation Assembly were handpicked by Jinnah himself. See "Back India Opposition," *New York Times*, November 26, 1946, 24. M. A. H. Ispahani would return to the United States three years later as Pakistan's first official ambassador to the United States.

121. Amir Saud, the crown prince of Saudi Arabia, was also a guest of Arizona's Indian Muslim community in January 1947.

122. Ronald Takaki, *Strangers from a Different Shore: A History of Asian Americans* (Boston: Little, Brown, 1998), 369.

Chapter Three

1. U.S. House Committee on Immigration and Naturalization, *To Authorize the Naturalization of Filipinos Who Are Permanent Residents of the U.S.*, 76th Cong., 3rd sess. (1940), 50–53.

2. Among U.S. sources on the wartime naturalization campaigns, Philippine American newspapers and accounts written by participants including labor leader and author Carlos Bulosan remain some of the most accessible and most widely used primary sources. Joseph Fry, *Dixie Looks Abroad: The South and US Foreign Relations, 1789–1973* (Baton Rouge: Louisiana State University Press, 2002). Historian Dawn Bohulano Mabalon has written about the community-based lobbying of Filipino American labor-leftists and radicals (who included Bulosan) as part of a community study of Little Manila in Stockton, California, while H. Brett Melendy and Rick Baldoz have documented the legislative history. Howard Brett Melendy, *Asians in America: Filipinos, Koreans, and East Indians* (Boston: Twayne, 1977), 46–57; Rick Baldoz, *The Third Asiatic Invasion: Migration and Empire in Filipino America, 1898-1946* (New York: New York University Press, 2011), 194–236; Dawn Bohulano Mabalon, *Little Manila Is in the Heart: The Making of the Filipina/o American Community in Stockton, California* (Durham, NC: Duke University Press, 2013), 226–29.

3. Scholars widely agree that the desire for Philippine exclusion made Philippine independence politically possible. See, for example, James Sobredo, "The 1934 Tydings-McDuffie Act and Filipino Exclusion: Social, Political, and Economic Context Revisited," in *Studies in Pacific History: Economics, Politics, and Migration* (Farnham, U.K.: Ashgate, 2002), 155–69; Mae M. Ngai, *Impossible Subjects: Illegal Aliens and the Making of Modern America* (Princeton, NJ: Princeton University Press, 2004), 116–20; Paul A. Kramer, *The Blood of Government: Race, Empire, the United States, and the Philippines* (Chapel Hill: University of North Carolina Press, 2006), 423–31.

4. The Tydings-McDuffie Act (1934) reversed a provision of the 1924 Immigration Act (Section 28[b]) that specifically exempted Filipina/os from the category of "alien."

5. Paul A. Kramer, *The Blood of Government*, 357.

6. Many historians have traced the islands' transformation from a colony to a client state in the years after 1946. I have found Nick Cullather's work particularly helpful in documenting how Filipina/os "found ways to work around, subvert, or deflect U.S. power" in spite of their relative position of economic and military dependency. JoAnna Poblete, *Islanders in the Empire: Filipino and Puerto Rican Laborers in Hawai'i* (Chicago: University of Illinois Press, 2014). See also H. W. Brands, *Bound to Empire: The United States and the Philippines* (New York: Oxford University Press, 1992).

7. For an example of the Philippines being described as a textbook case of U.S. empire's shift from formal to informal modes after World War II, see Julian Go, *Patterns*

of Empire: The British and American Empires, 1688 to the Present (New York: Cambridge University Press, 2011), 145–58, especially 153.

8. See, for example, Robert J. McMahon, *The Limits of Empire: The United States and Southeast Asia since World War II* (New York: Columbia University Press, 1999), 10.

9. Takashi Fujitani, "A Different Kind of 'Asia Pivot,'" *Amerasia Journal* 42, no. 3 (2016): 21. Along similar lines, Go describes how one mode of empire involved the decolonization of a territory "only to replace formal colonialism with informal control." Go, *Patterns of Empire*, 11.

10. The United States' annexation of the Philippines has long captivated scholars, who have attributed the decision to a plethora of factors: the desire for markets, racial and religious beliefs and the "civilizing mission," late nineteenth-century gender anxieties, and even, in the case of historian Ernest May, the absence of a foreign policy consensus organized and strong enough to prevent annexation. See, for example, Kramer, *The Blood of Government*, 2006; Kristin L. Hoganson, *Fighting for American Manhood: How Gender Politics Provoked the Spanish-American and Philippine-American Wars* (New Haven, CT: Yale University Press, 1998); Ernest R. May, *American Imperialism: A Speculative Essay* (New York: Atheneum, 1968).

11. Indeed, some U.S. officials cited the Jones Act (1916) declaring Washington's intention to grant the Philippines independence as a reason to withhold U.S. citizenship. For more on the differential treatment of U.S. territories and colonial peoples, see Baldoz and Ayala, "The Bordering of America: Colonialism and Citizenship in the Philippines and Puerto Rico," *Centro Journal* 25, no. 1 (2013): 76–105.

12. Charles J. McClain, "Tortuous Path, Elusive Goal: The Asian Quest for American Citizenship," *Asian Law Journal* 2 (1995): 53.

13. Baldoz, *The Third Asiatic Invasion*, 14.

14. Two acts of Congress—one passed shortly after World War I and the Nye-Lea Act of 1934—permitted the naturalization of Filipino veterans as a special dispensation granted by Congress to recognize their military service and bodily sacrifice in the fight against Germany. See Lucy E. Salyer, "Baptism by Fire: Race, Military Service, and U.S. Citizenship Policy, 1918–1935," *Journal of American History* 91, no. 3 (December 2004): 847–76.

15. Bill Ong Hing, *Making and Remaking Asian America through Immigration Policy: 1850-1990* (Palo Alto, CA: Stanford University Press, 1993), 61.

16. The first so-called invasion saw an influx of Chinese, while the second brought South Asians, Japanese, and other Asians to the United States. Compared with tens of thousands of Filipina/os, by 1940 the U.S. census recorded only 1,502 Filipinas living in the United States. That number grew significantly after the Luce-Celler Act was passed, with nearly 22,000 Filipinas immigrating to the United States between 1946 and 1960. Much of the increase was due to newly naturalized Filipino soldiers, now citizens, who brought their wives, mothers, and daughters to the United States in record numbers. See Mabalon, *Little Manila Is in the Heart*, 247.

17. Maximo C. Manzon, *The Strange Case of the Filipinos in the United States* (New York: American Committee for Protection of Foreign Born, 1938), 4, 17–18.

18. *Time*, October 3, 1938, 10.

19. Manzon, *Strange Case*, 4–7, 12, 16–17, 22.

20. While the ACPFB had historically focused on European groups, its attention to Filipina/os was part of a sustained, if secondary, concern about the unique legal plight Asians faced due to their alienage under racially restricted U.S. naturalization laws.

21. U.S. House Committee on Immigration and Naturalization, *To Authorize the Naturalization of Filipinos Who Are Permanent Residents of the U.S.* (1940), 57–59.

22. Carlos Bulosan, *America Is in the Heart: A Personal History* (New York: Harcourt, Brace and Co, 1946), 284, 287, 289.

23. During the final year of the CPFR, Bulosan writes that some members tried to convert the group into a "separate unit" of the Communist Party of the USA, but their efforts proved unsuccessful. See Bulosan, *America Is in the Heart*, 289.

24. Nick Cullather, *Illusions of Influence: The Political Economy of United States-Philippines Relations, 1942-1960* (Stanford, CA: Stanford University Press, 1994), 10.

25. Cullather, 11, 44.

26. According to sociologist Miriam Sharma, the level of remittances, or monies sent by overseas Filipina/os to the Philippines, had already "elevated the profile of overseas workers and set the stage for even more outmigration." They also gave overseas employment an "added cachet" and "quelled further attempts by Philippine officials to restrict emigration," at least until the 1934 Tydings-McDuffie Act brought Filipino migration under quota for the first time. Miriam Sharma, "Labor Migration and Class Formation among Filipinos in Hawaii, 1906-1946," in *Labor Immigration under Capitalism: Asian Workers in the United States before World War II*, ed. L. Cheng and Edna Bonacich (Berkeley: University of California Press, 1984), 591–92.

27. Quoted in Mabalon, *Little Manila Is in the Heart*, 142–43.

28. Brands, *Bound to Empire*, 166, 172–74.

29. JoAnna Poblete, *Islanders in the Empire*, 102–3.

30. Manuel Adeva to Joaquin Elizalde, January 7, 1943, Series 7, Box 132, Manuel Quezon Papers, Philippine National Library, Manila, Philippines (hereafter, Quezon Papers).

31. Trinidad A. Rojo, "Introduction Coast-to-Coast Survey of Fil-American Communities, 1937-1948," Diosdado Yap Papers, Filipino American Historical Society, Seattle, WA.

32. Mabalon, *Little Manila Is the Heart*, 219.

33. It is unclear whether the savings plan idea was ever implemented on a large scale. Manuel Adeva to Joaquin Elizalde, January 7, 1943, Series 7, Box 132, Quezon Papers.

34. See Baldoz, *The Third Asiatic Invasion*, 50–60; Poblete, *Islanders in the Empire*, 95–120; Kramer, *The Blood of Government*, 325–27.

35. Poblete, *Islanders in the Empire*, 95.

36. Poblete, 113.

37. To be clear, quoted in Mabalon, *Little Manila Is in the Heart*, 143; "Filipinos Held to Blame for Plight Abroad," *Wheeling News-Register*, September 2, 1938. For more on Varona's death, see Mabalon, *Little Manila Is in the Heart*, 229–30.

38. Brands, *Bound to Empire*, 162. The late historian Dawn Mabalon described Elizalde as a "largely ineffectual" member of the Filipino elite "for whom the position was a political plum." Mabalon, *Little Manila Is in the Heart*, 219.

39. Carlos Bulosan, "Filipinos Deserve a Break: Little Brown Brothers Have Earned U.S. Gratitude in War against Japan," *Pic*, March 3, 1942.

40. Brands, *Bound to Empire*, 162.

41. "Elizalde Called 'Unqualified' in Court Suit," *Washington Post*, October 18, 1938, X7; "Court Refuses to Consider Elizalde Case," *Washington Post*, April 16, 1940, 23.

42. U.S. House Committee on Immigration and Naturalization, *To Authorize the Naturalization of Filipinos* (1940), 1.

43. Memorandum of Conversation, Ex-Senator Hawes and Mr. Jacobs, April 24, 1939, Entry 1062, Records of the Joint Preparatory Committee on Philippine Affairs, 1937–40, Records Regarding the Philippine Independence Act, RG 59, NARA II.

44. Cordell Hull to Richard Russell, June 10, 1938; Cordell Hull to Dickstein, March 30, 1940, Box 112, RG 233, NARA I.

45. U.S. House Committee on Immigration and Naturalization, *To Authorize the Naturalization of Filipinos Who Are Permanent Residents*, 3.

46. U.S. House Committee on Immigration and Naturalization, *To Authorize the Naturalization of Filipinos* (1940), 14–15, 30.

47. Fry, *Dixie Looks Abroad*, 128.

48. U.S. House Committee on Immigration and Naturalization, *To Authorize the Naturalization of Filipinos* (1940), 25.

49. See, for example, Rhacel Salazar Parreñas, "'White Trash' Meets the 'Little Brown Monkeys': The Taxi Dance Hall as a Site of Interracial and Gender Alliances between White Working Class Women and Filipino Immigrant Men in the 1920s and 30s," *Amerasia Journal* 24, no. 2 (1998): 115–34.

50. Bruno Lasker, *Filipino Immigration to Continental United States and to Hawaii* (Chicago: University of Chicago Press, 1931).

51. Scholars have shown how the mass incarceration of West Coast Japanese Americans benefited some Filipina/os on the local level. Filipina/os in California's Central Valley found new opportunities opened to them in employment, the leasing of land, business entrepreneurship, and even social relations with whites. In 1942, the California legislature amended the state Alien Land Law to allow noncitizen Filipina/os, Mexicans, and Chinese to lease agricultural land. See Mabalon, *Little Manila Is in the Heart*, 217–46, especially 235–40. On the federal level, Public Law 360 opened government and war industry jobs to Filipina/os; the law eased some of the employment constraints that had prompted Marcantonio to introduce his naturalization bill in the first place. This was also true for Chinese Americans. See, for example, K. Scott Wong, *Americans First: Chinese Americans and the Second World War* (Cambridge, MA: Harvard University Press, 2009).

52. Salyer, "Baptism by Fire." See chapter 4 for more on the Nye-Lea Act (1935).

53. U.S. House Committee on Immigration and Naturalization, *To Authorize the Naturalization of Filipinos Who Are Permanent Residents of the U.S.*, 77th Cong., 2nd sess. (1942), 6–7, 33.

54. More shocking to observers in Washington, DC, was General MacArthur's written endorsement of the plan, which reversed his previous position opposing an earlier independence date. Brands states that Quezon took this action, in part, to

preempt a Japanese proclamation of Philippine independence, which he rightly predicted was forthcoming. Brands, *Bound to Empire*, 193–95.

55. Brands, *Bound to Empire*, 163. See, for example, "The Filipinos Surrender to Dictatorship," *Christian Century*, September 25, 1940.

56. Cullather, *Illusions of Influence*, 13.

57. Quoted in Brands, *Bound to Empire*, 213. Another Washington observer described him as a "rather pathetic figure." Brands, 212.

58. For example, during the negotiations over the Hawes-Hare-Cutting bill providing for Philippine independence, Quezon argued against a complete ban on Filipino immigration after independence on the grounds that it would become a source of "widespread ill-feeling" with the potential to "make or mar future Filipino-American relations." The bill, absent provisions fully banning Filipino migration, passed the U.S. Congress in 1933 over President Hoover's veto but was rejected by the Philippine Senate. Box 136, Quezon Papers.

59. Quezon and the PRC's office also initiated a lawsuit challenging the constitutionality of the restrictions. It never went to trial. Elizalde to Quezon, August 17, 1943; October 15, 1943; December 22, 1943; Series 7, Box 132, Quezon Papers.

60. J. C. Dionisio to Manuel Quezon, February 15, 1944, Box 1.1, Carlos Romulo Papers, University of Philippines-Dilliman, Quezon City, Philippines (hereafter, CPR Papers).

61. Dionisio to Quezon, February 15, 1944, emphasis in original, Box 1.2, CPR Papers.

62. "Participation of Filipinos in the United States and Hawaii in the Post-War Reconstruction of the Philippines," August 4, 1943, Box 131, Series 7, Quezon Papers.

63. The list of sponsors notably included two representatives from California, which had been a center of opposition just a few years earlier. In addition to McGehee, bills were introduced by Harry Sheppard and C. Norris Poulson of California, Joseph Farrington of Hawaii, Jennings Randolph of West Virginia, and Vito Marcantonio of New York. Filipino American leaders including writer Diosdado Yap aligned themselves behind a bill introduced by Rep. Jennings Randolph of West Virginia, while the House Committee on Immigration and Naturalization favored the McGehee bill. In early 1943, Marcantonio had introduced an even more sweeping measure proposing to open U.S. citizenship to all persons regardless of "race, color, creed, or national origin." The implications of the bill, namely, to extend naturalization rights to *all* Asian peoples—including the Japanese enemy—stirred great controversy and caused other proponents of legislative change to distance themselves from the New York Democrat for fear of irreversibly sullying their own efforts with the taint of radicalism. From this point onward, few Filipino leaders actively sought or courted Marcantonio's sponsorship of legislation on their behalf, though he reintroduced his Filipino naturalization bill in 1944 anyway.

64. For more on the Bataan Death March, see Michael Norman, *Tears in the Darkness: The Story of the Bataan Death March and Its Aftermath* (New York: Macmillan, 2009).

65. Quoted in "Romulo Bids 'Au Revoir' to Colleagues in Congress before Leaving for Philippines," October 1944, *Bataan*, 12–13.

66. The CPFR could have theoretically served in this capacity, but it had gone defunct by 1944, and not all Filipina/os were willing to work with leftists such as Bulosan.

67. Jaime Hernandez, Secretary of Finance, Commonwealth of Philippines, to Samuel Dickstein, November 21, 1944, HR76A-D11-D12, Box 76, RG 233, NARA I.

68. Adeva to Romulo, November 20, 1944, Box 1.1, CPR Papers.

69. For more on the *pensionado* system, see Teodoro, "Pensionados and Workers: The Filipinos in the United States, 1903-1956," no. 1/2 (1999): 157-78.

70. Carlos Romulo, *My Brother Americans* (New York: Doubleday, 1945), 170.

71. Augusto Espiritu, *Five Faces of Exile: The Nation and Filipino American Intellectuals* (Palo Alto, CA: Stanford University Press, 2005), 25-26.

72. Romulo to Ms. Kirchwey of the *Nation* magazine, July 28, 1945, Folder 15, Box 1.1, CPR Papers.

73. Romulo ran for president of the Philippines in 1953 and lost in the primary stage.

74. In general, nonresident or overseas Filipina/os did not have the right to vote in Philippine elections until passage of the Overseas Absentee Voting Act, or Republic Act No. 9189, in 2003.

75. "Territorial Council Delegates Visit Capitol City," *Bataan*, July 1945, 18.

76. According to the Hawaiian Sugar Planters Association, which proposed the plan to the secretary of the interior, the new workers would both "relieve the shortage of farm labor" in Hawaii and "relieve thousands of distressed families" in the Philippines. "Territorial Council Delegates Visit Capitol City," July 1945, 18.

77. The Bracero Program, created in 1942 by Congress, was a notable exception; it would continue to operate in some form until 1964.

78. Together with South Carolina Senator Strom Thurmond, Russell would go on to coauthor the 1956 Southern Manifesto, a statement opposing the Supreme Court order for school desegregation across the American South. Andrew Escalona to Leonides Virata, December 29, 1945; Virata to Escalona, January 22, 1946, Folder 21, Box 1.2, CPR Papers.

79. Romulo to Osmena, August 28, 1945, Box 8, Series 1, Sergio Osmena Papers, Philippine National Library, Manila, Philippines.

80. By contrast, most U.S. officials in Washington preferred Osmena to Roxas, who had worked with the Japanese occupation government while supplying secret intelligence to both the local resistance and the Americans. U.S. officials had long seen Osmena as the "real workhorse" of the Philippine government, especially as Quezon's failing health left him unable to perform his official duties. Osmena had also generally been regarded as more loyal to the United States and reliable than Quezon. General MacArthur's support of Roxas was thus a notable exception. Brands, *Bound to Empire*, 213.

81. Cullather, *Illusions of Influence*, 43-47.

82. Brands, *Bound to Empire*, 213.

83. The executive order described the challenges facing "Filipinos who are stranded in United States." "President Osmena Creates Committee for the Relief of Filipinos in America," *Bataan*, October 1944, 30.

84. R. R. Tugade, "Let Us Look for Real Leaders," *The People*, September 15, 1945.

85. Richard Keech of the White House to Secretary of State James Byrnes, February 1, 1946, Box 151, Office Files (OF) Philippines, Truman Library.

86. Frank H. Golay, *Face of Empire: United States-Philippine Relations, 1898-1946* (Madison: University of Wisconsin Press, 1998), 461-62.

87. Stephen R. Shalom, "Philippine Acceptance of the Bell Trade Act of 1946: A Study of Manipulatory Democracy," *Pacific Historical Review* 49, no. 3 (1980): 499–517; Brands, *Bound to Empire*, 228.

88. Shalom, "Philippine Acceptance of the Bell Trade Act of 1946," 505.

89. See, for example, Michael Adas, "Improving on the Civilising Mission? Assumptions of United States Exceptionalism in the Colonisation of the Philippines," *Itinerario* 22, no. 04 (1998): 44–66; Paul A. Kramer, "Empires, Exceptions, and Anglo-Saxons: Race and Rule between the British and United States Empires, 1880–1910," *The Journal of American History* 88, no. 4 (2002): 1315–1353.

90. "Gamponia Champions Filipino Legislation on Naturalization, Labor; Past Efforts Reviewed," *Bataan*, July 1946, 45–47.

91. Born in Luzon, Philippines, Abaya came to the United States in 1927 and had been working for the U.S. Immigration Service for seventeen years by the time he applied to become a U.S. citizen. "Chicago Filipino First to Obtain U.S. Citizenship," *Bataan*, September 1946, 32.

92. Other concerns included how to resolve infighting and factionalism within Filipina/o American communities. Jose de los Reyes, "Filipino Inter-Community Convention to Be Held in San Diego; Numerous Problems to Be Solved," *Bataan*, August 1946, 6–7.

93. For more on exile in the context of Philippine Americans, see Espiritu, *Five Faces of Exile*.

94. As part of its general crackdown on overseas critics, the Marcos government censored Santos's novels and confiscated his property. See Espiritu, *Five Faces of Exile*, 158–61.

95. Espiritu, 29–30, 98, 134.

96. Along these lines, historian Nick Cullather describes Manila's "feeble control" over the Philippine economy by the postwar years. See Cullather, *Illusions of Influence*, 66–69.

97. "Philippines is 3rd Top Remittance Receiving Country in the World," *Philippine Star*, April 2, 2018.

98. Robyn Magalit Rodriguez, *Migrants for Export: How the Philippine State Brokers Labor to the World* (Minneapolis: University of Minnesota Press, 2010), xxi, xxvi.

99. In early 1942, Congress passed the First War Powers Act removing and incentivizing Filipinos in the United States to enlist in exchange for U.S. citizenship eligibility; the Second War Powers Act expanded naturalization eligibility to Filipino soldiers enlisting from the Philippines. Public Law 360, which took effect on the same day that Manila fell to the Japanese, also made Filipinos living in the United States, regardless of citizenship, eligible for voluntary U.S. military service as well as for the draft; it removed the obstacles that Filipinos in the United States initially encountered in their efforts to enlist. Mabalon, *Little Manila Is in the Heart*, 233, 388–89n91. Baldoz, *The Third Asiatic Invasion*, 199.

100. These figures were taken from Baldoz, *The Third Asiatic Invasion*, 235.

101. Baldoz, *The Third Asiatic Invasion*, 199, 233. For more on the 1946–49 Rescission Acts and the contemporary movement for redress, see Michael A. Cabotaje, "Equity Denied: Historical and Legal Analyses in Support of the Extension of US Veterans' Benefits to Filipino World War II Veterans," *Asian Law Journal* 6 (1999): 67–97; Mi-

chael Honda, "Justice for Filipino Veterans, at Long Last," *Asian American Law Journal* 16 (2009): 193–96.

102. After decades of activism, the Immigration and Nationality Act of 1990 granted citizenship rights to all Filipino veterans of World War II. In 2009, a section of the American Recovery and Reinvestment Act extended veterans' benefits to Filipino World War II veterans. In addition, the Filipino Veterans Equity Compensation Act of 2009 made Filipino American veterans of World War II who fought in the Philippines eligible for a one-time lump sum payment of $15,000 if they lived in the United States and $9,000 if they still lived in the Philippines, but the law has run into serious bureaucratic issues. As of this book's writing, of the more than 250,000 Filipinos who served, few than 10 percent have been officially recognized and deemed eligible for the payments. Additional legislation has been introduced to extend these benefits to the survivors of veterans, in line with the treatment that current U.S. veterans and their families receive.

Chapter Four

1. Scholars have charted this change in popular culture, official discourse, and media representations, among other sites. See, for example, Naoko Shibusawa, *America's Geisha Ally: Reimagining the Japanese Enemy* (Cambridge, MA: Harvard University Press, 2006).

2. Under the 1952 act's security provisions, scores of foreign-born Asians, Europeans, and others faced state harassment and even deportation for their alleged communist sympathies. Many of the 1952 McCarran-Walter Act's national security provisions, including those related to deportation, remain good law today.

3. While scholars have written extensively about the consequences of the McCarran-Walter Act to increase state repression, less work has been done on the legislation's Asian immigration and naturalization provisions. Charlotte Brooks's discussion of Chinese American protests to the Judd bill is a notable exception. See Charlotte Brooks, *Between Mao and McCarthy: Chinese American Politics in the Cold War Years* (Chicago: University of Chicago Press, 2015), 93–97.

4. The 1952 act further imposed an annual ceiling of 2,000 on immigration to the United States from the Asia-Pacific Triangle as a whole.

5. Historian Takashi Fujitani has described the strategic link between Japanese Americans' status in the United States and American occupation projects in postwar Japan, stating that their inclusion was "coupled to the imperial ambition to incorporate Japan and Asia into a new postwar hegemony in the Asia-Pacific region." Precisely because the "fate of Japanese Americans was overdetermined by global and national forces," he argues, the "question of Japanese Americans' rights as citizens and of redress for racist acts against them . . . cannot be completely understood within the narrow frame of national history." At the same time, Fujitani takes care to note that he is not claiming that "international factors outweighed domestic ones" in shaping Japanese Americans' status. Takashi Fujitani, *Race for Empire: Koreans as Japanese and Japanese as Americans during World War II* (Berkeley: University of California Press, 2011), 101, 107, 109. See also Shibusawa, *America's Geisha Ally*, 144. More recently, Di-

ane Fujino coined the term "Japanese American exceptionalism" to refer to the process whereby the "image of Japanese Americans as model minorities was used to counter charges of U.S. racism, to delegitimize anti-imperialist freedom movements, and to affirm the exportation of American-style expansionism abroad." See Diane Fujino, "Cold War Activism and Japanese American Exceptionalism: Contested Solidarities and Decolonial Alternatives to Freedom," *Pacific Historical Review* 87, no. 2 (2018): 267.

6. Matthew Connelly, "Taking Off the Cold War Lens: Visions of North South Conflict during the Algerian War for Independence," *American Historical Review* 105, no. 3 (2000): 739–69.

7. See, for example, Izumi Hirobe, *Japanese Pride, American Prejudice: Modifying the Exclusion Clause of the 1924 Immigration Act* (Palo Alto, CA: Stanford University Press, 2001); Naoko Shimazu, *Japan, Race and Equality: The Racial Equality Proposal of 1919* (New York: Psychology Press, 2009).

8. President Roosevelt recommended a bill making Japanese eligible for U.S. citizenship as a possible way of resolving a San Francisco public school matter while averting a diplomatic crisis with Japan in the wake of its unexpected victory over a European power in the Russo-Japanese War. Under pressure from the Asiatic Exclusion League, the San Francisco school board was attempting to force the ninety-three Japanese students enrolled in the city's public schools to attend the segregated Chinese school; Japanese officials were appalled at the insult. Roosevelt had a vested interest, having just negotiated the Treaty of Portsmouth that ended the Russo-Japanese War and won a Nobel Prize for his work. See Ian Haney Lopez, *White by Law: The Legal Construction of Race* (New York: New York University Press, 1997), 3.

9. U.S. Supreme Court, *Ozawa v. United States*, 260 U.S. 178 (1922).

10. According to Hirobe, Americans' general ignorance of Asia coupled with the close ties of many private interests with U.S. media and government meant that private actors such as businessmen and missionaries were "always in the forefront of American expansion" in East Asia. See Hirobe, *Japanese Pride*, 10.

11. Salyer estimates that about 2,200 noncitizen Asians served in the U.S. military during World War I, though it is hard to know the actual numbers. Lucy E. Salyer, "Baptism by Fire: Race, Military Service, and U.S. Citizenship Policy, 1918-1935," *Journal of American History* 91, no. 3 (December 2004): 866, 871, 876. For more on the JACL's role in the 1930s Nye-Lea campaign, see Salyer, 866–76.

12. Mae Ngai has called this second-class citizenship "alien citizenship." See Mae M. Ngai, *Impossible Subjects: Illegal Aliens and the Making of Modern America: Illegal Aliens and the Making of Modern America* (Princeton, NJ: Princeton University Press, 2004), 8, 81. Challenges to the constitutionality of Executive Order 9066 included *Korematsu v. U.S.* (1944), *Hirabayashi v. U.S.* (1943), and *Yasui v. U.S.* (1943).

13. Estimates of JACL's prewar membership vary. According to historian Ellen D. Wu, it was 8,000 before the Pearl Harbor attack. JACL accounts indicate much higher numbers. Ellen D. Wu, *The Color of Success: Asian Americans and the Origins of the Model Minority* (Princeton, NJ: Princeton University Press, 2013), 76; Bill Hosokawa, *JACL in Quest of Justice: The History of the Japanese American Citizens League* (New York: William Morrow, 1982).

14. Paul R. Spickard, "The Nisei Assume Power: The Japanese American Citizens League, 1941-1942," *Pacific Historical Review* 52, no. 2 (May 1983): 147–74, especially 169.

15. Hosokawa, *JACL in Quest of Justice*, 210.

16. In a now infamous episode, JACL's national board worked with WRA (War Relocation Authority) officials to administer loyalty questionnaires to military-age nisei males being held in the camps in an effort to identify those loyal enough to be drafted. The outcome was widespread protest and pandemonium, as the poorly worded and even more poorly administered loyalty questionnaires divided Japanese American communities and prompted death threats against JACL leaders within the camps. Reflecting on this episode, JACL leaders have remarked on the "unfairness" and lack of sensitivity the questionnaires betrayed. In his 1987 memoir, Masaoka called the WRA questionnaires a "dumb mistake." For more discussion of the JACL's role in the drafting of nisei soldiers, see Wu, *The Color of Success*, 150–80; Hosokawa, *JACL in Quest of Justice*, 197–201, 209–17; Mike Masaoka and Bill Hosokawa, *They Call Me Moses Masaoka: An American Saga* (New York: William Morrow, 1987), 123–38, 161–79.

17. Fujitani, *Race for Empire*, 101–8, 118–19.

18. Wu, *The Color of Success*, 150–80.

19. Having served as a Mormon missionary in Japan during his youth before earning a doctorate in East Asian studies, Thomas remained deeply interested in Japan and greater East Asia throughout his academic and congressional career as a U.S. senator representing Utah from 1933 to 1951. For more on Thomas and Japan, see Hayashi Yoshikatsu, "Elbert D. Thomas in the Context of U.S.-Japanese Relations," *Nanzan Review of American Studies* 29 (2007): 125–30.

20. Formed by President Truman in 1946, the committee had fifteen members—a mix of former state officials, academics, community and labor leaders, civil rights activists, religious leaders, and businesspersons.

21. Though undeniably aspirational, the report laid out an ambitious legislative agenda outlining how the U.S. government might strengthen and better protect the rights of minority communities. It condemned injustices facing persons of African, Asian, Mexican, and Native descent, framing the problem of civil rights in the United States as "complex" and multiracial in scope. Immigration was not explicitly included in the report's final policy platforms, but in a separate section on immigration, the president's committee lamented how racial and ethnic differences were "too often . . . seized upon as justification for discrimination." U.S. President's Committee on Civil Rights, *To Secure These Rights* (Washington, DC: U.S. Government Printing Office, 1947), 13–14, 32–33.

22. JACL leaders originally courted Joseph Farrington, a territorial delegate to Congress from Hawaii, who introduced the first two broad-based repeal bills to the House at the league's request. By the spring of 1947, however, they decided that Farrington could not be counted on to "carry the ball or provide the necessary leadership" for the campaign due to his primary commitment to Hawaii's ongoing fight for statehood. As a voting member of the House, Judd was also preferable to Farrington, a nonvoting territorial delegate who could introduce bills but could not vote on them. Progress Report #4, February 9, 1947, Box 64, Folder 9, Mike Masaoka Papers, Marriott Library, University of Utah, Salt Lake City, Utah (hereafter, Masaoka Papers). Other would-be sponsors were even more problematic. Vito Marcantonio (D-NY), then of the American Labor Party, introduced a similar bill to remove the racial barriers

against naturalization. As the India League had done during the Luce-Celler campaign, the JACL-ADC (Japanese American Citizens League–Anti-Discrimination Committee) deliberately distanced itself to avoid the taint of Marcantonio's radical reputation. According to Masaoka, Marcantonio's bill was "not solicited, nor welcome, since he is persona non grata to both parties. As little publicity and attention should be given to this bill as possible." ADC office memo, May 10, 1947, Box 5, Folder 4, Mike Masaoka Papers.

23. In its various iterations, the Judd bill was introduced as H.R. 4824 in 1947, H.R. 5004 in 1948, and H.R. 6809, as passed by the House that year.

24. Bill Hosokawa, Nisei: The Quiet Americans (New York: William Morrow, 1969), 287.

25. Progress Report #1, January 18, 1947, Box 64, Folder 9, Mike Masaoka Papers.

26. Progress Report #1, Mike Masaoka Papers.

27. Salyer, "Baptism by Fire," 871.

28. Hosokawa, JACL in Quest of Justice, 280–81.

29. U.S. House, Committee on the Judiciary, Subcommittee on Immigration, Providing for Equality under Naturalization and Immigration Laws, 80th Congress, 2nd sess. (1948), 118.

30. JACL–Anti-Discrimination Committee (ADC) Progress Report, March 1947, Box 64, Folder 9, Mike Masaoka Papers, University of Utah, Salt Lake City.

31. The idea of martial or militaristic patriotism has a long history in the United States. See Salyer, "Baptism by Fire"; Cecilia Elizabeth O'Leary, To Die for: The Paradox of American Patriotism (Princeton, NJ: Princeton University Press, 1999); Wu, The Color of Success, 72–110.

32. For more on the JACL's martial patriotism in the 1940s, see Wu, The Color of Success; Fujitani, Race for Empire.

33. For more on this idea, see Cindy I-Fen Cheng, Citizens of Asian America: Democracy and Race during the Cold War (New York: New York University Press, 2013), 149–90.

34. Pacific Citizen, December 25, 1948 (emphasis added).

35. My thanks to Judy Tzu-Chun Wu for pointing out the importance of maternal themes in JACL appeals. Ellen D. Wu has also described how some allies of the Japanese American community described "Issei women as republican mothers." Wu, The Color of Success, 98.

36. U.S. House, Committee on the Judiciary, Subcommittee on Immigration, Providing for Equality under Naturalization and Immigration Laws, 120–21.

37. Go for Broke actor Van Johnson, quoted in Naoko Shibusawa, America's Geisha Ally, 269.

38. U.S. House, Committee on the Judiciary, Subcommittee on Immigration, Providing for Equality under Naturalization and Immigration Laws, 116–18.

39. Alfred Steinberg, "Washington's Most Successful Lobbyist," Reader's Digest, May 1949, 125, 128. The piece was condensed from a longer article that originally appeared in the April 1949 issue of the national Catholic magazine The Sign.

40. According to Robert Divine, this was the last time during the war and immediate postwar years that a reduction proposal received serious consideration. The opposition of organized labor ultimately doomed the clause's chances of passage, but the

final vote was close. See Robert A. Divine, *American Immigration Policy, 1924-1952* (New Haven, CT: Yale University Press, 1957), 158–60.

41. Masaoka to JACL Headquarters, March 19, 1948, Box 2, Folder 14, Masaoka Papers.

42. See, for example, NAACP, "An Appeal to the World: A Statement on the Denial of Human Rights to Minorities in the Case of Citizens of Negro Descent in the United States of America and an Appeal to the United Nations for Redress," 1947.

43. Penny M. Von Eschen, *Race against Empire: Black Americans and Anticolonialism, 1937-1957* (Ithaca, NY: Cornell University Press, 1997); Mary L. Dudziak, *Cold War Civil Rights: Race and the Image of American Democracy* (Princeton, NJ: Princeton University Press, 2000); Thomas Borstelmann, *The Cold War and the Color Line: American Race Relations in the Global Arena* (Cambridge, MA: Harvard University Press, 2001).

44. U.S. House, Committee on the Judiciary, Subcommittee on Immigration, *Providing for Equality under Naturalization and Immigration Laws*, 9–10.

45. John W. Dower, *Embracing Defeat: Japan in the Wake of World War II* (New York: W. W. Norton, 2000), 23.

46. For more on the reverse-course, see Michael Schaller, *The American Occupation of Japan: The Origins of the Cold War in Asia* (New York: Oxford University Press, 1985). It is widely agreed that the reverse-course in U.S. Japan policy was already happening by 1948. Historians Mark Caprio and Yoneyuki Sugita argue that the shift began earlier. Mark E. Caprio and Yoneyuki Sugita, *Democracy in Occupied Japan: The U.S. Occupation and Japanese Politics and Society* (New York: Routledge, 2007), 14–15. For more on Grew's role in shaping SCAP occupation policy, see Howard Schonberger, "The Japan Lobby in American Diplomacy, 1947-1952," *Pacific Historical Review* 46, no. 3 (1977): 327–59.

47. Grew had an outsized role in shaping America's postwar occupation policy in Japan. Even after leaving his ambassador's post, he remained highly influential as an advisor to the State Department and an unofficial leader of the so-called Japan Lobby in Washington, DC, which was active during the years of the SCAP Occupation (1945–52). For a positive treatment of Grew's tenure, see Waldo H. Heinrichs, *American Ambassador: Joseph C. Grew and the Development of the United States Diplomatic Tradition* (New York: Oxford University Press, 1986). For a more critical assessment, see Fujitani, *Race for Empire*, 106–7.

48. U.S. House, Committee on the Judiciary, Subcommittee on Immigration, *Providing for Equality under Naturalization and Immigration Laws*, 43.

49. Yukiko Koshiro, *Trans-Pacific Racisms and the U.S. Occupation of Japan* (New York: Columbia University Press, 1999), 33–48.

50. President's Committee on Civil Rights, *To Secure These Rights*, 137. Fujitani notes how Reischauer's writings outlining his strategy of how the U.S. government could use nisei soldiers as a propaganda tool exhibited a similar disregard for Japanese Americans. See Fujitani, *Race for Empire*, 104–5.

51. Walter Judd to Mrs. Chris Carlson, May 14, 1943, Box 60, Walter Judd Papers, Minnesota History Society (MHS), St. Paul, MN.

52. Walter Judd to William Ziegler, January 14, 1943, Box 60, Walter Judd Papers, MHS.

53. U.S. House, Committee on the Judiciary, Subcommittee on Immigration, *Providing for Equality under Naturalization and Immigration Laws*, 40, 66. Some scholars have suggested that actual equality would have required Asian countries to receive much larger immigration quotas both to compensate for past restrictions and to account for their much higher populations with respect to European countries also under quota. This builds on historian Mae Ngai's critique of the "politics of symbolic reform," whereby a "discourse of formal equality" could result in a "substantively unequal" policy that failed to consider important differences "in size and needs among countries" or the "particular historical relations between some countries and the United States." Mae Ngai, "The Unlovely Residue of Outworn Prejudices: The Hart-Celler Act and the Politics of Immigration Reform, 1945–65," in *Americanism: New Perspectives on the History of an Ideal*, ed. M. Kazin and J. McCartin (Chapel Hill: University of North Carolina Press, 2006), 108–27; Ngai, *Impossible Subjects*, 245.

54. U.S. House, Committee on the Judiciary, Subcommittee on Immigration, *Providing for Equality under Naturalization and Immigration Laws*, 37.

55. Divine, *American Immigration Policy*, 155.

56. The Filipina wives of U.S. citizens were also affected, prompting protest from the Spring 1948 House hearing's two Filipino witnesses.

57. More than 150,000 black persons immigrated to the United States from the Caribbean and Africa between 1890 and 1937. Between 1900 and 1932, 88,000 persons entered the United States from the Caribbean. By 1914, Afro-Caribbean immigration had become significant enough that the U.S. Senate passed an exclusion bill barring black peoples from immigrating to the United States, but the measure failed in the House of Representatives. By the end of World War II, there were over a quarter of a million Afro-Caribbeans living in the United States, with the majority concentrated in New York City and Chicago. See Winston James, *Holding Aloft the Banner of Ethiopia: Caribbean Radicalism in Early Twentieth-Century America* (New York: Verso, 1998), 7–8; Mary C. Waters, *Black Identities* (Cambridge, MA: Harvard University Press, 2009), 3437.

58. The provision in question, Section 12(c), read: "Provided, that not more than one hundred persons born in any one colony or other dependent area shall be chargeable to the quota of its governing country in any one year." While frequently cited in discussions of the 1952 McCarran-Walter Act and its oversights, the colonial quota has not been the subject of any close study; consequently, we continue to know little about its origins or the many years of efforts to block its inclusion in legislation, or later, to remove it from existing law.

59. The most prominent case involved a Minneapolis-born African American soldier disciplined for requesting changes in the army's treatment of black enlisted soldiers. Judd wrote to U.S. Army leaders in the soldier's defense.

60. Writing to a constituent in March 1943, Judd suggested that the only viable solution to the problem of "racial prejudice" was the "long, long process of educating the minds and changing the hearts of human beings." Judd to Mrs. Blanche Hayes, March 29, 1943, Box 41, MHS.

61. As one of few black lawmakers serving in Congress, Powell bore the burden of representing black interests on a broad range of issues. In the years before the Judd

bill, Vito Marcantonio introduced several unsuccessful bills to remove racial restrictions to U.S. immigration and naturalization; due to his radical reputation, many immigration advocates, including most Indian and Japanese Americans, kept a distance for fear of being tainted by his far-left socialist and communist sympathies.

62. Rep. Adam Clayton Powell Jr., speaking on HR 199, on March 1, 1949, 81st Cong., 1st sess., *Congressional Record*, H1688-1689.

63. U.S. House, Committee on the Judiciary, Subcommittee on Immigration, *Providing for Equality under Naturalization and Immigration Laws*, 40, 66.

64. Rep. Adam Clayton Powell Jr., speaking on HR 199, on March 1, 1949, 81st Cong., 1st sess., *Congressional Record*, H1678.

65. Under the 1946 Congressional Reorganization Act, jurisdiction over immigration and naturalization matters moved from a dedicated Committee on Immigration and Naturalization to fall under the aegis of the House and Senate Judiciary Committees. For more on Chinese Americans in World War II, see K. Scott Wong, *Americans First: Chinese Americans and the Second World War* (Cambridge, MA: Harvard University Press, 2005).

66. U.S. Senate, Committee on the Judiciary, *Naturalization of Asian and Pacific Peoples, Volume 1: Hearings on H.R. 199*, 81st Cong., 1st sess. (1949), 177. Japanese American soldiers in the segregated 442nd and 100th military battalions were some of the most highly decorated in U.S. military history.

67. While historically not a major participant in immigration debates, in 1915 the NAACP helped block an amendment barring "all members of the African or black race" from entering the country; its campaign against the colonial quota followed in the same tradition. For more, see Jake C. Miller, "The NAACP and Global Human Rights," *Western Journal of Black Studies* 26, no. 1 (Spring 2002), 22–28.

68. Charles Houston, "Our Civil Rights," February 23, 1949, *Afro-American, St Louis American, Minneapolis Spokesman, Kansas City Call*, Box 33, Folder 22, RG 18, National Council of Churches Papers, Presbyterian Historical Society, Philadelphia. For more on the history of African Americans and U.S. immigration policy, see Jeff Diamond, "African-American Attitudes towards United States Immigration Policy," *International Migration Review* 32, no. 2 (1998): 451–70.

69. NAACP press release, March 3, 1949, Box 33, Folder 22, RG 18, National Council of Churches Papers, Presbyterian Historical Society, Philadelphia. In part, the NAACP's interest in the issue complemented its postwar focus on anticolonialism and the close relationships African American leaders had begun cultivating with West Indian political leaders during World War II. Rep. Powell's 1948 trip to Jamaica was one in a series of visits between the United States and the islands; NAACP president Walter White hosted Jamaican politician Norman Manley in New York in 1947, and civil rights activist and entertainer Paul Robeson toured Jamaica the following year. The NAACP's involvement was consistent with its ongoing efforts to court these men, who were widely expected to lead their respective homelands after they gained independence. Jason Parker refers to this network of transnational black activists based around New York City as the "Harlem Nexus," comprising a "diasporan community" of African Americans and West Indians who fought not only for black rights in the United States and Caribbean decolonization but freedom for black peoples

globally. See Jason Parker, "'Capital of the Caribbean': The African American-West Indian 'Harlem Nexus' and the Transnational Drive for Black Freedom, 1940–1948," *Journal of African American History* (2004): 98–117. For more on the NAACP's anticolonialism, see Carol Anderson, *Bourgeois Radicals: The NAACP and the Struggle for Colonial Liberation, 1941–1960* (New York: Cambridge University Press, 2014).

70. Founded in the late 1940s, the UCAC was technically anticommunist, but its ties with the decidedly leftist Caribbean Labor Congress and other leftist figures in the region may have sullied its image in the minds of U.S. government observers familiar with the group.

71. U.S. Senate Committee on the Judiciary, *Naturalization of Asian and Pacific Peoples, Volume 2: Hearings on H.R. 199*, 81st Cong., 1st sess. (1949), 203, 244.

72. U.S. Senate Committee on the Judiciary, *Naturalization of Asian and Pacific Peoples*, 112, 200–203, 225.

73. U.S. Senate Committee on the Judiciary, *Naturalization of Asian and Pacific Peoples*, 200.

74. Examples include the 1947 Rio Pact and the 1949 creation of the Organization of American States.

75. As historian Brian Harrison writes, Britain's relinquishing of India was "widely viewed as an unavoidable and unique development that demanded compensation elsewhere." See Brian Harrison, *Seeking a Role: The United Kingdom 1951–1970* (London: Oxford University Press, 2009), 27.

76. Jason C. Parker, *Brother's Keeper: The United States, Race, and Empire in the British Caribbean, 1937–1962* (New York: Oxford University Press, 2008), 84.

77. Jason Parker, "Remapping the Cold War in the Tropics: Race, Communism, and National Security in the West Indies," *International History Review* 24, no. 2 (2002): 329.

78. U.S. Senate Committee on the Judiciary, *Naturalization of Asian and Pacific Peoples*, 203, 225.

79. As scholars have shown, many of the same restrictionist southern Democrats who opposed black civil rights measures used their influential positions on the Senate Judiciary Committees overseeing immigration to stall liberalizing measures such as the Judd bill. Southern Democrats blocked legislation by filibuster or, more often, by quietly burying them in committee. See Steven F. Lawson, ed., *To Secure These Rights: The Report of President Harry S Truman's Committee on Civil Rights* (Boston: Bedford/St. Martin's, 2004), 32.

80. See, for example, Greg Robinson, *After Camp: Portraits in Midcentury Japanese American Life and Politics* (Berkeley: University of California Press, 2012); Mark Brilliant, *The Color of America Has Changed: How Racial Diversity Shaped Civil Rights Reform in California, 1941–1978* (New York: Oxford University Press, 2010).

81. For more on the NAACP in Washington, DC, see Denton L. Watson, *Lion in the Lobby: A Biography of Clarence Mitchell* (New York: William Morrow, 1990).

82. For all those groups who had experienced the "awful horrors of mob rule," "waited in fear for rifle shots in the night," and "seen [their] homes and properties burned and dynamited," Masaoka testified that a federal antilynching law would make "human life more worthwhile and property more secure." The bill proposed to broaden federal statutes to make state inaction to lynching crimes a prosecutable

offense. U.S. Senate Committee on the Judiciary, *Crime of Lynching*, 80th Cong., 2nd sess. (1948), 64, 68. 72.

83. Robinson, *After Camp*, 222–23.

84. Progress Report #2, December 12, 1948, Box 64, Folder 9, Masaoka Papers.

85. Progress Report #5, March 31, 1949, Box 64, Folder 11, Masaoka Papers.

86. The 1946 Legislative Reorganization Act strengthened southern Democrats' hold on key committees by giving greater weight to lawmakers' seniority.

87. Divine, *American Immigration Policy*, 156–60.

88. David Reimers, *Still the Golden Door: The Third World Comes to America* (New York: Columbia University Press, 1992), 16–20.

89. Tichenor, *Dividing Lines*, 191–95, especially 192.

90. The first few months of 1951 saw more than five repeal bills introduced to Congress, including another version of the Judd bill. Judd, a Republican, reportedly stepped aside to allow Francis Walter, a Democrat, to take credit for the legislation at the request of Democratic House Speaker Sam Rayburn, who wanted his party to get credit. JACL historian Bill Hosokawa praised Judd's willingness to forego recognition for his part in passing the measure that, Hosokawa suggests, testified to Judd's commitment to the cause and was evidence of how, after almost a decade of laboring for repeal, he was willing to prioritize passage of the bill over his own ability to claim credit. See Hosokawa, *JACL: In Quest of Justice*, 295–96.

91. U.S. Senate Committee on the Judiciary, *Revision of Immigration, Naturalization, and Nationality Laws* (1951), 31, 33–34, 49.

92. U.S. Senate Committee on the Judiciary, *Revision of Immigration, Naturalization, and Nationality Laws* (1951), 74.

93. Wu, *The Color of Success*, 97.

94. This term was taken from Greg Fritz Umbach and Dan Wishnoff, "Strategic Self-Orientalism: Urban Planning Policies and the Shaping of New York City's Chinatown, 1950–2005," *Journal of Planning History* 7, no. 3 (August 2008), 214–38.

95. U.S. Senate Committee on the Judiciary, *Revision of Immigration, Naturalization, and Nationality Laws* (1951), 74.

96. Masaoka and Hosokawa, *They Call Me Moses Masaoka*, 203.

97. Masaoka's experiences exemplified what historian Mae Ngai has described as the lot of "alien citizens," those who lived in the United States legally and possessed the legal rights of citizenship but who nevertheless "remain[ed] alien in the eyes of the nation." See Ngai, *Impossible Subjects*, 8.

98. Mary Alice Baldinger of the ACLU to JACL National Headquarters, March 20, 1947, reprinted in JACL Headquarters memo, April 18, 1947, Box 16, Folder 12, JANL (Japanese American National Library), San Francisco, CA.

99. Bill Hosokawa, "MASAOKA: Nisei of the Year," *Pacific Citizen*, December 23, 1950, 7.

100. Wu, *The Color of Success*, 74–97.

101. Celler's bill, which followed McCarran's by a month, called for the pooling of unused quota slots so as to relieve the oversubscribed quotas of eastern and southern European countries. Supporters of liberalization were heartened. They anticipated

that as chairman of the House Judiciary Committee, Celler would have some leverage in the discussion, but much to their chagrin, his countermeasure went nowhere. The Humphrey–Lehman bills, introduced to Congress in early 1952, likewise failed, but their main ideas are encapsulated in the 1952 report of the President's Commission on Immigration and Naturalization and are discussed in chapter 5.

102. Maddalena Marinari, "Divided and Conquered: Immigration Reform Advocates and the Passage of the 1952 Immigration and Nationality Act," *Journal of American Ethnic History* 35, no. 3 (2016): 32.

103. Marinari, "Divided and Conquered," 16, 19, 22.

104. The JACL was not the only group that ultimately decided to endorse the McCarran-Walter bills as an acceptable step toward greater gains. Others included Read Lewis's Common Council for American Unity, the National Catholic Welfare Council (NCWC), and the National Catholic Rural Conference. See Marinari, "Divided and Conquered," 22, 32. Gráinne McEvoy has traced the split within Catholic circles that followed the NCWC's decision. Gráinne McEvoy, "Justice and Order: American Catholic Social Thought and the Immigration Question in the Restriction Era, 1917–1965" (PhD diss., Boston College, 2014), 208–16.

105. Y. C. Hong, Randolf M. Sakada, Hilario Moncado, and Chin Ha Choy to Pat McCarran, May 20, 1952, Hong Business Files, Huntington Library, San Marino, CA.

106. Hyung-chan Kim, *Asian Americans and Congress: A Documentary History* (Westport, CT: Greenwood, 1996); Robinson, *After Camp*; Brooks, *Between Mao and McCarthy*; Fujino, "Cold War Activism and Japanese American Exceptionalism: Contested Solidarities and Decolonial Alternatives to Freedom."

107. For more, see Fujino, "Cold War Activism and Japanese American Exceptionalism: Contested Solidarities and Decolonial Alternatives to Freedom."

108. In one of the only close studies of the JACL's work in the Judd and McCarran-Walter campaigns, Diane Fujino contrasts the JACL's "light solidarity" with the "deep solidarity" of the Nisei Progressives, which she defines as the "willingness to assume the risk or sacrifice of standing with targeted groups even when it conflicts with direct self-interest." See Fujino, "Cold War Activism and Japanese American Exceptionalism," 298; "Omnibus Bill Takes 1 Step Forward, Two Steps Back," *Hokubei Shimpo*, June 5, 1952, 1. For more on the Nisei Progressives, see also Diane Fujino, "The Indivisibility of Freedom: The Nisei Progressives, Deep Solidarities, and Cold War Alternatives," *Journal of Asian American Studies* 21, no. 2 (2018): 171–208.

109. The three students were Morgan Yamanaka, Anne Kunikani, and Kimi Fugita. Eugene Block of San Francisco to Truman, May 16, 1952, Box 682, White House File: Office File (WHF:OF) 133, Truman Papers, Truman Library, Independence, MO (hereafter, Truman Papers).

110. Bishop Reginald Barrow to Truman, February 6, 1952, Box 682, WHCF:OF 133; Ms. Eveline Hollar of New York to Truman, February 26, 1952, Box 682, WHCF:OF 133, Truman Papers.

111. Felix A. Cummings, President of the British Guiana Development League of America in New York, to Truman, April 9, 1952, Box 682, WHCF:OF 133, Truman Papers.

112. Walter to Rep. John W. McCormack, April 2, 1952, Box 314, File H.R. 5678, RG 233, NARA I, Washington, DC.

113. In the 1920s, labor leader A. Philip Randolph opposed West Indian migration on the grounds that Caribbean immigrants did not become U.S. citizens and therefore did not help the black movement critically. He was also concerned that West Indian migrants, along with Indians and Chinese, would undercut black workers within the U.S. labor market. A. Philip Randolph of Brotherhood of Sleeping Car Porters to Truman, May 29, 1952, Box 682, WHCF:OF 133, Truman Papers.

114. According to Masaoka, the bill reflected the "evolutionary nature" of legislative reform in a democracy. See Mike Masaoka, "McCarran Bill Upheld," *New York Times*, April 27, 1952, E8.

115. Masaoka to Truman, June 13, 1952, Box 682, WHCF:OF 133, Truman Papers.

116. According to Takashi Fujitani, the 1952 act's dual audiences reflected the United States' domestic and international racial projects to "mobilize an ever greater diversity and number of people for national projects," on the one hand, and to "win allies of color" overseas, on the other. Fujitani, *Race for Empire*, 13.

117. Truman's veto message to the House (Confidential Memorandum), June 25, 1952, Box 682, OF 133: 1952 McCarran-Walter bills, Truman Library.

118. Masaoka and Hosokawa, *They Call Me Moses Masaoka*, 235, 256–57.

119. Robinson, *After Camp*, 97–98; Greg Robinson, "The Great Unknown and the Unknown Great: Remembering the McCarran-Walter Act," *Nichi Bei*, July 11, 2013.

120. Hayakawa, quoted in President's Commission on Immigration and Naturalization, *Hearings before the President's Commission on Immigration and Naturalization* (Washington, DC, 1952), 843–44.

121. For more on the JACL's campaign of self-justification, see William R. Tamayo, "Asian Americans and the McCarran-Walter Act," in *Asian Americans and Congress*, ed. Hyung-Chan Kim (Westport, CT: Greenwood Press, 1996), 363n92, for a reference to what he alleged was Judd's "deliberate misrepresentation" that "no group of Asians . . . protested" the creation of the Asia-Pacific Triangle, 83rd Cong. Rec—Appendix, A217, January 19, 1953; Masaoka and Hosokawa, *They Call Me Moses Masaoka*, 227–37.

122. U.S. President's Commission on Immigration and Naturalization, *Emigration and Immigration Law* (Hearings), Los Angeles, CA, October 1952, 1737; Hosokawa, *JACL: In Quest of Justice*, 294.

123. Dower, *Embracing Defeat*, 23, 552; Simeon Man, *Soldiering through Empire: Race and the Making of the Decolonizing Pacific* (Berkeley: University of California Press, 2018), 8.

124. Jennifer M. Miller, "Fractured Alliance: Anti-Base Protests and Postwar US–Japanese Relations," *Diplomatic History* 38, no. 5 (2013): 953–86.

125. Bill Ong Hing, *Making and Remaking Asian America through Immigration Policy: 1850–1990* (Palo Alto, CA: Stanford University Press, 1993), 55–56.

126. After the 1952 law's enactment curtailed black migration to the United States, the number of Jamaicans and other West Indians migrating to Great Britain jumped in proportion. See Iyiola Solanke, "Black Women Workers and Discrimination: Exit, Voice, and Loyalty . . . or 'Shifting'"?, in *Migrants at Work: Immigration and Vulnerability in Labour Law*, ed. Cathryn Costello and Mark Freedland (London: Oxford University Press, 2014), 314n78.

127. Hosokawa, *JACL: In Quest of Justice*, 294, 298.

Chapter Five

1. U.S. President's Commission on Immigration and Naturalization, *Whom We Shall Welcome: Report of the President's Commission on Immigration and Naturalization* (Washington, DC: U.S. Government Printing Office, 1953), 44–46.

2. U.S. President's Committee on Civil Rights, *To Secure These Rights* (Washington, DC: U.S. Government Printing Office, 1947).

3. U.S. President's Commission on Immigration and Naturalization, *Whom We Shall Welcome*, 63.

4. Meredith Oyen, *The Diplomacy of Migration: Transnational Lives and the Making of U.S.-Chinese Relations in the Cold War* (Ithaca, NY: Cornell University Press, 2015), 155.

5. By this time, the India League of America was more focused on issues of U.S.-India relations and no other Indian American organization rivaled its reputation and wide network of influential supporters. Similar to the 1940s, Filipina/o Americans had only inconsistent national representation in Washington, DC. Korean community organizations in Hawaii had previously sponsored a national representative named Walter Jhung to lobby for a Korean immigration and naturalization bill on Capitol Hill. Between 1947 and 1949, Jhung served as the Washington representative of a group called the Korean Immigration and Naturalization Committee. When the group went defunct in 1949, Jhung moved to South Korea, where by 1953, he was serving as a special assistant to the Republic of Korea's (ROK) prime minister as part of ROK president Syngman Rhee's cabinet.

6. Yen Espiritu, *Asian American Panethnicity: Bridging Institutions and Identities* (Philadelphia: Temple University Press, 1993).

7. Gretchen Heefner, "A Symbol of the New Frontier," *Pacific Historical Review* 74, no. 4 (2005): 545–74.

8. Historian Simeon Man, for example, contends that Hawaiian statehood was a U.S. state project to "preserve empire in the name of freedom." In his telling, the denial of sovereignty for the islands encapsulated the limitations of racial liberalism. Takashi Fujitani described Hawaiian statehood an example of "decolonization through nationalization." Simeon Man, *Soldiering through Empire: Race and the Making of the Decolonizing Pacific* (Berkeley: University of California Press, 2018), 77–102, especially 82; Takashi Fujitani, "A Different Kind of Asia Pivot," *Amerasia Journal* 42, no. 3 (2016): 17–22. See also Dean Saranillio, *Unsustainable Empire: Alternative Histories of Hawai'i Statehood* (Durham, NC: Duke University Press, 2018).

9. See, for example, Rebekah Barber, "How the Civil Rights Movement Opened the Door to Immigrants of Color," *Facing South*, February 3, 2017. Law professors Gabriel Chin and Rose Cuison Villazor have called the 1965 act a "sibling" of the 1964 and 1965 laws. Gabriel J. Chin and Rose Cuison Villazor, *The Immigration and Nationality Act of 1965: Legislating a New America* (New York: Cambridge University Press, 2015), 4.

10. Daniel J. Tichenor, *Dividing Lines: The Politics of Immigration Control in America* (Princeton, NJ: Princeton University Press, 2002), 208–10.

11. For more on these campaigns, see Robert L. Fleegler, *Ellis Island Nation: Immigration Policy and American Identity in the Twentieth Century* (Philadelphia: University of Pennsylvania Press, 2013); Danielle Battisti, *Whom We Shall Welcome: Italian Americans and Immigration Reform, 1945–1965* (New York: Fordham Univer-

sity Press, 2019); Maddalena Marinari, *Unwanted: Italian and Jewish Mobilization against Restrictive Immigration Laws, 1882–1965* (Chapel Hill: University of North Carolina Press, 2020).

12. Tichenor, *Dividing Lines*, 197–98.

13. Oscar Handlin, "The Immigration Fight Has Only Begun," *Commentary* 14 (July 1952): 1, 6. As Ngai writes, "Handlin did not entirely ignore immigrants from Asia or Mexico, but he did not believe they were part of the central story of American history in the way that Europeans were." See Mae M. Ngai, "Oscar Handlin and Immigration Policy Reform in the 1950s and 1960s," *Journal of American Ethnic History* 32, no. 3 (2013): 63.

14. Mae Ngai, "The Unlovely Residue of Outworn Prejudices: The Hart-Celler Act and the Politics of Immigration Reform, 1945–1965," in *Americanism: New Perspectives on the History of an Ideal*, ed. Michael Kazin and Joseph McCartin (Chapel Hill: University of North Carolina Press, 1996), 117–18.

15. U.S. President's Commission on Immigration and Naturalization, *Whom We Shall Welcome*, 52.

16. Carl J. Bon Tempo, *Americans at the Gate: The United States and Refugees during the Cold War* (Princeton, NJ: Princeton University Press, 2008), 8.

17. Oyen, *The Diplomacy of Migration*, 304.

18. U.S. President's Commission on Immigration and Naturalization, *Whom We Shall Welcome*, 61–64.

19. The focus of refugee admissions shifted somewhat during the 1960s. Over this decade, the United States accepted more than 15,000 Chinese and 360,000 Cubans as refugees. See Oyen, *The Diplomacy of Migration*, 182; Bon Tempo, *Americans at the Gate*.

20. Oyen, *The Diplomacy of Migration*, 247. Washington also directed such efforts at Chinese Americans, many of whom embraced an association with the ROC after 1949 out of self-protection as well as in pursuit of their own interests, but with no particular impact on immigration policy. See Cindy Cheng, *Citizens of Asian America: Democracy and Race during the Cold War* (New York: New York University Press, 2013), 154–89; Charlotte Brooks, *Between Mao and McCarthy: Chinese American Politics in the Cold War Years* (Chicago: University of Chicago Press, 2015).

21. With roots dating to World War II, the China Lobby, comprising former missionaries, state officials, journalists, and other white elites, successfully fought to prevent the United States and the United Nations from formally recognizing the PRC until the 1970s.

22. U.S. House Committee on the Judiciary, *Emergency Immigration Program: Hearings before Subcommittee No. 1*, 83rd Cong., 1st sess. (1953), 227–29.

23. Brooks, *Between Mao and McCarthy*, 5.

24. Madeline Y. Hsu, *The Good Immigrants: How the Yellow Peril Became the Model Minority* (Princeton, NJ: Princeton University Press, 2015), 140.

25. Hsu, *The Good Immigrants*, 135. For more on the founding of ARCI, see Hsu, 137–43; Meredith Oyen, "'Thunder without Rain': ARCI, the Far East Refugee Program, and the US Response to Hong Kong Refugees," *Journal of Cold War Studies* 16:4 (2014), 197–201. Hsu writes that ARCI was created "solely to address the Cold War refugee crisis." Hsu, *The Good Immigrants*, 136, 140.

26. Along similar lines, historian Cindy Cheng has described how the geopolitics of the early Cold War "differentially impacted the social standings of Asian Americans," giving the "inclusion and exclusion" of Chinese Americans "greater political significance" than that of Japanese Americans and other groups. See Cheng, *Citizens of Asian America*, 11.

27. In a prime example of the Eisenhower administration's policy of neglect, despite mounting Japanese protests to the 1951 Mutual Cooperation and Security Treaty, U.S. officials took no action to modify it until years later. As Japanese critics were quick to note, Tokyo's ratification of a 1951 Security Treaty giving the United States control over Japanese military operations had been one of the conditions for ending the U.S. occupation. See Nick Kapur, "Mending the 'Broken Dialogue': US-Japan Alliance Diplomacy in the Aftermath of the 1960 Security Treaty Crisis," *Diplomatic History* 41, no. 3 (2017): 492.

28. Simeon Man, *Soldiering through Empire: Race and the Making of the Decolonizing Pacific* (Berkeley: University of California Press, 2018), 8. While scholars have noted and sought to explain Japanese Americans' rapid transformation in the media and minds of U.S. officials from disloyal and pernicious enemies during World War II to model Americans and patriotic soldiers soon after it, much less is known about Japanese American activism during the Eisenhower and Kennedy years, when the Japan–U.S. relationship soured. See Naoko Shibusawa, *America's Geisha Ally: Reimagining the Japanese Enemy* (Cambridge, MA: Harvard University Press, 2006).

29. By early 1952, repeated attacks by an angry General Douglas McArthur, who accused Japan lobbyists of undermining his authority in Japan, coupled with the folding of the American Council on Japan, the lobby's best-known member group, meant that its influence in shaping U.S. Japan policy after occupation remained limited at best. In one notable exception, the Japan and China Lobbies joined forces to assure Japan's nonrecognition policy of the PRC. See Howard Schonberger, "The Japan Lobby in American Diplomacy, 1947–1952," *Pacific Historical Review* 46, no. 3 (1977): 342–57. Lingering enmity against former Japanese enemies also played a role, but it was arguably more pronounced among the American public than among congressional lawmakers.

30. Mike Masaoka and Bill Hosokawa, *They Call Me Moses Masaoka: An American Saga* (New York: William Morrow, 1987), 259–66.

31. In 1951, the United Nations Refugee Convention defined refugees as people "unable or unwilling to return to their country of origin owing to a well-founded fear of being persecuted for reasons of race, religion, nationality, membership of a particular social group, or political opinion." But U.S. law would not officially adopt this definition until the 1980 Refugee Act, leaving the term open for wide and varying interpretation.

32. U.S. House Committee on the Judiciary, *Emergency Immigration Program*, 167.

33. This group of POWs would have been familiar to congressional lawmakers, as it had become a focus of increasing international, and especially U.N., attention during this time.

34. U.S. House Committee on the Judiciary, *Emergency Immigration Program*, 169. Edward N. Barnhart, "Japanese Internees from Peru," *Pacific Historical Review*

31, no. 2 (1962): 169–78; Lika C. Miyake, "Forsaken and Forgotten: The US Internment of Japanese Peruvians during World War II," *Asian Law Journal* 9 (2002): 163–93.

35. The White House had authorized their removal from the Western Hemisphere under the terms of a pan-American agreement. Peru was the first and main Latin American destination for Japanese immigrants after the Gentleman's Agreement of 1907 effectively eliminated the United States as an option for Japanese workers, mostly farmers, seeking to emigrate. For an overview of Japanese migration to Peru, see Ayumi Takenaka, "The Japanese in Peru: History of Immigration, Settlement, and Racialization," *Latin American Perspectives* 31, no. 3 (2004): 77–98.

36. While it is unclear whether Congress ever formally resolved the administrative issues of quota allotment that Masaoka described, it did pass a law one year later granting formerly incarcerated (or stranded) Latin Americans the right to apply for the status of permanent resident, thereby ending any ambiguity in the problem of Peruvian Japanese legal status by qualifying them for U.S. citizenship. Public Law 751 (1954).

37. According to Meredith Oyen, this usage was "much less in line with the philosophical origins of the act," but during the 1950s, the INS was receptive to Cold War arguments that the program could help contain communism in Japan by reducing rural poverty. Oyen, *The Diplomacy of Migration*, 170; Masaoka and Hosokawa, *They Call Me Moses Masaoka*, 248.

38. JAWP has historically received little scholarly attention, though this has begun to change. See, for instance, Mireya Loza, "The Japanese Agricultural Workers' Program: Race, Labor, and Cold War Diplomacy in the Fields, 1956–1965," *Pacific Historical Review* 86, no. 4 (2017): 661–90. Loza has described how California growers and other supporters of the program enlisted the media in distinguishing Japanese workers from Mexican braceros as a superior and more desirable workforce, even appealing to "nascent model-minority discourses" portraying Japanese guest workers as students rather than laborers.

39. Masaoka claimed that the monies JAWP workers sent to their families in Japan had "turn[ed] the tide against communism" in Japan's Kagoshima prefecture.

40. U.S. House, Committee on the Judiciary, Special Subcommittee on Japanese Temporary Workers, *Japanese Temporary Workers* (1957), 41, 43, 47.

41. Juan Garcia, *Operation Wetback: The Mass Deportation of Mexican Undocumented Workers in 1954* (Westport, CT: Greenwood Press, 1980); Kelly Lytle Hernández, "The Crimes and Consequences of Illegal Immigration: A Cross-Border Examination of Operation Wetback, 1943 to 1954," *Western Historical Quarterly* 37, no. 4 (2006): 421–44.

42. Masaoka and Hosokawa, *They Call Me Moses Masaoka*, 270–71.

43. Tichenor, *Dividing Lines*, 204–5. The two lawmakers were a study in contrasts. Forty-four-year-old Humphrey was at the beginning of his Washington political career; he would later serve as vice president under Lyndon B. Johnson. More than thirty years his senior, Lehman was ending a long and often frustrated career spent fighting for race reform. Both men shared a passion for civil rights and fought for revision of the national origins quota system as an extension of their support for racial equality and civil rights. Lehman had introduced the civil rights platform adopted by the Democratic Party leadership at its 1948 convention that caused southern delegates to

walk out in protest. Humphrey would later become a chief author of the 1964 Civil Rights Act. While Lehman would not live to see the 1964 law pass, he spent much of his 1950s Senate term fighting to revise the rules for ending filibusters, the tool of choice for southern senators seeking to block civil rights measures.

44. Political scientist Daniel Tichenor underscores the importance of the AFL's decision to support immigration reform upon its merger with the CIO in 1955. In his telling, the shift dealt a "serious blow to postwar nativists," who had long depended on the opposition of unions to resist change. See Tichenor, *Dividing Lines*, 204.

45. One writer described it as a "compromise bill" representing a "token gesture in the direction of [Eisenhower's] proposals." Allen Drury, "Immigration Bill Passed by Senate," *New York Times*, July 28, 1956, 35.

46. As then-senator John F. Kennedy (D-MA) warned Majority Leader Lyndon B. Johnson (D-TX), Democrats stood to lose white ethnic voters in the large northern cities if Congress did not abolish the national origins quota. For their part, Republicans hoped to close slight Democratic majorities in the House and Senate by riding on President Eisenhower's popularity during his reelection campaign; like their Democratic counterparts, GOP party strategists saw winning white ethnic voters in the North as the key to making this happen.

47. Instead of applying for admission once they arrived on American soil, Chinese applicants now had to obtain travel documents from U.S. diplomatic agencies first. The main U.S. consul in Hong Kong was now able to "double-check" the identity of each nonquota derivative applicant even as it "processed fewer than twenty quota applications each year," causing a significant backlog in applications. The consulate's use of blood tests beginning in 1951 also made securing admission more difficult while easing U.S. officials' attempts to rout out Chinese seeking entry using false identities. See Xiaojian Zhao, *Remaking Chinese America: Immigration, Family, and Community, 1940-1965* (New Brunswick, NJ: Rutgers University Press, 2002), 153.

48. Zhao, *Remaking Chinese America*, 156, 159; U.S. Senate, Committee on the Judiciary, Subcommittee on Immigration, *Review of Immigration Laws, Volume 4*, 84th Cong., 1st session (1955), 321.

49. U.S. Senate, Committee on the Judiciary, Subcommittee on Immigration, *Review of Immigration Laws*, 313–14, 353, 356, 469.

50. As the first secretary of the Chinese American Democratic Club of San Francisco, Chinn was part of an early generation of Bay Area Chinese to take advantage of the patronage networks associated with mainstream party politics in the state. Chinn was a Democrat, and appearing with him was CCBA president Earl Sun Louie, one of the first Chinese Americans to serve in the California Republican Assembly and on the San Francisco Republican Party County Committee.

51. Chin arguably sought to invoke a proviso of the McCarran Act (1950) giving the U.S. attorney general discretion to suspend the deportation of aliens to countries where they were likely to face physical persecution or harm. U.S. Senate, Committee on the Judiciary, Subcommittee on Immigration, *Review of Immigration Laws*, 313–14,

353, 356, 469. For other examples of this strategy, see Cheng, *Citizens of Asian America*, 132–36.

52. See Brooks, *Between Mao and McCarthy*. The American Committee for the Protection of the Foreign Born (ACPFB) was one such example. See also Rachel Ida Buff, *Against the Deportation Terror: Organizing for Immigrant Rights in the Twentieth Century* (Philadelphia: Temple University Press, 2017).

53. Mae Ngai, "The Unlovely Residue of Outworn Prejudices," 117–18.

54. U.S. Senate, Committee on the Judiciary, Subcommittee on Immigration, *Review of Immigration Laws*, 446, 450, 459.

55. Joyce Mao, *Asia First: China and the Making of American Conservatism* (Chicago: University of Chicago Press, 2015).

56. U.S. Senate, Committee on the Judiciary, Subcommittee on Immigration, *Review of Immigration Laws*, 447, 455, 453.

57. Mike Masaoka to Senator Harley Kilgore, November 2, 1955, Box 1005, RG 46, NARA I, Washington, DC.

58. U.S. Senate, Committee on the Judiciary, Subcommittee on Immigration, *Review of Immigration Laws*, 443, 446, 450, 459.

59. See, for example, Larry Tajiri, "The Chinese Americans," *Pacific Citizen*, January 13, 1951.

60. See Joan S. Wang, "The Double Burdens of Immigrant Nationalism: The Relationship between Chinese and Japanese in the American West, 1880s–1920s," *Journal of American Ethnic History* 27, no. 2 (Winter 2008): 28–58. On economic competition between Japanese and other Asian American groups, see Charlotte Brooks, "The War on Grant Avenue: Business Competition and Ethnic Rivalry in San Francisco's Chinatown, 1937–1942," *Journal of Urban History* 37, no. 3 (May 2011): 311–30.

61. K. Scott Wong, *Americans First: Chinese Americans and the Second World War* (Cambridge, MA: Harvard University Press, 2005), 82–86.

62. See Shibusawa, *America's Geisha Ally*.

63. After years of contention among league members, delegates to the JACL's 1954 annual conference adopted a hands-off policy asking league members to avoid "participating or intervening in any matters" relating to U.S. foreign affairs, "including those with Japan," except in cases where the "welfare" of Japanese Americans was under threat. But this policy proved thorny in practice. A series of tests over the late 1950s revealed that many members were unwilling to comply, and the debate flared up again several years later in a very public way, suggesting that an organizational policy alone would not resolve the issue. See Ellen D. Wu, *The Color of Success: Asian Americans and the Origins of the Model Minority* (Princeton, NJ: Princeton University Press, 2013), 101–7; Naoko Shibusawa, "Femininity, Race and Treachery: How 'Tokyo Rose' Became a Traitor to the United States after the Second World War," *Gender & History* 22, no. 1 (2010): 169–88.

64. Cheng, *Citizens of Asian America*, 79.

65. Chinese Americans in San Francisco eventually found relief with the help of white allies; a district court judge quashed the government subpoena and ended the witch hunt. Lacking the same strong connections, members of the New York City Chi-

nese community suffered longer. Quoted in Brooks, *Between Mao and McCarthy*, 162; see also Brooks, 159–63.

66. Cheng, *Citizens of Asian America*, 251.

67. Memo from Mike Masaoka to Roy Nishikawa, September 16, 1957, Box 5, Folder 15, JACL Papers.

68. Harold Gordon to Masaoka, May 13, 1958, Folder 30, Box 6, JACL Papers.

69. Julius Edelstein, a longtime aide of Senator Herbert Lehman and member of the American Jewish Congress, had inaugurated the NCIC in April 1956 in conjunction with other liberal immigration reformers.

70. In a sign of things to come, future president Lyndon B. Johnson was one of the lead Democratic supporters in the debate. His show of support was significant, especially because he had voted for McCarran-Walter.

71. Tichenor, *Dividing Lines*, 207.

72. Christina Klein, *Cold War Orientalism: Asia in the Middlebrow Imagination, 1945–1961* (Berkeley: University of California Press, 2003), 6.

73. To the chagrin of many liberal reformers, Kennedy had delayed action in both arenas after taking office in early 1961 for fear of upsetting southern members of his own party. Immigration reformers were especially disappointed in light of Kennedy's strong record of support for abolition of the national origins quota system. As a U.S. senator, Kennedy had published *A Nation of Immigrants* (New York: Anti-Defamation League, 1959), which celebrated the United States' immigrant past and laid out his vision for a "fair" and "flexible" immigration policy that "turned to the world." Assured by Rep. Walter and Senator James Eastland, a well-known restrictionist and segregationist, that an immigration bill had no chance of passing so long as they controlled the committees overseeing it, Kennedy spent the first two years in office on other parts of his agenda, mostly related to foreign policy and Cold War crises in Cuba, Germany, and elsewhere.

74. Maddalena Marinari, "'Americans Must Show Justice in Immigration Policies Too': The Passage of the 1965 Immigration Act," *Journal of Policy History* 26, no. 2 (2014): 219–45.

75. They were not the first Asian Americans to be elected to Congress, however. That honor belongs to Dalip Singh Saund, who in 1956 became the first person of Indian descent specifically and of Asian descent generally to serve in the U.S. House of Representatives.

76. Wu, *The Color of Success*, 235.

77. Fong's amendment proposed to allow the attorney general to parole up to 2,250 refugees who were not under the United Nations High Commissioner for Refugees mandate into the United States at his discretion. It was dropped at Rep. Walter's insistence. Davis erroneously claimed that Fong was the first lawmaker in Congress to lobby for the admission of Asian refugees; as discussed earlier in the chapter, Walter Judd (R-MN) had done so seven years earlier in the lead-up to the Refugee Relief Act (1953). See Michael G. Davis, "Impetus for Immigration Reform: Asian Refugees and the Cold War," *Journal of American-East Asian Relations* 7, no. 3/4 (1998): 134–36. See also David M. Reimers, "An Unintended Reform: The 1965 Immigration Act and Third World Immigration to the United States," *Journal of American Ethnic History* 3, no. 1 (1983): 13–14.

78. After Congress declined to act, Kennedy used his presidential parole power to admit over 15,000 Chinese refugees from Hong Kong the following year. U.S. Senate Committee on the Judiciary, *To Investigate Problems Connected with Refugees and Escapees*, 87th Cong., 1st sess. (July 12–14, 1961), 81–83.

79. President Johnson granted an immigration quota to Tonga by presidential proclamation in January 1964. Fong's actions were in keeping with a longer political tradition in Hawaii of representatives championing the rights of Pacific Islanders in Washington, DC. Before statehood, for example, territorial delegates such as Joseph Farrington repeatedly sponsored migration and naturalization measures on behalf of residents of American Samoa and Guam, among other groups. While Farrington's bills failed to pass the House, Congress did eventually enact the Organic Act of 1950, which made Guamanians eligible for U.S. citizenship. 48 U.S.C. § 1421 et seq.

80. Richard Halloran, *Sparky: Warrior, Peacemaker, Poet, Patriot: A Portrait of Senator Spark M. Matsunaga* (Honolulu, HI: Watermark, 2002).

81. A. S. "Doc" Young, "The Big Beat," *Los Angeles Sentinel*, September 3, 1959, C1, C3.

82. P. L. Prattis, "Horizon: Senator Fong," *New Pittsburgh Courier (1959-1965)*, National Edition; Pittsburgh, Pa., November 21, 1959, 13.

83. For more on southern opposition to Hawaiian statehood, see Ann K. Ziker, "Segregationists Confront American Empire: The Conservative White South and the Question of Hawaiian Statehood, 1947–1959," *Pacific Historical Review* 76, no. 3 (2007): 439–66.

84. Ziker, "Segregationists Confront American Empire," 441.

85. Joseph Fry, *Dixie Looks Abroad: The South and US Foreign Relations, 1789–1973* (Baton Rouge: Louisiana State University Press, 2002), 128–30.

86. Roger John Bell, *Last among Equals: Hawaiian Statehood and American Politics* (Honolulu: University of Hawaii Press, 1984), 133–35, especially 134. Historian Ann Ziker has shown how southern opposition to Hawaiian statehood extended beyond Congress to grassroots resistance among ordinary people. See Ziker, "Segregationists Confront American Empire."

87. "Hawaii's Statehood," *Chicago Defender*, March 18, 1959, A11; quoted in Wu, *The Color of Success*, 234.

88. "Hawaii Legislators Pledge Rights Aid," *Tri-State Defender* [Memphis, TN], August 15, 1959, 13.

89. Eleanor C. Nordyke, "Blacks in Hawai'i: A Demographic and Historical Perspective," *Hawaiian Journal of History* 22 (1988): 242.

90. Sponsored by Minnesota Republican Clark MacGregor, the amendment proposed to place a numerical quota of 115,000 on immigration from the Western Hemisphere; the ceiling in the final bill imposed a ceiling of 120,000.

91. Tichenor, *Dividing Lines*, 213; Marinari, "'Americans Must Show Justice in Immigration Policies Too.'"

92. At least this is how Masaoka reported the exchange in a letter to Fong himself. Masaoka to Fong, August 31, 1965, Immigration: Subject Series, Folder 13, Box 299, Spark Matsunaga Papers, Hawaii Congressional Papers Collection, University of Hawaii, Honolulu.

93. This shift, which was much more complicated than described here, will be discussed further in the epilogue.

94. Like his better-known colleague, future U.S. senator Daniel Inouye, Matsunaga served in an all-nisei regiment during World War II, but Matsunaga was injured before his outfit joined the famed 442nd Regimental Combat Team on which Inouye served. Widely popular, Matsunaga represented Hawaii in the House for four terms before going on to take Hiram Fong's seat when he left the Senate in 1977. Matsunaga developed a reputation for being bold and brash at times, such as when he demanded a public apology from vice-presidential candidate Spiro Agnew for using the term "Jap" in a speech. For more on this episode, see Jules Witcover, *Very Strange Bedfellows: The Short and Unhappy Marriage of Richard Nixon and Spiro Agnew* (New York: Public Affairs Press, 2007), 43–44.

95. U.S. House, Committee on the Judiciary, Subcommittee on Immigration and Naturalization, *Immigration. Part 1*, 88th Cong., 1st sess. (June 11, 18–19, 22–23, 25–26, 29–30, 1964), 259.

96. Matsunaga had become aware of the deportation issue through the case of Los Angeles Korean architect David Hyun, who had grown up in Hawaii and had many close family connections there. In 1963, Matsunaga petitioned the U.S. attorney general to cancel the deportation proceedings against Hyun. Hyun's deportation was ultimately stayed indefinitely and he passed away in Los Angeles in 2012. For more on Hyun's deportation case and others like it, see Cindy Cheng, *Citizens of Asian America*, 117–47.

97. Wu, *The Color of Success*, 232.

98. U.S. Senate, Committee on the Judiciary, Subcommittee on Immigration and Naturalization, *S. 1932 and Other Legislation Relating to Immigration Quota System*, vol. 2, 88th Cong., 2nd sess. (January 14, 1964), 96, 99.

99. U.S. House Committee on the Judiciary, *Immigration*, 1965, 89th Cong., 1st sess., 199.

100. U.S. House Committee on the Judiciary, Subcommittee No. 1, *Immigration Part 1*, 88th Cong., 1st sess. (1964), 257.

101. Fong did so enthusiastically, while Matsunaga, a decorated World War II veteran, expressed reservations about the U.S. role.

102. *Public Papers of the Presidents of the United States: Lyndon B. Johnson, 1965. Volume II, entry 546* (Washington, DC: Government Printing Office, 1966), 1037.

103. This more critical view complements a large body of work by scholars across disciplines highlighting the illiberal dimensions of the 1965 law. See, for example, Kevin Johnson, *The Huddled Masses Myth: Immigration and Civil Rights* (Philadelphia: Temple University Press, 2004); Mae M. Ngai, *Impossible Subjects: Illegal Aliens and the Making of Modern America* (Princeton, NJ: Princeton University Press, 2004).

104. Quoted in David M. Reimers, *Still the Golden Door: The Third World Comes to America* (New York: Columbia University Press, 1992), 73.

105. Quoted in Reimers, 73.

106. U.S. House, Committee on the Judiciary, Subcommittee on Immigration, *Immigration*, 89th Cong., 1st sess. (March 3, 8, 10–11, 18, 31, April 6, May 18, 20, 26–27, June 1, 1965), 200.

107. "Statement of JACL Endorsing Administration's Immigration Bill" (S. 599, H.R. 2580), submitted by Mike Masaoka on behalf of the JACL, Box 38, Folder 11: Statement, 1965 bill, Mike Masaoka Papers, University of Utah, Salt Lake City.

108. U.S. Senate, *Congressional Record*, September 20, 1965, 111:24503. For more general views, see Reimers, "An Unintended Reform," 15–16.

109. Morrison G. Wong, "Post-1965 Asian Immigrants: Where Do They Come from, Where Are They Now, and Where Are They Going?," *Annals of the American Academy of Political and Social Science* 487, no. 1 (1986): 151.

110. Sabrina Tavernise, "U.S. Has Highest Share of Foreign-Born since 1910, with More Coming from Asia," *New York Times*, September 13, 2018.

111. This more critical view complements a large body of work by scholars across disciplines highlighting the illiberal dimensions of the 1965 law. See, for example, Johnson, *The Huddled Masses Myth*; Ngai, *Impossible Subjects*.

Epilogue

1. Michael Lind, *Next American Nation: The New Nationalism and the Fourth American Revolution* (New York: Simon and Schuster, 1995), 133.

2. Sabrina Tavernise, "U.S. Has Highest Share of Foreign-Born since 1910, with More Coming from Asia," *New York Times*, September 13, 2018.

3. Douglas S. Massey and Karen A. Pren, "Unintended Consequences of US Immigration Policy: Explaining the Post-1965 Surge from Latin America," *Population and Development Review* 38, no. 1 (2012): 1–29.

4. Peter S. Canellos, "Obama Victory Took Root in Kennedy-Inspired Immigration," *Boston Globe*, November 11, 2008.

5. Theodore Schultz, *The Economic Value of Education* (New York: Columbia University Press, 1963); Gary Becker, *Human Capital: A Theoretical and Empirical Analysis, with Special Reference to Education* (New York: National Bureau of Economic Research, 1964).

6. UNESCO, "The Problem of Emigration of Scientists and Technologists (Brain Drain)" (Paris: February 29, 1968).

7. U.S. House Committee on Government Operations, *Scientific Brain Drain from the Developing Countries*, 90th Cong., 2nd sess. (March 1968).

8. Man Singh Das, "The 'Brain Drain' Controversy in a Comparative Perspective," *International Review of Sociology* 1, no. 1 (1971): 55–65.

9. U.S. Senate, Committee on the Judiciary, Subcommittee on Immigration and Naturalization, *International Migration of Talent and Skills*, 90th Cong., 1st sess. (March 1967), 102.

10. For more on modernization theory, also known as "development doctrine," see Michael E. Latham, *Modernization as Ideology: American Social Science and "Nation Building" in the Kennedy Era* (Chapel Hill: University of North Carolina Press, 2000); Nils Gilman, *Mandarins of the Future: Modernization Theory in Cold War America* (Baltimore, MD: Johns Hopkins University Press, 2003).

11. U.S. Senate, Committee on the Judiciary, Subcommittee on Immigration and Naturalization, *International Migration of Talent and Skills*, 102.

12. U.S. Senate, Committee on the Judiciary, Subcommittee on Immigration and Naturalization, *International Migration of Talent and Skills*, 111.

13. UNESCO, "The Problem of Emigration," 20, 45.

14. The Health Professions Educational Assistance Act severely reduced the number of foreign medical graduates entering the United States in response to protests by American medical graduates concerned about their employment prospects. In fact, the 1976 act was one in a series of laws designed to reduce the United States' dependence on foreign medical labor by making it easier for Americans to seek medical training and find employment. Earlier laws included the 1963 Health Professions Educational Assistance Act, the Nurse Training Act of 1964, the Allied Health Professions Personnel Training Act of 1966, and the Health Manpower Act of 1968. For more on the migration of foreign medical graduates as a legacy of U.S. imperialism, see Catherine Ceniza Choy, *Empire of Care: Nursing and Migration in Filipino American History* (Durham, NC: Duke University Press, 2003).

15. George B. Baldwin, "Brain Drain or Overflow?," *Foreign Affairs* 48, no. 2 (1970): 358–72.

16. Lewis M. Stern, "Response to Vietnamese Refugees: Surveys of Public Opinion," *Social Work* 26, no. 4 (1981): 306–11; Alan Gomez, "Fewer Americans Believe U.S. Should Accept Refugees," *USA Today*, May 24, 2018.

Selected Bibliography

Archival Sources and Document Collections

Charles E. Young Research Library, Special Collections, University of California, Los Angeles
    Japanese American Research Project
Ethnic Studies Library, University of California, Berkeley, Berkeley
    Asian American Studies Collection
Filipino American Historical Society, Seattle, WA
    Diosdado Yap Papers
Harry S. Truman Presidential Library, Independence, MO
    White House Office Files
Hawaii State Archives, Honolulu
    Joseph Farrington Jr. Papers
Hoover Institute, Stanford University, Stanford, CA
    Walter H. Judd Papers
Huntington Library, San Marino, CA
    Y.C. Hong Family Papers
Japanese American National Library (JANL), San Francisco, CA
    Japanese American Citizens League (JACL) Papers
Library of Congress, Washington, DC
    Clare Boothe Luce Papers
    Henry Luce Papers
Marriott Library, Special Collections, University of Utah, Salt Lake City
    Mike Masaoka Papers
Minnesota History Center (MHC), St. Paul, MN
    Walter H. Judd Papers
National Archives I (NARA I), Washington, DC
    Records of the U.S. House of Representatives (RG [Record Group] 233)
National Archives II (NARA II), College Park, MD
    General Records of the Department of State (RG 59)
    Records of the War Department General and Special Staffs (RG 165)
National Archives of India, Delhi
    Records of the Office of External Affairs
Nehru Memorial Museum and Library (NMML), Delhi, India
    Jawaharlal Nehru Papers
    J.J. Singh Papers
Philippine National Library, Manila, Philippines
    Manuel Quezon Papers
    Sergio Osmena Papers

Presbyterian Historical Society, Philadelphia
  National Council of Churches Papers
University Archives, University of Hawaii, Manoa, Honolulu
  Romanzo Adams Social Research Laboratory Student Papers
  Spark Matsunaga Papers
University Library, Special Collections, University of California, Santa Cruz
  Kilsoo Haan Papers
University of the Philippines, Quezon City, Philippines
  Carlos Romulo Papers (CPR Papers)

U.S. Government Publications

U.S. Census Reports, 1940–2010.
U.S. Congress. House, Committee on Foreign Affairs. *American Neutrality*, 76th
  Congress, 2nd session. Washington, DC: Government Printing Office (GPO), 1939.
U.S. Congress. House, Committee on Immigration and Naturalization. *Hearings on*
  Bills to Grant a Quota to Eastern Hemisphere Indians and to Make Them Racially Eligible
  for Naturalization, 79th Congress, 1st session. Washington, DC: GPO, 1943.
———. *India-Born Residents of the U.S. Request for Naturalization*, 76th Congress,
  1st session. Washington, DC: GPO, 1939.
———. *Naturalization of India-Born Immigrants: Hearing on H.R. 7110*, 76th Congress,
  3rd session. Washington, DC: GPO, 1940.
———. *Repeal of the Chinese Exclusion Acts: Hearings on H.R. 1882 and H.R. 2309*,
  78th Congress, 1st session. Washington, DC: GPO, 1943.
———. *Samples of Japanese-Controlled Radio Comments on America's Exclusion Act*,
  78th Congress, 1st session. Washington, DC: GPO, 1943.
———. *To Authorize the Naturalization of Filipinos Who Are Permanent Residents of the*
  U.S., 76th Congress, 3rd session. Washington, DC: GPO, 1940.
———. *To Authorize the Naturalization of Filipinos Who Are Permanent Residents of the*
  U.S., 77th Congress, 2nd session. Washington, DC: GPO, 1942.
U.S. Congress. House, Committee on the Judiciary, Special Subcommittee on
  Japanese Temporary Workers. *Japanese Temporary Workers*, 1957.
U.S. Congress. House, Committee on the Judiciary, Subcommittee on Immigration.
  Emergency Immigration Program: Hearings before Subcommittee No. 1,
  83rd Congress, 1st session. Washington, DC: GPO, 1953.
———. *Immigration, Part 2: Hearings on H.R. 1629, H.R. 1654*, et al.,
  88nd Congress, 2nd session. Washington, DC: GPO, 1964.
———. *Providing for Equality under Naturalization and Immigration Laws*,
  80th Congress, 2nd session. Washington, DC: GPO, 1948.
U.S. Congress. House, Committees on the Judiciary, Joint Subcommittees.
  Revision of Immigration, Naturalization, and Nationality Laws: Hearings on S. 716,
  H.R. 2379, and H.R. 2816, 82nd Congress, 1st session. Washington, DC: GPO,
  1951.
U.S. Congress. Senate, Committee on the Judiciary. *Naturalization of Asian and*
  Pacific Peoples, Volume 1: Hearings on H.R. 199, 81st Congress, 1st session.
  Washington, DC: GPO, 1949.

U.S. Congress. Senate, Committee on the Judiciary, Subcommittee on Immigration. *Review of Immigration Laws, Volume 4*, 84th Cong., 1st session, 1955.

U.S. Congress. Senate, Committee on the Judiciary, Subcommittee on Immigration. *To Permit the Naturalization of Approximately Three Thousand Natives of India: Hearing before the Senate Committee on Immigration*, 78th Congress, 2nd session. Washington, DC: GPO, 1944.

U.S. President's Commission on Immigration and Naturalization. *Whom Shall We Welcome*. Washington, DC: GPO, 1953.

U.S. President's Committee on Civil Rights. *To Secure These Rights*. Washington, DC: U.S. GPO, 1947.

U.S. Government Serial Publications

Congressional Record

Department of State Bulletin

INS Annual Yearbooks

Newspapers and Periodicals

Asia and the Americas
Bataan (Washington, DC)
Boston Globe
Chicago Defender
Christian Century
Christian Science Monitor
Commentary
Common Ground
Contemporary China

Far Eastern Survey
Hindustan Times (India)
India Today (New York)
Los Angeles Sentinel
Los Angeles Times
Nation
New India Bulletin (New York)
New Pittsburgh Courier

New York Times
New Yorker
Pacific Citizen
Reader's Digest
Time
Washington Post

Published Primary Sources

Kennedy, John F. *A Nation of Immigrants*. New York: Anti-Defamation League, 1959.

Manzon, Maximo C. *The Strange Case of the Filipinos in the United States*. New York: American Committee for Protection of Foreign Born, 1938.

Masaoka, Mike, and Bill Hosokawa. *They Call Me Moses Masaoka: An American Saga*. New York: William Morrow, 1987.

Muzumdar, Haridas. *America's Contribution to India's Freedom*. Allahabad, India: Central Book Depot, 1962.

Romulo, Carlos. *My Brother Americans*. New York: Doubleday, 1945.

Saund, Dalip Singh. *Congressman from India*. New York: Dutton, 1960.

Secondary Sources

Aiyar, Sana. "Anticolonial Homelands across the Indian Ocean: The Politics of the Indian Diaspora in Kenya, ca. 1930–1950." *American Historical Review* 116, no. 4 (October 1, 2011): 987–1013.

Anderson, Carol. *Bourgeois Radicals: The NAACP and the Struggle for Colonial Liberation, 1941–1960*. New York: Cambridge University Press, 2014.

———. *Eyes Off the Prize: The United Nations and the African American Struggle for Human Rights, 1944–1955*. New York: Cambridge University Press, 2003.

Atkinson, David. *The Burden of White Supremacy: Containing Asian Migration in the British Empire and the United States*. Chapel Hill: University of North Carolina Press, 2017.

Azuma, Eiichiro. *Between Two Empires: Race, History, and Transnationalism in Japanese America*. New York: Oxford University Press, 2005.

———. *In Search of Our Frontier: Japanese America and Settler Colonialism in the Construction of Japan's Borderless Empire*. Berkeley: University of California Press, 2019.

Bald, Vivek. *Bengali Harlem and the Lost Histories of South Asian America*. Cambridge, MA: Harvard University Press, 2013.

Bald, Vivek, Miabi Chatterji, Sujani Reddy, and Manu Vimalassery. *The Sun Never Sets: South Asian Migrants in an Age of U. S. Power*. New York: New York University Press, 2013.

Baldoz, Rick. *The Third Asiatic Invasion: Migration and Empire in Filipino America, 1898–1946*. New York: New York University Press, 2011.

Baldoz, Rick, and César Ayala. "The Bordering of America: Colonialism and Citizenship in the Philippines and Puerto Rico." *Centro Journal* 25, no. 1 (2013): 76–105.

Bangarth, Stephanie D. "'We Are Not Asking You to Open Wide the Gates for Chinese Immigration': The Committee for the Repeal of the Chinese Immigration Act and Early Human Rights Activism in Canada." *Canadian Historical Review* 84, no. 3 (2003): 395–422.

Barnhart, Edward N. "Japanese Internees from Peru." *Pacific Historical Review* 31, no. 2 (1962): 169–78.

Battisti, Danielle. *Whom We Shall Welcome: Italian Americans and Immigration Reform, 1945–1965*. New York: Fordham University Press, 2019.

Bell, Roger John. *Last among Equals: Hawaiian Statehood and American Politics*. Honolulu: University of Hawaii Press, 1984.

Bernstein, Shana. *Bridges of Reform: Interracial Civil Rights Activism in Twentieth-Century Los Angeles*. New York: Oxford University Press, 2010.

Bhagavan, Manu. "A New Hope: India, the United Nations and the Making of the Universal Declaration of Human Rights." *Modern Asian Studies* 44, no. 2 (2010): 311–47.

Bon Tempo, Carl J. *Americans at the Gate: The United States and Refugees during the Cold War*. Princeton, NJ: Princeton University Press, 2008.

Borstelmann, Thomas. *The Cold War and the Color Line: American Race Relations in the Global Arena*. Cambridge, MA: Harvard University Press, 2001.

Brands, H. W. *Bound to Empire: The United States and the Philippines*. New York: Oxford University Press, 1992.

Brawley, Sean. *The White Peril: Foreign Relations and Asian Immigration to Australasia and North America, 1919–1978*. Sydney, Australia: University of New South Wales Press, 1995.

Brilliant, Mark. *The Color of America Has Changed: How Racial Diversity Shaped Civil Rights Reform in California, 1941-1978*. New York: Oxford University Press, 2010.

Brooks, Charlotte. *Alien Neighbors, Foreign Friends: Asian Americans, Housing, and the Transformation of Urban California*. Chicago: University of Chicago Press, 2009.

———. *Between Mao and McCarthy: Chinese American Politics in the Cold War Years*. Chicago: University of Chicago Press, 2015.

———. "The Rise and Fall of a Front Group: The National Chinese Welfare Council, 1957-1991." *Chinese America: History and Perspectives* 83 (2015): 47-59.

———. "The War on Grant Avenue: Business Competition and Ethnic Rivalry in San Francisco's Chinatown, 1937-1942." *Journal of Urban History* 37, no. 3 (May 2011): 311-30.

Buff, Rachel Ida. *Against the Deportation Terror: Organizing for Immigrant Rights in the Twentieth Century*. Philadelphia: Temple University Press, 2017.

Cabotaje, Michael A. "Equity Denied: Historical and Legal Analyses in Support of the Extension of US Veterans' Benefits to Filipino World War II Veterans." *Asian Law Journal* 6 (1999): 67-97.

Campomanes, Oscar V. "New Formations of Asian American Studies and the Question of U.S. Imperialism." *Positions* 5, no. 2 (1997): 523-50.

Celler, Emanuel. *You Never Leave Brooklyn: The Autobiography of Emanuel Celler*. New York: John Day, 1953.

Chan, Sucheng. *Asian Americans: An Interpretive History*. Boston: Twayne, 1991.

———, ed. *Entry Denied: Exclusion and the Chinese American Community, 1882-1943*. Philadelphia: Temple University Press, 1991.

———. "The Exclusion of Chinese Women." In *Entry Denied: Exclusion and the Chinese Community in America, 1882-1943*, 94-146. Philadelphia: Temple University Press, 1991.

Chan, Sucheng, and K. Scott Wong, eds. *Claiming America: Constructing Chinese American Identities during the Exclusion Era*. Philadelphia: Temple University Press, 1998.

Chang, Gordon H. "China and the Pursuit of America's Destiny: Nineteenth-Century Imagining and Why Immigration Restriction Took So Long." *Journal of Asian American Studies* 15, no. 2 (2012): 145-69.

Chang, Kornel. *Pacific Connections: The Making of the US-Canadian Borderlands*. Berkeley: University of California Press, 2012.

———. "Reconsidering Asian Exclusion in the United States." In *The Oxford Handbook of Asian American History*, David K. Yoo and Eiichiro Azuma, eds., 154-70. New York: Oxford University Press, 2016.

Cheng, Cindy I-Fen. *Citizens of Asian America: Democracy and Race during the Cold War*. New York: New York University Press, 2013.

Cheng, Lucie, and Edna Bonacich. *Labor Immigration under Capitalism: Asian Workers in the United States before World War II*. Berkeley: University of California Press, 1984.

Chin, Gabriel J. "The Civil Rights Revolution Comes to Immigration Law: A New Look at the Immigration and Nationality Act of 1965." *North Carolina Law Review* 75 (1996): 273–94.

Chin, Gabriel J., and Rose Cuison Villazor. *The Immigration and Nationality Act of 1965: Legislating a New America*. New York: Cambridge University Press, 2015.

Choy, Catherine Ceniza. *Empire of Care: Nursing and Migration in Filipino American History*. Durham, NC: Duke University Press, 2003.

Chung, Sue Fawn. "Fighting for Their American Rights: A History of the Chinese American Citizens Alliance." *Claiming America: Constructing Chinese American Identities during the Exclusion Era* (1998): 95–126.

Clymer, Kenton J. "Jawaharlal Nehru and the United States: The Preindependence Years." *Diplomatic History* 14, no. 2 (1990): 143–62.

———. *Quest for Freedom: The United States and India's Independence*. New York: Columbia University Press, 2010.

Cohen, Warren I. *Pacific Passage: The Study of American–East Asian Relations on the Eve of the Twenty-First Century*. New York: Columbia University Press, 1996.

Conn, Peter J. *Pearl S. Buck: A Cultural Biography*. New York: Cambridge University Press, 1998.

Connelly, Matthew. "Taking Off the Cold War Lens: Visions of North-South Conflict during the Algerian War for Independence." *American Historical Review* 105, no. 3 (2000): 739–69.

Cullather, Nick. *Illusions of Influence: The Political Economy of United States-Philippines Relations, 1942-1960*. Stanford, CA: Stanford University Press, 1994.

Daniels, Roger. *Guarding the Golden Door: American Immigration Policy and Immigrants since 1882*. New York: Hill and Wang, 2004.

———. *The Politics of Prejudice: The Anti-Japanese Movement in California and the Struggle for Japanese Exclusion*. Berkeley: University of California Press, 1977.

———. *Prisoners without Trial: Japanese Americans in World War II*. New York: Hill and Wang, 1993.

Das, Man Singh. "The 'Brain Drain' Controversy in a Comparative Perspective." *International Review of Sociology* 1, no. 1 (1971): 55–65.

Davis, Arthur K. "Review of Whom Shall We Welcome. Report of the President's Commission on Immigration and Naturalization." *Science & Society* 17, no. 4 (1953): 360–63.

Davis, Michael G. "Impetus for Immigration Reform: Asian Refugees and the Cold War." *Journal of American-East Asian Relations* 7, no. 3/4 (1998): 127–56.

Divine, Robert A. *American Immigration Policy, 1924-1952*. New Haven, CT: Yale University Press, 1957.

Dong, Lorraine. "Song Meiling in America 1943." In *The Repeal and Its Legacy: Proceedings of the Conference on the 50th Anniversary of the Repeal of the Exclusion Acts*, 39–46. San Francisco: Chinese Historical Society of America, 1994.

Dudziak, Mary L. *Cold War Civil Rights: Race and the Image of American Democracy*. Princeton, NJ: Princeton University Press, 2000.

Edwards, Jerome E. *Pat McCarran, Political Boss of Nevada*. Reno: University of Nevada Press, 1982.

Edwards, Lee. *Missionary for Freedom: The Life and Times of Walter Judd*. St. Paul, MN: Paragon House, 1990.

Espiritu, Augusto. *Five Faces of Exile: The Nation and Filipino American Intellectuals*. Palo Alto, CA: Stanford University Press, 2005.

———. "'To Carry Water on Both Shoulders': Carlos P. Romulo, American Empire, and the Meanings of Bandung." *Radical History Review*, no. 95 (May 1, 2006): 173–90.

Espiritu, Yen. *Asian American Panethnicity: Bridging Institutions and Identities*. Philadelphia: Temple University Press, 1993.

Fite, Gilbert C. *Richard B. Russell, Jr., Senator from Georgia*. Chapel Hill: University of North Carolina Press, 2002.

Fleegler, Robert. *Ellis Island Nation: Immigration Policy and American Identity in the Twentieth Century*. Philadelphia: University of Pennsylvania Press, 2013.

Flores, Lori A. *Grounds for Dreaming: Mexican Americans, Mexican Immigrants, and the California Farmworker Movement*. New Haven, CT: Yale University Press, 2016.

Fry, Joseph. *Dixie Looks Abroad: The South and US Foreign Relations, 1789–1973*. Baton Rouge: Louisiana State University Press, 2002.

Fujino, Diane C. "Cold War Activism and Japanese American Exceptionalism: Contested Solidarities and Decolonial Alternatives to Freedom." *Pacific Historical Review* 87:2 (Spring 2018): 264–304.

Fujitani, Takashi. "A Different Kind of 'Asia Pivot.'" *Amerasia Journal* 42, no. 3 (2016): 17–22.

———. *Race for Empire: Koreans as Japanese and Japanese as Americans during World War II*. Berkeley: University of California Press, 2011.

Fujita-Rony, Dorothy B. *American Workers, Colonial Power*. Berkeley: University of California Press, 2003.

Gabaccia, Donna. *Foreign Relations: American Immigration in Global Perspective*. Princeton, NJ: Princeton University Press, 2012.

Garcia, Juan. *Operation Wetback: The Mass Deportation of Mexican Undocumented Workers in 1954*. Westport, CT: Greenwood Press, 1980.

Go, Julian. *Patterns of Empire: The British and American Empires, 1688 to the Present*. New York: Cambridge University Press, 2011.

Golay, Frank H. *Face of Empire: United States–Philippine Relations, 1898–1946*. Madison: University of Wisconsin Press, 1998.

Gotanda, Neil. "Exclusion and Inclusion: Immigration and American Orientalism." In *Across the Pacific: Asian Americans and Globalization*, edited by Evelyn Hu-Dehart. Philadelphia: Temple University Press, 1999.

———. "Towards Repeal of Asian Exclusion." In *Asian Americans and Congress: A Documentary History*, edited by Hyung-Chan Kim. Westport, CT: Greenwood Press, 1996.

Gould, Harold A. *Sikhs, Swamis, Students, and Spies: The India Lobby in the United States, 1900–1946*. New Delhi, India: Sage, 2006.

Graham, Sarah Ellen. "American Propaganda, the Anglo-American Alliance, and the 'Delicate Question' of Indian Self-Determination." *Diplomatic History* 33, no. 2 (2009): 223–59.

Gyory, Andrew. *Closing the Gate: Race, Politics, and the Chinese Exclusion Act.* Chapel Hill: University of North Carolina Press, 1998.

Halloran, Richard. *Sparky: Warrior, Peacemaker, Poet, Patriot: A Portrait of Senator Spark M. Matsunaga.* Honolulu, HI: Watermark, 2002.

Heefner, Gretchen. "A Symbol of the New Frontier." *Pacific Historical Review* 74, no. 4 (2005): 545–74.

Hellwig, David J. "Black Leaders and United States Immigration Policy, 1917–1929." *Journal of Negro History* (1981): 110–27.

Herzstein, Robert E. *Henry R. Luce, Time, and the American Crusade in Asia.* New York: Cambridge University Press, 2005.

Hess, Gary R. *America Encounters India, 1941–1947.* Baltimore, MD: Johns Hopkins University Press, 1971.

———. "The Forgotten Asian Americans: The East Indian Community in the United States." *Pacific Historical Review* 43:4 (November 1974): 576–96.

———. "The 'Hindu' in America: Immigration and Naturalization Policies and India, 1917–1946." *Pacific Historical Review* (1969): 59–79.

Hing, Bill Ong. *Making and Remaking Asian America through Immigration Policy: 1850–1990.* Palo Alto, CA: Stanford University Press, 1993.

Hirobe, Izumi. *Japanese Pride, American Prejudice: Modifying the Exclusion Clause of the 1924 Immigration Act.* Palo Alto, CA: Stanford University Press, 2001.

Hoganson, Kristin L. *Fighting for American Manhood: How Gender Politics Provoked the Spanish-American and Philippine-American Wars.* New Haven, CT: Yale University Press, 1998.

Hollinger, David A. *Protestants Abroad: How Missionaries Tried to Change the World but Changed America.* Princeton, NJ: Princeton University Press, 2017.

Honda, Michael. "Justice for Filipino Veterans, at Long Last." *Asian American Law Journal* 16 (2009): 193–96.

Horne, Gerald. *Black and Red: WEB Du Bois and the Afro-American Response to the Cold War, 1944–1963.* Albany, NY: SUNY Press, 1986.

Hoskins, Janet, and Viet Thanh Nguyen. *Transpacific Studies: Framing an Emerging Field.* Honolulu: University of Hawai'i Press, 2014.

Hosokawa, Bill. *JACL in Quest of Justice: The History of the Japanese American Citizens League.* New York: William Morrow, 1982.

———. *Nisei: The Quiet Americans.* New York: William Morrow, 1969.

Hsu, Madeline Y. *The Good Immigrants: How the Yellow Peril Became the Model Minority.* Princeton, NJ: Princeton University Press, 2015.

Hsu, Madeline Y., and Ellen D. Wu. "'Smoke and Mirrors': Conditional Inclusion, Model Minorities, and the Pre-1965 Dismantling of Asian Exclusion." *Journal of American Ethnic History* 34, no. 4 (2015): 43–65.

Hunt, Michael H. *The Making of a Special Relationship: The United States and China to 1914.* New York: Columbia University Press, 1983.

Ichioka, Yuji. *The Issei: The World of the First Generation Japanese Immigrants, 1885–1924.* New York: Free Press, 1988.

Iriye, Akira. *Across the Pacific: An Inner History of American-East Asian Relations.* Chicago: Imprint, 1992.

James, Winston. *Holding Aloft the Banner of Ethiopia: Caribbean Radicalism in Early Twentieth-Century America*. New York: Verso, 1998.

Jensen, Joan M. *Passage from India: Asian Indian Immigrants in North America*. New Haven, CT: Yale University Press, 1988.

Johnson, Howard. "The Anglo-American Caribbean Commission and the Extension of American Influence in the British Caribbean, 1942–1945." *Journal of Commonwealth & Comparative Politics* 22, no. 2 (1984): 180–203.

Johnson, Kevin. *The Huddled Masses Myth: Immigration and Civil Rights*. Philadelphia: Temple University Press, 2004.

Jose, Ricardo T. "Governments in Exile." *Asian and Pacific Migration Journal* 8, no. 1/2 (1999): 179–93.

Jou, Chin. "Contesting Nativism: The New York Congressional Delegation's Case against the Immigration Act of 1924." *Federal History* 3 (2011).

Juergensmeyer, Mark. "The Ghadar Syndrome: Nationalism in an Immigrant Community." *Punjab Journal of Politics* 1, no. 1 (1977): 1–22.

Jung, Moon-Ho. *Coolies and Cane: Race, Labor, and Sugar in the Age of Emancipation*. Baltimore: Johns Hopkins University Press, 2006.

Kapur, Nick. "Mending the 'Broken Dialogue': US-Japan Alliance Diplomacy in the Aftermath of the 1960 Security Treaty Crisis." *Diplomatic History* 41, no. 3 (2017): 489–517.

Kennedy, Paul. *The Rise and Fall of the Great Powers: Economic Change and Military Conflict from 1500 to 2000*. New York: Random House, 1987.

Kim, Hyung-chan. *Asian Americans and Congress: A Documentary History*. Westport, CT: Greenwood, 1996.

Kim, Richard S. *The Quest for Statehood: Korean Immigrant Nationalism and US Sovereignty, 1905-1945*. New York: Oxford University Press, 2011.

King, Desmond. *Making Americans: Immigration, Race, and the Origins of the Diverse Democracy*. Cambridge, MA: Harvard University Press, 2009.

Klein, Christina. *Cold War Orientalism: Asia in the Middlebrow Imagination, 1945–1961*. Berkeley: University of California Press, 2003.

Koshiro, Yukiko. *Trans-Pacific Racisms and the U.S. Occupation of Japan*. New York: Columbia University Press, 1999.

Kramer, Paul. *The Blood of Government: Race, Empire, the United States, and the Philippines*. Chapel Hill: University of North Carolina Press, 2006.

———. "Geopolitics of Mobility: Immigration Policy and American Global Power in the Long Twentieth Century." *American Historical Review* 123, no. 1 (April 2018): 393–438.

———. "Imperial Openings: Civilization, Exemption, and the Geopolitics of Mobility in the History of Chinese Exclusion, 1868–1910." *Journal of the Gilded Age and Progressive Era* 14, no. 3 (2015): 317–47.

———. "Power and Connection: Imperial Histories of the United States in the World." *American Historical Review* 116, no. 5 (2011): 1348–91.

Krenn, Michael L. *Race and U.S. Foreign Policy during the Cold War*. New York: Taylor & Francis, 1998.

Kurashige, Lon. *Japanese American Celebration and Conflict: A History of Ethnic Identity and Festival, 1934-1990*. Berkeley: University of California Press, 2002.

————. *Two Faces of Exclusion: The Untold History of Anti-Asian Racism in the United States*. Chapel Hill: University of North Carolina Press, 2016.

Ladd, Tony, and Patricia Neils. "Mission to Capitol Hill: A Study of the Impact of Missionary Idealism on the Congressional Career of Walter H. Judd." In *United States Attitudes and Policies toward China: The Impact of American Missionaries*. Armonk, NY: M.E. Sharpe, 1990.

LaFeber, Walter. *The Clash: US-Japanese Relations throughout History*. New York: W. W. Norton, 1998.

Lake, Marilyn, and Henry Reynolds. *Drawing the Global Colour Line: White Men's Countries and the International Challenge of Racial Equality*. London: Cambridge University Press, 2008.

Lasker, Bruno. *Filipino Immigration to Continental United States and to Hawaii*. Chicago: University of Chicago Press, 1931.

Latham, Michael E. *Modernization as Ideology: American Social Science and "Nation Building" in the Kennedy Era*. Chapel Hill: University of North Carolina Press, 2000.

Lauren, Paul Gordon. *Power and Prejudice: The Politics and Diplomacy of Racial Discrimination*. Boulder, CO: Westview Press, 1996.

Le Espiritu, Yen. *Asian American Panethnicity: Bridging Institutions and Identities*. Philadelphia: Temple University Press, 1993.

Lee, Erika. *At America's Gates: Chinese Immigration during the Exclusion Era, 1882–1943*. Chapel Hill: University of North Carolina Press, 2003.

————. "Orientalisms in the Americas: A Hemispheric Approach to Asian American History." *Journal of Asian American Studies* 8, no. 3 (2005): 235–56.

————. "The 'Yellow Peril' and Asian Exclusion in the Americas." *Pacific Historical Review* 76, no. 4 (2007): 537–62.

Leffler, Melvyn P. *A Preponderance of Power: National Security, the Truman Administration, and the Cold War*. Palo Alto, CA: Stanford University Press, 1992.

Lemelin, Bernard. "Emanuel Celler of Brooklyn: Leading Advocate of Liberal Immigration Policy, 1945–52." *Canadian Review of American Studies* 24, no. 1 (1994): 81–112.

Leonard, Karen. *Making Ethnic Choices: California's Punjabi Mexican Americans*. Philadelphia: Temple University Press, 2010.

Leong, Karen J. "Foreign Policy, National Identity, and Citizenship: The Roosevelt White House and the Expediency of Repeal." *Journal of American Ethnic History* 22, no. 4 (2003): 3–30.

Levenstein, Lisa. *A Movement without Marches: African American Women and the Politics of Poverty in Postwar Philadelphia*. Chapel Hill: University of North Carolina Press, 2009.

Lew-Williams, Beth. "Before Restriction Became Exclusion." *Pacific Historical Review* 83, no. 1 (2014): 24–56.

————. *The Chinese Must Go: Violence, Exclusion, and the Making of the Alien in America*. Cambridge, MA: Harvard University Press, 2018.

Lind, Michael. *Next American Nation: The New Nationalism and the Fourth American Revolution*. New York: Simon and Schuster, 1995.

Liu, Haiming. "The Trans-Pacific Family: A Case Study of Sam Chang's Family History." *Amerasia Journal* 18, no. 2 (1992): 1–34.

Lopez, Ian Haney. *White by Law: The Legal Construction of Race.* New York: New York University Press, 1997.

Lowe, Lisa. *Immigrant Acts: On Asian American Cultural Politics.* Durham, NC: Duke University Press, 1996.

Loza, Mireya. "The Japanese Agricultural Workers' Program: Race, Labor, and Cold War Diplomacy in the Fields, 1956–1965." *Pacific Historical Review* 86, no. 4 (2017): 661–90.

Ma, Xiaohua. "The Sino-American Alliance during World War II and the Lifting of the Chinese Exclusion Acts." *American Studies International* 38, no. 2 (2000): 39–61.

Mabalon, Dawn Bohulano. *Little Manila Is in the Heart: The Making of the Filipina/o American Community in Stockton, California.* Durham, NC: Duke University Press, 2013.

Man, Simeon. *Soldiering through Empire: Race and the Making of the Decolonizing Pacific.* Berkeley, CA: University of California Press, 2018.

Manela, Erez. *The Wilsonian Moment: Self-Determination and the International Origins of Anticolonial Nationalism.* New York: Oxford University Press, 2007.

Mao, Joyce. *Asia First: China and the Making of American Conservatism.* Chicago: University of Chicago Press, 2015.

Marinari, Maddalena. "'Americans Must Show Justice in Immigration Policies Too': The Passage of the 1965 Immigration Act." *Journal of Policy History* 26, no. 2 (2014): 219–45.

———. "Divided and Conquered: Immigration Reform Advocates and the Passage of the 1952 Immigration and Nationality Act." *Journal of American Ethnic History* 35, no. 3 (2016): 9–40.

———. *Unwanted: Italian and Jewish Mobilization against Restrictive Immigration Laws, 1882–1965.* Chapel Hill: University of North Carolina Press, 2020.

Masaoka, Mike, and Bill Hosokawa. *They Call Me Moses Masaoka: An American Saga.* New York: William Morrow, 1987.

Massey, Douglas S., and Karen A. Pren. "Unintended Consequences of US Immigration Policy: Explaining the Post-1965 Surge from Latin America." *Population and Development Review* 38, no. 1 (2012): 1–29.

May, Ernest R. *American Imperialism: A Speculative Essay.* New York: Atheneum, 1968.

McAdam, Doug. "On the International Origins of Domestic Political Opportunities." In Anne Costain and Andrew McFarland, eds., *Social Movements and American Political Institutions.* Totowa, NJ: Rowman and Littlefield, 1998.

McClain, Charles J. *In Search of Equality: The Chinese Struggle against Discrimination in Nineteenth-Century America.* Berkeley: University of California Press, 1994.

———. "Tortuous Path, Elusive Goal: The Asian Quest for American Citizenship." *Asian Law Journal* 2 (1995): 33.

McEvoy, Gráinne. "Justice and Order: American Catholic Social Thought and the Immigration Question in the Restriction Era, 1917–1965." PhD diss., Boston College, 2014.

McKee, Delber L. "The Chinese Boycott of 1905–1906 Reconsidered: The Role of Chinese Americans." *Pacific Historical Review* 55, no. 2 (1986): 165–91.

McKeown, Adam. "Transnational Chinese Families and Chinese Exclusion, 1875–1943." *Journal of American Ethnic History* 18:2 (Winter 1999): 73–110.

McKercher, Brian. *Transition of Power: Britain's Loss of Global Pre-Eminence to the United States, 1930–1945.* New York: Cambridge University Press, 1999.

McMahon, Robert J. *The Limits of Empire: The United States and Southeast Asia since World War II.* New York: Columbia University Press, 1999.

Melendy, H. Brett. *Asians in America: Filipinos, Koreans, and East Indians.* Boston: Twayne, 1977.

Miller, Jake C. "The NAACP and Global Human Rights." *Western Journal of Black Studies* 26, no. 1 (2002): 22.

Miller, Jennifer M. "Fractured Alliance: Anti-Base Protests and Postwar US–Japanese Relations." *Diplomatic History* 38, no. 5 (2013): 953–86.

Miyake, Lika C. "Forsaken and Forgotten: The US Internment of Japanese Peruvians during World War II." *Asian Law Journal* 9 (2002): 163–93.

Molina, Natalia. *How Race Is Made in America: Immigration, Citizenship, and the Historical Power of Racial Scripts.* Berkeley: University of California Press, 2014.

Narayanan, Sikh R. "Indian Immigration and the India League of America." *Indian Journal of American Studies* 2, no. 1 (1969).

Neils, Patricia, ed. *United States Attitudes and Policies Toward China: The Impact of American Missionaries.* Armonk, NY: M.E. Sharpe, 1990.

Ngai, Mae M. "Chinese Gold Miners and the 'Chinese Question' in Nineteenth-Century California and Victoria." *Journal of American History* 101, no. 4 (2015): 1082–1105.

———. *Impossible Subjects: Illegal Aliens and the Making of Modern America: Illegal Aliens and the Making of Modern America.* Princeton, NJ: Princeton University Press, 2004.

———. "Oscar Handlin and Immigration Policy Reform in the 1950s and 1960s." *Journal of American Ethnic History* 32, no. 3 (2013): 62–67.

Nkrumah, Kwame. *Neo-Colonialism: The Last Stage of Imperialism. 1965.* New York: International Publishers, 1966.

Nordyke, Eleanor C. "Blacks in Hawai'i: A Demographic and Historical Perspective." *Hawaiian Journal of History* 22 (1988): 241–55.

Norman, Michael, and Elizabeth M. Norman. *Tears in the Darkness: The Story of the Bataan Death March and Its Aftermath.* New York: Farrar, Straus, and Giroux, 2009.

Oda, Meredith. "Rebuilding Japantown: Japanese Americans in Transpacific San Francisco during the Cold War." *Pacific Historical Review* 83, no. 1 (2014): 57–91.

Okihiro, Gary Y. *American History Unbound: Asians and Pacific Islanders.* Berkeley: University of California Press, 2015.

———. *Margins and Mainstreams: Asians in American History and Culture.* Seattle: University of Washington Press, 1994.

O'Leary, Cecilia Elizabeth. *To Die for: The Paradox of American Patriotism.* Princeton, NJ: Princeton University Press, 1999.

Onishi, Yuichiro. *Transpacific Antiracism: Afro-Asian Solidarity in 20th-Century Black America, Japan, and Okinawa.* New York: New York University Press, 2013.

Oyen, Meredith. *The Diplomacy of Migration: Transnational Lives and the Making of U.S.-Chinese Relations in the Cold War.* Ithaca, NY: Cornell University Press, 2015.

————. "'Thunder without Rain': ARCI, the Far East Refugee Program, and the US Response to Hong Kong Refugees." *Journal of Cold War Studies* 16, no. 4 (2014): 189–211.

Pakula, Hannah. *The Last Empress: Madame Chiang Kai-Shek and the Birth of Modern China*. New York: Simon and Schuster, 2009.

Parker, Jason C. *Brother's Keeper: The United States, Race, and Empire in the British Caribbean, 1937–1962*. New York: Oxford University Press, 2008.

————. "Cold War II: The Eisenhower Administration, the Bandung Conference, and the Reperiodization of the Postwar Era." *Diplomatic History* 30, no. 5 (2006): 867–92.

————. "Remapping the Cold War in the Tropics: Race, Communism, and National Security in the West Indies." *International History Review* 24, no. 2 (2002): 318–47.

Parreñas, Rhacel Salazar. "'White Trash' Meets the 'Little Brown Monkeys': The Taxi Dance Hall as a Site of Interracial and Gender Alliances between White Working Class Women and Filipino Immigrant Men in the 1920s and 30s." *Amerasia Journal* 24, no. 2 (1998): 115–34.

Plummer, Brenda Gayle. *Rising Wind: Black Americans and US Foreign Affairs, 1935–1960*. Chapel Hill: University of North Carolina Press, 1996.

Poblete, JoAnna. *Islanders in the Empire: Filipino and Puerto Rican Laborers in Hawai'i*. Chicago: University of Illinois Press, 2014.

Prashad, Vijay, et al., eds. *The Sun Never Sets: South Asian Migrants in an Age of US Power*. New York: New York University Press, 2013.

Raimundo, Antonio. "The Filipino Veterans Equity Movement: A Case Study in Reparations Theory." *California Law Review* 98, no. 2 (2010): 575–623.

Reimers, David M. *Still the Golden Door: The Third World Comes to America*. New York: Columbia University Press, 1992.

————. "An Unintended Reform: The 1965 Immigration Act and Third World Immigration to the United States." *Journal of American Ethnic History* 3, no. 1 (1983): 9–28.

Riggs, Fred. *Pressures on Congress: A Study of the Repeal of Chinese Exclusion*. New York: King's Crown Press, 1950.

Robinson, Greg. *After Camp: Portraits in Midcentury Japanese American Life and Politics*. Berkeley: University of California Press, 2012.

Rodriguez, Robyn Magalit. *Migrants for Export: How the Philippine State Brokers Labor to the World*. Minneapolis: University of Minnesota Press, 2010.

Salyer, Lucy E. "Baptism by Fire: Race, Military Service, and U.S. Citizenship Policy, 1918–1935." *Journal of American History* 91, no. 3 (December 2004): 847–76.

————. *Laws Harsh as Tigers: Chinese Immigrants and the Shaping of Modern Immigration Law*. Chapel Hill: University of North Carolina Press, 1995.

Sandmeyer, Elmer Clarence. *The Anti-Chinese Movement in California*. Urbana: University of Illinois Press, 1991.

Saranillio, Dean. *Unsustainable Empire: Alternative Histories of Hawai'i Statehood*. Durham, NC: Duke University Press, 2018.

Savage, Timothy L. "The American Response to the Korean Independence Movement, 1910–1945." *Korean Studies* 20/21 (1996): 189–231.

Saxton, Alexander. *The Indispensable Enemy: Labor and the Anti-Chinese Movement in California*. Berkeley: University of California Press, 1975.

Schaller, Michael. *The American Occupation of Japan: The Origins of the Cold War in Asia*. New York: Oxford University Press, 1985.

Schonberger, Howard. "The Japan Lobby in American Diplomacy, 1947–1952." *Pacific Historical Review* 46, no. 3 (1977): 327–59.

Shaffer, Robert. "J.J. Singh and the India League of America, 1945–1959: Pressing at the Margins of the Cold War Consensus." *Journal of American Ethnic History* 31, no. 2 (Winter 2012): 68–103.

Shalom, Stephen R. "Philippine Acceptance of the Bell Trade Act of 1946: A Study of Manipulatory Democracy." *Pacific Historical Review* 49, no. 3 (1980): 499–517.

Sherwood, Marika. "India at the Founding of the United Nations." *International Studies* 33, no. 4 (October 1, 1996): 407–28.

Shibusawa, Naoko. *America's Geisha Ally: Reimagining the Japanese Enemy*. Cambridge, MA: Harvard University Press, 2006.

——. "Femininity, Race and Treachery: How 'Tokyo Rose' Became a Traitor to the United States after the Second World War." *Gender & History* 22, no. 1 (2010): 169–88.

Shimazu, Naoko. *Japan, Race and Equality: The Racial Equality Proposal of 1919*. New York: Psychology Press, 2009.

Simpson, Caroline Chung. *An Absent Presence: Japanese Americans in Postwar American Culture, 1945–1960*. Durham, NC: Duke University Press, 2001.

Slate, Nico. *Colored Cosmopolitanism: The Shared Struggle for Freedom in the United States and India*. Cambridge, MA: Harvard University Press, 2012.

Snow, Jennifer. *Protestant Missionaries, Asian Immigrants, and Ideologies of Race in America, 1850–1924*. New York: Routledge, 2006.

Sobredo, James. "The 1934 Tydings-McDuffie Act and Filipino Exclusion: Social, Political, and Economic Context Revisited." In *Studies in Pacific History: Economics, Politics, and Migration*, 155–69. Farnham, U.K.: Ashgate, 2002.

Sohi, Seema. *Echoes of Mutiny: Race, Empire, and Indian Anticolonialism in North America*. New York: Oxford University Press, 2014.

Sohoni, Deenesh. "Unsuitable Suitors: Anti-Miscegenation Laws, Naturalization Laws, and the Construction of Asian Identities." *Law & Society Review* 41, no. 3 (2007): 587–618.

Spickard, Paul. *Almost All Aliens: Immigration, Race, and Colonialism in American History and Identity*. New York: Routledge, 2009.

——. "The Nisei Assume Power: The Japanese American Citizens League, 1941–1942." *Pacific Historical Review* 52, no. 2 (1983): 147–74.

Stern, Lewis M. "Response to Vietnamese Refugees: Surveys of Public Opinion." *Social Work* 26, no. 4 (1981): 306–11.

Takaki, Ronald. *Strangers from a Different Shore: A History of Asian Americans*. Boston, MA: Little, Brown, 1989.

Takenaka, Ayumi. "The Japanese in Peru: History of Immigration, Settlement, and Racialization." *Latin American Perspectives* 31, no. 3 (2004): 77–98.

Taylor, Sandra. *Advocate of Understanding: Sidney Gulick and the Search for Peace with Japan*. Kent, OH: Kent State University Press, 1984.

Teodoro, Noel V. "Pensionados and Workers: The Filipinos in the United States, 1903–1956." *Asian and Pacific Migration Journal* 8, no. 1/2 (1999): 157–78.

Thorne, Christopher. *Allies of a Kind: The United States, Britain, and the War against Japan, 1941–1945*. New York: Oxford University Press, 1978.

Tichenor, Daniel J. *Dividing Lines: The Politics of Immigration Control in America*. Princeton, NJ: Princeton University Press, 2002.

Tinker, Hugh. *Race, Conflict, and the International Order: From Empire to United Nations*. New York: Macmillan, 1977.

———. *Separate and Unequal: India and the Indians in the British Commonwealth, 1920–1950*. Vancouver: University of British Columbia Press, 1976.

Torok, John Hayakawa. "'Interest Convergence' and the Liberalization of Discriminatory Immigration and Naturalization…." *Chinese America: History & Perspectives* (January 1995): 1–28.

Varma, Premdatta. *Indian Immigrants in USA: Struggle for Equality*. New Delhi, India: Heritage, 1995.

Volpp, Leti. "'Obnoxious to Their Very Nature': Asian Americans and Constitutional Citizenship." *Citizenship Studies* 5, no. 1 (2001): 57–71.

Von Eschen, Penny M. *Race against Empire: Black Americans and Anticolonialism, 1937–1957*. Ithaca, NY: Cornell University Press, 1997.

Wang, Joan S. "The Double Burdens of Immigrant Nationalism: The Relationship between Chinese and Japanese in the American West, 1880s–1920s." *Journal of American Ethnic History* 27, no. 2 (2008): 28–58.

Wang, L. Ling-chi. "Politics of the Repeal of the Chinese Exclusion Laws." In *Remembering 1882: Fighting for Civil Rights in the Shadow of the Chinese Exclusion Act*, edited by Connie Young Yu. San Francisco: Chinese Historical Society of America, 1993.

Weinstein, Allen, Alexander Vassiliev, and Bill Wallace. *The Haunted Wood: Soviet Espionage in America—the Stalin Era*. New York: Random House, 1999.

Wong, K. Scott, and Sucheng Chan. *Claiming America: Constructing Chinese American Identities during the Exclusion Era*. Philadelphia: Temple University Press, 1998.

Wong, K. Scott. *Americans First: Chinese Americans and the Second World War*. Cambridge, MA: Harvard University Press, 2005.

Wong, Sau-ling C. "Denationalization Reconsidered: Asian American Cultural Criticism at a Theoretical Crossroads." *Amerasia Journal* 21, no. 1/2 (1995): 1–27.

Wu, Ellen D. "'America's Chinese': Anti-Communism, Citizenship, and Cultural Diplomacy during the Cold War." *Pacific Historical Review* 77, no. 3 (2008): 391–422.

———. *The Color of Success: Asian Americans and the Origins of the Model Minority*. Princeton, NJ: Princeton University Press, 2013.

Yanli, Gao. "Judd's China: A Missionary Congressman and US–China Policy." *Journal of Modern Chinese History* 2, no. 2 (2008): 197–219.

Yoo, David K., and Eiichiro Azuma, eds. *The Oxford Handbook of Asian American History*. New York: Oxford University Press, 2016.

Yu, Renqiu. "Little Heard Voices: The Chinese Hand Laundry Alliance and the *China Daily News* Appeal for Repeal of the Chinese Exclusion Act in 1943." *Chinese America: History & Perspectives* (1990): 21–35.

Yui, Daizaburo. "From Exclusion to Integration: Search for Postwar Hegemony and Repeal of the Oriental Exclusion Acts." *Hitotsubashi Journal of Social Studies* 25, no. 2 (1993): 95–101.

Zhao, Xiaojian. *Remaking Chinese America: Immigration, Family, and Community, 1940–1965*. New Brunswick, NJ: Rutgers University Press, 2002.

Ziker, Ann K. "Segregationists Confront American Empire: The Conservative White South and the Question of Hawaiian Statehood, 1947–1959." *Pacific Historical Review* 76, no. 3 (2007): 439–66.

Zolberg, Aristide R. *A Nation by Design: Immigration Policy in the Fashioning of America*. Cambridge, MA: Harvard University Press, 2009.

Index

442nd Regimental Combat Team, 122, 130

Walsh, Richard, 33–35, 38, 57–58, 64, 119

Walter, Francis (Rep.), 129, 134–35, 142, 155, 162–63; and Afro-Caribbean groups, 139

war brides, 145

Wartime Evacuation Claims Act (1948), 122

White, Walter, 59–60, 140

Whitehall, 49, 61, 67–68, 70, 72–73, 75–76

World War II, 2–4, 9, 11–13, 17, 19; and Chinese exclusion repeal, 22, 25–26, 29–30, 36, 39, 42; and Indian independence, 49–51, 56, 59, 62, 65, 68–69, 77; and Philippine Independence, 82, 84–85, 94, 100, 105, 108, 110; and refugees, 150, 152–53, 154, 160, 165–67

Yee, Fred, 40, 43